Reading the Contemporary Irish Novel
1987–2007

Nottingham Trent University
CLIFTON LIBRARY
www.ntu.ac.uk/llr

Enquiries: 0115 848 2175

READING THE NOVEL

General Editor: **Daniel R. Schwarz**

The aim of this series is to provide practical introductions to reading the novel in both the British and Irish, and the American traditions.

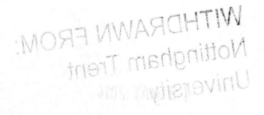

Reading the Contemporary Irish Novel 1987–2007

Liam Harte

WILEY Blackwell

This edition first published 2014
© 2014 Liam Harte

Registered Office
John Wiley & Sons Ltd, The Atrium, Southern Gate, Chichester, West Sussex, PO19 8SQ, UK

Editorial Offices
350 Main Street, Malden, MA 02148-5020, USA
9600 Garsington Road, Oxford, OX4 2DQ, UK
The Atrium, Southern Gate, Chichester, West Sussex, PO19 8SQ, UK

For details of our global editorial offices, for customer services, and for information about how to apply for permission to reuse the copyright material in this book please see our website at www.wiley.com/wiley-blackwell.

The right of Liam Harte to be identified as the author of this work has been asserted in accordance with the UK Copyright, Designs and Patents Act 1988.

Library of Congress Cataloging-in-Publication Data

Harte, Liam.
   Reading the contemporary Irish novel 1987–2007 / Liam Harte.
     pages cm – (Reading the novel)
   ISBN 978-1-4443-3619-1 (hardback) – ISBN 978-1-4443-3620-7 (paper)   1. English fiction–Irish authors–History and criticism.   2. English fiction–20th century–History and criticism.   3. English fiction–21st century–History and criticism.   4. Social change in literature.   5. Social problems in literature.   6. Ireland–In literature.   7. Northern Ireland–In literature.   I. Title.
   PR8803.H37 2014
   823'.914099415–dc23
                                                                          2013025426

A catalogue record for this book is available from the British Library.

Cover image: Martin Gale, *By Pass 2*, oil on canvas, 2003. Reproduced courtesy of the artist, www.martingale.ie
Cover design by Nicki Averill Design & Illustration

Typeset in 10/12.5pt Minion by Aptara Inc., New Delhi, India
Printed and bound in Malaysia by Vivar Printing Sdn Bhd

1   2014

For Yvonne and Oisín

Contents

Acknowledgements

This book began its journey into print in university classrooms, so I must begin by thanking the many students who have taken my undergraduate and postgraduate courses on contemporary Irish fiction over the past two decades at the University of Manchester, the University of Ulster and St Mary's University College, Twickenham. I have had the pleasure of teaching many bright minds in all three institutions and several of the textual readings I put forward in these pages have their origins in seminar discussions and tutorials. Friends and colleagues in these universities, and others, have also shaped my thinking about the contemporary Irish novel, in particular Lance Pettitt, Patrick Crotty, John Wilson Foster, Declan Kiberd, John McAuliffe, Kelly McGovern, Murray Pittock, Stephen Regan, Michael Parker and George O'Brien.

I am very grateful to Professor Daniel R. Schwarz at Cornell University who, as General Editor of the Reading the Novel Series, put his faith in me to bring this book to fruition. My thanks also go to Emma Bennett, commissioning editor at Wiley Blackwell, and project editor Ben Thatcher for their patience and encouragement during the book's evolution. I am also indebted to the three anonymous readers at Wiley Blackwell who offered valuable insights and suggestions on reading an earlier version of my manuscript. Thanks, too, to Martin Gale for kindly granting permission to reproduce his *By Pass 2* on the cover.

My deepest debt, as ever, is to the dedicatees of this book, my wife Yvonne and my son Oisín, who are my richest sources of support, inspiration and joy.

Some parts of this book have been previously published, though all have been revised and expanded for publication here. Different versions of the Introduction and Chapters 4, 5, 8 and 9 have appeared in the following forms: "'Tomorrow we will change our names, invent ourselves again': Irish fiction and autobiography since 1990," in *Irish Literature Since 1990: Diverse Voices*, eds Scott Brewster and Michael Parker (Manchester: Manchester University Press, 2009), 201–215; "Uncertain Terms, Unstable Sands: *The Heather Blazing*," in *Reading Colm Tóibín*, ed. Paul Delaney (Dublin: Liffey Press, 2008), 53–68; "Material and Symbolic Geographies in William Trevor's *Felicia's Journey*," *PLL: Papers on Language and Literature. A Quarterly Journal for Scholars and Critics of Language and Literature*, 48:4 (Winter 2012), 411–440; "The Politics of Pity in Sebastian Barry's *A Long Long Way*," *South Carolina Review*, 44:2 (Spring 2012), 103–116; "Mourning Remains Unresolved: Trauma and Survival in Anne Enright's *The Gathering*," *LIT: Literature Interpretation Theory*, 21:3 (2010), 187–204.

Introduction: Reading the Contemporary Irish Novel 1987–2007

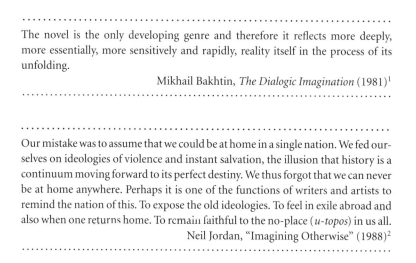

The novel is the only developing genre and therefore it reflects more deeply, more essentially, more sensitively and rapidly, reality itself in the process of its unfolding.

Mikhail Bakhtin, *The Dialogic Imagination* (1981)[1]

Our mistake was to assume that we could be at home in a single nation. We fed ourselves on ideologies of violence and instant salvation, the illusion that history is a continuum moving forward to its perfect destiny. We thus forgot that we can never be at home anywhere. Perhaps it is one of the functions of writers and artists to remind the nation of this. To expose the old ideologies. To feel in exile abroad and also when one returns home. To remain faithful to the no-place (*u-topos*) in us all.

Neil Jordan, "Imagining Otherwise" (1988)[2]

This book examines some of the most well-known and critically feted works of contemporary Irish literary fiction, all of which were published during a twenty-year period that witnessed accelerated change in virtually every sphere of the country's economic, social, cultural, political, and religious life, and which was paralleled by an uncommon flourishing of literary and artistic creativity.[3]

Reading the Contemporary Irish Novel 1987–2007, First Edition. Liam Harte.
© 2014 Liam Harte. Published 2014 by John Wiley & Sons, Ltd.

It is written primarily for third-level students of Irish literature and culture, and as such my textual choices have been significantly influenced by university syllabi at home and abroad, though my chief guide has been my sense of the moral and aesthetic quality of the fiction itself. I have also drawn on my extensive experience of teaching and writing about Irish fiction outwith Ireland over the past two decades, of which this book is the latest fruit. As the select number of novels chosen for analysis indicates, this study does not purport to be comprehensive in its scope or set out to offer a final account of a subject whose defining characteristic is its thematic and stylistic diversity. Nor am I trying to recommend a canon of contemporary Irish fiction: we are much too close in time to this literary corpus to achieve anything approaching a settled perspective on it. Moreover, eight of the nine novelists whose work is discussed in this study are still flourishing, and I suspect every reader will wish certain authors had been represented by a different novel.

In terms of its methodology, this book does not advocate any one critical approach to the Irish novel or seek to clothe it in an overarching theory, not least because most of my chosen works resist or exceed conventional critical categories. Instead, I adopt freely as I see fit from a range of theoretical and disciplinary perspectives, guided by the resonances and refractions of each text. Such a pluralistic approach means that no single thesis or expository framework governs my analysis. Direct, close engagement with the individual texts matters more to me than elaborating a fixed critical position or adhering to a particular academic mandate. Rather than provide a stocktaking of literary trends or parse the contemporary canon according to various "isms," my aim has been to offer substantial and detailed critical readings of some of the works I consider to be the most sharply provocative and keenly insightful recent fictional enquiries into particular aspects of Irish history, culture, and society. That "some" is worth stressing: the book could easily have expanded to twice its eventual size, given the richness of the primary sources from which to choose. As it is, all nine of the novelists discussed here have won international acclaim for the literary excellence of their human and social portraiture. Between them, they have garnered an array of prestigious citations and awards, including the Costa Book of the Year Award (Sebastian Barry), the European Prize for Literature (Edna O'Brien), the *Guardian* Fiction Prize (Seamus Deane), the Impac Dublin Literary Award (Colm Tóibín), the *Irish Times*/Aer Lingus Literary Award (John McGahern and Patrick McCabe), the Man Booker Prize (Roddy Doyle and Anne Enright), and the Whitbread Book of the Year Award (William Trevor).

But even without such garlands, there are good grounds for ranking the accomplishments of the contemporary cohort of Irish novelists highly and for devoting serious critical attention to their contribution to the unsettling and remaking of the national imagination that has accompanied the country's reinvention of itself since the 1980s. The artistry, diversity, and incisiveness of these and other novelists' narrative responses to the changing life of the times in general, and to the complexities of a mutating Irish culture and identity in particular, has made for universally compelling works of fiction that have extended and consolidated the Irish novelistic tradition after Joyce, intellectually, affectively, and imaginatively. "The Irish novel is intensely related to the body politic,"[4] observes Colm Tóibín, and in the work of the nine novelists under discussion here the narration of the nation takes on a heightened interrogative and sociological complexion. Each of these writers strategically collapses the boundaries between the personal and the national in an attempt to capture the fractured, conflictual nature of contemporary Irish experience and to explore the gap between lived realities and inherited narratives of origin, identity, and place. The interconnected themes of history, memory, and belonging – all fiercely contested categories in Irish cultural discourse – are therefore central to the book's focus. So too is the ideology of the nuclear family, which circulates through these eleven novels with cyclonic persistence, fanning the warring energies that permeate the parent-child relationships they portray. Although they exceed any single story we might wish to tell about them, all of these novels were composed at a time when the artificially constructed narratives of Irishness that claimed cultural authority since the foundation of the state were giving way to a rich diffusion of voices and perspectives, inflected by a complex interplay of competing artistic, political, and social agendas. Each of these authors participates in this process of renegotiating received meanings of nationality and creating spaces for a revised rhetoric of Irishness, just as each seeks a literary language, rhythm, and form that might match what Fintan O'Toole described as "the angular, discontinuous, spliced-together nature of contemporary Irish reality."[5] Some do it by offering charged portrayals of individuals and communities in chronic crisis; others by fashioning scenarios that foreground contradiction, contingency, and open-endedness; and others still by focusing on protagonists whose singular choices and stigmatized identities unsettle authorized narratives of belonging. Generational and attitudinal differences notwithstanding, all nine novelists find deficiencies in totalizing narratives of the past, refuse to fix the nation in unambiguous paradigms, and pose awkward, complex questions about the adequacy of nationality as a foundational fiction for the self.

Having situated my chosen novels within a particular sociohistorical matrix, it behoves me to provide some calibration of the realities with which they engage, though I do so in the full knowledge that any scene-setting survey can but skim the surface. A small sampling of social and political contexts must be made nonetheless. Few cultural critics would disagree that the Ireland of 1987 was a society in the throes of political and economic crisis, with optimism in short supply within both jurisdictions on the island. Writing in July of that year, the journalist Tim Pat Coogan described the country as "a world trouble spot" that infiltrates "the subconscious of television viewers and newspaper readers [through] such words as 'hunger strikes', 'IRA', 'Paisley', 'murder.'"[6] He was, of course, referring to Northern Ireland, which was still mired in an intractable bloody struggle between two mutually exclusive sets of nationalisms. The situation got bleaker still on November 8, 1987, when 11 people were killed by an IRA bomb at a Remembrance Day ceremony in the Fermanagh town of Enniskillen, an atrocity that inflamed murderous sectarian divisions even further. Meanwhile, the Republic was enduring its own social and economic purgatory, as Coogan noted: "at the time of writing, there are more people unemployed (240,000) than work in manufacturing industry or as farmers. Forty percent of the Irish population depends to some extent on social welfare."[7] These statistics would have been much worse were it not for emigration, the "mirror in which the Irish nation can always see its true face,"[8] as Liam Ryan so aptly described it at the time. The latest – so-called "third wave" – of emigration peaked in the 1987–1989 period, during which an estimated 172,000 people left the Republic, the great majority of whom went to Britain.[9] Coogan's account of his chance meeting with six recently arrived Irish graduates on a London bus in September 1986 provides a snapshot of the nature and scale of this scattering:

. . . .

All six had just qualified as civil engineers and they had with them the previous Sunday's *Sunday Press*, which carried a large picture of their graduating class – of the 47 beaming young faces in the photograph, only one had a permanent job in Ireland, two had temporary work, and the other 44 were emigrants. Very few, initially at least, were working as engineers. My six had worked as labourers, temporary barmen, whatever they could get, in some cases at jobs lasting only four or six days each. [. . .] They had been doubling up in friends' bedsitters, sneaking into hostels after hours with illegally-held keys, and generally subsisting in a variety of ways never envisaged by themselves or their parents as they worked their way through sixteen difficult, costly years of education.[10]
. . . .

Seven years later, in late 1993, the commentator John Waters was so dismayed by the ongoing effects of this still-unstanched human exodus that he sounded an extravagant death knell for a moribund nation:

. . . .

Walk into almost any town in the west of Ireland and take a deep breath. You will *inhale* the smell of the decomposition of the Irish economy. This is the smell of Appalachia. If you do not believe the evidence of your own lungs, look up the most recent census figures which show that every county and town in the west of Ireland suffered dramatic population losses in the five years to 1991. We are losing our people at a frightening rate. [...] This country is finished. A year or two ago, I might have added an 'unless we do X or Y ...' But the time for unlesses has run out. Our condition is terminal; it is just a matter of a few years.[11]

While it is easy in retrospect to smile at how spectacularly wrong Waters' controversy-courting pronouncement was soon proved to be, his despair is a useful barometer of national morale on the eve of the Republic's improbable 1990s economic revival. For by the time the few years in question had elapsed, this seemingly doomed polity had transformed itself into a booming high-tech economy, one suffused with optimism and cultural confidence and experiencing previously unheard-of levels of prosperity. Ireland's astonishing makeover from pauper to prince was driven by a variety of factors, some of which originated from outside the country and some from earlier political choices and shifts in government economic policy (though time would expose the profound, and profoundly consequential, lack of political vision behind the country's slavish embrace of global capitalism). Economist Daniel McCoy summarizes the key drivers of growth as follows:

EU membership and access to the Single Market; Ireland's low corporation tax rate and a large multinational presence, particularly from the U.S.; a high proportion of the population of working age; increased participation in the labor market, especially by females; a reversal of the trend of emigration toward immigration; sustained investment in education and training; coordinated social partnership agreements; and a more stable public finance position.[12]

The social effects of sudden prosperity soon became graphically apparent in the form of hyperconsumerism, urban gridlock, breakneck building projects, soaring property prices, and a dramatic increase in immigration from central Europe, Asia, and Africa, which peaked at almost 110,000 in the twelve months to April 2007, and was both the herald of a multicultural future and a trigger for racially motivated attacks on foreigners.[13] The benefits of the boom were far from evenly distributed, however, and the exclusionary processes it produced fuelled rising levels of social inequality, criminality, homelessness, alcohol consumption, and suicide.[14] Nevertheless, by the century's end, Ireland Inc. was being touted as the poster child of globalization, topping the index of the most globalized nations on earth in 2000 and 2001, as measured by the Washington-based *Foreign Policy* magazine.[15] With an annual average growth rate of 6.5% throughout the 1990s, the Republic's economic resurrection drew favorable comparisons with the "tiger" economies of East Asia, prompting a London-based economist with the investment bank Morgan Stanley to coin the appellation "Celtic Tiger" on August 31, 1994,[16] a term that, as Colin Coulter notes, would soon "slip its moorings" and "come to operate as a widely recognized and understood master signifier for a very particular and essentially hegemonic reading of the nature of contemporary Irish society."[17]

By coincidence, August 31, 1994 was also the day on which the IRA declared "a complete cessation of military operations," an announcement that proved to be the first of several watershed moments in the Northern Ireland "peace process," shorthand for the province's tortuously slow transition from protracted civil conflict to a negotiated political settlement between unionism, nationalism, and the Irish and British governments. When the resultant Belfast Agreement of 1998 created the conditions for economic regeneration north of the border, many were persuaded that a tamer cousin of the phantasmal beast running amok down south had emerged. Nine years later, just before the rampant Tiger vanished like the Cheshire cat's grin, the world's media again reverberated with the words "IRA" and "Paisley," but this time in circumstances that would have been utterly unimaginable to Coogan and his readers two decades earlier. In May 2007 Sinn Féin (the IRA's political alter ego) and the Democratic Unionist Party, still led by Ian Paisley, reached a historic agreement to share power in the devolved Northern Ireland Assembly, thus clearing the way for the cogovernance of the province by the "extremes" of nationalism and unionism. Both parties were returned to power in the 2011 Assembly elections and, at the time of writing (spring 2013), still lead a multiparty coalition. Bone-deep ethnic and sectarian divisions persist behind these power-sharing arrangements, however, and sporadic paramilitary violence continues to threaten the province's political and economic future, as does the embittered alienation of those socially deprived communities that have not felt the benefit of any peace dividend.

These, then, are some of the significant milestones on Ireland's journey from the "creeping catastrophe" and "petty apocalypse"[18] of the 1980s to socioeconomic and cultural revitalization in the 2000s, during which Irishness became for a time a fashionable global brand, having been "sanitised and made remarkably accommodating to the dominant elitist project of subservient assimilation into multinational capitalism; robbed of reference points from a rich and subversive history."[19] The story of societal and attitudinal change is much more complex than this limited summary allows, however, and, as in any society, whether "in transition" or not, a proliferation of continuities and countercurrents complicate conventional linear notions of change and development. From many (poorer) people's perspective, little changed fundamentally during the years of Ireland's intensive economic growth and it wasn't hard to discern the undertow of nineteenth-century currents beneath globalized surfaces. So while it is necessary to acknowledge the radical displacement of long-standing historical patterns, we should also bear in mind the enduring antinomies of modernity and tradition in the new Irish commercial culture of the 1990s and 2000s. Take the example of Catholic religiosity in the Republic. On the face of it, the sudden surge in levels of personal affluence in the 1990s quickened the trend toward secularism and accelerated the jettisoning of traditional social and moral orthodoxies, although money was not the sole or even the primary factor in these developments. The decline in the authority of Catholic churchmen on state and society was already underway by the time the nation's coffers began to swell, as a more critically aware and less deferential populace rejected the idea that civil law in a pluralist society should be based on the teachings of one religion. The scandal generated by the revelation in 1992 that Eamon Casey, the high-profile Bishop of Galway, had fathered a son with an Irish-American divorcée eighteen years earlier had a seismic impact on the ordinary faithful, exposing the moral hypocrisy of an all-pervading institution in Irish life. To observers such as Colm Tóibín, the news was not wholly unexpected:

For years, it had been clear that something like this would have to come into the open. In the mid-eighties, rancorous battles had been fought over divorce and abortion, and the liberal side – our side – had lost. There were times when we felt the country was going to burst at the seams with hypocrisy.[20]

Yet as Tóibín goes on to note, the scandal proved to be "only one of several previously unimaginable incidents that began to transform both the moral and the political climate of Holy Catholic Ireland."[21] The bishop's transgression soon paled beside the litany of horrific crimes committed against children and vulnerable young adults by pedophile priests and religious leaders, which were routinely covered up by the church hierarchy until their widespread media exposure in the 1990s and 2000s. Years of official investigation into the chronic emotional, physical, and sexual abuse inflicted upon children in various religious-run institutions culminated in the publication in 2009 of the Report of the Commission to Inquire into Child Abuse, commonly known as the Ryan Report, which outlined the crimes of more than 800 known abusers in over 200 institutions during a period of thirty-five years. An *Irish Times* editorial described the Report as "the map of an Irish hell" and starkly set out the consequences of the findings for the nation's self-image: "We have to deal with the now-established fact that, alongside the warmth and intimacy, the kindness and generosity of Irish life, there was, for most of the history of the State, a deliberately maintained structure of vile and vicious abuse. [. . .] [A]buse was not a failure of the system. It was the system."[22] "Never before," observed one commentator, "has a single, formerly powerful, and highly respected sector of Irish society turned, within little more than a decade, into a focus for almost universal contempt and condemnation."[23]

And yet despite the damage done to its temporal power and influence by these clerical scandals, the Catholic Church did not wither. Catholicism remains the dominant religion in the state, in spite of the church's crisis of credibility and the rise of religious pluralism. Census results from 2002 and 2006 showed that, although religious practice was in decline, the great majority of the population (90% and 87%, respectively) still identified themselves as Catholic, and pilgrimage sites such as Lough Derg in County Donegal and Knock in County Mayo have continued to thrive.[24] Indeed, Knock, the site of a reported Marian apparition in 1879, made national headlines in late 2009 and again in 2010 when several thousand people flocked there in response to predictions by a self-proclaimed visionary of an imminent apparition by the Virgin Mary. In scenes that recalled earlier outbreaks of magical devotionalism at times of socioeconomic crisis, the credulous and the curious stared at the sun for hours, camera phones and digital recorders in hand. From this, one might conclude that whereas the Catholic Church's psychosexual stranglehold has weakened, the grip of folk religion on many Irish minds endures.

Any account of the peculiar nature of Irish modernity must therefore attend to what sociologist Carmen Kuhling terms "the diverse and antagonistic character of the transformations that have accompanied Ireland's experience of accelerated modernization."[25] She herself borrows Zygmunt Bauman's notion of "liquid modernity" to make sense of the contradictory cultural tendencies that characterize a society being reshaped in the furnace of globalization and the communications revolution. Her claim that "The experience of living in contemporary Ireland is that of living in an in-between world, in between cultures and identities – an experience of liminality,"[26] chimes with film historian Martin McLoone's memorable assertion that Ireland in the swinging 1990s inhabited "a cultural space somewhere between its nationalist past, its European future and its American imagination."[27] Such diagnoses speak to the pervasive sense of fragmentation and unease that was one of the most notable corollaries of the country's newfound prosperity and economic self-confidence. Reflecting on the international marketing of Irish cultural distinctiveness in the 1990s through such forms as the theme pub and the musical extravaganza *Riverdance*, Terence Brown concluded: "In such phenomena, Irish identity, rather than remaking itself in acts of imagination, seemed bereft of significance, a simulacrum in a world of simulacra, where meaning had been hollowed out to allow for the easy transportation and assembly of Ireland Lite."[28] But perhaps the most succinct summary of the depthless nature of Irish capitalist modernity was provided by the commentator who declared that "Everywhere in the mentality of the Irish people are flux and uncertainty. Our national consciousness may be described, in a native phrase, as a quaking sod. It gives no footing. It is not English, not Irish, nor Anglo-Irish."[29] A vivid verdict to be sure, but not a recent one, considering the writer was Daniel Corkery and the year not 1991 or 2001 but 1931. I cite his remarks as a reminder that anxieties about the instability and inauthenticity of Irish cultural identity are by no means new. Flux rather than fixity has been the historical norm, a point that should be borne in mind at the same time as we acknowledge that each generation fashions its own diverse set of responses to an identity that has long been perceived as being out of joint.

The specific novelistic challenges presented by the splintering of the grand *récit* of Irishness under the impact of 1990s globalization were succinctly set out by Fintan O'Toole in a 2001 *Irish Times* article:

. . . .

What has happened, essentially, is that the emergence of a frantic, globalised, dislocated Ireland has deprived fiction writers of some of their traditional tools. One is a distinctive sense of place. To write honestly of where most of us live now is to describe everywhere and nowhere [. . .]. The other troublesome change is the collapse of the very notion of a national narrative. Throughout the 20th century, it was possible for Irish writers to tell stories which seemed in one way or another to relate to a bigger story of revival, revolution, repression and collapse. [. . .] These days, it is by no means clear what the big story of Ireland actually is, or indeed that the whole notion of 'Ireland' as a single framework has any validity.[30]

. . . .

Given these challenges, critical evaluations of the effectiveness of literary novelists' negotiation of the relationship between the social and the imaginary orders during this era of long-term cultural shifts have tended to be quite negative. Before the 1990s were out, George O'Brien was expressing concern at the lack of concerted fictional treatment of social change: "All too few contemporary Irish literary novels portray the shifts in class structure, the political fallout, the moral challenges, the conflict of outlooks that have typified Irish life of late, and in doing so has lent the airs and graces of modern democracy to Ireland at the present time."[31] While sympathizing with the novelist's predicament, Declan

Kiberd also bemoaned the paucity of meaningful fictive engagement with the dynamics of a rapidly changing society:

> There is no Trollopian *The Way We Live Now*, much less a Tom Wolfe-style *Bonfire of the Vanities* even among our younger writers. The pace of change may be just too fast for most, for it is never easy to take a clear photograph of a moving object, especially when you are up close to it. Nothing, after all, is more difficult to realise than the present – we are always at its mercy more than we are its masters.[32]

Others took a more critical line, indicting the contemporary generation of novelists for their stubborn fixation with the past. In a 2010 broadside, the Berlin-based novelist Julian Gough stirred up controversy by caricaturing Irish "literary writers" as "a priestly caste, scribbling by candlelight, cut off from the electric current of the culture,"[33] an analogy that recalled Joe Cleary's critique of Irish literary and cinematic production during the 1990s:

> Far from suggesting a climate of radical innovation or dramatic new departures, nearly all the most critically lauded and commercially successful Irish works of that decade continued to be very strikingly invested in 'the dark ages' of the mid-twentieth century rural Ireland that the country had supposedly left behind. [...] The Celtic Tiger of the 1990s may have been attempting to get as far away as fast as it possibly could from de Valera's Ireland, but in the literary, dramatic and cinematic worlds that Ireland continued to be the biggest business in town.[34]

While it is true that Ireland's difficult history, including the revolutionary ferment of the 1916–1923 period, has been the focus of much recent Irish literary fiction, such criticisms miss several key points about novelists' uses of the past, the most obvious being that the turn to history and to personal and collective memory is directly related to the need for a fuller, more historicized understanding of the present. Steven Connor's observation that in the postwar English novel "every representation of the past is a historicizing of the present, making it possible to inhabit or belong to one's present differently,"[35] is no less applicable to the contemporary Irish novel. Furthermore, to speak of the recent past as if it were unproblematically knowable and definitively "over" is surely misguided. As Hilary Mantel reminds us: "The past is not dead ground, and to traverse it is not a sterile exercise. History is always changing behind us, and the past changes a little every time we retell it."[36] We must also acknowledge the degree to which contemporary Irish novelists have been self-consciously preoccupied by the conditions of possibility under which history is narratable, by the methods by which a conflict-laden past can be known, and by the ethics of historical representation. Recent years have seen the publication of several notable metahistorical novels – Roddy Doyle's *A Star Called Henry* (1999), Jamie O'Neill's *At Swim, Two Boys* (2001), Joseph O'Connor's *Star of the Sea* (2003) – that self-reflexively grapple with the problems of historicism and ironize the uses of historical memory in the formation of modern Irish identities, individual and collective. While none of the works discussed in this study fall directly into this category, at least three – *The Butcher Boy, Reading in the Dark* and *The Gathering* – foreground, at the level of form as well as theme, the challenges of narrating obscure, not-fully-known, and still-troubling histories in socially realistic modes. These three novels are also among the most striking fictional renderings of one of the defining preoccupations of contemporary Irish novelists: the damaging psychic and cultural legacies of violent histories of both the hidden and overt kinds. The haunting repercussions of sublimated memories, unspeakable secrets, and unprocessed histories run like a dark thread through the fabric of recent Irish fiction, making the wounded, traumatized subject one of its most representative figures. Traumatized individuals, claims Cathy Caruth, "carry an impossible history with them, or they become themselves the symptom of a history that they cannot entirely possess," a pathological condition that is bound up with a profound epistemological crisis that "extends beyond the question of individual cure and asks how we in this era can have access to our own historical experience, to a history that is in its immediacy a crisis to whose truth there is no simple access."[37] Caruth might be describing here the crisis that afflicts the protagonists of several recent Irish novels, in which there is a sustained attempt to explore the psychological and political effects of repressed or unknown histories and lay bare the social forces and cultural institutions that reinforce trauma at a national level.

Not all contemporary Irish writers deal in catastrophic histories and traumatic memories, however, or promote a view of the past as deeply operative in the present. Such themes are wearyingly burdensome to a postnationalist novelist such as Colm Tóibín, who would like to see the culture rid itself of its "terrible obsession about Ireland and Irishness, about tradition, identity and history."[38] For Tóibín and others, the emergence of a posthistorical Irish consciousness proves more imaginatively quickening than a brooding preoccupation with national identity and the postcolonial agendas that are often associated with it. The fault lines between those who cling to the traditional markers of cultural distinctiveness and authenticity and those who espouse a new cosmopolitan individualism are beginning to be mapped fictionally with varying degrees of seriousness and levity. For example, in Harry Clifton's short story, "A Visitor from the Future" (2007), the depthlessness of Ireland's globalized culture perturbs Ann, a disaffected university tutor. Her attempt to interest her students in an older Ireland, one in which "people were continuous with themselves, and everything could be named," exposes deep attitudinal and generational schisms, leaving her with a "strange sense that the country she came from was levitating into a weightless, valueless space where everything equalled everything else. These things – disintegration, discontinuity – are not threatening but good, the best of them told her. Tomorrow we will change our names, invent ourselves again."[39] Anne Haverty's *The Free and Easy* (2006) offers a more caustic critique of this vision of a present and, by implication, a future from which history has been evacuated. The novel, which satirizes the pretensions and snobberies of the Dublin *nouveaux riches*, stages a contest between those who want to preserve and opportunistically reinvent the nation's heritage as a saleable commodity and those who wish to jettison tradition completely. What unites these seemingly polarized positions is a postmodern view of the past as an agreed-upon fiction. Affluent Irish modernity, the novel suggests, is underpinned by a willful amnesia and a pernicious effacement of history, traits personified by Seoda Fitzgibbon, the glamorous wife of a corrupt businessman, for whom the perpetual present is the primary ground of personal and socioeconomic success:

. . . .

'You can forget the last century. And you can definitely forget the century before. Ireland as we know it – and let's thank whoever or whatever – was born some time around nineteen ninety-four. Or ninety-six?' She smiled. 'Let the historians fight about the year. Historians like to have something to fight about.'[40]

. . . .

There is a caveat to enter here, however, lest we pin the social realist label too firmly to the lapels of contemporary Irish novelists or predicate our analysis of a diverse literary corpus on a simple correspondence between literary text and social text. The hiatus between the phenomenal world and the fictive universe, between language and reality, complicates realism's implicit claims to transparent representation. So while it is perfectly valid to argue that "the novel is not simply the product and the reflection of certain social conditions but actively contributes to producing them as the very conditions of its own reception,"[41] we must also acknowledge that there is more to fiction than social realism, and none of the writers included in this study would want their work to be read solely or perhaps even primarily in terms of its relation to sociohistorical realities. Patrick McCabe, for instance, observed that "naturalism or realism only really provides maybe a third of the story"[42] and John McGahern remarked in a late interview that "life is of very little use to fiction; it has to be re-imagined or changed or altered in some way."[43] Then there is the striking passage in Edna O'Brien's memoir, *Country Girl* (2012), in which she recalls how, as a budding writer, she antagonized her writer-husband, Ernest Gébler, by describing a road as blue in a short story:

....

He erupted, saying there was no such thing as a blue road, but I knew that there was. I had seen them, I had walked on one, the hot tar smearing the white canvas of my new shoes. Roads were every colour, blue, grey, gold, sandstone and carmine. He was categorical about it. It was as if by saying it, I had defied some inalienable truth. He had to be right about everything and if he was crossed, a look of hatred came into his eyes, but to be crossed by me, a literary flibbertigibbet, was ridiculous, believing as he did that he owned me.

But in secret I clung to the blue road, while knowing that somewhere, in the distance, like a glacier, it would come between us.[44]

....

The scene has a paradigmatic quality about it: to express herself, the apprentice female novelist must struggle against the patriarchal monopoly of literary realism and be prepared to pay an emotional price for adhering to her personal artistic vision.

Such moments remind us of the ambiguous nature of the relationship between the literary imagination and social reality in Ireland. Historically, realism has "never been less than profoundly problematic"[45] for Irish novelists, successive generations of whom have cavilled at the rebarbative anomalies and inadequacies of society and bemoaned their resistance to figuration within the representational frame of the realist text. In the 1830s Maria Edgeworth famously found it "impossible to draw Ireland as she now is in a book of fiction – realities are too strong, party passions too violent to bear to see."[46] Over a century later, Sean O'Faolain complained that the postrevolutionary social milieu was too "unshaped" to yield to the realist novelist's pen and wrote it off as "stuff for the anthropologist rather than the man of letters."[47] That this argument about Ireland's lack of social density hasn't gone away is evidenced by the remarks about language, form, and representation made by several of the novelists under discussion here. Tóibín, for instance, has spoken of his sense of being involved in the creation of an Ireland "which hasn't yet solidified"[48] and Anne Enright has expressed her impatience with culturally determined notions of realism in Ireland, explaining: "My impulse is towards the real. That's where I am trying to get."[49] The frustration of this same impulse – the struggle to render in prose fiction the texture of what O'Faolain called a "thin"[50] society – bears heavily on the novel that we shall consider in Chapter 2, McGahern's *Amongst Women*, about which the author said in a 1990 interview:

Ireland isn't like other places where the novel has flourished, in that it is so structureless. It has no formed society, no tradition of manners. Because of that, the form of the novel or the shape of a sonnet aren't available to an Irish writer in the same way, which is a pain in the arse because they are a great saving of time. This is true of the novel more than any other form: by its history and nature, a novel is a whole world, it is more social than other forms. Here, though, you don't have a proper society. The whole country is made up of families, each family a kind of independent republic. In *Amongst Women*, the family is a kind of half-way house between the individual and the society.[51]

It is difficult to gauge the extent to which this perception of the inadequacy of Irish society has affected contemporary novelists' confidence in moving between the social and the aesthetic domains. Certainly, the diversity of views held by these nine writers on the role of social commentary and commitment in fiction is quite striking, the primacy of politics and history in their work notwithstanding. Anne Enright, the youngest of the nine, is reluctant to have her work appreciated only for the light it throws on contemporary Irish society, explaining: "I don't write about Ireland so much as from Ireland."[52] The reverse is true, arguably, of Edna O'Brien who, although she left the country in 1958, has rarely strayed from Ireland in her imagination, and whose *House of Splendid Isolation*, discussed in Chapter 6, is part of a provocative 1990s trilogy based on headline-grabbing real-life events. Roddy Doyle is in the O'Brien mold, though he shares Enright's resistance to rigid national categorization: "I would say, rather than being an Irish writer, I'm a writer who happens to be in Ireland. But having said that, I've been here for more than fifty years. And I've seen some extraordinary social changes."[53] Coming from a Dublin working-class background, Doyle forthrightly embraced an *engagé* position from the outset of his career, seeing himself as "socially committed and politically engaged" and believing that it is "important to upset and outrage people."[54] Contrast this with William Trevor's presentation of himself as an unaligned storyteller: "I don't really want to make any statement. I see the writing of a story as creating an impression, and that impression is going to communicate itself to somebody else. That's all I seek to do."[55] Even if we allow for a measure of disingenuousness, Trevor's outlook is far removed from that of Seamus Deane. A product of post-partition working-class Derry, Deane has always championed politically committed art and criticism, and since the 1970s has been a combative arbiter of the terms in which Irish cultural history can be retrieved and appraised. Moreover, his anti-revisionist and anti-unionist politics are the antithesis of those espoused by Sebastian Barry, Enright, and Tóibín, the last of whom was one of the most trenchant critics of Deane's groundbreaking *The Field Day Anthology of Irish Writing* (1991), which Tóibín regarded as canonizing a narrow and anachronistic version of Irish literary nationalism.[56]

Curiously, Tóibín himself tends to regard his own fiction as something of a politics-free zone, telling one interviewer:

> I think society in my novels is like the background colour in a portrait. I am more interested in the intricacies and secrecies of the self than I am in politics and society. They have to be there but most of the thinking I do is about character itself. [...] I think I feel free not to bother too much with large political questions in the novel, or dramatisations of change, because I am, when not writing novels, really alert to them, and interested in them. I follow them and I know them. But I keep the novels pure.[57]

Not only is the concept of purity that Tóibín invokes here puzzling – especially when one considers Edna O'Brien's observation that "everything is political: one's upbringing, the culture in which one grows up, even religion is political, whether we like it or not"[58] – it is also undercut by the novel of his we shall discuss in Chapter 4, *The Heather Blazing*, which is an intensely political work. This discussion is preceded by a critical appraisal of *The Butcher Boy* by McCabe, whose reflections on the relationship between societal change and the artistic imagination wryly warn against myopically reading novels as social or political bulletins:

> I have always been of the opinion that the fictional chroniclers of epoch-making, glacial movements of history will tend to be authors who, when they first sat down at their desk, were convinced that their chosen subject involved being bitten by a crab at the age of seven or rejected by a woman at the age of 21, theirs among the first eyebrows to raise when it emerges their story is, in fact, about the displacement of millions and the collapse of empire.[59]

In the textual readings that follow, therefore, I try to provide contextual interpretations of my chosen texts and attend to the particularities of the writing itself, while remaining alert to the fact that these novels are as much about the state of being alive as they are about the state of the nation. Often, of course, ontological and national concerns go hand in hand. The trilogy of novels by Doyle that is the subject of Chapter 1 appears to be much more invested in representing the alienated lives and relationships of working-class denizens of 1980s Dublin than in calibrating the nation's political or cultural health, until we realize that Doyle's privileging of the raw, colloquial utterance of his culturally invisible Dubliners carries a pungent political statement about social inequality and class prejudice before the influx of global capital during the boom years. Context also incorporates matters of literary tradition and influence and, as one would expect, the work of these nine novelists bears the marks of many antecedents, from Stendhal and Henry James to Ernest Hemingway, James Baldwin, Angela Carter and, inevitably, James Joyce. Back in the mid-1970s Denis Donoghue claimed that "The contemporary Irish novelist looks for a tradition capable of telling him what has been done and how he ought to proceed: instead he finds Joyce, an overbearing presence."[60] Forty years on, this is no longer a truth that can be universally acknowledged. While it remains the case that some contemporary Irish novelists continue to regard Joyce as a tutelary figure – chief among them Edna O'Brien, who said of her stylistic and moral mentor that "In the constellation of geniuses, he is a blinding light and father of us all"[61] – I suspect few would now speak of Joyce as possessing a "peculiar, impregnable, *frightening* authority,"[62] as John Banville did in 1990. The easing of this monumental anxiety of influence is audible in Deane's response to a question about literary models for *Reading in the Dark* – "I tried not to think of Joyce but of course he was there anyway"[63] – and in McCabe's sense of Joyce as an enabling contemporary rather than a stifling predecessor: "I remember picking up a copy of *Dubliners* and thinking 'This could have been written yesterday'. [...] [S]omehow just the sheer brilliance, the art of Joyce made it seem so contemporary, it was absolutely mindblowing."[64] Enright is even more animated about the liberating impact of Joyce's example and keen to seize the opportunity to possess and extend his legacy through her own work: "I pilfer freely from Joyce, I have no problem doing that. [...] It's not a competition with Joyce. [...]. Joyce did not throw a shadow, he cast a great light. He made it possible to write about anything at all."[65] But it is perhaps Tóibín who provides the most radical updating of Donoghue's thesis. Echoing Samuel Beckett's claim that "The artist who stakes his being is from nowhere, has no kith,"[66] Tóibín insists on the necessary solitariness of the creative imagination and reminds us that every artistic work is its own freshly created universe:

· ·

The imagination at work is always alone, no matter how strong a tradition or sense of community. The mind making images does so singly, in moments of fierce concentration, suddenly, as though this had never been done before, as though the task of now were the only task there ever would be.[67]

· ·

The critical challenge, then, is to honor the imaginative integrity and idiomatic uniqueness of each of these eleven novels, while investigating the distinctive features and deeper meanings of their retelling of the Irish national narrative; to explore the new directions plotted by these texts, while remaining attuned to the intertextual dialogues they conduct with those that came before; and to examine these writers' representation of the personal and the sociopolitical, while recognizing that literature, in the end, serves "Only the pure circle of itself."[68]

Notes

1. Mikhail Bakhtin, *The Dialogic Imagination: Four Essays*, trans. Caryl Emerson and Michael Holquist, ed. Michael Holquist (Austin: University of Texas Press, 1981), 7.

2. Neil Jordan, "Imagining Otherwise," in *Across the Frontiers: Ireland in the 1990s*, ed. Richard Kearney (Dublin: Wolfhound Press, 1988), 199.

3. This study does not concern itself with Irish genre fiction, of which there has been a significant outpouring in recent decades. For example, the 1990s witnessed an explosion of Irish popular romantic fiction by authors such as Patricia Scanlan and Marian Keyes, who followed the groundbreaking example of Maeve Binchy in becoming best-selling novelists, nationally and internationally. For a discussion of this publishing phenomenon, see Kathy Cremin, "The Dispersed and Dismissed: The World of Irish Women's Best-sellers," *Critical Survey*, 15:1 (2003), 60–76. The 1990s also marked the appearance of a distinctive subgenre of Irish crime fiction spearheaded by Ken Bruen, John Connolly, and Adrian McKinty, and described as "a hybrid of hard-boiled detective, forensic thriller and crime mystery" by Andrew Kincaid in "'Down These Mean Streets': The City and Critique in Contemporary Irish Noir," *Éire-Ireland*, 45:1&2 (Spring/Summer 2010), 39–55. Meanwhile, the political violence in Northern Ireland continued to fuel the production of so-called "Troubles thrillers," approximately 400 of which have been published since 1970, the majority by British and American writers. This literary corpus is expertly surveyed by Aaron Kelly in *The Thriller in Northern Ireland since 1969: Utterly Resigned Terror* (Aldershot: Ashgate, 2005).

4. Lynne Tillman, "Colm Tóibín," *Bomb*, 38 (Winter 1992), 23.

5. Fintan O'Toole, "Writing the boom," *Irish Times*, January 25, 2001, 12.

6. Tim Pat Coogan, *Disillusioned Decades: Ireland 1966–1987* (Dublin: Gill and Macmillan, 1987), unpaginated preface. The Paisley in question was the Reverend Ian, leader of the Democratic Unionist Party from 1971 to 2008.

7. Coogan, *Disillusioned Decades*, unpaginated preface.

8. Liam Ryan, "Irish Emigration to Britain since World War II," in *Migrations: The Irish at Home and Abroad*, ed. Richard Kearney (Dublin: Wolfhound Press, 1990), 46.

9. Bronwen Walter, "From 'flood' to 'trickle': Irish migration to Britain 1987–2006," *Irish Geography*, 41:2 (2008), 185–86.

10. Coogan, *Disillusioned Decades*, 150–151.

11. John Waters, "The smell of Appalachia," *Irish Times*, November 23, 1993, original emphasis. Reproduced in his *Every Day Like Sunday?* (Dublin: Poolbeg Press, 1995), 74.

12. Daniel McCoy, "Ireland's Spectacular, If Delayed, Convergence," *Radharc: A Journal of Irish and Irish-American Studies*, 5–7 (2004–2006), 183.

13. Emma Quinn, John Stanley, Corona Joyce, and Philip J. O'Connell, *Handbook of Immigration and Asylum in Ireland 2007* (Dublin: Economic and Social Research Institute, 2008), 5–6. The killing of a Chinese man, Zhao Liu Tao, on a Dublin street in January 2002 was widely reported as Ireland's first racially motivated murder. See *Racism and Anti-racism in Ireland*, eds Ronit Lentin and Robbie McVeigh (Belfast: Beyond the Pale, 2002).

14. In a 2009 interview Colm Tóibín linked the suicide rate in his home town of Enniscorthy to the collapse of traditional sources of authority in contemporary Ireland: "What has changed more than anything else is the death of authority, not only the church's authority but, say, the family's authority, the doctor's and the politician's authority, and the employer's authority. That has brought with it great freedom for people. But it has also meant that if anybody had loose moorings, they could be really unprotected. There have been a large number of suicides in the town. Some of them very disturbing, really disturbing." See Joseph Wiesenfarth, "An Interview with Colm Tóibín," *Contemporary Literature*, 50:1 (Spring 2009), 19.

15. Fintan O'Toole, "Irish Culture in a Globalised World," in *Kaleidoscopic Views of Ireland*, eds Munira H. Mutran and Laura P. Z. Izarra (São Paulo: Humanitas/FFLCH /USP, 2003), 77.

16. Denis O'Hearn, "The Celtic Tiger: the role of the multinationals," in *Under the Belly of the Tiger: Class, Race, Identity and Culture in the Global Ireland*, eds Ethel Crowley and Jim Mac Laughlin (Dublin: Irish Reporter Publications, 1997), 21. The Irish economy continued to grow at an average rate of 5.5% during the 2000s, until the disastrous economic crash of 2008.

17. Colin Coulter, "The end of Irish history? An introduction to the book," in *The End of Irish History?: Critical Reflections on the Celtic Tiger*, eds Colin Coulter and Steve Coleman (Manchester: Manchester University Press, 2003), 4.

18. Fintan O'Toole, *A Mass for Jesse James: A Journey Through 1980s Ireland* (Dublin: Raven Arts Press, 1990), 9.

19. Peadar Kirby, "Contested Pedigrees of the Celtic Tiger," in *Reinventing Ireland: Culture, Society and the Global Economy*, eds Peadar Kirby, Luke Gibbons, and Michael Cronin (London: Pluto Press, 2002), 27.

20. Colm Tóibín, "Dublin's Epiphany," *The New Yorker Magazine*, April 13, 1995, 46.

21. Tóibín, "Dublin's Epiphany", 47.
22. Editorial, "The savage reality of our darkest days," *Irish Times*, May 21, 2009, 19.
23. Terry Prone, "Bricks on the Road to Hell," in *Responding to the Ryan Report*, ed. Tony Flannery (Dublin: Columba Press, 2009), 84.
24. Data drawn from the Central Statistics Office, Dublin.
25. Carmen Kuhling, "'Liquid Modernity' and Irish Identity: Irishness in Guinness, Jameson and Ballygowan Advertisements," *Advertising and Society Review*, 9:3 (2008). http://muse.jhu.edu/journals/advertising_and_society_review/v009/9.3.kuhling.html
26. Kuhling, "'Liquid Modernity' and Irish Identity."
27. Martin McLoone, *Irish Film: The Emergence of a Contemporary Cinema* (London: British Film Institute, 2000), 7.
28. Terence Brown, *Ireland: A Social and Cultural History 1922–2002* (London: Harper Perennial, 2004), 400.
29. Daniel Corkery, *Synge and Anglo-Irish Literature* [1931] (Cork: Mercier Press, 1966), 14.
30. O'Toole, "Writing the boom," 12.
31. George O'Brien, "Worlds of Their Own: Autonomy and Anxiety in Contemporary Irish Fiction," *Colby Quarterly*, 35:3 (September 1999), 133–134.
32. Declan Kiberd, *The Irish Writer and the World* (Cambridge: Cambridge University Press, 2005), 276.
33. Julian Gough, "The State of Irish Literature 2010." http://www.juliangough.com/journal/2010/2/10/the-state-of-irish-literature-2010.html
34. Joe Cleary, *Outrageous Fortune: Capital and Culture in Modern Ireland* (Dublin: Field Day Publications, 2006), 160–161.
35. Steven Connor, *The English Novel in History: 1950–1995* (London: Routledge, 1996), 140.
36. Hilary Mantel, "Booker winner Hilary Mantel on dealing with history in fiction," *Guardian*, October 17, 2009.
37. Cathy Caruth (ed.), *Trauma: Explorations in Memory* (Baltimore: Johns Hopkins University Press, 1995), 5–6.
38. Jody Allen Randolph (ed.), *Close to the Next Moment: Interviews from a Changing Ireland* (Manchester: Carcanet, 2010), 175.
39. Harry Clifton, "A Visitor from the Future," in *The Faber Book of Best New Irish Short Stories 2006–7*, ed. David Marcus (London: Faber and Faber, 2007), 173.
40. Anne Haverty, *The Free and Easy* (London: Chatto & Windus, 2006), 112.
41. David Lloyd, *Anomalous States: Irish Writing and the Post-Colonial Moment* (Dublin: Lilliput Press, 1993), 131.
42. Pat McCabe and Maurice Fitzpatrick, "An Interview with Pat McCabe," *Journal of Irish Studies*, 23 (2008), 55.

43. Linda Collinge and Emmanuel Vernadakis, "John McGahern—b.1934," *Journal of the Short Story in English*, 41 (Autumn 2003), online edition. http://jsse.revues.org/ index314.html

44. Edna O'Brien, *Country Girl* (London: Faber and Faber, 2012), 125.

45. Terry Eagleton, *Heathcliff and the Great Hunger: Studies in Irish Culture* (London: Verso, 1995), 225. This was especially so in the nineteenth century. As Lloyd points out in *Anomalous States*: "One of the problems of the [nineteenth-century] Irish novel, precisely insofar as it conforms to the symbolic mode of realism, is the sheer volume of inassimilable residue that it can neither properly contain not entirely exclude" (152–153).

46. Maria Edgeworth to Michael Pakenham Edgeworth, February 19, 1834. Cited in Derek Hand, *A History of the Irish Novel* (Cambridge: Cambridge University Press, 2011), 68.

47. Sean O'Faolain, "The Dilemma of Irish Letters," *The Month*, 2:6 (1949), 375–376.

48. Alex Clark, "Songs of Experience," *Guardian*, March 13, 2004, review section, 22.

49. Hedwig Schwall, "Muscular Metaphors in Anne Enright: An Interview," *The European English Messenger*, 17:1 (2008), 21–22.

50. O'Faolain, "The Dilemma of Irish Letters," 376.

51. Fintan O'Toole, "The family as independent republic," *Irish Times*, October 13, 1990, review section, 2.

52. Miranda Popkey, "Anne Enright on *The Forgotten Waltz*," *The Paris Review Daily*, October 25, 2011. http://www.theparisreview.org/blog/2011/10/25/anne-enright-on-the-forgotten-waltz/

53. Randolph, *Close to the Next Moment*, 146.

54. Stephen J. Costello (ed.), *The Irish Soul: In Dialogue* (Dublin: Liffey Press, 2001), 91.

55. Mira Stout, "The Art of Fiction CVIII: William Trevor," *Paris Review*, 110 (1989), 151. In the same interview Trevor was asked about his relationship to the Irish literary tradition, to which he replied: "I always call myself an Irish writer. I'm one of the few Irish writers who actually likes the phrase. [...] I don't really feel that being Irish is the important thing. What is important is to take Irish provincialism – which is what I happen to know about because it's what I come from – and to make it universal" (127).

56. See Tóibín's review of *The Field Day Anthology of Irish Writing* in the *Canadian Journal of Irish Studies*, 18:2 (December 1992), 121–124, in which he characterized Field Day's governing ideology as "an old-fashioned and unreconstructed version of Irish nationalism which has a deep contempt for the Irish state and anything that has happened within its confines" (123).

57. Randolph, *Close to the Next Moment*, 170–171.

58. Helen Thompson, "Edna O'Brien," in *Irish Women Writers Speak Out: Voices from the Field*, eds Catriona Moloney and Helen Thompson (Syracuse: Syracuse University Press, 2003), 200.
59. Patrick McCabe, "The Republic of the Soul," *Irish Times*, December 29, 1999, 10.
60. Denis Donoghue, "Together," in his *We Irish: Essays on Irish Literature and Society* (Berkeley: University of California Press, 1986), 149–150.
61. Philip Roth, "A Conversation with Edna O'Brien: 'The Body Contains the Life Story,'" *New York Times Book Review*, November 18, 1984, 39. O'Brien also paid homage to Joyce through her 1999 biography of him, which lays bare the extent of his influence on her own aesthetic strategies.
62. John Banville, "Survivors of Joyce," in *James Joyce: The Artist and the Labyrinth*, ed. Augustine Martin (London: Ryan Publishing, 1990), 80, original emphasis.
63. Seamus Deane and Maurice Fitzpatrick, "An Interview with Seamus Deane," *Journal of Irish Studies*, 22 (2007), 90.
64. Christopher FitzSimon, "St Macartan, Minnie the Minx and Mondo Movies: Elliptical Peregrinations Through the Subconscious of a Monaghan Writer Traumatised by Cows and the Brilliance of James Joyce," *Irish University Review*, 28:1 (Spring/Summer 1998), 182–183.
65. Schwall, "Muscular Metaphors in Anne Enright," 20.
66. Samuel Beckett, "Homage to Jack B. Yeats," in his *Disjecta: Miscellaneous Writings and a Dramatic Fragment*, ed. Ruby Cohn (London: Calder, 1983), 149.
67. Quoted in Stacey D'Erasmo, "About Colm Tóibín: A Profile by Stacey D'Erasmo," *Ploughshares*, 37:1 (Spring 2011), 168.
68. Tom Paulin, "The Other Voice," *The Strange Museum* (London: Faber and Faber, 1980), 45.

Chapter 1

In the Family Way: Roddy Doyle's Barrytown Trilogy (1987–1991)

I

If, as has been claimed, the origins of contemporary Irish drama can be traced to September 28, 1964, the date Brian Friel's *Philadelphia, Here I Come!* premiered at Dublin's Gate Theatre,[1] then one might legitimately nominate March 27, 1987, as the inaugurating moment of contemporary Irish fiction, if by "contemporary" we mean writing that is "characterised by an increasing sense of democratisation, of challenges, from previously marginalised constituencies, to the values and judgements that historically had governed the formation of the literary canon."[2] On that date, a twenty-eight-year-old Dublin schoolteacher named Roddy Doyle published *The Commitments*, a debut novel that vibrates with the exuberance, enterprise, and humanity of characters previously unheard in Irish fiction: disaffected youths from the impoverished working-class suburbs of 1980s Dublin. Unlike Friel two decades earlier, Doyle could not count on the backing of a major Irish cultural institution to promote his work nor did he have a successful literary apprenticeship behind him. On the contrary, his first novelistic attempt, the unpropitiously titled *Your Granny is a Hunger Striker*, written during the early 1980s, failed to attract the interest of a single publisher.[3] Determined to avoid this fate for his second novel, and in keeping with the entrepreneurial, do-it-yourself ethic of the book's protagonists, Doyle and his friend, John Sutton, decided to bypass the publishing establishment and issue

Reading the Contemporary Irish Novel 1987–2007, First Edition. Liam Harte.
© 2014 Liam Harte. Published 2014 by John Wiley & Sons, Ltd.

The Commitments under their own imprint, King Farouk Publishing, a name supposedly inspired by Dublin rhyming slang for "book." This nod of allegiance to the urban demotic was reinforced by a short but combative manifesto in which the patrimony of the contemporary Irish novelist was unceremoniously jettisoned. As an exercise in symbolic patricide, it is stingingly pithy:

> King Farouk is a new company and will be publishing fiction by young Irish writers. King Farouk stories will be popular and direct. King Farouk novels will definitely NOT explore any of the following well-chewed Irish themes: the provincial upbringing of the protagonist, often the author in disguise, in the fifties and sixties; the absence of love in the home, usually the fault of the father; the brutality of the Christian Brothers' education, or the more subtle brutality of the Holy nuns or the Jesuits; the suffocating influence of the Church; the smallness of provincial town life; and, of course, the various frustrations that torment sensitive young men growing up in provincial towns in the fifties and sixties. Too many 'new' Irish novelists seem to have used the pages of their books to help rid themselves of their neuroses. King Farouk authors will keep their neuroses to themselves. King Farouk stories will entertain. King Farouk fiction will be just that: fiction – made up, direct and funny.[4]

With this audacious statement of intent, Doyle self-consciously set his face against what he saw as the anachronistic realist fictions of an older generation of Irish novelists, collectively characterized as chroniclers of the miseries of a repressive Catholic ruralism and national traumas that were foreign to him and his generation. The corollary of such impatience with moribund tradition was a desire to recuperate for fiction the voices and values of a new, disregarded generation of urbanized and internationalized working-class youth, specifically those from Dublin's socioeconomically disadvantaged northside, who had little affinity for the traditional pieties or priorities of Catholic nationalist Irishness. This was a "hidden Ireland" that Doyle knew intimately, having been born in 1958 in the fledgling suburb of Kilbarrack and raised there during a defining period of social, economic, and physical transformation. Kilbarrack was one of those "frontier" sites that Fintan O'Toole would later identify as seedbeds of postnationalist forms of cultural identity, places that broke inherited molds and buffeted the preconceptions of the ruling elites:

> New places have been born, places without history, without the accumulated resonances of centuries, places that prefigure the end of the fierce notion of Irishness that sustained the state for seventy years. Sex and drugs and rock 'n roll

are more important in the new places than the old totems of Land, Nationality and Catholicism.[5]

....

As this suggests, for the children of these anonymous suburbs, cosmopolitan Anglo-American popular culture held far greater appeal than anything provincial Ireland had to offer, and it is the multivalent effects of these youngsters' absorption and appropriation of external cultural influences that much of Doyle's early fiction seeks to process. Although King Farouk Publishing passed quickly into obscurity, the iconoclastic spirit that informed Doyle's brash manifesto became the catalyst for the production of three of the most enduringly popular contemporary Irish novels, which established him as the country's preeminent comic novelist. That all three works went on to be successfully adapted for the screen by English directors Alan Parker (*The Commitments*, 1991) and Stephen Frears (*The Snapper*, 1993; *The Van*, 1996) meant that Doyle's vision of a working-class Dublin in transition became as internationally influential at the end of the twentieth century as James Joyce's searchingly realist *Dubliners* (1914) was at the beginning.

Doyle's own childhood memories of Kilbarrack reveal the structural and demographic shifts that underpinned the foundational changes O'Toole describes above. This was indeed frontier territory, where Dublin's metamorphosis from compact city to sprawling conurbation was visible in the raw:

....

When I was a kid it [Kilbarrack] was bang at the edge of the city. Quite literally, on my side of the road you were in Dublin 5 postal district, and then you crossed the road and you were in County Dublin – you'd left the city. The city limits were right down the middle of the street. There was a farm across the road from us. [. . .] As I grew up, the city cooperations [sic] bought out the farms, and the private developers bought out the other farms, and it gradually grew more inner city.[6]

....

What Doyle is describing here are the local effects of the radical refashioning of the capital's urban infrastructure during the 1960s, which led to "the building of hundreds of modernist office blocks in the capital, the destruction of many of Dublin's Georgian houses, and the construction of vast, low-density suburbs around Dublin to cater to an expanding and industrializing economy."[7] This spate of urban renewal was driven by a new doctrine of economic modernization, the stimulus for which was a 1958 Department of Finance report, *Economic Development*, which called time on the protectionist policies of autarkic nationalism and accentuated the need for foreign direct investment to boost industrialization and entrepreneurship. This report formed the basis of the Programme for Economic Expansion (1959–1963) implemented by Taoiseach Seán Lemass when he came to power as head of the new Fianna Fáil government in 1959. The economic revival that followed, which saw the country's annual growth rate soar to 4% by 1963, not only raised many people's living standards and expectations but also set in train a protracted process of uneven modernization that would create a "new Irish reality [that] was ambiguous, transitional, increasingly urban or suburban, disturbingly at variance with the cultural aspirations of the revolutionaries who had given birth to the state."[8]

While many parts of this society resisted the gospel of consumer capitalism and remained wedded to traditional values, the burgeoning cities began to show a more marked degree of openness to consumerist aspirations and international cultural influences, especially from Britain and America. As the decade progressed, evidence that the Republic was beginning a slow mutation into a less conservative, more outward-looking society took many forms, from the government's first (failed) application for membership of the European Economic Community in 1961, to the inauguration of a domestic television service (RTÉ) in 1962, to the relaxation of the literary censorship laws in 1967. In the education sphere, the introduction of free post-primary education in 1967 benefited many less well-off children, including Doyle himself, who went on to graduate with a degree in English and Geography from University College Dublin in 1979, after which he returned to Kilbarrack to teach in Greendale Community School until becoming a full-time writer in 1993, the year in which his fourth novel, *Paddy Clarke Ha Ha Ha* (1993), won the Booker Prize.

The fruits of 1960s prosperity were not equitably apportioned, however, nor were the levers of social mobility within everyone's reach. From Doyle's own lower-middle-class perspective, it was the ambivalent allegiances and value systems of those in the buffer zone between classes that drew him in as he sought to express the contemporary realities of a modernizing society and the altered identities that were emerging therein:

. . . .

For people of my generation there was a huge grey area between working and middle-class and a lot of us occupied that area. We benefited from free education and the rising standard of living in the sixties and the surplus cash. And though we might have been regarded as middle-class, one leg was firmly on the working-class side of things and it's that grey area that most of my work inhabits.[9]

. . . .

The Kilbarrack to which Doyle returned after university provided a rich canvas in this regard, since its gray areas were becoming ever darker as the gap between the optimistic rhetoric of the 1960s and the stagnating realities of the recessionary 1980s widened. Not only were such economically blighted suburbs airbrushed from tourist-board images of Dublin, they also remained beyond the pale of literary representation. As O'Toole noted in 1992: "The great tradition of Irish writing is silent on the subject of the suburbs, so you can slip out from under its shadow. No one has ever mythologized this housing estate, this footbridge over the motorway, that video rental shop. It is, for the writer, virgin territory."[10] It was here that Doyle would find the material for his trilogy of novels about Barrytown, the fictional working-class neighborhood for which Kilbarrack was the template. Through the vehicle of the noisy, rambunctious Rabbitte family, Doyle sought to give "working-class people a voice and a vibrancy of life that's often missing in literary representation,"[11] as he himself put it. In addition, he sought to challenge through the trilogy the long-standing hegemony of the rural over the urban in Irish culture. To Doyle, the view that "Dublin was a garrison town that wasn't quite Irish enough, the real Ireland was west of the Shannon and if you wanted to write, to paint or to create music that was the source to draw on,"[12] needed to be emphatically debunked. But whereas many of his fellow "northside realists"[13] marinaded their accounts of urban experience in anger, pessimism, and despair, Doyle chose to write about everyday life in corporation housing estates in a mode of comic social realism, influenced by his friend and dramatist, Paul Mercier, whom Doyle first met at UCD and who was a staffroom colleague at Greendale in the early 1980s. Seeing a rehearsal of Mercier's *Wasters* in November 1985 was a revelation and an inspiration to the novelist manqué:

It was fast and funny and wonderful but that wasn't it: for the first time in my life I saw characters I recognised, people I met every day, the language I heard every day. It was like watching an old cine-film; I could point out people I knew and remember them saying what they said. The way they dressed, walked, held their cans of lager – it was all very familiar.[14]

The spur to creativity was instantaneous and the evolution of what became the Barrytown trilogy organic. By June 1986 Doyle had completed *The Commitments*, which follows the exploits of Jimmy Rabbitte Jr as he attempts to build a band from scratch by appropriating and "Dublinising" the ethos, aesthetic and energy of African-American soul music. Keen to "continue the energy of the first book," but also to write a "more intimate" family narrative,[15] Doyle immediately began work on *The Snapper* (1990), in which the focus shifts to the wider Rabbitte family and the domestic and social dissension provoked by twenty-year-old Sharon's unplanned pregnancy, the result of drunken sex with the father of one of her best friends. The novel took three years to complete, in which time Doyle also wrote two plays, *Brownbread* and *War*, for Mercier's Passion Machine theatre company. *The Van* (1991), by contrast, was written "very quickly"[16] in 1990 and short-listed for the 1991 Booker Prize, a development that marked Doyle's acceptance by the British literary establishment and intensified the antipathy of some in the Irish literary media towards him.[17] The comic notes are necessarily scarcer in this novel, in which a critical spotlight is shone on the corrosive effects of unemployment and ageing on Jimmy Rabbitte Sr's masculine identity and male friendships, in a working-class community threatened by change.

In fact, it is only when we have reached the end of the trilogy that we realize that what we have been reading all along properly belongs to a tradition of Irish tragicomedy that stretches back through Brendan Behan to Joyce and Sean O'Casey, in which the bonds of family and community are continually tested by manifold internal and external stresses. Like his Dublin predecessors, Doyle's cultural and political project in the trilogy is at once defiantly parochial and determinedly international, even though the books' social and cultural coordinates are very different from those of his literary forebears. As he explained in a 1996 interview: "All my stories have a universal quality – like grief, birth and so on – but they're solidly founded on a couple of square miles of Dublin."[18] Doyle knows his home patch as intimately as any sociologist and he also understands what is politically at stake in his act of cultural self-representation. His core aim in the Barrytown trilogy is to reinvigorate fictive views of contemporary Dublin and rescue its socially marginalized inhabitants from their subordination to pejorative images and stereotypes. "Ireland" *per se*, which at the time the novels were written mostly meant the Troubles, the North, and the IRA, doesn't get a look-in and there is no rhetorical obeisance to those iconic cultural forces of nationalism, religion, and the land. Barrytown is, quite simply, a priest-, peasant-, and politician-free zone. But by its very silence on such topics the trilogy sharply challenges secure but outmoded notions of what it meant to be Irish in the 1980s and 1990s and instead shows us what the conflicted, fissured future might look like from the perspectives of, respectively, a working-class teenager, a single mother, a housewife, and an unemployed plasterer. It is with the savvy teenager, Jimmy Rabbitte Jr, that we shall begin, a youngster who exudes a chutzpah and swagger hitherto unseen in the pages of an Irish novel.

II

The Commitments dramatizes the personal and musical tensions that beset a disparate group of unruly Dublin youths who come together under the management of Jimmy Jr to form a soul band in Barrytown. The novel instantly divided critics. For every reviewer who praised its raw colloquial utterance and rumbustious humor there was one who castigated Doyle for his profanity and accused him of patronizing or exploiting ordinary Dubliners. Yet even dissenting critics applauded the way the narrative commends the protagonists' vim and spirit, and more perceptive commentators saw in the book the emergence of a daring new literary talent. Doyle's voice was, in Fintan O'Toole's words, "not just the voice of a new author, but the voice of a radically different country from the Ireland of traditional stories," whose "way of telling a story is different: there is no single hero on whom the action focuses, there are no passages of descriptive writing, and there is no assumption that everything happens in a simple, understandable place called Ireland."[19] The formal and stylistic differences alluded to here are signaled before the narrative even begins, in the novel's framing devices, which feature three idiomatically distinct voices. The first is that of the author, heard in the dedication, who follows common custom by inscribing his book to his parents. Convention is immediately disrupted, however, by having one of the novel's characters, Joey The Lips Fagan, deliver a supplementary exhortation: "Honour thy parents, Brothers and Sisters. They were hip to the groove too once you know. Parents are soul."[20] The epigraph introduces a third voice, that of the soul singer James Brown, whose lyrics not only add another linguistic register but also derive a special voltage from their typographical appearance on the page:

··

—SOMETIMES I FEEL SO NICE——

GOOD GOD————
I JUMP BACK———

I WANNA KISS MYSELF———————!
I GOT—
SOU—OU—OUL—
AN' I'M SUPERBAD————
··

With these paratexts, Doyle advertises key elements of the determinedly democratic conception of fiction that informs his debut novel and shapes the trilogy as a whole. Not only does he prefigure the vernacular energy of the voices that will shortly regale us, he also displays a subtle disregard for narrative hierarchy by presenting his own voice as simply one among several. This the first clue to the text's polyphonic nature, the polyphonic novel being "a democratic one, in which equality of utterance is central."[21] Equality of utterance is embedded in the novel at every turn, from the narrator's refusal to make moral pronouncements on the characters to his allowing himself to be interrupted by snatches of their conversation, as in this early example, where a past exchange between Jimmy and Outspan intrudes upon the narrative present like an abrupt burst of radio wave interference:

. . . .

The last time Outspan had flicked through Jimmy's records he'd seen names like Microdisney, Eddie and the Hot Rods, Otis Redding, The Screaming Blue Messiahs, Scraping Foetus off the Wheel (– Foetus, said Outspan. – That's the little fella inside the woman, isn't it?
– Yeah, said Jimmy
– Aah, that's fuckin' horrible, tha' is.); groups Outspan had never heard of, never mind heard. (7)

. . . .

The implicit challenge to convention signaled by this abdication of narratorial control is reinforced by Doyle's choice of epigraph. If, as Gérard Genette argues, a writer "chooses his peers and thus his place in the pantheon"[22] by means of his epigraph, then Doyle's decision to quote the utterances of an African-American music icon is a pointedly anti-elitist gesture calculated to unsettle readerly, middle-class expectations. It is also a bold cue to the proliferation of non-Irish influences and international popular cultural practices that shape the characters' mindsets. More than any other novel of its era, *The Commitments* heralds the advent of a globalized, postmodern Irish culture by provocatively registering the disparate cultural forces – none of which are compatible with traditional determinants of Irishness – now molding the mindsets of working-class urban youth. There is also subversive intent in Doyle's use of capital letters, exclamation marks, and long and short dashes to replicate orthographically the vocal cadence and rhythmic pulse of soul music, which is one of the novel's most eye-catching stylistic features. Once the narrative proper begins, it quickly becomes evident that the author's readiness to experiment with conventional stylistics to capture the dynamism of soul music is part of his wider ideological agenda as a comic social realist: to give authentic expression to the distinctive accents and speech rhythms of a working-class Dublin demotic, irrespective of the dictates of literary propriety and eschewing a condescendingly superior narratorial point of view.

Doyle's innovative treatment of narratorial voice is a crucial part of the novel's democratic realism and one of the qualities that, for all the author's literary inexperience, made *The Commitments* the most remarkable Irish fiction debut of the 1980s. The style of the novel is unashamedly anti-literary insofar as Doyle, in an attempt at unpremeditated authenticity, avoids retrospective and introspective narration and restricts himself to a vocabulary and idiom that mimic those of working-class youths of limited education and means. From the opening sentence, the prose is shaped by a desire to replicate the oral demotic of working-class subjects accurately and graphically. The most remarked-upon manifestations of this are the stripped-down, script-like form of the novel, in which character is defined through quick-fire, expletive-laden dialogue rather than detailed description, and the vernacular speech patterns and idioms of the novel's protagonists, virtually all of whom speak in a broad northside Dublin dialect. That the narrator also speaks in the living voice of his characters underscores Doyle's ideological commitment to representing his subjects faithfully in their own demotic, powerfully fusing voice, character, and place in the process. His ability to capture the authentic sound and lexical peculiarities of this dialect means that much of the novel's levity stems from colloquial deviations from expressive norms. Our eyes and ears are continually arrested by the preponderance of phonetically rendered words ("righ'", "annymore", "scarleh'"), phrases ("prickin' around", "puked me ring"), obscenities ("fuckin'", "Jaysis"), syntax ("Keep the suits on but"), and slang terms ("ride", "gee", "gaff", "redner"), all of which imbue the prose with a musicality derived from a decidedly local source.

Doyle's desire to make the narrative bear the imprint of the spoken (and sung) voice makes him chafe against the barriers that separate the oral and textual forms of the language, as evidenced by his use of dashes of varying length rather than inverted commas to convey direct speech. These dashes function like musical notation, complementing the poetic cadence and metrical stresses of the dialogue, particularly the resonant repetition of "workin'" and "fuckin'" and the echoing rhyme of such memorable phrases as "say it loud, I'm black an' I'm proud."[23] In interviews, Doyle has spoken of the role this loose style of oral narration plays in enabling the reader to *hear* the dialogue, since "Sometimes just writing a sentence by itself doesn't quite capture the way you want the sentence to be heard."[24] There is also a definite anti-hierarchical impetus in play, as his comments to Karen Sbrockey reveal:

· ·

I didn't want there to be too big a division between the narrative and the dialogue. I thought by just using a dash it would advertise the fact that people were talking, but that there wouldn't be a huge gap between the narrative and the dialogue. I want it to be, at times, irrelevant.[25]

· ·

Critics have rightly noted correspondences between Doyle's demotic style and that of contemporaries such as Irvine Welsh and James Kelman, whose recreation of the actual sound of working-class Scottish voices and accents leads to the artful elision of the distinction between the spoken and the written.[26] Indeed, Cairns Craig's comments on the significance of Kelman's rejection of inverted commas as speech markers are equally applicable to Doyle's practice throughout the Barrytown trilogy:

> The text is designed visually to resist that moment of arrest in which the reader switches between the narrative voice of the text and the represented speech of a character, and what this does is to create a linguistic equality between speech and narration which allows the narrator to adopt the speech idioms of his characters or the characters to think or speak in 'standard English' with no sense of disruption.[27]

A similar equalizing ethos informs Doyle's decision to replace an omniscient narrator with an immanent one who occupies the same plane as the characters and whose voice is infected by their oral idiolect. He explained to Caramine White:

> I've always wanted to bring the books down closer and closer to the characters – to get myself, the narrator, out of it as much as I can. And one of the ways to do this is to use the language that the characters actually speak, to use the vernacular, and not ignoring the grammar, the formality of it, to bend it, to twist it, so you get a sense that you are hearing it, not reading it. That you are listening to the characters. You get in really close to the characters.[28]

What Doyle is describing here is free indirect style, whereby "the voice of the character becomes embedded in the voice of the narrator; thus, the character's habit of speech is present, but direct imitation and quotation marks are not."[29] *The Commitments* brilliantly exploits one of the great strengths of this narratorial mode, its ability "to suggest the precise flavor of the original utterance or consciousness that is 'true' to the character's mind."[30] The qualities of oral performance are so powerfully preserved by the elision of the idiomatic divide between narrator and character that the reader has little sense of *The Commitments* being a *written* narrative. Rather, the novel's tone and structure are those of overheard oral storytelling, the effects of which are manifold. Most obviously, this style means that the voice and speech idiom of the narrator are virtually interchangeable with those of the characters, so that when the narrator explains that "He was getting air from further down" (32) or "The time flew in" (67), it could just as easily be one of the characters speaking. This leads to a blurring of individual voices and identities and sometimes to confusion as to the source of particular utterances. Doyle's distinctive use of free indirect style also means that the narrator is presented as having no superior knowledge to his characters, but rather shares their limitations of expression, thought, and outlook. So close, indeed, is the non-omniscient narrator to the characters that he is tacitly on their side, in sympathy with their opinions and aspirations. Doyle's remark that he wanted "to write about the type of kids I taught and had become charmed by, really, and whose company I enjoyed, who are typical of the type of place I came from"[31] is revealing in this regard. Here is a novelist who is so enamored of his characters, so indulgent of their foibles and follies, that the critical distance between author, narrator, and protagonist that usually sustains a novel has all but disappeared. The narrative voice that results from this elision has a distinctly partisan, even proselytizing, quality about it, in that it exerts a tangible emotional pressure on readers, asking that we too succumb to these characters' charm and share the narrator's warm feelings for them.

For many readers, this mode of narration is the perfect complement to Doyle's descriptive minimalism and an added source of pleasure and delight. Yet it presents some significant interpretive challenges, making it difficult to decode the specific targets of Doyle's comic scrutiny and gauge the precise points at which his comedic voice shifts between registers. Comedy, he has said, "is an extremely serious business; it's never casual, it has to be precise, it has to have a point."[32] What then, apart from giving pleasure, is the point of the high jinks and freewheeling anarchy of *The Commitments*? Doyle himself has repeatedly stressed his celebratory motives, claiming in one interview that his aim in the trilogy was to "capture and celebrate crudity, loudness, linguistic flair and slang, which is the property of working-class people."[33] The text itself tells a more complex tale, however, in that the actual language users and music makers, and the views they express, are not univocally celebrated. On the contrary, characters are subjected to a subtle mixture of sympathy and satire that blends high-octane entertainment with mockery and social critique. Doyle's narrative irony is perhaps best exemplified by his double-edged portrayal of Jimmy Rabbitte Jr, would-be impresario and orchestrator of the novel's most celebrated scene, in which he tries to convert Outspan and Derek to the ideology behind his proposition that they form a soul band:

. . . .

– Where are yis from? (He answered the question himself.)
– Dublin. (He asked another one.) – Wha' part o' Dublin? Barrytown. Wha' class are yis? Workin' class. Are yis proud of it? Yeah, yis are. (Then a practical question.)
– Who buys the most records? The workin' class. Are yis with me? (Not really.)
– Your music should be abou' where you're from an' the sort o' people yeh come from. ———— Say it once, say it loud, I'm black an' I'm proud.

> They looked at him.
> – James Brown. Did yis know ————— never mind. He sang tha'. ————- An' he made a fuckin' bomb.
> They were stunned by what came next.
> – The Irish are the niggers of Europe, lads.
> They nearly gasped: it was so true.
> – An' Dubliners are the niggers of Ireland. The culchies have fuckin' everythin'. An' the northside Dubliners are the niggers o' Dublin. ————— Say it loud, I'm black an' I'm proud.
> He grinned. He'd impressed himself again. (13–14)

Stylistically, the narrator's fugitive, *sotto voce* interjections work here to facilitate Jimmy's attempt to establish his intellectual authority over his credulous and speechless listeners, while the closed nature of his rapid question-and-answer routine suggests that he alone is capable of sophisticated, strategic thought. But what of the substance of Jimmy's bold manifesto and his plausibility as a self-styled postcolonial prophet? Are we to accept at face value his startling assertion of a symbolic kinship between white Irish people and black Americans, based on a shared experience of oppression and discrimination? The novelist's own comments reveal a contradictory mixture of comic and serious intent in composing this key set-piece scene. Asked in 1995 if he agreed with Jimmy's view of the Irish as "the niggers of Europe," Doyle replied: "No. There's some tongue-in-cheek there. I deliberately put it down because, one, it's bullshit, utter crap; two, it's funny; and three, there's a certain wisdom there."[34] His remarks in a later interview did little to clarify matters: "In one way it's a joke and in another it's all about Jimmy trying to motivate his band: he is trying to instil some sort of purpose in them. It's about overcoming the legacy of colonisation and it's also there to shock people out of their respectable, middle-class positions."[35]

These discrepant responses have not deterred critics from accepting the basic validity and felicity of Jimmy's ethnic analogy, which touches directly upon Ireland's contested status as a postcolonial country and the nationalist implications that flow from this, a topic that was beginning to excite much intellectual debate at the time the novel appeared. Luke Gibbons, for example, claims that "the legitimacy of the claim that the Irish are 'the niggers of Europe', and so on, only makes sense by reconnecting with a colonial legacy in which Ireland was indeed a Third World at the back door of Europe."[36] Michael Cronin is also sympathetic to this reading, though he insists that Jimmy's homily needs "to be set in the context of a rights discourse that can and did travel from Alabama to Antrim"[37] in the 1960s. For Elizabeth Cullingford, however, the Irish/black analogy is historically misleading because it overlooks "the dismal history of Irish-American hostility to African-Americans," which complicates in turn any notion of "the Catholics as the white Negroes of Northern Ireland."[38] And yet, as Lauren Onkey and Timothy Taylor have observed, historical evidence to support this cultural correspondence can be found not only in the political wall murals of Derry and West Belfast but also in the utterances of leading figures in the 1920s Harlem Renaissance, who looked to the Irish literary revival for artistic models.[39] Onkey also alludes to remarks made in 1988 by a real-life music maker from Dublin's northside – Paul Hewson, a.k.a. Bono – which contain a striking echo of Jimmy's sentiments. Describing how he found "passports home" in American gospel and blues, the U2 singer identified "soul" as the quality that unites the musical traditions of Ireland and black America, and proceeded to link this to a shared history of subjection: "I was called a 'White Nigger' once by a black musician, and I took it as he meant it, as a compliment. The Irish, like the blacks, feel like outsiders."[40] Of course, in Jimmy's case, the paradox of white working-class Dubliners being labeled "niggers" is based on an unspoken and unnuanced substitution of class for race as a marker of difference. As Dermot McCarthy points out: "Jimmy pushes identification with African-Americans because he sees the working-class urban Irish to be systemically *economically* disadvantaged in the same way that African-Americans are racially."[41] More specifically, the band's "blackness" is presented as a function of their systemic economic disenfranchisement by two Irish social groups perceived as being more privileged: the "southsiders" who live in the more affluent southern sub- urbs of Dublin city and "culchies" or "rednecks," disparaging terms for Irish country people. Jimmy's appropriation of the race-based injustices visited on black America, then, is less about Ireland's past history of colonialism and more about the deep-seated internal inequities of the postcolonial nation.

But we should pause here and look again at the role of narrative irony in the presentation of Jimmy's galvanizing pep talk, since we are already in danger of overempowering him by uncritically accepting his political *bona fides*. Even as he is propounding it, Jimmy's tendentious thesis is being ironized by the narrator's hyperbolic remark that "it was so true," just as Jimmy himself is surely being lampooned for his creamy smugness. Doyle's political subtext is thus exposed: glib identifications between the Catholic Irish and African Americans to bolster a sense of enduring Irish victimhood are bogus and meretricious. McCarthy bluntly states the case for the prosecution: "The narrator's ironic comment emphasises the improvisatory nature of Jimmy's language and behaviour. He is a 'bullshitter' and a 'chancer', and the 'niggers of Europe' analogy is a 'con' – a 'pitch'; and the narrator's deflation of Jimmy's rhetorical balloon should prevent anyone from ascending into the ideological ozone."[42] Evidence to support this judgment mounts as the band takes shape. The credibility of Jimmy's "black pride" message is undermined by the crude racist stereotyping that he and others casually indulge in; his criticism of The Commitmentettes for singing in their "ordin'y accents" (34) flatly contradicts his earlier valorization of working-class pride; and his motivational concept of "Dublin soul" becomes so nebulous and elastic as to be meaningless. It is, in fact, the blatant glibness with which the "soul" label is applied to everything from democracy to a bingo caller's kidneys by Jimmy and his disingenuous mentor, Joey, that lays bare the true *raison d'être* of their "soul politics": financial gain. Jimmy and Joey are classic micks on the make, opportunistically prepared to tailor their rhetoric to maximize the market potential of their impressionable, wayward protégées. What appears to be a principled "commitment" to working-class empowerment through local music-making is in reality a profit-seeking enterprise, and when money beckons, everything is negotiable: note how quickly Jimmy's northside solidarity evaporates when a residency for the group materializes on the much-derided southside. As Mary McGlynn accurately points out, such pragmatism suggests that our hero's strident localism is little more than "a pose, something to be dropped once economics are at stake."[43]

Jimmy's response to the band's acrimonious disintegration at the end of the novel shows that his seemingly evangelistic attachment to the emancipatory politics of soul music is equally disposable. Undaunted by the band's demise, and with Joey's valedictory verdict that "soul isn't right for Ireland" (133) ringing in his ears, he sets about forming a "country-punk" (138) group from the embers of The Commitments, with a view to exploiting a more lucrative niche in the wider Irish market. Rednecks are now fair game, commercially speaking: "You've got to remember tha' half the country is fuckin' farmers. This is the type of stuff they all listen to. —— Only they listen to it at the wrong speed" (139). But while the same musical formula will be employed – the lyrics of "Night Train" are already being "culchified" – Jimmy insists that this time the band will be an ideology-free zone. This cheerfully cynical *volte face* renders his whole political vision comically preposterous and suggests that he and Joey are ultimately to be regarded as blustering rogues bent on market exploitation, rather than "savvy entrepreneurs," "cannily employing the capitalist strategies that have left them disenfranchised."[44] The proposed name of his new group, The Brassers, obliquely suggests as much, "brasser" being Dublin slang for a prostitute or woman of dubious morality. Having first sold his "soul" without scruple, Jimmy now resolves to sell his "country" with equal relish.

This ending also casts a retrospective shadow over Jimmy's initial inspirational motto that "Your music should be abou' where you're from an' the sort o' people yeh come from." Although the proclaimer of this creed is discredited in the end, the creed itself survives as a gentle rebuke to these aspiring musicians' failure to live up to its emancipatory potential by creating original music. From the outset, Jimmy's assertion of "difference" is predicated on an aesthetic of accurate reproduction rather than original production, the "Dublinization" of American soul music being the band's sole concession to newness. Indeed, it is "the Dublin bits" (73) that Derek points to on the one occasion when Outspan laments the fact that they don't write their own material. As Gerry Smyth astutely notes, the band members are conspicuously devoid of the desire to compose "original material that would express (in a soul idiom) something of their own individual and/or collective identity."[45] When, early in the novel, Jimmy is challenged by Derek and Outspan to name a proper alternative to their "doin' bad versions of other people's poxy songs" (11), his retort that "It's not the other people's songs so much [. . .] It's which ones yis do" (12) tellingly exposes his lack of commitment to genuinely original modes of creative expression and underscores the fundamental paradox of a group striving to be "authentic" using borrowed forms and idioms – which is, of course, the classic dilemma of a colonized mentality. That the musically "superior" culture being imitated is that of subaltern black America rather than postimperialist white Britain complicates, but does not nullify, the force of this comic portrait of a community's inability to develop an independent identity under the neocolonial pressure of a globalized American popular culture.[46] Jimmy's swapping of soul for country music confirms this cultural hegemony. Indigenous music traditions have as little to offer these youths as Catholicism, nationalism, or the party politics of "Fianna fuckin' Fail or annythin' like tha'" (13).

What we have in *The Commitments*, then, is a portrait of a culturally disregarded segment of Irish society that blends empathy with mockery and celebration with subtle social commentary. Beneath its verbal exuberance, irreverence, and earthy contemporaneity, Doyle's comic vision of working-class Dublin is fundamentally good-natured and optimistic, but also mischievously tongue-in-cheek; hence the warm, knowing glow that many readers are left with at the end of the novel. Whether his humane vision is reductive or patronizing is another matter, however. Perhaps only a humorless reader could accuse Doyle of perpetuating the negative stereotype of the cocky streetwise Dubliner who is not to be trusted, least of all by credulous culchies. That said, the characterization of Jimmy Jr and Joey as blathering chancers comes uncomfortably close to reinforcing hoary pejorative markers of Irishness. Ultimately, however, *The Commitments*'s novelty, buoyant charm, and somewhat unusual frame of reference – band-formation being a relatively uncommon working-class pursuit – protect it from the harsher criticisms leveled at *The Snapper*, in which Doyle seeks to recreate the feel-good factor of his debut novel while delving more deeply into the disjunctures and contradictions of social change in this urban subculture.

Although widely praised for the color of its language and its fast-paced narration, *The Snapper* led some critics to complain that its author was now succumbing to stereotypical images of the work-classing Irish as "happy-go-lucky slobs with sharp tongues and gutter vocabularies,"[47] thus sidestepping meaningful engagement with vexed sociopolitical issues. In his acerbic review of the novel, George O'Brien blamed Doyle's "ethnographic" approach to his subject matter for turning his characters into simplistic "stage-lumpens" who inhabit a self-contained enclave that is "detached from the society that built it,"[48] while Shaun Richards accused *The Snapper* of presenting "an urban reality as partial in its representations as was Yeats's Celtic Twilight – rendered the subject of comic indulgence rather than critical concern."[49] Both critics clearly felt that Doyle's use of the comic mode was neither dexterous nor incisive enough to do justice to the complexities of the issues broached in the novel: alcohol-fuelled rape, out-of-wedlock pregnancy, and potentially shambolic single motherhood. However, in a later contribution to this debate Brian Donnelly defended Doyle against such criticisms, arguing that the comic novelist is under no obligation to present a worked-through critique of the darker side of these dilemmas because he is operating within comic conventions that presuppose a happy ending.[50]

It seems to me that both sides of this argument underestimate Doyle's deepening appreciation of comedy as a vehicle for the nuanced representation of a culture and society in the throes of turbulent transition. In both *The Snapper* and *The Van*, Doyle's use of the comic form as a tool with which to dissect the complexity of his protagonists' experience becomes ever more sophisticated. While these novels share several stylistic features with *The Commitments*, they also show Doyle developing more refined skills of characterization and narrative development. Although localized dialect and profane speech still proliferate, *The Snapper* and *The Van* are more nourished by focalized narration than *The Commitments*, chiefly because of Doyle's willingness to probe more fully the inner life and feelings of his protagonists. The process begins in *The Snapper* with his exploration of the internal dynamics of the Rabbitte family in the wake of the dramatic news with which the novel opens: Jimmy and Veronica's eldest, unmarried daughter, Sharon, has fallen pregnant but refuses to disclose the identity of the baby's father. Immediately, the spotlight is fixed on the issue of pregnancy outside of marriage, which is further complicated by the fact that Sharon conceived as a result of drunken, non-consensual sex – it is left to the reader to decide whether she was raped – with George Burgess, the father of one of her best friends. Thus, the family kitchen, a space traditionally associated with cozy conviviality in Irish culture, becomes a microcosmic testing ground for changing social, sexual, and moral attitudes.[51] Whereas Veronica's latent Catholicism is audible in her murmured remark that her daughter's actions are "not right" (149), Jimmy's gauche question about abortion, prompted by "something he'd heard a good few times on the telly" (149), indicates that his is not a conscience conditioned to agonize over church teaching on sexual morality. Sharon's own moral outlook is an intriguing mixture of unreconciled impulses. On the one hand, her brusque declaration that "Abortion's murder"

(150) suggests a rigid conservatism that recalls the zeal with which activists on the Catholic right resisted efforts to liberalize Ireland's abortion laws in the 1980s. On the other hand, her farcical attempts to pray reveal the irrelevance of institutionalized religion to her everyday concerns: "She tried to remember the Hail Mary but she couldn't get past Hello Be Thy Name, and anyway, she didn't believe in it, not really; so she stopped trying to remember the rest of it. It was just something to do" (168). Yet the very fact that in a time of crisis she should resort to prayer, however ineptly, suggests that part of her continues to be governed by values in which she no longer believes.

It is a measure of Doyle's maturing practice that he sustains this complex characterization of Sharon for most of the novel, making her an engrossing embodiment of conflicted contemporary Irish womanhood. Although her acquiescence in the moral relativism of the community at large, where unmarried motherhood is accepted as the social norm, is made plain – "The baby was nothing. It happened. It was alright. Barrytown was good that way. Nobody minded. Guess the daddy was a hobby" (253) – this does not make her an unequivocally "modern girl" (205). Indeed, her reluctance to contemplate raising the baby on her own and her desire to remain in the family home so that her child would have "a proper family" (287) reveal as much about Sharon's ingrained traditionalism as it does her economic dependency, even though her poorly paid job provides enough disposable income for boozy nights out with her girlfriends. Sharon's latent conservatism also means that she colludes in her father's growing appropriation of her pregnancy, a product of his guilt-ridden, belated appreciation of that which he himself failed to practise as a young father: attentive, hands-on parenting. However, just as Doyle hesitates to make Sharon's rape explicit, this narrative strand shows him fudging the more problematic implications of her predicament. So intent is he on "Celebrating pregnancy outside marriage"[52] that, when push comes to shove, he must make this daughter as soft-hearted and family-loving as her father. Consequently, *The Snapper* assimilates rather than confronts the issue of teenage pregnancy. By having Jimmy co-own his daughter's pregnancy, "the threat of the single mother bringing up her child in a non-paternalistic family unit is dispelled."[53]

Yet in spite of this evasiveness, the novel successfully uses the social reality of single motherhood to portray the unresolved dilemmas thrown up by social change in a working-class context, where the undertow of conservative value systems continues to trouble the liberal stream. Just because one-parent families diverge starkly from the de Valeran ideal of the nuclear family as "a moral institution possessing inalienable and imprescriptible rights,"[54] it does not necessarily follow that older belief structures have been wholly supplanted. *The Snapper* also skillfully dramatizes the refiguring of traditional gender roles through its depiction of Jimmy Sr's struggles to reconcile his preconceived notions of what fatherhood entails with the changes happening around him. From the outset, his shortcomings as a husband and father are comically skewered, rendering him a domestically clueless figure of fun. There is much of the pantomime father about him, from his puerile jokes and reflex prejudices to his incontinent swearing and cringe-inducing malapropisms. The juvenility of so much of his banter and behavior – both at home and in the Hikers pub, his home from home – defines him as an outsized boy, as when, for example, he seeks to appease Veronica by buying her an ice cream, a childish gesture that preempts Burgess's pathetic offer of money for "sweets" to Sharon. Such tactics are part of the adolescent gamesmanship that Jimmy practises in all his relationships, since for him "paternal authority and respect are all about 'winning' and 'losing' and these come down to keeping up appearances."[55] Hence his need to punish Sharon by coercing her into admitting that she has "disgraced the family" (286), only for her to outmaneuver him by insincerely threatening to move out, a ploy that results in their mutual "victory." But whereas there may be humor in Jimmy's attempts to save face domestically and socially, his persistent abdication of parental responsibility raises fewer smiles. The frequency of his pub excursions makes the Rabbittes resemble a single-parent family – a foreshadowing of Sharon's own – and his disingenuous justification for refusing to assist Veronica in the moral guidance of the twins betrays an exasperating platitudinous evasiveness: "They'd only laugh at me. I'm only their da. Anyway, it'd sound better comin' from a woman, wouldn't it?" (189). Jimmy's propensity for self-pity is equally unappealing. His rash disregard for what the neighbors might say about Sharon soon curdles into selfish resentment when he comes to believe that "his life was being ruined because of her" (278–279).

Yet for all his flaws, Jimmy Rabbitte undoubtedly commands a special affection on account of his amiable openness, good-natured solidarity, and shambolic indefatigability, qualities that set him apart from an arch-patriarch like McGahern's Michael Moran, about whom we shall hear more in the next chapter. Whereas Moran rules his wife and family with an iron will, Jimmy Sr seems destined never to come into his patrimony as "the head of the fuckin' house" (186) but is all the more endearing for it. The starkness of the contrast is nicely captured by the oblique way in which Jimmy's offhand quip, "The family tha' eats together – How does it go?" (236), parodically deflates the pious solemnity of Moran's controlling mantra, "the family that prays together stays together."[56]

That is not to say, however, that Jimmy has transcended his cultural conditioning and transformed himself into an enlightened paterfamilias, despite his claims of having done so following a sudden bout of critical self-appraisal as Sharon's due date approaches. In truth, he is no more a "new man" at the end of the novel than he was an unalloyed patriarch at the beginning. He remains in thrall to prescribed notions of what these roles entail, constantly struggling to pass the "paternity test." From the novel's opening exchanges, we see how much fatherhood is for him a matter of "manly" performance. On hearing Sharon's news, for example, he instantly feels he should "throw a wobbler or somethin'" (146) and is reassured when his anger starts to grow. The stunting effects of his having internalized the expectations and assumptions that accompany a culturally sanctioned version of macho Irish manhood are again revealed when he hesitates to kiss his wife in front of his sons for fear they'd "slag" (180) him, a sure sign that these young men have already begun to conform to the same oppressive cultural norms. Jimmy's crooning of "The Great Pretender" in the novel's closing scenes carries much symbolic truth in the light of this masquerade of masculinity, as does his reading of Alexander Dumas's *The Man in the Iron Mask* in the early part of *The Van*, for by the time this novel opens the strain of faking it has begun to take a corrosive toll. The notion of masculinity in transition that is comically explored in *The Snapper* takes on a much darker coloration in *The Van*, as serious and disquieting questions are raised about what happens to contemporary working-class masculinities when they are subjected to sustained economic, social, and psychological stresses.

In the final installment of the Barrytown trilogy the recessionary realities of the late 1980s come more fully into focus, darkening the devil-may-care mood and complicating characters' attempts to improvise their way around personal and economic difficulties. *The Van* is mainly concerned with the plight of Jimmy Rabbitte Sr as he faces into a financially precarious middle age, having lost his job in the economic downturn. That his changed status as an unemployed plasterer is having a profound impact on his sense of self and his relationships with family and community is crisply captured in the novel's opening scene, which establishes the bass notes of despondency and diminution that resonate through the first third of the novel (like its two predecessors, *The Van* is chapterless). Having already been cooped up in his kitchen because the other rooms in the house are occupied, Jimmy symbolically evicts himself when he gives up this space to Darren and drifts outside to sit on the front step, hoping to find it a more congenial place in which to kill time. Instead, his feelings of homelessness and isolation are amplified by the November chill and the sight of passing motorists he doesn't recognize. Precisely because it is so understated, there is real pathos in this vignette of a redundant plasterer searching the streets in vain for a familiar face that might lessen the pain of his loneliness.

In a culture where masculinity is defined not in terms of being but of doing, Jimmy's alienation and bewilderment cannot easily be shrugged off with a whimsical one-liner. While he is still capable of acting the buffoon, there is now a hollowness to his clowning, as it becomes increasingly clear to him that he is being pushed to the side of his own life while those close to him get on with theirs. Sharon is absorbed by single motherhood; Darren has outgrown his childish interests and no longer talks to his father "properly" (353); Jimmy Jr has moved into a bedsit with his girlfriend; and the wayward Leslie is "in England, somewhere" (359). Veronica, too, gives off an air of emotional detachment and confident self-reliance. Having started studying part-time for her Leaving Certificate, she is determined to achieve her educational goals without interference from her husband and pointedly prioritizes her studies over babysitting Sharon's snapper, thus forcing Jimmy to assume the role of feminized caregiver, leaving him literally holding the baby. His abortive attempt to kick-start his own educational journey by joining a library merely compounds his sense of futility and plummeting self-esteem: "He was useless; couldn't even read a book properly" (372). Within moments of Jimmy admitting this to himself, Jimmy Jr drops by and hastily stuffs a fiver in his father's pocket (373), a gesture made all the more poignant by its feigned casualness. When, afterwards, Sharon finds her father in a kind of fugue state, his diminishment is palpable:

. . . .

– Are yeh alrigh'?
He looked miserable, and small and kind of beaten looking.
– I'm grand, he said.
He looked around him, as if for a reason for being there. (374)

. . . .

Scenes such as these showcase Doyle's maturing ability to manage the representation of emotional nuance and complexity without lapsing into sentimentality or heavy-handedness. Cumulatively, they contribute to the suasive force with which the novel evokes the ramifying effects of redundancy on Jimmy Rabbitte Sr, which, as we have already hinted, go far beyond the mere fact of his ceasing to be the family breadwinner. The profound sense of male inadequacy Jimmy feels as a result of his loss of economic status is intimately connected to other psychosocial anxieties and insecurities that are contingent upon changing socioeconomic conditions, shifting gender relations, and his keen awareness of the losses being wrought by ageing and mortality. To say that he has slid into depression is too simplistic a diagnosis. Self-destructive feelings of anger, envy, frustration, and aggression are also welling up in this out-of-work father in ways and for reasons that he cannot fully understand, but which we as readers recognize as a deepening crisis of old-style, patriarchal masculinity. That an overwhelming sense of fear is at the root of this crisis is made clear in the scene where Jimmy is described as having days when he is plagued by "a feeling in his guts all the time, like a fart building up only it wasn't that at all" (395). It is a sensation that reminds him of the silent terror he felt as a child, when he was forced by his mother to "go through the whole day scared shitless, waiting for his da to come home" (395) and sadistically beat him for some reported misdemeanor – a rare and deeply affecting vignette of Jimmy's boyhood. But whereas his childhood anguish had form and focus, Jimmy's visceral sense of dread as an adult is more inchoate and diffuse.

Little by little, this fear is revealed to be bound up with an anxiety about the potential redundancy of his phallic power and a corresponding horror of emasculation – the dread prospect of becoming a feminized man. This anxiety is memorably crystallized in the scene where Jimmy is overtaken by a sudden and, to him, bewildering compulsion to try out Maggie's electric razor when he finds himself in the Reeves' bathroom on Christmas Day: "He felt weak, hopeless, like he'd been caught. Was something happening to him?" (405). Characteristically, he shies away from further introspection, but we have seen enough to recognize that this furtive flirtation with femininity is as much a product of Jimmy's sense of himself as a member of the contemptible "weaker sex" now that he is jobless as it is an expression of suppressed sexual desire for Bertie's wife, Vera, about whom Jimmy fantasizes, Leopold Bloom-like, as he shaves his shins: "She was a bit of a brasser, Vera, but Jimmy Sr liked that. [. . .] He looked at the door again. Vera probably used one of these, when she was shaving her legs" (404–405).

Probing a little deeper, we can see in Jimmy's disgusted reaction to his "lapse" into womanliness while coveting his neighbor's wife the lineaments of his male fear of, and hostility towards, women's sexual power over him. Psychiatrist Anthony Clare's analysis of the roots of contemporary male insecurity and its relationship to the masculine need for control speaks directly to Jimmy Rabbitte's predicament here. As Clare explains, the fact that some men "regard every woman as a potential whore who has it within her sexual power to ennoble or degrade him" means that

. . . .

That which is desired is detested, for that which is desired exercises a terrible, nagging, insistent, irresistible temptation and poses an immense challenge to the male sense of control. The preoccupation of men with pornography provides an example of how men can and do turn their own self-disgust against women. [. . .] Men know only too well how tragic they appear, know too the extent to which they feel enslaved by their libidos. [. . .] Men in thrall to sex exhibit self-disgust and disgust with what is seen to be the cause of their degradation: women.[57]

. . . .

The result of this swirl of destructive emotions is a neurotic aggression, directed against the self and against others, since men "are not just fearful of, and angry with, women. They are fearful of, and angry with, each other. Men repudiate the feminine not only in women but in themselves. [. . .] If a man feels he does not have *it* – masculine strength, masculine bravery, masculine achievement – he is a castrated male. He is a woman."[58]

And so it is with Jimmy Rabbitte. Enslaved by his libido and oppressed by feelings of inadequacy, his renascent need for power and control in his jobless middle age fuels his embarrassingly desperate quest to shore up his impaired and weakened manhood. One of the most striking developments in Jimmy Sr's character between *The Snapper* and *The Van* is his heightened sexual awareness of young women, whom he lasciviously inspects at every turn, including Darren's girlfriend, Miranda: "A ride; she was. It was weird thinking it; his son was going out with a ride; but it was true. [. . .] He'd never gone out with a young one like that" (395). Still more disturbing for him is the realization that Miranda's generation is far less beholden to men, financially and emotionally, than the women he grew up with were. The evidence practically overwhelms him on a trip into the city center, where he counts "fifty-four great-looking young ones going by in only a quarter of an hour; brilliant-looking women now, and all of them dressed beautifully, the height of style; they must have paid fortunes for the stuff they had on them; you could tell" (409–410). Against this background, the aggressive male chauvinism exhibited by Jimmy and his friends is symptomatic of their reactionary response to feminism's displacement of the certainties and privileges of traditional patriarchy. The unraveling of the old fictions of Irish masculinity has bred in these marginalized men a kind of siege mentality, which expresses itself in their preference for all-male company and their wish to protect the bar of the Hikers from territorial invasion by couples. Here in this public space, which Bertie paradoxically claims as the men's private nation state, women are verbally demeaned and traits identified as feminine routinely mocked as signs of weakness and dependence. Insofar as women are appreciated by these "lads" – to use Veronica's telling characterization of them – it is almost exclusively in terms of their looks and perceived willingness to indulge in casual sex. Banter it may be, but there is a sinister undertow to Bertie's leering account of his sexual intimidation of sixteen-year-old Mandy in the local newsagent, which culminates in his misogynistic declaration that "All women are prostitutes" (418).

Although he joins in the laughter, Jimmy is discomfited by such talk, which makes him feel "dirty; kind of. And then stupid. Talking about young ones like that, very young ones" (417). These feelings of self-disgust, which are inextricably bound up with his resentment of women's sexual power over him, later resurface when he recalls his own erotic interest in the teenage girls who work in the sewing factory. Surreptitiously watching them from his bedroom window, "he'd felt the blood rushing through his head, walloping off the sides, like he was watching a blue video and he was afraid that Veronica would come in and catch him" (448). Afterwards, he'd felt "like a fuckin' pervert," but convinces himself that "he just liked looking at them, that was all" (449). As the porn analogy indicates, however, the objectifying mind does not escape unscathed. Increasingly, we see Jimmy mentally comparing his wife's slack flesh to the nubile bodies of these miniskirted teenagers and to the coiffed and sculpted figures of the "brassers" in the blue movie Bertie loans him. The aggression and self-hatred this provokes in Jimmy shockingly materializes in his impulsive desire to lash out at Veronica one boozy night, while she is helping him to untie his shoelaces. Even though Jimmy stops himself from hitting her, his sudden switch from silent contempt to unspoken smugness is no less dismaying: "It was nice as well sometimes, being mothered by Veronica" (384). In this moment of reprehensible self-satisfaction, Jimmy shows himself to be a regressive male in every sense, willfully resistant to making the transition from boy to man.

It is this same quality of incorrigible childlike egocentricity that is ultimately responsible for Jimmy's bust-up with Bimbo, after the two men have worked hard to build up a lucrative fast-food business in Barrytown. Once again, Jimmy's narcissism and control-freakery wreak havoc on a relationship. The fact that Bimbo owns the burger-and-chips van and is therefore Jimmy's employer rankles to the point where the latter is unable to endure his subordinate status and takes his frustration out on his best friend and his "wagon of a wife" (616), Maggie. Being a dependent employee of the man he is used to bossing as he would a wife is incompatible with Jimmy's fragile machismo. Revealingly, we are told that the dissolution of their partnership "was like a film about a marriage breaking up" (615). No amount of barroom overtures from Bimbo can heal the rift, and the men's friendship is already doomed by the time Bimbo sabotages the business by driving the divisive van into the sea at Dollymount, the place where Stephen Dedalus recognized his artistic destiny in *A Portrait of the Artist as a Young Man* (1916).

The novel ends with Jimmy returning home to Veronica after this sacrificial act of "vanslaughter" and asking her for a hug, a gesture which Dermot McCarthy reads as the logical consequence of Jimmy's "inability to change" and "a poignant but pathetic emblem of his defeat."[59] And yet it may be that, in a faint nod to Joyce, Doyle is hinting at some possible signs of transformation here, given that this unemployed-again husband has, for the first time in the novel, decided to verbalize his need for emotional comfort and support rather than bottle it up. In one sense he is back where he started, jobless and dejected, yet it is also possible that, by opening up emotionally and expressing his vulnerability and need for love, Jimmy Rabbitte Sr may just have begun the process of liberating himself from the insistent need to dominate and master that which he fears and loathes. While he is far from being on the threshold of a transfigured new life, as Stephen is in *Portrait*, Jimmy's admission that he has learned his lesson may not be all cliché.

Notes

1. Richard Pine, "Brian Friel and Contemporary Irish Drama," *Colby Quarterly*, 27:4 (December 1991), 190. Cited in Anthony Roche, *Contemporary Irish Drama* (Dublin: Gill and Macmillan, 1994), 2.
2. Steve Padley, *Key Concepts in Contemporary Literature* (Basingstoke: Palgrave Macmillan, 2006), xii.
3. Gene Kerrigan, "Catching the Rhythm," *Magill* (April 1987), 43.
4. King Farouk press release, April 30, 1987, unpaginated, original emphasis. It seems likely that this press release was misdated, given that the novel was actually published in late March.
5. Fintan O'Toole, "Introduction: On the Frontier," in *A Dublin Quartet*, Dermot Bolger (London: Penguin, 1992), 1.
6. Caramine White, *Reading Roddy Doyle* (Syracuse: Syracuse University Press, 2001), 176–177.
7. Andrew Kincaid, *Postcolonial Dublin: Imperial Legacies and the Built Environment* (Minneapolis: University of Minnesota Press, 2006), 128.
8. Terence Brown, *Ireland: A Social and Cultural History 1922–2002* (London: Harper Perennial, 2004), 299.
9. Stephen J. Costello (ed.), *The Irish Soul: In Dialogue* (Dublin: Liffey Press, 2001), 91–92.
10. O'Toole, "Introduction", 1–2.
11. Pat Wheeler and Jenny Newman, "Roddy Doyle," in *Contemporary Irish and British Fiction: An Introduction Through Interviews*, eds Sharon Monteith, Jenny Newman and Pat Wheeler (London: Arnold, 2004), 68.
12. Ulrike Paschel, *No Mean City?: The Image of Dublin in the Novels of Dermot Bolger, Roddy Doyle and Val Mulkerns* (Frankfurt am Main: Peter Lang, 1998), 148.
13. This label was applied to Doyle and Finglas-based Dermot Bolger by Shaun Richards in "Northside Realism and the Twilight's Last Gleaming," *Irish Studies Review*, 2 (Winter 1992), 18–22.
14. Roddy Doyle, "Introduction," *Brownbread* and *War* [1989] (London: Secker and Warburg, 1992), 1.
15. Costello, *The Irish Soul*, 88.
16. Costello, *The Irish Soul*, 89.
17. Despite his popularity with the reading public, critical reaction to Doyle's early novels in Ireland was far from fulsome and often openly hostile. See, for example, Justine Cunningham's scathing review of *The Van* in the *Sunday Business Post*, August 11, 1991.
18. Gerry Smyth, "Appendix: An Interview with Roddy Doyle, September 16, 1996," in his *The Novel and the Nation* (London: Pluto, 1997), 100.
19. Fintan O'Toole, "Brave New World," *Sunday Tribune*, April 12, 1987, 21.

20. Roddy Doyle, *The Barrytown Trilogy* [1992] (London: Minerva, 1993), unpaginated dedication. Subsequent page numbers are cited parenthetically in the text.

21. Sue Vice, *Introducing Bakhtin* (Manchester: Manchester University Press, 1997), 112.

22. Gérard Genette, *Paratexts: Thresholds of Interpretation*, trans. Jane E. Lewin (Cambridge: Cambridge University Press, 1997), 160.

23. See Penelope Fitzgerald, "Fried Nappy," *London Review of Books*, September 12, 1991, 16.

24. Wheeler and Newman, "Roddy Doyle," 62.

25. Karen Sbrockey, "Something of a Hero: An Interview with Roddy Doyle," *Literary Review*, 42:4 (Summer 1999), 547.

26. See, for example, Matt Maguire, "Dialect(ic) Nationalism?: The Fiction of James Kelman and Roddy Doyle," *Scottish Studies Review*, 7:1 (2006), 80–94.

27. Cairns Craig, "Resisting Arrest: James Kelman," in *The Scottish Novel Since the Seventies*, eds Gavin Wallace and Randall Stevenson (Edinburgh: Edinburgh University Press, 1993), 103.

28. White, *Reading Roddy Doyle*, 181–182.

29. Paul Cobley, *Narrative* (London: Routledge, 2001), 231.

30. Monika Fludernik, *The Fictions of Language and the Languages of Fiction* (London: Routledge, 1993), 260.

31. Sbrockey, "Something of a Hero," 544.

32. James Drewett, "An Interview with Roddy Doyle," *Irish Studies Review*, 11:3 (December 2003), 347.

33. Costello, *The Irish Soul*, 91.

34. Niam McArdle, "An Interview with Roddy Doyle," *New Orleans Review*, 21:3–4 (1995), 117.

35. Wheeler and Newman, "Roddy Doyle," 57.

36. Luke Gibbons, "The Global Cure?: History, Therapy and the Celtic Tiger," in *Reinventing Ireland: Culture, Society and the Global Economy*, eds Peadar Kirby, Luke Gibbons and Michael Cronin (London: Pluto Press, 2002), 94.

37. Michael Cronin, *The Barrytown Trilogy* (Cork: Cork University Press, 2006), 20.

38. Elizabeth Butler Cullingford, *Ireland's Others: Ethnicity and Gender in Irish Literature and Popular Culture* (Cork: Cork University Press, 2001), 159–160. It is notable that both Cronin and Cullingford silently elide the political differences that distinguish north Dublin youths from Northern Irish Catholics.

39. See Lauren Onkey, "Celtic Soul Rebels," *Éire-Ireland*, 28:3 (Fall 1993), 147–158; Timothy D. Taylor, "Living in a Postcolonial World: Class and Soul in *The Commitments*," *Irish Studies Review*, 6:3 (1998), 291–302.

40. Paul Hewson, "Bono: The White Nigger," in *Across the Frontiers: Ireland in the 1990s*, ed. Richard Kearney (Dublin: Wolfhound Press, 1988), 189–190.

41. Dermot McCarthy, *Roddy Doyle: Raining on the Parade* (Dublin, Liffey Press, 2003), 33, original emphasis.
42. McCarthy, *Roddy Doyle*, 39.
43. Mary M. McGlynn, *Narratives of Class in New Irish and Scottish Literature: From Joyce to Kelman, Doyle, Galloway, and McNamee* (Basingstoke: Palgrave Macmillan, 2008), 91.
44. Mary McGlynn, "Why Jimmy Wears a Suit: White, Black, and Working Class in *The Commitments*," *Studies in the Novel*, 36:2 (Summer 2004), 234.
45. Gerry Smyth, *Music in Irish Cultural History* (Dublin: Irish Academic Press, 2009), 82.
46. See M. Keith Booker, "Late Capitalism Comes to Dublin: 'American' Popular Culture in the Novels of Roddy Doyle," *Ariel: A Review of International English Literature*, 28:3 (July 1997), 27–45. There is a latent irony in the fact that what in the novel is described as the "back to basics" (9) ethos of the British punk and postpunk eras, to which Jimmy is ideologically opposed, would appear to be more suited to the lives of aspiring musicians from a north Dublin working-class background than soul music. Arguably, the music produced by young working-class musicians in 1980s London and Manchester has as much if not more to say to these youths than 1960s Motown. If they were to write, one imagines that they would to be more likely to compose songs about "meetin' mots in supermarkets an' McDonald's" (12) than about sexual liberation and political revolution.
47. Charles Foran, 'The Troubles of Roddy Doyle', *Saturday Night*, 111:3 (April 1996), 64.
48. George O'Brien, "Aspects of the Novelist," *Irish Review*, 10 (Spring 1991), 116–117.
49. Richards, "Northside Realism and the Twilight's Last Gleaming," 19.
50. Brian Donnelly, "Roddy Doyle: From Barrytown to the GPO," *Irish University Review*, 30:1 (Spring/Summer 2000), 17–31.
51. In *A History of the Irish Novel* (Cambridge: Cambridge University Press, 2011), Derek Hand makes the valid point that "While the teenage pregnancy in *The Snapper* is somewhat unconventional, it merely reflected the social reality, not only of working-class Ireland but also of the middle classes at a time when the political realm was being constantly buffeted by demands for a liberalisation of the constitution with regards to both divorce and abortion" (266).
52. Sbrockey, "Something of a Hero," 538.
53. Ruth Barton, "Feisty Colleens and Faithful Sons: Gender in Irish Cinema," *Cinéaste*, 24:2–3 (1999), 42.
54. http://legislationline.org/documents/action/popup/id/5284.
55. McCarthy, *Roddy Doyle*, 66.
56. John McGahern, *Amongst Women* [1990] (London: Faber and Faber, 1991), 137.

57. Anthony Clare, *On Men: Masculinity in Crisis* (London: Chatto and Windus, 2000), 200–201. There are signs that Darren is also beginning to exhibit an ambivalence towards girls he fancies, such as the buxom Mandy Lawless, who we are told "often took her jumper off in school and wrapped it around her waist, even when it wasn't all that hot. Darren liked that, and it annoyed him as well sometimes" (370).

58. Clare, *On Men*, 205, original emphasis.

59. McCarthy, *Roddy Doyle*, 90, 96.

Chapter 2

House Arrest: John McGahern's *Amongst Women* (1990)

I

One could hardly imagine a starker counterpoint to the Rabbittes of Barrytown than the Morans of Great Meadow, the west-of-Ireland farming family at the center of what is arguably the finest novel in the contemporary Irish canon, *Amongst Women*. To close *The Van* and open this novel is to exchange the ceaseless bustle and chatter of a corporation housing estate for an isolated rural idyll where placid surfaces seal in emotion; it is to leave behind a recently pieced-together place and enter a society that exudes oaklike tradition and organic connectedness; and it is to swap a richly demotic conversational style for prose of cool, crystalline intensity. The change of milieu can perhaps be encapsulated by a single vignette from *Amongst Women*: "Nothing but the years changed in Great Meadow. Rain came down outside for days at a time as Rose moved carefully about within. When the soaked ground dried in hard winds and Moran moved slowly about outside she had breathing space again."[1]

And yet beneath the many differences that separate these fictive worlds, some telling points of contact are discernible. Although Barrytown and Great Meadow are presented as self-contained microrealities, existing apart from society at large, the fact that the tides of social and cultural change are lapping all around means that nothing happens in isolation in either of these emblematic locales. Furthermore, the dramas between the individual and the group that are played out in the Rabbitte and Moran households offer a condensed cultural analysis of Irish family values in transition. Though reflecting different scales of difficulty, the marital tensions that beset Michael and Rose Moran in the 1950s and Jimmy

Reading the Contemporary Irish Novel 1987–2007, First Edition. Liam Harte.
© 2014 Liam Harte. Published 2014 by John Wiley & Sons, Ltd.

and Veronica Rabbitte in the 1980s highlight significant shifts in the dynamics of dominance and submission, and a still wider set of intergenerational fault lines are exposed by the contrasting ways in which the children of these couples respond to family conflicts and crises.[2] In all four novels, the questions of what it means to belong to a family and the price such belonging exacts are opened up to sharp scrutiny. At an important level, the politics of family is where these novels' cutting edges lie.

Long before his death from cancer in March 2006, *Amongst Women* (the novel's title is taken from the *Ave Maria* or *Hail Mary*, as it is more commonly known in Ireland) had come to be regarded as John McGahern's literary master-piece. In fact, its enduring qualities were already being proclaimed by reviewers in the month of its publication. Seamus Deane judged it to be a "millimetre away from perfection;"[3] Thomas Kilroy wrote that it "expresses a great toler-ance and wisdom about living that is at once lambent and profound, the type of distillation that is only possible from a great writer writing out of the full-ness of his gift;"[4] and John Banville hailed it as "an example of the novelist's art at its finest, a work the heart of which beats to the rhythm of the world and of life itself. It will endure."[5] Such glowing assessments set the tone for the novel's subsequent reception by the Irish reading public, which ranked *Amongst Women* third behind Joyce's *Ulysses* (1922) and *A Portrait of the Artist as a Young Man* in a 2003 *Irish Times* poll to find the greatest Irish novel.[6] Three years later, obituarists were virtually unanimous in identifying *Amongst Women* as McGahern's *chef-d'oeuvre*, with novelist Joseph O'Connor deeming it "the most important Irish novel of the late 20th century."[7]

Many of these obituarists also noted the significance of the novel's rapturous reception for McGahern's literary rehabilitation within Irish society, where his name had once been synonymous with scandal and sexual permissiveness. His debut novel, *The Barracks* (1963), attracted critical acclaim even before pub-lication: extracts from it won McGahern the AE Memorial Award of the Irish Arts Council in 1962 and two years later he was awarded a prestigious Macauley Fellowship. But his second novel, *The Dark* (1965), in which depictions of ado-lescent masturbation are explicit and clerical homosexuality implicit, brought about a stark and very public reversal of fortune when it was banned by the Irish Censorship Board, a body established in 1929 under stringent legislation to pro-hibit the circulation of material deemed to be "in [. . .] general tendency indecent or obscene."[8] Many mid-twentieth-century Irish writers regarded being banned as a badge of artistic integrity or even heroic dissent; McGahern himself said he felt that "the Censorship Board and the whole business was a joke."[9] The extent of his misjudgment became painfully clear when in 1965, on the orders of the Archbishop of Dublin, he was dismissed from his teaching post in the

Dublin primary school where he had been employed since 1955. "In a way I was almost an official writer when *The Dark* was banned,"[10] he later said of this episode, which made him not only angry but "a little ashamed that our own independent country was making a fool of itself yet again."[11] His sacking prompted him to move to London, where he worked as a supply teacher, but found that he was unable to write fiction for several years. He later taught at the University of Reading and at Colgate University in New York before returning to Ireland in the early 1970s and settling on a farm in County Leitrim with his second wife, Madeline Green. McGahern was to spend the rest of his life there, combining the activities of farming and writing with periods spent as a visiting fellow at universities in Ireland and the United States. As a farmer–writer, he produced a further four novels – *The Leavetaking* (1974), *The Pornographer* (1979), *Amongst Women,* and *That They May Face the Rising Sun* (2002) – as well as several short stories, a play, and an autobiography, *Memoir* (2005), his last published work during his lifetime.

McGahern's return to his rural roots after years in exile mimicked the circular journeys that structure so much of his fiction. As *The Pornographer*'s nameless narrator acknowledges, "the road away became the road back."[12] McGahern was born near Ballinamore in County Leitrim to a mother who was a primary school teacher and a father a police sergeant who, having fought with the IRA during the War of Independence (1919–1921), was among the first intake of recruits to the Gárda Síochána, the new police force established by the Irish Free State in 1922.[13] Although married, his parents lived apart, so that John spent the school year with his adored mother in Ballinamore and the summer holidays with his father in the police barracks in Cootehall, County Roscommon, where he was sergeant. This unconventional domestic arrangement lasted until Susan McGahern was hospitalized with breast cancer when John was seven. Her death in 1944 meant that the family of five girls and two boys came under Frank McGahern's "direct rule,"[14] and with it exposure to the full force of his volcanic temperament. In *Memoir* McGahern chronicles his complicated, acrimonious relationship with his domineering father, whom he confessed to have never fully understood, "so changeable was he, so violent, so self-absorbed, so many-faced."[15] But the leitmotif of the book is his unconditional love for his devout mother, whose death marked the end of her son's childhood Eden. McGahern's fiction bears the deep imprint of his contrasting experiences of parental nurture, most obviously in the perpetual contest it stages between a damaged patriarchal masculinity and an affirmative feminine life force.

Already, we have touched upon the thorny topic that readers and critics have long puzzled over: the nature of the relationship between McGahern's life experiences and his art. Given that his fiction is deeply rooted in the individual's relation to history, critics such as Patrick Crotty have argued that "almost all of the extensions of McGahern's fictional world beyond the immediate domestic circumstances of the author's childhood are based on experiences in the earlier part of his life."[16] *Memoir* appeared to confirm this verdict by laying bare the biographical roots of the fiction. The book's status as a valedictory opus tempts us to read it as a definitive sourcebook for the fiction, with *Amongst Women* being the novel most consistently brought to mind. The biographical depiction of Frank McGahern in *Memoir* maps onto the fictional portrait of Michael Moran, the novel's widowed anti-hero, with uncanny accuracy through a host of shared circumstantial details and psychological traits. These include their youthful IRA activism; their mercurial temperaments; their thinly veiled misogyny; their concealment of their selfish desires behind a rhetoric of family-centered altruism; their fondness for referring to their children as "troops;" even their habit of rotating their thumbs when in agitated contemplation. No reader familiar with McGahern's *oeuvre* will be surprised by such correspondences, as he is a novelist of persistent repetitions and returns who knows that "all true stories are essentially the same story in the same way as they are different: they reflect the laws of life in both its sameness and its endless variations."[17]

Yet we must be careful here not to lapse into reductive, overly biographical readings of the fiction. McGahern was quick to take issue with critics such as John Halperin who practised such methods on other artists, wondering aloud "if the overall result is not to turn those works back into the confusion and trivia and brittleness out of which they somehow contrived, magically, to emerge. We do not need knowledge of Shakespeare's 'obscure hurt' to enjoy or suffer with Falstaff or Ophelia or Hamlet or Lear."[18] Furthermore, McGahern consistently challenged attempts to pigeonhole him as an autobiographical writer, often doing so as part of his wider critique of romantic conceptions of art as self-expression, insisting that a richer kind of truth is revealed through the imaginative transformation and amplification of raw materials. In one interview he claimed that his most serious literary mistakes occurred when he drew from life and "actually stuck to the way things happen,"[19] and in another explained that "40%–60% of every character is one's self and the point is that the fiction would be a truer picture of my spiritual life than my own life."[20] It was a paradox he was fond of repeating: "the more the material is worked into an artifice, the more true feeling is set free."[21]

Chief among the most poignant passages in *Memoir* are those in which McGahern recounts his childhood wish to honor his mother by becoming a priest. In strikingly romantic language, he recreates the passion with which he imagined a prayerful life with his "beloved":

· ·

We'd live together in the priest's house and she'd attend each morning Mass and take communion from my hands. When she died, I'd include her in all the Masses that I'd say until we were united in the joy of heaven, when time would cease as we were gathered into the mind of God.[22]

· ·

In early adulthood, art displaced religion as the focus for such passionate feeling, an apostasy that is partly attributable to McGahern's loss of religious faith and partly to the intellectual awakening sparked by his being given access as an adolescent to the library of a local Protestant family. "Instead of being a priest of God, I would be the god of a small, vivid world,"[23] he recalled, which meant that the people and landscapes of counties Leitrim and Roscommon became his *locus amoenus* – they were, he said, "like my breathing"[24] – though his imagination was also keenly attuned to the experiences of the Irish in Britain, and to the chance that separates the emigrant from the stay-at-home.[25]

McGahern's fidelity to capturing the physical, moral, and psychological textures of particular lives lived in particular places is one of his most admired qualities and has led critics to compare his spare stylistics to the "scrupulous meanness" of Joyce, though he also has important affinities with Yeats.[26] Honesty was for McGahern a core, non-negotiable duty of authorship. Advice offered by one of his earliest readers, the Belfast writer Michael McLaverty, could stand as a distillation of his own aesthetic principles: "Saturate yourself in the material and the quintessential will take care of itself."[27] Verisimilitude and stylistic simplicity are qualities he consistently commends in the work of authors he admires, from Flaubert and Proust to Alistair MacLeod and Tomás O'Crohan, whose classic Irish-language autobiography, *The Islandman* (1929), was one of McGahern's artistic touchstones. Indeed, his celebration of *The Islandman* as a work anchored in truth reads as an oblique manifesto of his own literary principles. In a much-reprinted essay, McGahern surveys the architecture of O'Crohan's prose for the secret of its "simple, heroic poetry" and finds it in his self-effacing style: "So persistent is the form of seeing and thinking that it seems always to find its right expression: unwittingly, through the island frame, we have been introduced into a complete representation of experience."[28] Such "sure instinct" underwrites the authenticity of the text's organic unity of place, action, and outlook and imbues the narrative with a resolute realism that has a timeless universality to it:

· ·

A field is described only as it is reclaimed and cultivated; a strand is there to be crossed, a sea to be fished, a town to be reached, a shore to be gained, walked upon, lived upon. These are all near and concrete realities but so stripped down to their essentials because of the necessities of the action as to seem free of all local characteristics. One conditions the other to the same simplicity of form.[29]

....

Such observations have a very suggestive relevance for McGahern's own aesthetic approach and ethical stance. The quest for elemental utterance, the attention to the irrefutable materiality of the world, the revelation of the emblematic through the particular, the intensely observed extraordinary ordinariness of an intimately known place – these are the hallmarks of his fiction across five decades. Part of him also responded to O'Crohan's deep respect for the steady force of life beyond human control and his stoic acceptance of the implacable cycle of birth, procreation, and death. Many of his own protagonists evince a preternatural awareness of the turning of this cycle or "wheel" (one of his favorite motifs) and of how "The christening party becomes the funeral, the shudder that makes us flesh becomes the shudder that makes us meat."[30] Such awareness seldom leads to enlightenment, however. Rather, as Crotty points out, "a McGahern epiphany characteristically involves heightened sensitivity to conditions over which the subject has no control."[31] Time's indifference to human suffering and endeavor is repeatedly borne in upon characters such as Elizabeth Reegan in *The Barracks*, who comes to regard life as a painful, purposeless maelstrom, the meaning of which forever recedes before her, disappearing into "The starkness of individual minutes passing among accidental doors and windows and chairs and flowers and trees."[32] The insistent refrain of her former lover Michael Halliday – "What is all this living and dying about anyway?"[33] – is a defining question that echoes across McGahern's entire corpus and elicits oblique rejoinders from many sources, including Mary Murphy in *That They May Face the Rising Sun* – "We're no more than a puff of wind out on the lake"[34] – and the novelist himself in *Memoir*: "We come from darkness into light and grow into light while at death we return to that original darkness."[35]

This recurring preoccupation with humanity's lack of agency in the face of transience and fate, which sometimes manifests itself as an immobilizing pessimism, is one of the factors that complicates any attempt to pigeonhole McGahern as an existential writer. Another is the distinctly metaphysical aspect of his moral outlook, in that his work is shaped as much by a yearning for transcendent vision as it is by a scrupulous attention to social fact and the determining power of those aforementioned near and concrete realities. Although he rejected the notion of literature as a substitute for religion, he once confided to McLaverty: "I often think the realest reason I write is, having lost my formal faith, I am self compelled to pray or praise," and asserted in a later letter that "all art approaches prayers."[36] Despite his religious unbelief and his antipathy toward what he saw as the hollow devotionalism of Irish Catholic practice, he could never disavow the spiritual and aesthetic importance of his early religious induction. In *Memoir* he speaks of the Catholic Church as "my first book" through which "I was introduced to all I have come to know of prayer and sacrament, ceremony and mystery, grace and ornament and the equality of all women and men underneath the sun of heaven."[37] This makes McGahern, in Denis Sampson's words, "a religious writer in the largest sense because he associates art with a metaphysical quest, with the recovery of traces of mystery and a sense of the sanctity of the person."[38] That such openness to spiritual mystery can coexist with an exacting emotional and intellectual honesty – an utter commitment to speak as he feels, not as he feels he should speak – makes McGahern's rare epiphanies seem all the more precious. This is especially so in *Amongst Women*, a novel in which redemptive energies are at a premium.

II

The opening episode of *Amongst Women* introduces the novel's core themes: the gendered psychological dynamics of power, fear, and love in a rural Irish Catholic family, and the formative effects of war, militarism, and traumatic memory on the articulation of masculine identity in a postcolonial context. The novel's circular time scheme braids these thematic strands into a densely textured, richly suggestive story, the full emotional force of which emerges only with the final sentence, which returns us to the first, which itself contains the ending: "As he weakened, Moran became afraid of his daughters" (1). Bookended between these narrative poles, which are anchored in the novel's fictive present, is an extended flashback sequence that chronicles the defining events in the life of Michael Moran: his friendship with James McQuaid, his former IRA comrade during the War of Independence; his courtship and marriage to his second wife, Rose Brady; his tempestuous relationships with his three teenage daughters and youngest son in Great Meadow, the austere family home that only welcomes its own; and his obsessional desire to reconnect with his eldest son Luke, whose exile in London makes him a traitor to the family in his father's eyes. "The decision to open and close the novel with the same event means that, above all else, *Amongst Women* is a novel about memory,"[39] observes Robert Garratt, and it is true that McGahern's non-linear ordering of events draws attention to the centrality of remembrance to any understanding of the novel. But McGahern goes further by exploring the perplexing interplay in Irish culture between traumatic memory and history, between experience and imagination, and between repression and revelation, using as his lens that much-eulogized entity, the family unit, about which we shall say more later. Before that, however, I wish to take a closer look at how the themes mentioned above are embedded in the opening sections of the novel.

A subtle battle is joined from the start of the narrative over the recollection and rendition of past events and their potential to answer specific emotional and psychological needs in the present. We first encounter Moran's three daughters, Sheila, Mona, and Maggie – the Shakespearean parallels are compelling throughout – in revivalist mode, filled with a collective resolve to remedy the present by redeeming the past. Their aim is to restage Monaghan Day, an annual domestic ritual that they recall as having sustained their father when they were young.[40] Monaghan Day was a personal day of remembrance for Moran and McQuaid, on which they would reminisce about their exploits in an IRA flying column.[41] Although McQuaid is long dead, the Moran girls believe that reviving this memorial rite will help rejuvenate their ailing father. That they insist on doing so "Against all reason" (2) is telling. Not only is the idea of a one-man Monaghan Day illogical and the daughters' hopes to cheat death delusional, they are also shown to be willfully sentimentalizing and sanitizing their family history: "Forgotten was the fearful nail-biting exercise Monaghan Day had always been for the whole house; with distance it had become large, heroic, blood-mystical, something from which the impossible could be snatched" (2). Here, their idealistic fervor and refusal to face reality is strikingly captured by the loaded phrase "blood-mystical," which recalls the redemptive romantic nationalism of Patrick Pearse, leader of the 1916 Rising. That this long-forgotten domestic rite, from which Moran's daughters were excluded when young, has become so hallowed in retrospect suggests an evangelical zeal on their part to reconfigure history as an enabling, regenerative fiction. Like Pearse, they appear to be in thrall to a myth of transfiguration and deliverance. Against the dissolution of time, they seek to mobilize memory to restore a sense of wholeness and living continuity, trusting to its miraculous powers.

Moran himself is opposed to "any dredging up of the past," seeing it as an affront to "the continuing present he felt his life to be" (3).[42] Remembrance has become his enemy, a disruptive force that unsettles his current sense of self by reminding him of his ambivalence about the war and his failure to prosper as an officer in the Free State Army, a disappointment that has hardened into an acute disaffection for those who rose to the top in the postrevolutionary state that he helped bring into being. From his aggrieved perspective, the revolution was a travesty, a bloody gesture that resulted in a polity that is little more than an inverted image of the colonial administration it replaced. His contempt for the "crowd of small-minded gangsters out for their own good" (18) who came to power after 1922 dwarfs whatever animosity he once felt toward the "auld enemy": "What did we get for it? A country, if you'd believe them. Some of our own johnnies in the top jobs instead of a few Englishmen. More than half of my own family work in England. What was it all for? The whole thing was a cod" (5).[43]

And yet with typical unpredictability, Moran suddenly breaks his long-standing "embargo on the past" (177) by speaking about the war and his role in it. His daughters offer cautious prompts, effectively ventriloquizing McQuaid by repeating approbatory remarks they once heard him make. Unlike them, however, their father will brook no idealization or mythologization of history. Describing the war as "a bad business" and his unit as "a bunch of killers," he excoriates those who, for politically and financially expedient ends, retrospectively disavow the ugly reality of armed insurrection, insisting:

· ·

Don't let them pull wool over your eyes. The war was the cold, the wet, standing to your neck in a drain for the whole night with bloodhounds on your trail, not knowing how you could manage the next step toward the end of a long march. That was the war: not when the band played and a bloody politician stepped forward to put flowers on the ground. (5)

· ·

Yet this truculent veteran also registers a residual nostalgia for the frisson of potency he experienced during his days as an IRA commandant: "For people like McQuaid and myself the war was the best part of our lives. Things were never so simple and clear again. I think we never rightly got the hang of it afterwards" (6).

This schizoid view of the independence struggle – at once a time of blood-soaked horror and of glorious self-realization – reveals not only the depths of Moran's subsequent disenchantment with the postrevolutionary dispensation but also the extent to which his subjectivity has been molded by a core ambiguity of warfare: the experience of intimate killing can excite feelings of exhilaration as well as anguish.[44] Having been "a guerrilla fighter from the time he was little more than a boy" (163), Moran was at an early age initiated into the godlike power that comes from having command of a lethal weapon and a fighting unit. It is a secret knowledge he shares only with McQuaid, as their Monaghan Day recollections reveal. McQuaid recounts his acts of guerrilla efficiency with particular relish, savoring the sense of omnipotence he derived from being able to look his unsuspecting target in the eye in the moment before he killed him. The veterans' joint recital of "the days of their glory" (14) during this first, strategically positioned flashback sequence is thematically important, therefore, because it raises questions that cut to the heart of the novel. What are the legacies, for self and society, of masculinities weaned on revolutionary violence and guerrilla combat? What happens to the martial imagination after

59

the war is over? How do minds shaped by idealistic certainties adapt to the inevitable compromises and power struggles of peacetime? And how does the psychological trauma of harrowing events play itself out in this afterlife?

Certainly, Moran's early exposure to guerrilla combat is shown to be deeply formative of his character and a source of chronic psychic damage. The opening scenes pointedly establish that he has lost none of the instincts that made him such an effective insurgent, while also highlighting the extent to which his psyche is constituted around an unworked-through trauma, figured as the violent intrusion of a troublesome past. Although we know that Moran's silence about the war has not been absolute, his long-delayed disclosure of his disdainful views on it to his daughters suggests an element of unspeakability that is consistent with traumatic neurosis.[45] Equally tellingly, we are told that the Moran girls' Monaghan Day ministrations resurrect only "a weak fanciful ghost of what had been" (7), a metaphor that calls to mind Pierre Janet's and Sigmund Freud's conception of trauma as a form of psychological possession, whereby an overwhelming event resists assimilation at the time that it occurs, only to return belatedly and intrusively to haunt the subject. McGahern's insinuation of the haunting aspect of Moran's experience is masterfully evoked when the old man abruptly shoots a jackdaw on the morning after the family gathering, just before his daughters' departure. His arrestingly elliptical remark when confronted – "The closest I ever got to any man was when I had him in the sights of my rifle and I never missed" (7) – suggests that the bird is the incarnation of a dissonant, recursive history, just as the shotgun's prominent presence in the house symbolizes the fact that the war has never really ended for this veteran and that he remains mentally organized for combat.[46]

The image of the gun being returned to "its usual place in the corner of the room" (7) underlines the continuing power of this unresolved past to intrude upon the perpetual present Moran inhabits, and further supports a reading of *Amongst Women* as a narrative of traumatic haunting. Here is a protagonist who carries unprocessed memories of his devastating capacity for deadly intimacy, one who is disturbed by the allure of human assassination and tormented by his inextricable abhorrence of, and admiration for, his lethal handiwork. This portrait accords with Cathy Caruth's theorization of trauma as "a symptom of history. The traumatized, we might say, carry an impossible history with them, or they become themselves the symptom of a history that they cannot entirely possess."[47] And it is not only lived history that will not stay buried. There are also suggestive clues that link individual suffering to a more pervasive sociohistorical trauma emanating from the catastrophe of the Irish Famine of the 1840s. For example, we learn that Moran's "racial fear of the poorhouse or famine was deep" (68), deep enough to be a possible factor in his pained denial of Sheila's educational aspirations and to make him fear penury even when, in old age, he and Rose "had more money now than they had life" (172).[48] Such glimpses of his hidden anguish transform this seemingly imperious tyrant into history's victim, a carrier of the transgeneration fear and shame that stemmed from the traumatization of a whole culture.

The depiction of these two veterans' last Monaghan Day together provides further evidence of the pervasive impact of the traumatic legacy of the War of Independence on Moran's life, particularly in the portrayal of him as an unreconstructed "outlaw" (37). His tense anticipation of McQuaid's arrival at Great Meadow resembles that of a gunman waiting to ambush a target, with Moran "instinctively" (10) taking cover in a fir plantation to watch the road. His covert surveillance is akin to a sniper tracking his quarry, but the redundancy of this mode of conduct in the new Ireland is starkly exposed when we see how the power balance between the ex-comrades has altered. Almost immediately, the bumptious visitor usurps Moran's domestic authority by occupying his fireside armchair, from where he covetously inspects Moran's "blooming" (11) daughters as he would heifers at auction. This symbolic emasculation is underscored by Moran's "boyish" (12) fascination with McQuaid's business acumen in the public realm. Whereas Moran has become a virtual recluse since his army career ended as a result of some unspecified "trouble" (23), his former subordinate has developed into a man of substance, driven by avarice, guile, and an "aggressive sureness" (11). Yet Moran's eunuch-like deference masks a seething resentment that is fuelled by the knowledge that McQuaid's business success is built on money borrowed from him. Moran's retreat from the public sphere into his "shell of self" (12) seems all the more impotent in this light, and his suppressed humiliated rage all the more corrosive.

As both Antoinette Quinn and Denis Sampson point out, the one quality that unites these ex-soldiers is their domestic tyranny.[49] Moran's domination of his family is exemplified throughout the narrative, whereas McQuaid's cavalier treatment of his wife is glancingly evoked in a masterly single snapshot: "There was never a hint of a blow. So persistent was the language [of abuse] that it had become no more remarkable than just another wayward manner of speaking and their sons paid so little attention to it that it might well have been one of the many private languages of love" (13).[50] The subtle differences between the men's respective forms of domestic despotism are sketched with commensurate deftness. McQuaid's smirking recollection of a fellow guerrilla who humiliated a girl who was relieving herself abroad by poking her with his gun barrel reveals much about his own chauvinism. The prudish Moran is not amused, though he is more critical of the guerrilla's shameless broadcasting of his unchivalrous antics than of the act itself. Moran's guarded response here is wholly in keeping with his concealment of his own "compulsion to dominate" (21), in a society "where dress was conservative, all violence hidden" (135).

This embittered former hero's supremacist instincts are given free rein once the bonds of friendship between the two men are acrimoniously severed. Having stubbornly rejected male friendship, Moran performs a deathly recoil from life, taking refuge in family, "more particularly that larger version of himself – *his* family" (22), which he transforms into his own private regiment of "troops" (3, 31). According to Kai Erikson, a reactive retreat of this nature is one of the clinical signatures of traumatic neurosis: "To describe people as traumatized is to say that they have withdrawn into a kind of protective envelope, a place of mute, aching loneliness, in which the traumatic experience is treated as a solitary burden that needs to be expunged by acts of denial and resistance."[51] In Moran's case, his reclusive tendencies are complicated by a countervailing need for others, a need he despises because he cannot conquer it. Abandonment is one of his deepest fears, attention his deepest craving – an oscillation that has itself been identified as a dialectic of trauma by Judith Lewis Herman.[52] Hence his distress at Luke's resolute indifference toward him and his corresponding hope that by marrying Rose his life might "glow again in the concentration of her attention" (27). The bitterness with which Moran resigns himself to this union is as much a symptom of his deep-seated contempt for his own vulnerability and inconsistency – that is, for his own humanness – as it is a sign of his hidden misogyny, which he passes on to his son Michael.[53] Such vulnerability can itself be traced to his thwarted desire for sovereign mastery, which originates in his unbearable exclusion from sites of public power in independent Ireland. Thus, the fact that Moran feels "vulnerable in the face of the power that rested in the hands of the outside" (77) drives him to exercise ever greater levels of authoritarian control over the private dominion he establishes at Great Meadow, where he seeks to replicate the aims of the republican project that betrayed him by converting the "many" into the "one." In the process, he betrays the republic in turn by molding his family into a kind of anti-society, a bastion of asocial detachment that is fundamentally inimical to the egalitarian ideals and participatory ethos of republicanism. Moran's cynical manipulation of the republican rhetoric of equality renders this betrayal all the more egregious, as we shall see. McGahern's own comments provide a suggestive gloss on this aspect of the novel: "The whole country is made up of families, each family a kind of independent republic. In *Amongst Women*, the family is a kind of half-way house between the individual and the society."[54]

In seeking to bend his wife and family to his will, Moran turns his safe house into a war zone where behavior and interaction are heavily strategized. Everyday life becomes an emotional minefield for his daughters, who must develop an armory of watchful attitudes as "camouflage [. . .] for safekeeping" (68). Moran's view of power is distinctly gendered. He equates Michael's initial docility with effeminacy, but when Sheila challenges her father's authority she becomes male in his eyes, thus confirming the truth of Luke's observation that "only women could live with Daddy" (133). Rose frequently finds herself in the firing line of her husband's accusatory tirades, never more so than when he speaks to her "as quietly as if he were taking rifle aim" (69). McGahern's use of the language of military and diplomatic engagement reveals the extent to which martial modes have infiltrated the marital domain – another legacy of combat neurosis – though Moran's "home rule" is far from uncontested.[55] Throughout the novel, Rose Brady is presented as a wily tactician in the arena of social relations, a woman whose "true instinct was always to work behind the usual social frameworks: family, connections, position, conventions, those established forms that can be used like weapons when they are mastered" (24). As a returned emigrant, she has known enough "false starts" (30) in life to "foresee failure" (25) if she remains a spinster in this valley of squinting windows, and is therefore forced to pursue Moran in "the open" (25) – a place of excruciating vulnerability for all – even at the risk of public ridicule. Her eventual success in ensnaring her quarry and establishing an emotional bridgehead from which to ingratiate herself with Moran's daughters is attributed to her skilful use of "tact," a word that underlines the circumscribed and precarious nature of her challenge to Moran's monolithic power.

Rose's strategy of "subversive subservience"[56] is one the daughters quickly learn from, as their discreet attempts to negotiate a measure of collective sovereignty show. Within hours of the wedding, stepmother and daughters perform a jig of complicity and resistance around the lordly paterfamilias: "Rose and the girls smiled as the tea and the plates circled around him. They were already conspirators. They were mastered and yet they were controlling together what they were mastered by" (46). This drama of mutual containment, which has about it a whiff of malignant intimacy – note the alacrity with which Rose colludes in the daughters' self-infantilizing use of the term "Daddy" – rehearses in microcosm the predicament of the subject under colonial rule and is one of several scenes in the novel that lends itself to a politicized reading. The episode recalls the daughters' furtive display of disobedience during their preparations for McQuaid's Monaghan Day visit, when they secretly mock Moran's clichéd complaints, and anticipates the deathbed scene, where the women's assumption of authority is symbolized by their taking control of the rosary, Moran's chief rhetorical weapon for so long. The old man's dying cry of protest – "*Shut up!*" (180) – suggests that the sound of "his" litany emanating from the mouths of his wife and daughters is for him an unbearable moment of menacing mimicry. He could even be said to be experiencing a Kurtz-like epiphany of horror here, a counterpoint to his earlier awareness of his suddenly unignorable mortality, framed against the durable life force that suffuses the natural world: "To die was never to look on all this again. It would live in others' eyes but not in his. He had never realized when he was in the midst of confident life what an amazing glory he was part of" (179).[57] If so, it is not only his daughters' power to "will this life free of death" (178) that horrifies Moran but also the prospect of his malign patrimony ramifying across the generations, propagated by his own *female* flesh and blood. Prior to this reversal of power relations, however, we are continually reminded of the frailty of the women's defenses, even after they recognize the patriarch's hidden vulnerabilities. The comparison of Rose and the girls to "a shoal of fish moving within a net" (79) evokes patriarchy's pervasive influence, and the maimed hen pheasant the women discover in the hayfield is a pitiful emblem of the annihilation of female potential. Such images underline the carefully calibrated nature of McGahern's feminist critique of patriarchy, which he himself spoke of in the following terms:

. . . .

If the novel suggests anything, it is how difficult it is for people, especially women who until very recently had no real power at all in our society, to try to create space to live and love in the shadow of violence. How they manage to do that in the novel becomes their uncertain triumph.[58]

. . . .

Within the fortress of Great Meadow, Moran's coercive exercise of power is discursive as well as physical. That is to say, his authority rests not only on the threat of violence but also on his self-serving appropriation of the normative ideology of the nuclear family in independent Ireland, as promulgated by church and state. The 1937 Constitution enshrined the family at the heart of national ideology, defining it as "a moral institution possessing inalienable and imprescriptible rights, antecedent and superior to all positive law,"[59] and pledging the state to the protection of its integrity and authority. Such was the influence of Catholic doctrine on politicians and policymakers in the fledgling state that this constitutional guarantee effectively codified Catholic social teaching on the family.[60] The novel subtly registers the deeply embedded nature of this social veneration of the family unit, including its influence on the ethos of the chief bureaucratic instrument of state administration, the Civil Service. Such was "the primacy of the idea of the family that everyone was able to leave work at once without incurring displeasure" (123), when a family crisis arose. The Constitution also configured the family as a sanctified space of female authority and fulfillment and idealized the home as the locus of maternal influence. Such national conservatism clearly facilitates Moran's strategic manipulation of this ideology in order to transform his family into a self-aggrandizing fiefdom in which women are chronically marginalized and disempowered. It is his own supreme authority he reaffirms when he promotes family solidarity, as it is when he invokes the need for collective prayer: "*We* have to try to work together as best we can and *pray*" (6).

It is also the case that Great Meadow's status as a place of "true virginity" (166) reflects prevailing discourses of sexual abstinence associated with the promotion of the cult of the Virgin Mary in twentieth-century Irish Catholicism, to which the rosary was central. McGahern's thematic use of this prayer exemplifies his consummate skill in tapping the symbolic potential of a mundane domestic ritual, without seeking, in Joyce's terms, "to alter in the presentment, still more to deform, whatever he has seen and heard."[61] On the face of it, Moran's devotion to the rosary accurately reflects its popularity with the 1950s Catholic generation to which he belongs, many of whom would share his familiarity with the slogan coined by Father Patrick Peyton as part of his worldwide crusade to promote the prayer: "The family that prays together stays together" (137). Strategically speaking, however, Moran's piety is another mask of power, behind which he exploits the prayer's citational force to bolster his coercive control. As Antoinette Quinn explains:

. . . .

Though the Rosary repeatedly pronounces Mary as 'blessed . . . amongst women,' because she was chosen to be the mother of Christ, in the Moran household, the character blessed amongst women is Moran himself. So the paternal symbolically ousts the maternal. Ironically, the misogynistic Moran pays daily lip service to motherhood. He even manages to die 'amongst women,' since his son Michael is temporarily absent.[62]

. . . .

Of course, this is not the only irony that simultaneously underpins and undermines Moran's performative reaffirmation of his authority through his fetishization of family and prayer. His own family unit is both profoundly dysfunctional and irreparably fractured by Luke's alienated absence and the unmentioned death of the children's mother. Moran's anguished awareness of this brokenness puts a strain on his rhetoric of unity, forcing him to recast Peyton's mantra to fit these altered circumstances: "I think that families can stay together even though they're scattered, if there's a will to do so. The will's the important thing" (137). But the very act of praying for the absent family member merely "drew uncomfortable attention to the disturbing bonds of their togetherness" (96), and no amount of willpower can stem the exodus of the other siblings or shore up Moran's autocracy, the increasing fragility of which is captured in the tableau of a diminished family kneeling in prayer on a stormy night: "For the first time the house seemed a frail defence against all that beat around it. The prayers had done nothing to dispel the sense of night and stirring trees outside, the splattering of rain on the glass" (90).

This section of the novel ends with Moran sitting in brooding silence, oppressed by a searing apprehension of abandonment, his muteness a sign of his growing realization that his authority is neither immutable nor endlessly supervisable.[63] There is a tragic quality to his solitary stillness, for what man need be afraid of his daughters when he becomes weak, except one who terrified them when he was strong? In reality, the displacement of power to the matriarchal realm is already underway, although, as the concluding paragraphs of the novel reveal, it is by no means a matter of simple transference. The image of Moran "emptied [. . .] into blankness" (91) is one of several that portray his existential bewilderment as an agonizing form of blindness. His exasperation at his pervasive inability to comprehend life's meaning is most fully focalized in the scene where, with his family scattered, he goes out to walk his land in the gathering dusk, "field by blind field" (129):

> It was like grasping water to think how quickly the years had passed here. They were nearly gone. It was in the nature of things and yet it brought a sense of betrayal and anger, of never having understood anything much. Instead of using the fields, he sometimes felt as if the fields had used him. Soon they would be using someone else in his place. It was unlikely to be either of his sons. He tried to imagine someone running the place after he was gone and could not. He continued walking the fields like a man trying to see. (130)

In moments such as these, Moran appears as a piteous figure, enveloped by anguish and existential ignorance. As Denis Sampson eloquently observes:

> This suffering figure, who is unlikeable in his hatred of life and his contempt for those close to him, gains a mythic stature from the depth of this anguish; he seems to touch the quick of the human condition, to ask questions about the meaning of his life for which no answers are available.[64]

Sampson convincingly reads these episodes of blindness as metaphors for Moran's frustrated "yearning for transcendent vision,"[65] but it seems equally valid to construe them as another manifestation of what Caruth calls the "endless impact"[66] of trauma on a life, the profound sense of incomprehensibility that is inescapably bound up with the ongoing experience of having survived a devastating event.

Moran's scattered offspring are prey to their own hauntings. From the perspective of those who leave, Great Meadow grows in strength and inviolability the greater their distance from it. For all except Luke, who has, tellingly, grown "straight and manly" (13) in exile, the house exists as a gravitational source of "healing" wherein "the pain of individuality" (85) is soothed. The father's continuing, charismatic hold over his children is "pure binding" (2); they have been rendered emotionally and psychologically captive by their condition of dependency. This is crystallized in Mona's worshipful reflection that "No matter what they say, Daddy can be wonderful" (129), and felt in the programmed ferocity with she and her sisters cleave to the perpetual ground of home, where "they grew again into the wholeness of being the unique and separate Morans" (94). Such quasi-pathological attachment to the primal site of disempowerment is consistent with the kinds of traumatic bonding that often develops between abuser and abused, and there are also echoes in it of the dynamics of the paradoxical colonizer–colonized relationship. Indeed, it is hard to resist seeing the Moran children (*sans* Luke) as emblems of the neocolonial condition, in that having been subjugated for so long, they struggle to sustain individual identities beyond the perimeters of the father's imperium. The more we hear of the siblings' incessant homecomings, the more the full range of resonance of the novel's opening metaphor is borne in upon us: Moran truly is "implanted" in his children's psyches, in the same way that colonized territory is planted with settlers for the purposes of governing it in a manner that may represent itself as nurturing but which is actually exploitative. Throughout their upbringing, all signs of sibling difference, individuality, and ambition have been crushed by Moran in the name of a spurious egalitarianism: "I consider all my family equal. I don't like to see a single one trying to outdistance another" (89). The legacies of such conditioning are complex. On the one hand, it fosters in the children a delusional but resilient pride in their "aristocratic" (2) difference and superiority; on the other, it negates their individual identities to the extent that they can only imagine agency in collective terms: "Together they were one world and could take on the world. Deprived of this sense they were nothing, scattered, individual things. They would put up with anything in order to have this sense of belonging. They would never let it go" (145). The children's constant need for paternal approval is consonant with such psychological disablement, as is the readiness with which they forgive Moran's "unpredictable violences" and the elation with which they greet his "moods of pure charm" (131).

Although Michael Moran's charismatic paternalism has no precedent in Irish fiction, his extraordinary hold over his children does have intriguing affinities with that of Godfrey Marshall over his offspring in D. H. Lawrence's 1915 short story, "England, My England." Like Moran, Marshall is a man of "rough, tough fibre, not without a vein of healthy cunning through it all."[67] The allusion to him having "an acrid faith like the sap of some not-to-be exterminated tree" calls to mind the poisonous yew tree at the entrance gate to Great Meadow, with which Moran is symbolically identified, and indeed the yew tree in the cemetery under which he is eventually laid to rest. But the similarities between these patriarchs are strongest in the realms of fatherhood and parenting. If Marshall is "the father of the old English type,"[68] then Moran is surely his Irish counterpart. In fact, Marshall's "life-and-death authority over his children: a great natural power,"[69] is so uncannily close to that of Moran's that the following passage would not look out of place in *Amongst Women*:

· ·

> In his own small circle he [Marshall] would emanate power, the single power of his own blind self. [. . .] He was too wise to make laws and to domineer in the abstract. But he had kept, and all honour to him, a certain primitive dominion over the souls of his children, the old, almost magic prestige of paternity. There it was, still burning in him, the old smoky torch of paternal godhead. And in the sacred glare of this torch his children had been brought up. He had given the girls every liberty, at last. But he had never really let them go beyond his power. And they, venturing out into the hard white light of our fatherless world, learned to see with the eyes of the world. They learned to criticise their father, even, from some effulgence of worldly white light, to see him as inferior. But this was all very well in the head. The moment they forgot their tricks of criticism, the old red glow of his authority came over them again. He was not to be quenched.[70]

· ·

Yet in the same way that colonial authority is haunted by inherent insecurities, Moran's hegemony is revealed to be fragile, fissured, and ultimately survivable. Its limits are most tellingly exposed in the insight we are granted into Sheila's ambivalent relationship to Great Meadow after she becomes a mother:

· ·

> She knew that her loyalty was probably ambiguous, that the deepest part of herself was bound to her sisters, this man and house. That could not be changed; but she wanted no part of it for her children: doors would be open to them that had been locked to her, their lives would be different. (170)

· ·

Here we see a daughter engaged in a head-on struggle with what Lawrence calls the prestige of paternity, knowing that she will never fully transcend the influence of the place where she was emotionally damaged, yet determined nevertheless that her "inheritance of fear and guilt"[71] will not be passed on to her children. It is through such individual acts of self-assertion, the novel suggests, that the cycle of psychological disablement may yet be broken and the future redeemed. In Lawrentian terms, "the cold white light of feminine independence" may one day outshine "the glow of male power."[72]

The import of this scene seems to me to be a crucial aid to our understanding of the hauntingly enigmatic closing movement of the novel, in which the ramifying force of Michael Moran's influence and legacy is exquisitely rendered as a paradox of a living absence. At the moment of his interment in the Leitrim clay, Moran's patriarchal essence is portrayed as having been translated into the consciousness of his wife and daughters, such that "each of them in their different ways had become Daddy" (183). As if to prove the point that becoming Daddy entails denigrating femininity, Sheila is shown casting a mildly reproving backward glance at her husband, brother, and brother-in-law as they leave the graveyard and likening them to "a crowd of women" (184), a disparagement that could have come from her father's mouth. Had we not witnessed her earlier protection of the next generation from Moran's harmful influence, this ending would gloomily suggest that the future will be, in Joyce's words, "the seim anew."[73] But Sheila's act of shielding, combined with her announcement that she and her family will not be staying overnight in Great Meadow after the funeral, work to offset pessimism and imply that the future will not necessarily be determined by "a triumphalist, masculinist ethic of dominance"[74] in the way that the past has been, or at least not for all of these women.

The temptation to extrapolate from the local to the national here is one to which many readers have understandably succumbed, given that *Amongst Women* appeared within months of the election of Ireland's first female president, the left-leaning Mary Robinson, which marked a symbolically significant milestone on Irish women's emancipatory journey and emboldened advocates of liberal pluralism. Even the novelist himself, for all his aversion to refracting his protagonists' lives through a prism of social critique, admitted to being intrigued by the suggestion that "one of Moran's daughters might now be Mrs Robinson – that would drive the old man crazy."[75] But McGahern is far too astute a cultural analyst to equate the death of Moran with the complete and unequivocal passing of the patriarchal dominion he embodies, just as he is too attuned to life's contingencies to insinuate that this autocratic father's influence in his children's lives will forever be "pure binding." In place of closure, the denouement balances severance and continuity, gloom and levity to create a gorgeously realized and wholly credible ending to this tense family psychodrama.

First, there is the multilayered symbolism of Moran's being buried not with his first wife but "in a new plot beneath a yew tree" (182). When we recall the yew's notorious toxicity, the inference that a *cordon sanitaire* is being drawn around Moran's pestilent legacy presents itself, yet the yew is also regarded as a protector and purifier of the dead, a tree whose famous longevity and evergreen nature made it such a revered symbol of immortality and renewal in Celtic folklore that tribal leaders were reputedly buried in the shadow of a yew. These paradoxical resonances are dexterously amplified by what happens immediately after the burial, for as the clay settles over Moran's coffin, his power over his female progeny seems more palpably irresistible than ever. "'He may be gone home but he'll always be with us,' Maggie spoke for them all. 'He'll never leave us now'" (183). Such certitude sounds ungainsayable, such consensus final, yet Maggie is not granted the final word. The spell her utterance threatens to cast over the mourners is forestalled by her stepmother, whose subtle body language outspeaks her words: "'Poor Daddy,' Rose echoed absently out of her own thoughts before waking and turning brightly towards the girls" (184). This lightening of mood is reciprocated and intensified by Michael, Sean, and Mark, who share the novel's final frame with the bereaved women and are pictured "chatting and laughing pleasantly together, their children around them," as if "coming from a dance" (184). The animated conviviality of the scene, which is suggestive of a great weight lifting, checks the fatalism of Moran's daughters having "become" their father and implies that the future is not altogether scripted or predetermined. The master's aura will endure – Sheila's chauvinistic remark about the men being "more like a crowd of women" (184) constitutes immediate proof – but what is yet to come will not exactly replicate what has gone before.

Notes

1. John McGahern, *Amongst Women* [1990] (London: Faber and Faber, 1991), 168. Subsequent page numbers are cited parenthetically in the text.
2. Although no dates are mentioned in *Amongst Women*, circumstantial evidence suggests that the Ireland recreated in the novel is that of the late 1940s and 1950s.
3. Seamus Deane, *Sunday Tribune*, May 7, 1990, cited on the dust jacket of the 1991 Faber edition of the novel.
4. Thomas Kilroy, "The steady pulse of the world," *Irish Times*, May 12, 1990, *Weekend* section, 9.
5. John Banville, "In violent times," *New York Review of Books*, December 6, 1990, 23.
6. Shane Hegarty, "Reading the public," *Irish Times*, October 18, 2003, *Weekend* section, 11.
7. Joseph O'Connor, whose short tribute to McGahern appeared after W. J. McCormack's *Independent* obituary of April 1, 2006, 44.
8. Cited in Julia Carlson (ed.), *Banned in Ireland: Censorship and the Irish Writer* (London: Routledge, 1990), 3.
9. Mike Murphy, "John McGahern," in *Reading the Future: Irish Writers in Conversation with Mike Murphy*, ed. Clíodhna Ní Anluain (Dublin: Lilliput Press, 2000), 144.

10. Carlson, *Banned in Ireland*, 55.
11. John McGahern, *Memoir* (London: Faber and Faber, 2005), 250. See also the interview with McGahern in Carlson, *Banned in Ireland*, 53–67.
12. John McGahern, *The Pornographer* [1979] (London: Faber and Faber, 1990), 203.
13. McGahern, *Memoir*, 48, 226–227.
14. McGahern, *Memoir*, 35.
15. McGahern, *Memoir*, 226.
16. Patrick Crotty, "'All Toppers': Children in the Fiction of John McGahern," *Irish University Review*, 35:1 (Spring/Summer 2005), 43.
17. McGahern, *Memoir*, 241.
18. John McGahern, "The Life, the Work and the Hurt," *Irish Times*, March 17, 1990, *Weekend* section, 9.
19. Denis Sampson, "A Conversation with John McGahern," *Canadian Journal of Irish Studies*, 17:1 (July 1991), 14.
20. Joe Jackson, "Tales from the Darkside," *Hot Press*, November 14, 1991, 19.
21. James Whyte, "Appendix: An Interview with John McGahern," in his *History, Myth, and Ritual in the Fiction of John McGahern: Strategies of Transcendence* (Lewiston, NY: Edwin Mellen Press, 2002), 235.
22. McGahern, *Memoir*, 62–63.
23. McGahern, *Memoir*, 205.
24. McGahern, *Memoir*, 260.
25. It is interesting to note in this context McGahern's admission that *Amongst Women* was originally conceived as "a novel about that lost Irish generation of the 1950s and 1960s, a lost generation that disappeared into England," and was composed as such until "All that English experience, which must have been about two hundred pages, got pushed out by that Irish family, the Morans, and the London scenes with which the novel began were completely marginalized" (Murphy, "John McGahern," 149).
26. Denis Sampson is thoroughly alert to the Yeatsian and Joycean echoes in McGahern's fiction in *Outstaring Nature's Eye: The Fiction of John McGahern* (Dublin: Lilliput Press, 1993). See also Maria DiBattista, "Joyce's ghost: the bogey of realism in John McGahern's *Amongst Women*," in *Transcultural Joyce*, ed. Karen R. Lawrence (Cambridge: Cambridge University Press, 1998), 21–36; Frank Shovlin, "The ghost of W. B. Yeats", in *The John McGahern Yearbook* 2, ed. John Kenny (Galway: NUI Galway, 2009), 42–51; John McAuliffe, "Fiction's poetry," in *The John McGahern Yearbook* 4, ed. John Kenny (Galway: NUI Galway, 2011), 108–113.
27. John Killen (ed.), *Dear Mr McLaverty: The Literary Correspondence of John McGahern and Michael McLaverty, 1959-1980* (Belfast: Linen Hall Library, 2006), 22.
28. John McGahern, "What Is My Language?," *Irish University Review*, 35:1 (Spring/Summer 2005), 10.

29. McGahern, "What Is My Language?," 4.

30. McGahern, *The Pornographer*, 30.

31. Crotty, "'All Toppers,'" 45.

32. John McGahern, *The Barracks* [1963] (London: Faber and Faber, 1983), 59.

33. McGahern, *The Barracks*, 94.

34. John McGahern, *That They May Face the Rising Sun* (London: Faber and Faber, 2002), 115.

35. McGahern, *Memoir*, 36.

36. Killen, *Dear Mr McLaverty*, 24, 26.

37. McGahern, *Memoir*, 203.

38. Sampson, *Outstaring Nature's Eye*, 9–10.

39. Robert F. Garratt, "John McGahern's *Amongst Women*: Representation, Memory and Trauma," *Irish University Review*, 35:1 (Spring/Summer 2005), 130.

40. "Monaghan Day" was McGahern's original choice of title for the novel, according to his publicist at Faber. See Joanna Mackle, "The publishing of *Amongst Women*," *The John McGahern Yearbook* 1, ed. John Kenny (Galway: NUI Galway, 2008), 88–91.

41. The fact that this annual get-together had no official status but was a purely private affair between two local veterans reveals much about the Irish state's complicated and ambivalent attitude toward the commemoration of the republican dead of the 1919–1922 period in late twentieth-century Ireland.

42. His antipathy extends into the personal sphere. When Rose asks Moran if he recalls their first meeting at the post office, the narrator informs us that "His aversion to the past was as strong as ever and their early life together was now the past" (173).

43. McGahern's remarks in a 1991 article, which was written in response to the commemoration of the seventy-fifth anniversary of the Easter Rising, suggest that Moran's embitterment is indicative of a more pervasive sense of betrayal. He wrote: "I think that the 1916 Rising was not considered to be of any importance in the country I grew up in. In fact, it was felt secretly to have been a mistake. 'What was it all for?' was a puzzlement as widespread as the Rosary" ("From a Glorious Dream to Wink and Nod," *Irish Times*, April 3, 1991, 9).

44. Historian Joanna Bourke analyses this ambiguity in *An Intimate History of Killing* (London: Granta, 1999). See especially Chapter 1. See also David Grossman, *On Killing: The Psychological Cost of Learning to Kill in War and Society* (New York: Back Bay Books, 1995).

45. See Garratt, "John McGahern's *Amongst Women*," 132–133.

46. Moran appears at times to be at war with the land itself, to judge by the way he "slaughters" (47) some trees on the evening of his wedding and later proceeds to "knock" (81) one of his meadows.

47. Cathy Caruth (ed.), *Trauma: Explorations in Memory* (Baltimore: Johns Hopkins University Press, 1995), 5.

48. It doesn't help that Sheila is drawn to a medical career, given her father's contempt for what he sees as the profiteering professional classes: "It was the priest and doctor and not the guerrilla fighters who had emerged as the bigwigs in the country Moran had fought for. For his own daughter to lay claim to such a position was an intolerable affront" (88).

49. Antoinette Quinn, "A Prayer for My Daughters: Patriarchy in *Amongst Women*," *Canadian Journal of Irish Studies*, 17:1 (July 1991), 83. Sampson, *Outstaring Nature's Eye*, 220.

50. These lines are glossed by a comment in *Memoir* about the punishment meted out by a violent teacher: "once anything is licensed it can grow monstrous and be scarcely noticed" (17).

51. Kai Erikson, "Notes on Trauma and Community," in Caruth, *Trauma*, 186.

52. See Judith Lewis Herman, *Trauma and Recovery* (London: Pandora, 2001), Chapter 3.

53. The disclosure that Michael inherited from his father "a certain contempt for women as well as a dependence on them" (91) links *Amongst Women* to the Barrytown trilogy, wherein we see a very similar father-to-son transmission of misogyny taking place.

54. Fintan O'Toole, "The family as independent republic," *Irish Times*, October 13, 1990, *Weekend* section, 2.

55. Antoinette Quinn aptly describes Moran's domination of his family as "a diminished form of home rule" ("A Prayer for My Daughters," 81).

56. Garratt, "John McGahern's *Amongst Women*," 126.

57. McGahern's presentation of Moran's epiphany is rich in irony and pathos. Gazing into a little meadow at end of his life, the ruler of Great Meadow realises that nature's indifferent plenitude makes a mockery of all human pretensions. And as Sampson notes, nature's "glory" stands in ironic contrasts to the "glory" of revolutionary struggle (*Outstaring Nature's Eye*, 240). Such fleeting insights into the mystery of time, death, and eternity prompt Moran's most poignant utterance: "I never knew how hard it is to die" (179).

58. John McGahern, "The Solitary Reader," *Canadian Journal of Irish Studies*, 17:1 (July 1991), 23.

59. http://legislationline.org/documents/action/popup/id/5284.

60. In *Memoir* McGahern deplores the collusion between clerics and politicians that underpinned the Catholic Church's power in the civic realm: "By 1950, against the whole spirit of the 1916 Proclamation, the State had become a theocracy in all but name. [. . .] Church and State worked hand in hand" (210).

61. James Joyce, *The Letters of James Joyce*, vol. 2, ed. Richard Ellmann (New York: Viking Press, 1966), 134.

62. Quinn, "A Prayer for My Daughters," 86. See also Siobhán Holland's discussion of Moran's use of prayer in "Re-citing the Rosary: Women, Catholicism and Agency in Brian Moore's *Cold Heaven* and John McGahern's *Amongst Women*,"

in *Contemporary Irish Fiction: Themes, Tropes, Theories*, eds Liam Harte and Michael Parker (Basingstoke: MacMillan, 2000), 56–78.

63. Later, McGahern brilliantly exposes the illusory nature of Moran's respectable public image when Annie, the postmistress, openly mocks him in the presence of customers after he leaves the post office, provoking a burst of laughter that "was so carelessly dismissive that it seemed to destroy at once an idea that Moran had tried to impose with ferocious will all his life" (173). This is one of a number of public deaths that Moran is forced to endure before he himself slips "evenly out of life" (180).

64. Sampson, *Outstaring Nature's Eye*, 236.

65. Sampson, *Outstaring Nature's Eye*, 239.

66. Cathy Caruth, *Unclaimed Experience: Trauma, Narrative, and History* (Baltimore: Johns Hopkins University Press, 1996), 7.

67. D. H. Lawrence, *England, My England and Other Stories* [1922], ed. Bruce Steele (Cambridge: Cambridge University Press, 1990), 15.

68. Lawrence, *England, My England*, 16.

69. Lawrence, *England, My England*, 16.

70. Lawrence, *England, My England*, 15–16.

71. Sampson, *Outstaring Nature's Eye*, 220.

72. Lawrence, *England, My England*, 16.

73. James Joyce, *Finnegans Wake* (New York, Viking Press, 1959), 215.

74. Quinn, "A Prayer for My Daughters," 90.

75. Rosa González, "'An Interview with John McGahern," in *Ireland in Writing: Interviews with Writers and Academics*, eds Jacqueline Hurtley, Rosa González, Inés Praga, and Esther Aliaga (Amsterdam: Rodopi, 1998), 43–44.

Chapter 3

Malignant Shame: Patrick McCabe's *The Butcher Boy* (1992)

I

Twelve years after *Amongst Women*, John McGahern produced his sixth and final novel, *That They May Face the Rising Sun* (2002), which was published in North America under the title *By the Lake*. This intensely poetic work remains steadfastly focused on the natural processes, inner rhythms, and densely woven social rituals that bind a rural community "marooned"[1] in time, existing at one remove, somehow, from the spirit of accelerated change that had come to define a country which, in the year of the novel's publication, could boast an economy that was officially the most globalized in the world. The gently lapping lake that is the novel's true protagonist enfolds the community in its redemptive elemental embrace and the natural world subsumes all to its relentless pulsion, such that the characters seem to be mostly engaged in "turning each day into the same day, making every Sunday into all the other Sundays."[2] In this way, linear time shades into cyclical time, which mutates in turn into a kind of transcendent timelessness of the kind McGahern found so exemplary in O'Crohan's *The Islandman*.

Yet in affirming a version of Irish pastoral that is at once consoling and increasingly anachronistic, *That They May Face the Rising Sun* also carries the germ of its own critique. A pivotal scene shows Patrick Ryan mocking the arcadian tranquility so cherished by Joe and Kate Ruttledge, before launching into a "burlesque of listening and stillness"[3] with Johnny Murphy. Ryan's acerbic overture – "Will you listen to the fucken quiet for a minute and see in the name of God if it wouldn't drive you mad?"[4] – might serve as an epigraph for the

Reading the Contemporary Irish Novel 1987–2007, First Edition. Liam Harte.
© 2014 Liam Harte. Published 2014 by John Wiley & Sons, Ltd.

many recent fictional portraits of rural and small-town Ireland as places that conceal scarifying dysfunction and maddening tedium behind a placid veneer. The particular inflection of Ryan's mordant remark certainly resonates with the vernacular cadences of Patrick McCabe's prodigal protagonists who, in walking a line between horror and hilarity, are among the most memorable in the contemporary canon.

Whereas McGahern's last novel elegizes a fading world of "broken-down gentlemen,"[5] McCabe's fiction charts the psychotic collapse of "bogmen with bony arses,"[6] whose identities are pulverized by various forms of cultural oppression and repressed histories. From one perspective, McCabe's outlandish tales echo and update earlier dissections of rural claustrophobia in the novels of Sean O'Faolain, Frank O'Connor, John Broderick, Edna O'Brien, and indeed McGahern himself. From another, however, his novels mark a definitive break with this realist tradition, which McCabe finds inadequate to the task of expressing the acute postcolonial anxieties and absurdities of contemporary Ireland. John Banville offers the following incisive long view of McCabe's place in the tradition:

. . . .

Like Roddy Doyle writing about life in working-class Dublin suburbs, McCabe has used stuff the rest of us didn't bother with and made a peculiar kind of rough poetry out of it. He catches the particular kind of bizarre, insane world of Irish country life in the 50s and 60s. People like O'Faolain and Frank O'Connor wrote about it in a lyrical mode, McGahern wrote about it in tragic mode, but McCabe writes about it in a kind of antic black comedy that is absolutely unique.[7]

. . . .

McCabe himself has amusingly likened his deviation from tradition to literary parricide. Recalling the excitement he felt on finding a freewheeling vernacular in which to capture the derangement of Francie Brady in *The Butcher Boy*, he said: "It was almost like killing Frank O'Connor. It was like asking Sean O'Faolain would he like to come out into the garden and then producing a Magnum 357 and blowing his pipe into the bush."[8] Such an arresting analogy instantly puts one in mind of the comic-book perspective and science-fiction sensibility of Francie himself, who lives within the sway of a mythology conjured up for him by the fantasy worlds of *Red River, Voyage to the Bottom of the Sea* and, in his own breathless words, "*Dandy Beano Topper Victor Hotspur Hornet Hurricane Diana Bunty Judy* and *Commandos*" (53). Hearing the novelist speak frequently of his own childhood love of films and comics – "there were all these different worlds, and the Irish world of daily reality was kind of mixed up with the comics in my mind. To this day, I still draw on them"[9] – invites us to consider the interplay between the art and the life of the artist, which is as intimate as it is complex. As with many writers, the stimulus of the local muse was multilayered and paradoxical, so we must be careful not to map McCabe's primary experiences directly on to those of his protagonists. Nevertheless, it is hard to avoid the conclusion that his fiction bears distinct traces of his experiential DNA.

In interviews, McCabe has sketched some of the elements of light and shade that shaped his social and imaginative universe, the epicenter of which was the family home in Clones, County Monaghan, where he was born in March 1955. His family was, he said, "outwardly quite normal, like any ordinary family, but inwardly – fireworks, catastrophic domestic stuff and all that. [. . .] I would say I was born into an extraordinary, ordinary family."[10] As one of five children raised by "poorly schooled but highly educated"[11] working-class parents, McCabe grew up surrounded by books, ballads, and music, which meant that pop-cultural influences were as important as literary ones. He recalls how his father "would equally go from *The Beano* to reading you sections from Dickens or *The Glory That Was Greece* or whatever. [. . .] The word 'art' meant nothing to me. They were inextricable, these things, whether it was Thackeray or Minnie the Minx; it was all part of the same thing."[12] Film and television characters were soon added to this *mélange*, thus intensifying the power of popular culture over his imagination. McCabe's childhood coincided with the arrival of television in Ireland, the influence of which was rapidly expanded after the inauguration of a domestic station, RTÉ, on New Year's Eve 1961. At the launch event, broadcaster Eamonn Andrews said that in the minds of many, "Cathleen Ní Houlihan [. . .] was in danger of becoming Cathode Ní Houlihan,"[13] a remark that was prescient indeed for McCabe's generation. As a teenager, McCabe became a fixture in the local cinema, where he would overdose on "eight or nine movies a week – everything, from Clint Eastwood, to Carry On movies, to the occasional art movie that would get in by mistake."[14] These celluloid worlds provided welcome escape from distressing events at home, where parental rows were not infrequent. In a short 2004 biographical essay, McCabe recalled his emotional response to one such row between "the two people I loved and who, purportedly, loved me":

. . . .

Where I was standing was the opposite of bright space. It was a place I'd find later on in *Dubliners* – that smelt of old rotted plants and ash pits, orchestrated by sad ballads, semi-comatose; never finished. Where your head flopped backwards but your mouth stayed open – its mute cry frozen.[15]

. . . .

The raw, animalistic feelings evoked here may owe something to another of McCabe's formative experiences, his having to pass an abattoir on his daily route to school, which confronted him with "brutality at a very early age."[16] Inevitably, one thinks of Francie at work in Leddy's slaughterhouse and also, perhaps, of the abattoir in Bernard MacLaverty's *Cal* (1983), which nauseates the eponymous protagonist and stands as a metonym for Northern Ireland at its most war-torn. I mention this because in his interview with Christopher FitzSimon, McCabe spoke of his early awareness of coming from "a brutalised culture" in which poverty was endemic and where "there was a deep hurt at all levels of society, certainly in the small town that I lived in. I mean, it wasn't overt but you were always conscious of it."[17] He goes on to cite as evidence the closure of the Great Northern Railway in the late 1950s, which devastated the Clones economy, and the eruption of the Troubles a decade later, which caused "a huge psychological wound,"[18] Clones being close enough to the border to become a flashpoint for violence as the conflict escalated during the 1970s. Although he doesn't make the connection explicit, both events were delayed consequences of the partition of Ireland in 1920, the arbitrary and undemocratic nature of which caused far-reaching social and economic disruption to many border communities. This sense of belated experience, coupled with McCabe's use of the language of cultural wounding, suggests a view of partition as having created traumatized communities of the kind Kai Erikson and other trauma theorists have written about. Hypothesizing that "one can speak of a damaged social organism in almost the same way that one would speak of a damaged body," Erikson argues that

....

the tissues of community can be damaged in much the same way as the tissues of mind and body, [...] but even when that does not happen, traumatic wounds inflicted on individuals can combine to create a mood, an ethos – a group culture, almost – that is different from (and more than) the sum of the private wounds that make it up.[19]

....

Employing similar metaphors, David Lloyd proposes that the partition of Ireland "functions as a tear in the body of the state that cannot easily be sutured," and so operates "like an unclosed wound, marking not only a past violence but one whose perpetuation in the daily practice of the state left it in a continual state of emergency."[20]

Such hypotheses seem to me to have a suggestive relevance for our reading of McCabe's counterrealist fiction, not only because most of his novels are set in the border territory from which he himself comes but also because so many of his protagonists are, like the two states created by partition, "afflicted by the sense of their own arbitrariness and by the compulsive return to the questions of history and identity."[21] I am thinking here not only of Francie Brady but also of the mutually doomed "twins" Malachy Dudgeon and Raphael Bell in *The Dead School* (1995); of the transvestite prostitute Patrick 'Pussy' Braden in *Breakfast on Pluto* (1998); of the delusional Joey Tallon in *Call Me the Breeze* (2002); and of the spectral pedophile Redmond Hatch/Ned Strange in *Winterwood* (2006). None of these characters has any fixed ground or stable essence. Instead, like the "line on the grass"[22] that separates Northern Ireland from the Republic, they share the symbolic ambiguities of the border, which divides without itself belonging to either division. In other words, McCabe's characters continually ask to be read allegorically. Their ruptured, crisis-ridden conditions tell more than one story at the same time and merge personal story with public history to comment on a national "history of incompletion and 'ruination,'"[23] as Lloyd has it. We might productively think of his creations, therefore, as "borderline cases" in Julia Kristeva's sense of the term: characters whose identities "do not exist or only barely so – double, fuzzy, heterogeneous, animal, metamorphosed, altered, abject."[24]

Kristeva's theory of abjection, as propounded in *Powers of Horror* (1982), provides one very useful lens through which to view McCabe's recurring fascination with the cultural and psychological anxieties that arise from indeterminate identities and histories that will not lie down. Kristeva speaks of the abject in deeply paradoxical terms as that which simultaneously founds and threatens the unity, purity, and coherence of subject and society. The abject, she contends, is "what disturbs identity, system, order. What does not respect borders, positions, rules. The in-between, the ambiguous, the composite."[25] In primordial terms, abjection manifests itself as the struggle to separate from the maternal body "in order to be," an act Kristeva characterizes as "a violent, clumsy breaking away, with the constant risk of falling back under the sway of a power as securing as it is stifling."[26] Threatened thus by dissolution and the loss of boundaries, the self – and, by mimetic extension, society – must expunge or "cast off" (*abjicere* means to "reject" or "cast off" in Latin) that which disturbs, in order to demarcate borders and maintain order. Just as waste is expelled from the human body so that it may function as a healthy organism, so too the abject is rendered loathsome and expunged by society, for fear of chaos and formlessness. For Kristeva, however, the expelled elements can never be fully jettisoned since the abject is "something rejected from which one does not part," something that "beckons to us, and ends up engulfing us."[27] This paradox is cogently summarized by Anne McClintock in the following terms:

The abject is everything that the subject seeks to expunge in order to become social; it is also a symptom of the failure of this ambition. [...] Abjection traces the silhouette of society on the unsteady edges of the self; it simultaneously imperils social order with the force of delirium and disintegration. This is Kristeva's brilliant insight: the expelled abject haunts the subject as its inner constitutive boundary; that which is repudiated forms the self's internal limit.[28]

This scenario, whereby "from its place of banishment, the abject does not cease challenging its master,"[29] is one that correlates strongly to the way in which modern Irish history and society are portrayed in the fiction of McCabe.[30] His is a postcolonial society that takes formative shape around the displaced and the denied, where the repudiated remains constitutive. It is a society associated with betwixt-and-between conditions, where political, metaphysical, and moral borders are precarious and blurred, and where the thrown-off persistently returns as the fearful uncanny, "that class of the terrifying which leads back to something long known to us, once very familiar."[31] History for McCabe's protagonists is often radically out of sync, its chronologies distorted by loops and repetitions, its temporal sequences undone by simultaneity and delay. And it is not only, or even primarily, the smoldering legacies of Ireland's historical experience of colonialism – what Francie refers to as "the English and all that" (37) – which intrude upon the present moment. If anything, McCabe is more interested in examining the acute crises that ensue when a still-decolonizing culture, which has not yet come to terms with its traumatic history of occupation and partition, undergoes an accelerated process of uneven modernization, as happened in Ireland during the period from the late 1950s to the early 1970s, which era coincided with McCabe's own formative years. The country's social and political elites at this time hoped that Ireland's embrace of modernity would bring about a loosening of the clammy grip of social conservatism and a shedding of the burden of history and its irrational, violent claims, thus enabling those same claims to be safely recycled for a rhetorical republicanism. However, as Luke Gibbons and others have pointed out, traditional values and principles – "myths of community, the sanctity of the family, devotion to faith and fatherland"[32] – did not simply vanish in the face of a newly industrializing society, nor did the ghosts of Civil War antagonisms suddenly become quiescent, nor deeply rooted socioeconomic inequities magically dissolve. Rather, the recalcitrant deposits of tradition shadowed modernity at every turn, ensuring that the repudiated past would never completely pass or the expelled abject fully disappear. McClintock speaks of "morbid symptoms"[33] appearing when this occurs, directly echoing Antonio Gramsci's description of what happens when the masses "become detached from their traditional ideologies, and no longer believe what they used to previously, etc. The crisis consists precisely in the fact that the old is dying and the new cannot be born; in this interregnum a great variety of morbid symptoms appear."[34] It is these very symptoms – the outcroppings of the dark side of the discourse and experience of postcolonial Irish modernity – that McCabe places under the microscope in his fiction, beginning with his breakthrough third novel, *The Butcher Boy*.

II

If trauma, abjection, and the urgent return of the repressed provide useful frames of reference through which to approach McCabe's negotiations with contemporary history, then perhaps the master frame is provided by the gothic. The gothic, indeed, has been characterized as a form that symbolizes the process of abjection, in that "it has come to deal, as one of its principal subjects, with how the middle class dissociates from itself, and then fears, the extremes of what surrounds it: the very high or the decadently aristocratic and the very low or the animalistic, working class, underfinanced, sexually deviant, childish, or carnivalesque."[35] Furthermore, as "a cyclical genre that reemerges in times of cultural stress in order to negotiate anxieties for its readership by working through them in displaced (sometimes supernaturalized) form,"[36] the gothic clearly speaks to many aspects of the contemporary Irish experience. Anne Fogarty, for example, has identified how Irish women novelists of the 1990s utilized gothic motifs "to reflect upon shifting and troubled understandings of the self, of the child, of the home, of mother-daughter relations, and of transgenerational bonds"[37] in a radically transformed social landscape. Her argument that the "recent, devastating revelations about the longstanding public failure to nurture and safeguard the interests of children and the more vulnerable members of the community are mirrored by the numerous specters of a monstrous maternity"[38] has clear relevance for our discussion of *The Butcher Boy*, which uses a postcolonial gothic optic to show that monstrous mothers are not the only narrative shapes that these shocking revelations have taken.

Evidence that we are reading contemporary gothic presents itself right at the start of the novel through the narrator's distorted sense of time. Whereas Francie Brady's first five words ("When I was a young lad") come straight out of the Gaelic storyteller tradition, mimicking the idiom of the traditional *seanchaí*, his next seven ("twenty or thirty or forty years ago") abruptly shatter the illusion of a shared time and place that typically unites teller and listener in the context of oral performance.[39] This temporal disjunction is glossed by David Punter's observation that gothic time is typically dialectical, with "past and present intertwined, and distorting [. . .] each other with the sheer effort of coming to grips."[40] It follows that "the protagonist of the contemporary Gothic often experiences history as mixed up, reversed, and caught in a simultaneity of past-present-future," usually because of "some horrifying event that profoundly affects them, destroying (at least temporarily) the norms that structure their lives and identities."[41] So it is with Francie, who is speaking to us from some point in the mid-to-late 1980s from an unnamed psychiatric institution where he has spent most of his adult life. Later textual evidence suggests that we can roughly date his incarceration to the early 1960s, a period synonymous with social and economic transition, during which Ireland began to emerge from its de Valera-shaped shell of protectionist nationalism and self-congratulatory insularity. In her incisive analysis of the novel, Patricia Horton explains the traumatic relay these suggestive opening sentences set up:

. . . .

McCabe's novel is, on one level, an interrogation of De Valera's vision, an attempt to penetrate its cosy domesticity and spirituality and to read the tales of violence, abuse and deprivation which have been elided and repressed by it. Francie's narrative is, however, a retrospective one, recounted to us from somewhere in the 1980s. The effect of this is to forge a link between these two historical moments, for Francie – infantilised, physically deformed and psychologically damaged by the end of the novel – can be read as a product of the 1940s and '50s, the repressed legacy of De Valera's Ireland which surfaced so shockingly in the 1980s.[42]

. . . .

As this reading suggests, Francie is not merely an unreliable narrator. His radical uncertainty about the chronology of his own – and, by extension, his country's – past suggests that he will be unable to tell any kind of complete story about himself. Moreover, the story he does tell will be as much about the act of remembering as it will be about the events remembered. This fractured temporality is a telling clue to the fact that we are embarking upon a trauma narrative – the gothic itself being a narrative of trauma[43] – in which the protagonist seems to be living in durational rather than chronological time, experiencing a painful past through abrupt shifts between different time periods, not all of which he has personally lived through. Francie's sense of his youth as being so temporally unlocatable as to be, in a sense, timeless, suggests that part of him has been frozen or fossilized, thus recalling Lawrence Langer's thesis that trauma "stops the chronological clock and fixes the moment permanently in memory and imagination, immune to the vicissitudes of time. The unfolding story brings relief, while the unfolding plot induces pain."[44]

The source of Francie's trauma and its effects on his psyche are immediately laid bare in a prose style that has much in common with the counterrealist aesthetics of gothic fiction. Having attempted a social-realist style in his first two novels, *Music on Clinton Street* (1986) and *Carn* (1989), McCabe switched to what he described as a "social fantastic"[45] style in *The Butcher Boy*, explaining: "If you're writing about a boy from the wrong side of the tracks the traditional way is to observe him through the parsonage window with a sense of pity. But I wanted to be on the floor with him and come from the inside out."[46] This intimate, inside-out style makes for an intensely subjective and unsettling reading experience, where everything is focalized through the eyes of a protagonist whose mind is so manifestly out of kilter that he is psychotically unable to distinguish between reality and fantasy, and whose version of events is beyond corroboration. And so we listen, with growing levels of horrified apprehension and pity, as Francie, speaking at breakneck speed in a jaunty, ecstatic register, "recalls" what happened when he and his best friend, Joe Purcell, tricked Philip Nugent out of his pristine collection of comics. On hearing of this schoolboy sting, Philip's mother confronts Mrs Brady and extravagantly denounces the entire family as "*Pigs – sure the whole town knows that!*" (4). These excoriating words light the touch paper on a fuse that rips apart the Brady family's fragile equilibrium, exposing a gamut of psychic vulnerabilities and uncovering deep and painful emotions that reach far back into the family's past. But the effects of this operatic outburst are far from unilateral: Mrs Nugent's choice of insult is also highly revealing of her own repressed anxieties about her cultural origins and social status, which are intimately bound up with those of the Bradys. So pivotal is this dramatic flashpoint to the spiral of disaster that unfolds that we must pause and take a closer look at the meanings and associations the epithet "pig" carries in this particular social context.

As critics have noted, the novel's porcine motif is heavily freighted with cultural and historical opprobrium. At the most obvious level, Mrs Nugent's insulting remarks brand the Bradys as subhuman by equating them with animals long regarded as base, abominable, and unclean. St. Mark's Gospel shows Christ displacing the "unclean spirits" from man to a herd of swine, which he then chokes in the sea, and the prohibition against eating pork in both the Jewish and Muslim faiths upholds the distinction between the animalistic and the human, the lesson being that to eat meat from a pig is to become one yourself.

The maintenance of this distinction was all the more necessary given pigs' troubling resemblance to human infants and the widespread historical practice of keeping pigs, which were valuable economic assets, in domestic spaces.[47] As Peter Stallybrass and Allon White point out:

. . . .

[P]igs were *almost*, but not quite, members of the household and they *almost*, but not quite, followed the dietary regimes of humans. [. . .] Its mode of life was not different from, but alarmingly imbricated with, the forms of life which betokened civility. It is precisely 'creatures of the threshold' which become the object of fear and fascination.[48]

. . . .

Viewed in these transgressive terms, pigs could be said to bear the attributes of the abject, reminding us human beings of our prior animal existence that threatens our human identity at an existential level. Moreover, Stallybrass and White's remarks open up suggestive parallels between the human–bestial binary and the ambivalent relationship between colonizer and colonized, which Homi K. Bhabha has theorized as mimicry. There is even an echo of Stallybrass and White's language in Bhabha's description of colonial mimicry as the colonizer's desire for a subject that is *"almost the same, but not quite"* or, recast in explicitly racial terms, *"Almost the same but not white."*[49] The menace of mimicry, then – the specter of the in-between, the neither-nor – is also consonant with the process of abjection.

One can take this line of thinking a stage further by adapting Bhabha's thesis about the fate of the black subject under imperialism – "Black skin splits under the racist gaze, displaced into signs of bestiality, genitalia, grotesquerie, which reveal the phobic myth of the undifferentiated white body"[50] – to that of the Irish under English rule. Indeed, a Belgian observer of Anglo-Irish affairs in the late 1800s noted the propensity of sections of the English press to characterize the Irish as "white negroes,"[51] a phrase that encapsulates their threateningly abject status as subjects that were neither fully inside or fully outside the pale of civility, and to whom Victorian Englishmen attributed those emotions which they had repressed within themselves.[52] Nor was this the only slur aimed at the Irish. By the late nineteenth century there was a well-entrenched tradition of using porcine motifs to signify the innate degeneracy and inferiority of a people perceived as seditious, which qualities provided a moral justification for the English colonial project in Ireland.[53] Discriminatory views of the Catholic Irish poor as irredeemably swinish took on a particularly pungent edge in Victorian Britain, which had to contend with the revolutionary republicanism of the Fenians and unprecedented levels of famine-fuelled Irish immigration in towns and cities. Friedrich Engels was among those who viewed these impoverished newcomers as carriers of a contagious beastliness which, he inferred, they contracted from the pigs that lived in close proximity to them.[54] His views were loudly echoed in the British press, with newspapers such as the *Bristol Mirror* opining:

> To squat down under a stone or mud cabin in the corner of a waste moor, with fuel from the bog, potatoes, and a few cattle, pigs and poultry sharing the cabin – half house, half stable, the filth within and around which is preserved like gold – that is the ordinary picture of Irish contentment.[55]

Reading *The Butcher Boy* with this grid of symbolic systems in mind enables us to see more deeply into the causes and the incendiary effects of Mrs Nugent's dramatic outburst in front of Mrs Brady and her son. Class anxieties are central to the reactions of all concerned. Whereas the Bradys are a chronically dysfunctional and impoverished family, plagued by an unemployed father's alcoholism and a mother's mental illness, the Nugents embody bourgeois refinement and professional solidity. Philip's father has a "high-up job" (51), his mother keeps up stylish appearances, and he himself exudes gold-braided privilege. Underpinning these inequities is the fact that the Nugents have bettered themselves through emigration. Until recently they lived in London, where they prospered financially and in the process adopted the behavior, manners, and values of the metropolitan middle classes. But that is not all they picked up. Mrs Nugent's use of "pig" to disparage her uncouth neighbors suggests that she has also internalized the cultural prejudices that came with this social transformation and taken them back home. In fact, she exhibits textbook symptoms of the psychopathology Liam Greenslade argues is inherent in Irish migrants in the former "mother" country, who are compelled to adopt the identity of the racialized Other by internalizing "the pathological projections of the colonist's assumptions and fears."[56] Hence Mrs Nugent's extreme sensitivity and vehement reaction to the threat of having her hard-won civility contaminated by a beastly and troublingly familiar underclass, the "likes" of which she had known "long before she went to England" (4). This latter remark betrays her lingering anxieties about her own status as a reformed "barbarian" and her fears of being wrenched back into a state of abjection through confrontation with "those fragile states where man strays on the territories of the *animal*."[57] Mrs Nugent's aim might therefore be said to be that of every educated bourgeois subject, as identified by Stallybrass and White: "to get as far away from the smell of the pig sty as possible,"[58] lest they be thought unclean and uncivilized. In the Bradys, she and the wider community on whose behalf she presumes to speak find their scapegoat, the hateful embodiment of all that they fear within themselves, yet one that is also unconsciously needed as a marker of their own civility. Horton cogently summarizes this dynamic in the following terms:

. . . .

Newly returned from England, Mrs Nugent's comments can be read as a form of 'displaced abjection', an internalisation of the colonial mentality which is then channelled into class tensions. Francie reminds Mrs Nugent of her own Irishness, her own pig nature. [. . .] Francie is, therefore, a spirit of disorder, representing the messy realms of sexuality and violence. He is a challenge and a threat to the very values upon which the community bases its integrity. In order to save itself from destruction the community casts Francie out, and turns him into a scapegoat or sacrifice.[59]

. . . .

While this perceptive reading is wholly valid, Horton and others who have analyzed the wider resonances of the novel's pig imagery tend to overlook *why* it is that Mrs Nugent's slur provokes such emotional and psychological ruin within the Brady family. To assert that "Francie Brady's interpellation as a 'pig' is the originary trauma of *The Butcher Boy*, it is the one from which all other traumas emanate"[60] is to miss a key point about his family history. The fact is that Mrs Nugent's intervention reinflames a preexisting condition that the Brady family has secretly borne for a long time and which Francie inherits: the trauma of familial shame and disgrace, whose origins lie deep in the past and whose effects take the form of despair, rage, and neurotic behavior in the present. The hidden nature of this stigma is a key factor in the family's catastrophic implosion and in Francie's tragic descent into violent paranoia and existential crisis. As we shall see, the insights of shame theorists can deepen our understanding of how this inner devastation unfolds after the psychological structures of the self are shattered by an unprecedented attack from without.

A pertinent point of departure is provided by Helen Block Lewis's thesis that whereas acknowledged shame forms a necessary and important part of normal social relationships, repressed or denied shame causes chronic pathological behavior. When this occurs, unacknowledged shame, which has both social and psychological components, precipitates a "feeling-trap" of "humiliated fury, or shame-rage," which leads in turn to feelings of guilt and destructive behavior.[61] Building on Lewis's insights, Thomas Scheff and Suzanne Retzinger conceptualize this feeling-trap as a "shame-rage spiral": "shame leads to anger – which in turn leads to further shame, creating unending feedback loops."[62] Such shame-rage spirals "may be brief, lasting a matter of minutes, or they can last for hours, days, or a lifetime, as bitter hatred or resentment."[63] Shame-rage can also be generationally transmitted, as Michael Lewis conjectures: "When their parents are shamed, children are likely to learn to experience shame through empathic shame induction. Simply being with a parent who is shame-prone is likely to lead to shame in children."[64] Furthermore, Scheff and Retzinger hypothesize that unacknowledged shame can be the cause of "revenge-based cycles of conflict" and that "shame-rage may escalate continually to the point that a person or a group can be in a permanent fit of shame-rage, a kind of madness."[65] Significantly, when one adds guilt to the mix, this madness may take on elements of paranoid behavior, which of course is another sign of the gothic.[66]

When read in the light of these psychoanalytical insights, *The Butcher Boy* emerges as a powerful dramatization of the corrosive impact of parentally transmitted shame-rage and its escalation into psychotic paranoia in the mind of a vulnerable boy. Mrs Nugent's disparaging remarks effectively trigger an "affective storm"[67] within the Brady family that exposes a prolonged history of abysmal shame, the origins of which lie in Francie's father's childhood experience of rejection, abandonment, and lovelessness. Benny Brady's insistent need to conceal his sense of woundedness and inferiority compels him and those close to him to compensate for this stigma in various ways, all the while harboring within themselves destructive forms of self-hatred and self-contempt. It is the sudden resurfacing of these repressed feelings, under the stimulus of an aggressive shaming attack from without, that propels the family into terminal crisis. Interestingly, in a 1993 interview, McCabe drew attention to this aspect of the novel, which he felt was already being overlooked:

· ·

One aspect of Francie that hasn't really been mentioned is that he suffers from what you might call malignant shame. He's ashamed of so many things – of what he's done to his mother, of his father's drunkenness, of the state in which his house is left and so on. Subconsciously he is deeply aware of his class and his position in that. So the Nugents, who are a perfectly ordinary, middle-class family, become the focus of his hatred, and of the longing for release, for revenge for this malignant shame with which he is saddled.[68]

· ·

McCabe's invocation of malignant shame here echoes Michael Lewis's thesis that the stigma of shame is "contagious," capable of spreading through a family like "an infectious disease."[69] We might even say, then, that Mrs Nugent functions as the fiery diagnostician of the Bradys' condition, proclaiming them to be carriers of the "triple flaw of weakness, defectiveness, and dirtiness,"[70] which Léon Wurmser identifies as one of shame's defining traits.

Francie's overwrought mother is the first to react to this unwanted diagnosis. Instantly, she feels "the hatred or scorn of the 'other' almost as if the 'other' and the self were one,"[71] which is what shamed individuals do. No sooner has Mrs Nugent spoken than Annie Brady administers a severe beating to her son for which she immediately and profusely apologizes, blaming her "nerves" (4). She then makes him promise never to let her down, as her alcoholic and abusive husband Benny has done, thus priming Francie for the inevitable moment when the stigma of guilt will compound that of debilitating shame. When, a short time later, his mother is admitted to a mental hospital following her first suicide attempt, Francie seeks to block out his pain and hide his shame by equating her breakdown to that of a car in need of a "service" in the "garage" (14). He is thwarted, however, by the sight of Mrs Nugent and Philip, whom he promptly propositions for the "Pig Poll Tax." Francie's account of the meeting is highly revealing of his accelerating descent into paranoia, his repeated use of the phrase "I knew" suggesting that he has already entered the realm of delusional psychosis, where certainty about the rightness of his thinking has replaced all doubt:

. . . .

I knew she thought I was going to turn back when I saw them. She leaned over and said something to Philip. I knew what she was saying but I don't think she knew I knew. She crinkled up her nose and said in a dead whisper: *Just stands there on the landing and lets the father do what he likes to her. You'd never do the like of that would you Philip? You'd always stand by me wouldn't you?* (11).

. . . .

The voice Francie hears here – and note the pig-like facial gesture he projects on to his accuser – is one that articulates his own feelings of shameful impotence. This voice is also inflected by anxieties about his filial inadequacy and inability to act like a "real" man, his templates for which are the mythic archetypes of the rugged frontiersman and doughty gunslinger, as seen in American westerns. This shows that the balance of Francie's mind is already shifting dangerously. He has begun to project his negative evaluation of himself into the minds of others, utterly convinced that his judgment of himself as a socially despised non-person is shared by them. Later, these cinematic archetypes blend in Francie's deranged imagination with the stentorian voiceovers of B movie trailers, as he mentally directs the film of his own deviance: "All the way down the street I kept thinking: Hunted from town to town for a crime he didn't commit – Francie Brady – The Fugitive!" (38).

Francie's burgeoning shame-anxiety is temporarily quelled, however, when his mother emerges from hospital in a blur of manic energy, vowing that "we'd never be run down in this town again we'd show them we were as good as any of them" (18). The news that his Uncle Alo is coming home from England for Christmas is a further fillip, providing Francie with the opportunity to master his shame through the illusion of pride, a pride that is in reality a neocolonial expression of his sense of social inferiority, since it rests on a view of Anglicized civility as the desirable norm. Alo appears to be the very acme of emigrant success, not in the promised land of the New World but in the heart of the old colonial power. In Francie's eyes this makes him an ideal agent with which to cleanse the stain of social disgrace placed on his family, especially since this resplendent "new gent" sounds even more "authentically" English than the Nugents: "I couldn't stop looking at him, the gold tiepin and his polished nails, the English voice. Nugent's was only half-English" (26–27).

It soon becomes painfully clear, however, that Alo's affluent persona is a sham designed to mask the family's chronic social shame, their abiding feelings of inadequacy and inferiority. Well before Benny Brady exposes the truth of his brother's London life – "Closing a gate in a backstreet factory that's what he's been from the day he landed there" (33) – Alo lapses into uncannily animalistic behavior while flirting with Mary, crouching, growling, and pretending to attack her in a manner not unlike that of a pig. The vaguely atavistic nature of his playacting engenders a sense of foreboding that climaxes when Alo refers to the Belfast "home" – meaning orphanage – to which he and his brother were consigned as children by their father. Benny's explosive emotional reaction to this word shows that he himself lives in a chronic state of shame-rage, his humiliated fury stemming from this severance of parental bonds and the social stigma that ensued. As Donald Nathanson points out, the shame experience is one of "utter isolation" and involves "sudden, unexpected separation; no matter what our age, shame resonates with the worst of our fears of abandonment."[72] Benny's lacerating response to his wife's observation that the orphanage "destroyed" him, even though it was "no shame" (35) that he was placed there, highlights the continuing corrosive effects of this experience. His cruel retort to Annie – "He said at least he never had to be took off to the madhouse to disgrace the whole family" (35) – is that of a man compelled to inflict on others the humiliating injuries he himself has suffered. Such responses suggest that buried deep within Benny is the traumatic conviction of his "essential unlovability,"[73] which Wurmser claims is at the very heart of the experience of shame. That Francie's violent response to Mrs Nugent's wounding slur is rooted in the same conviction is borne out by the events that follow.

After the Christmas tempests have subsided, Francie runs away from home, though he cannot escape the newly haunting connotations of the word itself. He obsessively replays the image of his father and uncle arriving at the orphanage all those years ago and being introduced not as the Brady brothers but as Bernard and Alo Pig, thus conflating his own shame with their humiliating stigmatization. It is through such acts of emotional transference that Francie's paranoia steadily gains a tenacious grip on his psyche. Of course, by fleeing to

Dublin in the first place, Francie is enacting the classic desire of the socially shamed individual, which is to hide or disappear.[74] He is also breaking the promise his mother earlier extracted from him, which means that searing guilt now fuses with his shame-rage, channeled through the voice of his nemesis: "Mrs Nugent said: I'll tell you one thing our Philip wouldn't do it. No son worth his salt would do what he did, disown his own family" (39). When this guilt makes him hallucinate the voice of his mother calling him home, Francie returns with a pathetic, propitiatory gift for her, a souvenir bearing the image of "an old woman in a red shawl rocking by the fireside" and the legend, "*A Mother's love's a blessing no matter where you roam*" (41). This is one of several stylized, sentimental representations of arcadian Irish plenitude that catches Francie's eye in the course of his wanderings, each of which echoes the land of cozy homesteads and comely maidens evoked by de Valera in his epoch-defining 1943 St. Patrick's Day radio broadcast on "The Ireland that we dreamed of." Shortly after this episode, Francie becomes fixated by Philip Nugent's music book, *Emerald Gems of Ireland*, the cover of which is adorned by an image of "an ass and cart going off into green mountains" (45). Later, the sight of this book in a Bundoran music shop delights him so much that the proprietor presents him with an even more potent title, *A Treasury of Irish Melodies*, which Francie excitedly offers to Joe in a last, desperate attempt to revive their friendship.

Each of these emotionally hypercharged objects evokes a nostalgia – the word comes from *nostos*, "to return home," and *algos*, "a painful condition" – for a time and place that never was, an illusory golden age of Irish cultural innocence and bucolic simplicity. At a cultural level, the often violent yearning these kitsch items give shape to is the product of a pervasive sense of thwarted gratification and disconnection from an unsatisfactory present, a condition once classified as *Heimweh*, which translates as "pain from missing the beauty of the homeland."[75] In essence, then, these objects are emblems of an Irishness in crisis. They are displaced relics of a society that is metaphysically homesick, one that finds adaptation to the uncertainties and stresses of modernity so troubling that it seeks refuge in a falsified version of the past. In the absence of a secure sense of national belonging, such synthetic images of home and rootedness are called upon to fill the vacuum. Seen thus, these evocative talismans are befitting emotional touchstones for a youth who is himself homesick on every level, possessed of a visceral, insatiable nostalgia for the protective nurture of Mother Ireland and the Virgin Mother, as much as that of the woman who gave birth to him.[76]

Tellingly, Francie is still clutching his emotionally charged souvenir when he arrives home to hear, from the mouth of Mrs Nugent, the devastating news that he has missed his mother's funeral, Annie Brady having killed herself in her son's absence. This catastrophic development consolidates a knot of interlocking and deeply conflictual emotions in Francie, the cumulative effect of which is to transform his inner being into an abject. Most immediately, this news deepens Francie's hostility toward Mrs Nugent, the woman who first brought shame to his door, while simultaneously stoking his violent fixation with her as a replacement mother. Probing further, we can see that his mother's death marks the point where Francie's nostalgia for mothering turns pathological, insofar as it becomes a substitute for mourning. We see the first manifestation of this when he attacks Philip Nugent in the chickenhouse, an act which, because it takes place in a symbolic site of womblike comfort, represents an attempt by a son manqué to usurp his rival.[77] The loss of the mother also defines the Brady family home as a guilt- and shame-ridden site of reciprocal abandonment, Francie's own "betrayal" of his mother having been answered by her "betrayal" of him. And at the same deep level, this experience of ultimate desertion convinces Francie of his essential, irredeemable unlovability, paranoiacally experienced through the contemptuous gaze of others: "I knew one thing. As long as I walked the streets under them stars there'd be only one thing anyone could say about me and that was: I hope he's proud of himself now, the pig, after what he did on his poor mother" (44). Again, Léon Wurmser's observations on the thought patterns of the shame-bound person provide an apt gloss on Francie's mental state at this pivotal moment:

Shame anxiety has characteristically a 'freezing' or, paradoxically, a burning ('searing'), numbing quality and is accompanied by a profound estrangement from world and self, past and present. All eyes seem to stare at the shamed one and pierce him like knives. Everyone seems full of taunts and mockery; everyone undoubtedly knows about his profound disgrace. This tendency for shame anxiety to spread from one situation to all situations makes it akin, even if not causally related, to paranoid ideas.[78]

This shame-filled boy now begins to appropriate the porcine identity assigned to him by Mrs Nugent and also that of the "butcher boy," the protagonist of his mother's favorite song, in which a mother commits suicide after being let down by her faithless lover. Now that Annie Brady has emulated this character – suicide being the most extreme response to the impulse to hide from shame – Francie assumes the mantle of betraying lover, thereby performing a Freudian role-swap that suggests he has convinced himself that he is no better than his father, that what's bred in the bone will, in true gothic fashion, triumph over the will. This maneuver is part of Francie's wider, spiraling Freudian obsession with the Nugents, as evidenced by his unprovoked assault on Philip and his menacing pig impersonation on Mrs Nugent's doorstep. In these scenes we see Francie aggressively act out both his ever-deepening conviction of his unlovability and the abject role scripted for him by a surrogate mother figure, one who has by now come to excite overwhelming feelings of fascination and horror, anxiety and arousal. As Horton succinctly explains: "While Mrs Nugent is the repository for all Francie's negative and vengeful feelings towards his own mother, she also represents the ideal mother in much the same way as Philip represents the ideal son and the Nugents' house represents the ideal home."[79] So whereas Francie previously recoiled from Mrs Nugent's quasi-porcine physicality – "she was so close I could see the wiry hairs on her chin and the pink make-up and powder on her cheeks" (43) – he is now drawn to a photograph that shows off her "cupid bow's lips like you'd see on an old time film star" (51).

What follows constitutes an even more richly layered one-man drama in which Francie plays the role of Rabelaisian defiler of the Nugents' domestic order and mocker of their bourgeois pretentions. After breaking into their house while they are away, he gives free rein to his conflictual fusion of catastrophic shame, envy, guilt, loneliness, self-loathing, and desire for retribution by acting out a sexualized fantasy through which he seeks to avenge his earlier dehumanization. Dressed up in Philip's private-school uniform, Francie hears accusing voices that ventriloquize the shame and guilt he feels in craving the physical nurturance of Mrs Nugent, who looms as the abject surrogate mother, her breast milk "as securing as it is stifling."[80] Shadowing this fantasy of maternal excess is Francie's unbearable knowledge that his own mother failed to nourish him in the womb: "You know you were only five pounds weight when you were born Francie" (8), was one of the last things Annie Brady told her only son. Continuing his sadomasochistic spree, Francie convenes an imaginary "pig school" (61) in which he instructs Philip and his mother in the ways of pigs, before bringing this highly Oedipal drama to an end by defecating in Mrs Nugent's bedroom in the guise of Philip. With this, Francie materializes and reverses the discourse of dirt and defilement attributed to him, since to shame somebody is "really to change the person into excrement."[81] Such behavior is an almost textbook expression of what Wurmser describes as the shamed person's "helpless attempt to change an experience of suffering into one of action or provocation" by acting out a "*fantasy of omnipotence* as a protection against the terror of helplessness."[82]

It is worth taking a moment here to appreciate how McCabe's hyperbolic style succeeds in evoking the incremental escalation of Francie's delusional paranoia and its relationship to a wider cultural millenarianism that shaped the particular world-historical moment he inhabits. In the episode discussed above, Francie's transformation of the Nugents' house into a pigsty begins with him watching *Voyage to the Bottom of the Sea*, in which "Admiral Nelson and his submarine gang" (57) defeat a giant octopus, and ends with Francie excreting a large turd, "shaped like a submarine" (62). The manner in which film and feces subliminally converge in Francie's febrile apocalyptic imagination recalls his earlier experience in a Dublin cinema, when the dialogue in an alien invasion movie reminded him of invasive forces much closer to home:

. . . .

Make no mistake he [the alien leader] says we will control the world and neither you nor anyone else in this town will stop us. It was him saying *in this town* made me think of the women and Mrs Nugent they were always saying that. Mrs Nugent said: I'll tell you one thing our Philip wouldn't do it. No son worth his salt would do what he did, disown his own family. (39)

. . . .

McCabe's quasi-expressionistic rendition of such hallucinatory moments brilliantly captures the process whereby Francie's individual psychosis mirrors and is magnified by a pervasive Cold War paranoia and conspiratorial mindset that grew in response to the threat of nuclear warfare after 1945, and which received vivid metaphorical expression in American science fiction cinema of the era. Both of the films Francie watches in the above scenes are thinly disguised Cold War allegories in which Americans battle grotesque monsters in order to save the "free" world from the totalitarian threat of communism, such monsters being cultural displacements of the West's fears, fantasies, and imagined enemies. Francie increasingly takes his bearings from such films. Their apocalyptic subtext – that the world could end in nuclear Armageddon at any moment – seeps into his hyperalert consciousness, his receptivity to such messages heightened by the fact that his own private Armageddon is already underway. Given that paranoia is symptomatic of a crisis of interpretation in which reality is perceived in terms of the interconnectedness of elements and events, the skewed perception of the world that such films dramatize feeds the compelling associative logic by which Francie sees correspondences where objectively there are none. At the same time, however, McCabe's alignment of his protagonist's spiraling psychosis with a generalized and insidious cultural paranoia makes us question just how irrational Francie Brady's orientation toward reality is. One is reminded of the radical ideas of the maverick 1960s psychiatrist R.D. Laing, who thought insanity a perfectly rational response to an insane world and believed that all so-called madness began in the confines of the traditional family unit. After all, if the political leaders and mass media of the most powerful nation on earth could detect mortal threats to liberty and democracy in various minority political and social movements, should we wonder that a woebegone Monaghan boy is visited by delusions of persecution and sees submarines in his own shit?

McCabe adds a further dimension by showing how his protagonist's exposure to movies about totalitarian conflicts abroad impinges upon his experience of authoritarian Catholicism at home, where Irish clergy, with messianic fervor, spearheaded a relentless campaign against communism during the Cold War era.[83] Not only does Francie lack the cultural conditioning that comes with a traditional Irish Catholic upbringing, he has nothing of the deferential piety that was so pervasive in 1950s Ireland. His sensibility is irreligious to the point of profanity and much of the novel's black comedy emanates from his irreverent take on the culture of hypocritical, even pathological, religiosity that surrounds him. So immersed is Francie in the aesthetics of the horror and sci-fi genres that he views Catholic beliefs and rituals through utterly desacralized eyes. Thus, the martyrdom of the seventeenth-century Catholic archbishop, Oliver Plunkett, is the stuff of a Hammer melodrama and the self-mortifying practices of Matt Talbot, a reformed Dublin alcoholic who became a temperance advocate, seem to Francie to be the actions of a "headcase" (80) rather than a saint. Holy visions and Marian apparitions are filtered through the same profane lens. Far from regarding the blood-red "tears" of a religious statue as a manifestation of God's supernatural power, Francie dismisses them as a waste of good tomato sauce. Through such knowing, Grand Guignolish satire, McCabe is doing more than merely skewering the credulous magical devotionalism of popular Catholicism in Ireland. He is also trying to express complex truths about the cultural interpenetration of the premodern and the postmodern in late twentieth-century Ireland, about the conflicting impulses toward enlightenment and atavism, and about a people's apparent capacity to dwell in contradiction and ambiguity. In one of the novel's many exquisite touches of black humor, McCabe shows how these dialectical impulses are catered for commercially by Mickey Traynor, the "holy telly man" (10), who sells religious pictures as well as television sets. In a culture as non-synchronous and dialectical as this, comfortable divisions between states cannot hold and are not to be trusted. Interestingly, it is these elusive aspects of the text that the writer and filmmaker Neil Jordan responded to when deciding to adapt *The Butcher Boy* for the screen – what he referred to as "the extraordinary mixture of paranoia and paralysis, madness and mysticism that was the Ireland I grew up in [during] the 1950s."[84]

Francie's defilement of the Nugents' well-kept house leads directly to his arrest and detention in an industrial school – aka the "School for Pigs" (72) – a development that echoes the committal of his father and uncle to "the Belfast school for pigs" (82) as children. This sense of Francie's entrapment within the fixed wheel of family history is further underscored when, having reprised his pig act in this "house of a hundred windows" (66), he suddenly plummets into a suicidal state, using a broken statuette of Jesus to slash his wrists. With this, it becomes graphically clear that all of Francie's pantomimic behavior is a mask for deep-seated traumatic shame, compounded by a profound sense of being bereft of loving nurture:

> ....
>
> There was a gaping hole in my stomach for I knew Joe would have heard all about the Nugents by now. I had let him down. I had nobody now that was for sure and it was all my own fault. I wouldn't blame him for not writing to me, why should he after what I'd done on him? (69)
>
> ....

This is the utter isolation and fear of abandonment of which Nathanson speaks, a sense of alienation so acute and inexpressible that punishment and oblivion are welcomed as perverse pleasures. In such moments of self-incrimination Francie comes face-to-face with his own unspeakable abjection, convinced as he now is that he deserves to be expelled from human company. Like the classic shame-bound person, he "has learned from others and now accuses himself of the 'crime' of being surplus, unwanted, and worthless."[85]

From this point forward, Francie's feelings of emptiness and abandonment, which are all the more destructive for being unutterable, intensify with stomach-churning inexorability. The pain of the sexual abuse he suffers in the industrial school at the hands of a pedophile priest – who, in true-to-life fashion, is shielded by the church from civil prosecution – is as nothing compared to the hurt he experiences at the thought of Joe Purcell transferring his friendship to Philip Nugent. The symbol of this new, exclusive bond, a carnival goldfish that Philip gifts to Joe, skewers Francie's brittle, yearning heart like a butcher's blade and deepens his desperation "to fix it some way or blank it out so that it hadn't happened" (105). However, his decision to tell Joe about his experiences in the school merely widens the gulf between them and further compounds Francie's sense of himself as a stigmatized outcast. Unable to accept these changing circumstances, and tortured by the sight of Joe and Philip enjoying a cushioned, middle-class adolescence from which he is firmly shut out, Francie increasingly falls back on a pathological nostalgia for "the way it used to be" (108) between Joe and himself, as a means of screening out his shame-rage and shoring up his floundering sense of self. Immersed in opprobrium, Francie becomes mentally fixated on reviving their lost friendship, now wholly idealized in retrospect as part of his adaptive strategy against the grief of loss. His is now "the magical thinking of pathological nostalgia,"[86] which suppresses the pain and shame of the past and which proves remarkably resilient in the face of repeated rebuffs from the Purcells and from Joe himself, who disavows his former friend in front of the cartoon-like henchmen, Buttsy and Devlin.

With less and less to lose, Francie sinks to the bottom of the social hierarchy to the point where he finally embraces his abject predestiny by taking a job in Leddy's abattoir. Reborn as "Brady the Pig Man" (137), he is now pig and butcher, victim and victimizer, executioner and executee in one.[87] In this new guise he revels in displays of drunken boorishness and delinquency, after which he returns to his house of abjection to commune with the maggot-infested corpse of his father: "I'd just sit there with dad thinking about things one thing I thought was dumb people must have black holes in their stomachs from not being able to cry out" (139). With typical gothic excess, his traumatic shame returns to haunt him in phantasmagorical form during his committal in a psychiatric hospital for "the treatment" (148). Heavily sedated, Francie experiences delusionally intense feelings of shameful exposure during an extended psychotic hallucination in which his personal and familial shame are on extravagant public display. This Dantean episode ends with Francie watching himself being sliced in half by Leddy and hung on a meat rack in the tenebrous slaughterhouse, while an indifferent Joe walks away from him toward the light. And yet for all that Francie is dead meat walking, he still clings compulsively to the nostalgic dream of restoring his friendship with Joe, about which he remains excruciatingly deluded. So even though the sound of "all these doors clicking shut" (163) in his face amplifies his sense of existential abandonment, his craving for the "narcissistic gratification of nostalgic memories"[88] propels him through a succession of searing blows to his terminally damaged self-esteem, until he reaches the point where he decides to travel to the Donegal resort of Bundoran, where Joe is at boarding school and where Francie's parents once courted and honeymooned.

It is here, in the place where he may well have been conceived, that Francie Brady's final mental and emotional unravelment occurs, as he fails in his twin objectives of regaining Joe's friendship and corroborating his father's claim that he and Annie were once happy and in love. First, he learns from the proprietor of the guesthouse in which his parents stayed that his father was "No better than a pig" and that he "disgraced himself" (181) by insulting a priest from a Belfast orphanage – testimony to a marriage doomed from the start. Stung by this fresh reminder of his shameful pedigree and his entrapment in an intergenerational cycle of shame-rage, Francie makes a final pathetic overture to Joe, only to be rejected once more, this time with Philip as a silent witness. Still unable to accept that this is the "real" Joe speaking, his psyche is reinvaded by paranoid thoughts and feelings of malevolent self-loathing that give life to an all-consuming vision of Mrs Nugent as the Machiavellian orchestrator of his final public humiliation. In this moment the fate of his nemesis is sealed, the transfer of blame being fundamentally a transfer of shame. With gruesome inevitability, the climax of this complicated drama of shame-reversal is played out in the home of the

96

ideal mother, Mrs Nugent, where Francie externalizes his own experiences of victimization by butchering the woman who unleashed in him a self-loathing desire for her, and then uses her blood to daub the word "PIGS" on her walls.

The closing scenes of *The Butcher Boy* graphically merge Francie's psychic disintegration with that of the wider community, which in his absence has begun to exhibit morbid symptoms of religious hysteria in response to fears of global cataclysm. The prospect of nuclear conflagration as a result of the escalating Cuban missile crisis causes an outbreak of mass piety among the townspeople, who believe that the appearance of the Virgin Mary is imminent.[89] Marian apparitions have long been associated with times of political or social upheaval, in Ireland and elsewhere, and this eruption of Monaghan Mariology speaks to the historical moment of the novel in more ways than one. October 1962 was not only the month in which political tensions between the United States and the Soviet Union brought the world to the brink of nuclear war. It also marked the start of the Second Vatican Council, which was to have "the most profound and pervasive effect on Irish life and the Irish mind in the 1960s."[90] And as we have already seen, 1962 was also the year in which a national television service began beaming seductive images of other, more glamorous lives into Irish people's living rooms, thus whetting consumerist appetites and further eroding the defenses of cultural nationalism. The townspeople's quest for signs and wonders, then, is as much a panicked response to the fear of fundamental change at home as it is to the prospect of nuclear annihilation. Everywhere the pious look, their unified, ordered world seems under threat from the onset of a modernity with chaos at its heart. Francie, who knows all about collapsing worlds and disappointing mothers, takes a grotesque delight in mocking this psychotic religious nostalgia, even as he is being interrogated about the murder of his own mother substitute: "Oh I said, this must be the end of the world. I hope the Blessed Virgin comes along to save me!" (201). Paradoxically, this abandoned orphan has never seemed more at home in his homesickness, now that the town has become engulfed by an unrequitable longing for the protective, reassuring embrace of the mother of all mothers, whose non-appearance bespeaks an existential degree of collective abjection in "this vale of tears in which we are all but wanderers searching for home" (203).

Ineluctably faced with the disappearance of all hope of maternal and fraternal consolation, let alone tenderness and love, it is entirely logical that Francie Brady should wish to incinerate both himself and his actual home, the site of so much chronic shame, guilt, and sorrow. The reemergence of traumatic memory is signaled by his playing of a recording of "The Butcher Boy," which comes to him in the voice of his dead mother, whom he now wishes to join in the grave. The song lyrics confirm the lesson his short, brutish life has imparted: "All the beautiful things of this world are lies. They count for nothing in the end"

(198). Everything must therefore be consigned to the pyre, not just his parents' furniture and effects but also the disillusioning myths and emblems of Irishness, as represented by the pictures of the Sacred Heart, Pope John XXIII, and John F. Kennedy. But society has not yet finished with its demonized outcast. The forces of law and order rescue Francie from a fiery death in order to inflict an institutional death on him by sentencing him to indefinite detention in a mental hospital, where he is kept in solitary confinement. Thus is the butcher boy banished from the conscience of community and nation, made invisible even to his fellow inmates in "*another* house of a hundred windows" (213).

McCabe reserves one last ironic twist for his conclusion. After years of seg-regation, Francie is told that his solitary confinement is about to end, the doctors having decided that he is unlikely "to take a humane killer to any of our patients" (214). Without shifting verbal register, this brutal and brutalized murderer responds with the disconcerting perspective of the madman who knows that the only true madness is the belief that this world is rational:

> *Humane* killer! I don't think Mrs Nugent would be too pleased to hear you call it that, doc, I said. Oh now now he says that's all over you must forget all about that next week your solitary finishes how about that hmm? I felt like laughing in his face: How can your solitary finish? That's the best laugh yet. (214)

Quietly but emphatically, McCabe endows the adult Francie Brady with an acuity of insight and a savviness of skepticism that have Shakespearean overtones: one is reminded of the Fool in *King Lear*, who sees through appearances and "speaks to (and out of) a quite different order of apprehension."[91] McCabe then overlays this glimpse of Francie's sharpness of perception with a final image of him weeping uncontrollably, still unhinged, still locked inside a childish fantasy world, bearing a grief so great as to be beyond articulation. This is not merely the conclusion of the action; it is the moment in which the enduring pathos of this "poor, bare forked animal," of whom family, community and society have "ta'en / Too little care,"[92] is crystallized.

Notes

1. John McGahern, *That They May Face the Rising Sun* (London: Faber and Faber, 2002), 51.
2. McGahern, *That They May Face the Rising Sun*, 41.
3. McGahern, *That They May Face the Rising Sun*, 77.
4. McGahern, *That They May Face the Rising Sun*, 77.
5. McGahern, *That They May Face the Rising Sun*, 2.

6. Patrick McCabe, *The Butcher Boy* [1992] (London: Picador, 1993), 76. Subsequent page numbers are cited parenthetically in the text.

7. Quoted in John O'Mahony, "King of Bog Gothic," *Guardian*, August 20, 2003.

8. *Patrick McCabe: Blood Relations*, dir. Dara McCluskey. Screened as part of the "Arts Lives" strand on RTÉ One television, June 3, 2008.

9. O'Mahony, "King of Bog Gothic."

10. Christopher FitzSimon, "St Macartan, Minnie the Minx and Mondo Movies: Elliptical Peregrinations Through the Subconscious of a Monaghan Writer Traumatised by Cows and the Brilliance of James Joyce," *Irish University Review*, 28:1 (Spring/Summer 1998), 177.

11. Marianne Brace, "Comic cuts from the butcher boys," *Independent*, January 20, 2001, review section, 9.

12. FitzSimon, "St Macartan, Minnie the Minx and Mondo Movies," 177. In the novel's closing scenes Francie Brady finds a copy of *The Glory That Was Greece* in the family home.

13. Quoted in Fintan O'Toole, "A very Irish box of tricks," *Irish Times*, December 31, 2011, *Weekend* section, 1. In Irish nationalist tradition, Cathleen Ní Houlihan is the female personification of Ireland.

14. Richard Kerridge, "Meat is Murder: Patrick McCabe talks to Richard Kerridge," *Irish Studies Review*, 3 (Spring 1993), 11.

15. Patrick McCabe, "Ships and shadows and invisible men," *Guardian*, September 4, 2004, review section, 27. There are echoes of this childhood memory in the scene in *The Butcher Boy* where Francie, standing on the landing, overhears his drunken father's verbal attack on his mother after he returns from the pub (6–7).

16. FitzSimon, "St Macartan, Minnie the Minx and Mondo Movies," 184. The boy-protagonist of Seamus Deane's *Reading in the Dark* (London: Vintage, 1997), discussed in Chapter 7 below, registers a similar response to the sounds emanating from a city abattoir in Derry: "Sometimes, when passing there, I would hear the terrified squealing of pigs from the slaughterhouse. They sounded so human I imagined they were going to break into words, screaming for mercy" (35).

17. FitzSimon, "St Macartan, Minnie the Minx and Mondo Movies," 180–181.

18. FitzSimon, "St Macartan, Minnie the Minx and Mondo Movies," 181. In "Partition and the Irish Boundary Commission: A Northern Nationalist Perspective," *Clogher Record*, 18:2 (2004), Paul Murray explains: "The railway map alone illustrated the significant disruption of normal traffic to which the 1920 partition gave rise. The Great Northern Railway system cut across the border in fifteen places, with six crossings between Clones and Redhills within seven miles, each necessitating customs arrangements and consequent extra costs" (189).

19. Kai Erikson, "Notes on Trauma and Community," in *Trauma: Explorations in Memory*, ed. Cathy Caruth (Baltimore: Johns Hopkins University Press, 1995), 188, 185.

20. David Lloyd, *Irish Times: Temporalities of Modernity* (Dublin: Field Day, 2008), 138, 132. We must, of course, tread carefully when extrapolating from abstract theory to specific cultural contexts and heed the words of historian Roy Foster, who, in "Something to Hate: Intimate Enmities in Irish History," *Irish Review*, 30 (Spring–Summer 2003), warns that "the very concept of 'collective memory', and still more 'collective trauma', can produce astonishingly crude and airbrushed impressions of our fractured history" (5).

21. Lloyd, *Irish Times*, 140.

22. Tom Paulin, "Line on the Grass," *The Strange Museum* (London: Faber and Faber, 1980), 20.

23. Lloyd, *Irish Times*, 131.

24. Julia Kristeva, *Powers of Horror: An Essay on Abjection*, trans. Leon S. Roudiez (New York: Columbia University Press, 1982), 207.

25. Kristeva, *Powers of Horror*, 4.

26. Kristeva, *Powers of Horror*, 10, 13.

27. Kristeva, *Powers of Horror*, 4.

28. Anne McClintock, *Imperial Leather: Race, Gender and Sexuality in the Colonial Contest* (London: Routledge, 1995), 71.

29. Kristeva, *Powers of Horror*, 2.

30. Laura G. Eldred has persuasively made the case that all of McCabe's fictional communities, including the one depicted in *The Butcher Boy*, tend toward the Kristevan abject. See her "Francie Pig vs. the Fat Green Blob from Outer Space: Horror Films and *The Butcher Boy*," *New Hibernia Review*, 10:3 (2006), 53–67. See also Ellen E. Sweeney, "Mrs Nugent's Little Piggy Went to Town: Abjected Identities and the Traumatic Return in Neil Jordan's *The Butcher Boy*," *Cultural Dynamics*, 15:3 (2003), 267–286, for insightful remarks about the role of abjection in *The Butcher Boy*.

31. Sigmund Freud, "The Uncanny," [1919] in his *On Creativity and the Unconscious*, trans. Alix Strachey (New York: Harper & Row, 1958), 123–124.

32. Luke Gibbons, "Coming Out of Hibernation: The Myth of Modernity in Irish Culture," in *Across the Frontiers: Ireland in the 1990s*, ed. Richard Kearney (Dublin: Wolfhound Press, 1988), 209.

33. McClintock, *Imperial Leather*, 270.

34. Antonio Gramsci, *Selections from the Prison Notebooks*, ed. and trans. Quintin Hoare and Geoffrey Nowell-Smith (London: Lawrence and Wishart, 1971), 276.

35. Jerrold E. Hogle, "Introduction: the Gothic in western culture," in *The Cambridge Companion to Gothic Fiction*, ed. Jerrold E. Hogle (Cambridge: Cambridge University Press, 2002), 9.

36. Kelly Hurley, "British Gothic fiction, 1885–1930," in Hogle, *The Cambridge Companion to Gothic Fiction*, 194.

37. Anne Fogarty, "Uncanny Families: Contemporary Irish Women's Fiction," *Irish University Review*, 30:1 (Spring/Summer 2000), 62.

38. Fogarty, "Uncanny Families," 81.

39. The Irish translation of "When I was a young lad" ("Nuair a bhí me ina bhuachaill óg") is a common overture to a formulaic chronicle of formative childhood experiences in Gaelic autobiography and as such would be familiar to many Irish ears.

40. David Punter, *The Literature of Terror: A History of Gothic Fictions from 1765 to the present day* (London: Longman, 1996), vol. 2, 198.

41. Steven Bruhm, "The contemporary Gothic: why we need it," in Hogle, *The Cambridge Companion to Gothic Fiction*, 194.

42. Patricia Horton, "'Absent from Home': Family, Community and National Identity in Patrick McCabe's *The Butcher Boy*," *Irish Journal of Feminist Studies*, 3:1 (December 1998), 76.

43. Bruhm, "The contemporary Gothic," 268.

44. Lawrence Langer, *Holocaust Testimonies: The Ruins of Memory* (New Haven: Yale University Press, 1991), 174–175.

45. FitzSimon, "St Macartan, Minnie the Minx and Mondo Movies," 176.

46. Brace, "Comic cuts from the butcher boys," 9.

47. Pigs were so central to the rural economy of nineteenth-century Ireland that the animal was sometimes euphemistically referred to as "the gentleman that pays the rent."

48. Peter Stallybrass and Allon White, *The Politics and Poetics of Transgression* (New York: Cornell University Press, 1986), 47, original emphasis. Horton was the first critic to apply these authors' cultural analysis of pigs and their symbolic meanings to the novel and my own reading is indebted to hers. See also Donna Potts, "From Tír na nóg to Tír na Muck: Patrick McCabe's *The Butcher Boy*," *New Hibernia Review*, 3:3 (1999), 83–95.

49. Homi K. Bhabha, *The Location of Culture* (London: Routledge, 1994), 86, 89, original emphasis. Cited in Jessica Scarlata, "Carnivals and Goldfish: History and Crisis in *The Butcher Boy*," in *Literature and Film: A Guide to the Theory and Practice of Film Adaptation*, eds Robert Stam and Alessandra Raengo (Oxford: Blackwell, 2005), 245–246.

50. Bhabha, *The Location of Culture*, 92.

51. L.P. Curtis explains in *Apes and Angels: The Irishman in Victorian Caricature* (Washington DC: Smithsonian Institution Press, 1997; 2nd edn), 1, that the phrase was used by Gustave de Molinari in an 1880 article on the condition of Ireland and reproduced in a *Times* leader in September of that year.

52. See Declan Kiberd, *Inventing Ireland: The Literature of the Modern Nation* (London: Jonathan Cape, 1995), 35ff.

53. Although one might assume that such crude stereotypes did not survive the Victorian era, they occasionally surfaced in later decades. One of the most high-profile examples comes from 1979 when, in the wake of the murder of her uncle, Lord Mountbatten, by the IRA in August of that year, Princess Margaret

is reputed to have described the Irish as pigs to the then Mayor of Chicago, who was himself of Irish descent. See "Margaret: A life of glamour and controversy," BBC News, February 9, 2002, http://news.bbc.co.uk/1/hi/uk/278463.stm.

54. In *The Condition of the Working Class in England* [1845] (London: Penguin, 1987), Engels wrote: "The lack of cleanliness, [...] which is the Irishman's second nature, becomes terrifying and gravely dangerous through its concentration here in the great cities. [...] He builds a pig-sty against the house wall as he did at home, and if he is prevented from doing this, he lets the pig sleep in the room with himself. This new and unnatural method of cattle-raising in cities is wholly of Irish origin. The Irishman loves his pig [...], he eats and sleeps with it, his children play with it, ride upon it, roll in the dirt with it, as anyone may see a thousand times repeated in all the great towns of England" (124–125).

55. Cited in Michael de Nie, *The Eternal Paddy: Irish Identity and the British Press, 1798–1882* (Madison: University of Wisconsin Press, 2004), 91. The racialization of the Irish reached its apogee in the late nineteenth and early twentieth centuries, notably in the political cartoons of *Punch* and other satirical magazines, which depicted Irish nationalists as pigs that were incorrigibly impervious to British reason and common sense. This was not a one-way street, however; James Joyce famously described Ireland as "the old sow that eats her farrow." As Horton notes, Mrs Nugent's insult also echoes Jonathan Swift's devastating satirical critique of England's colonial exploitation of Ireland, *A Modest Proposal* (1729), in which a speaker who poses as Ireland's benefactor sets out his relentlessly rational solution to the "problem" of Catholic overbreeding. His recommendation that the children of the poor be commodified for the tables of the rich, like "Sheep, black Cattle, or Swine," includes the chilling suggestion of "buying the Children alive, and dressing them hot for the Knife as we do Roasting-Pigs." Although we are not told why the Nugents moved back to Ireland from London, their situation to some degree mirrors that of Swift in 1714, when his hopes of advancement in London abruptly ended with the death of Queen Anne and he was forced to return to live in Ireland, a place he regarded as barbarous and uncivilised.

56. Liam Greenslade, "White skin, white masks: psychological distress among the Irish in Britain," in *The Irish World Wide: History, Heritage Identity*, vol. 2, ed. Patrick O'Sullivan (London: Leicester University Press, 1992), 215.

57. Kristeva, *Powers of Horror*, 12, original emphasis.

58. Stallybrass and White, *The Politics and Poetics of Transgression*, 52.

59. Horton, "Absent from Home," 87. See also Sweeney, "Mrs Nugent's Little Piggy Went to Town," 270–271. One might make an additional, admittedly tangential, connection here between notions of abjection and exclusion and a folkloric resonance buried deep within the term "pig." The boundary of the ancient, nine-county province of Ulster bears the name of the Valley of the Black Pig

or the Black Pig's Dyke in Irish folklore. Some scholars speculate that this boundary consists of a disparate series of prehistoric earthworks or ditches that stretches from Dundalk in County Louth to Bundoran in County Donegal, where Francie's parents spent their apparently happy honeymoon, and to where he himself walks to try to reestablish his exclusive friendship with Joe Purcell. Christopher J. Lynn's account of the origins of the boundary's name in *The Encyclopedia of Ireland*, ed. Brian Lalor (Dublin: Gill and Macmillan, 2003) sparks suggestive thoughts about its application to the novel: "The Black Pig is explained in local legend as a wicked schoolmaster who was transformed into a pig and banished; the pig created the ditches with its snout as it rampaged angrily across the countryside" (96).

60. Sweeney, "Mrs Nugent's Little Piggy Went to Town," 279.
61. Helen Block Lewis, *Shame and Guilt in Neurosis* (New York: International Universities Press, 1971), 222, 41.
62. Thomas Scheff and Suzanne Retzinger, *Emotions and Violence: Shame and Rage in Destructive Conflicts* (Lexington, MA: Lexington Books, 1991), 105.
63. Scheff and Retzinger, *Emotions and Violence*, 127.
64. Michael Lewis, *Shame: The Exposed Self* (New York: Free Press, Simon and Schuster, 1995), 113.
65. Scheff and Retzinger, *Emotions and Violence*, 148.
66. Helen Block Lewis argues in *Shame and Guilt*: "With regards to symptom formation, undischarged shame tends to evoke affect disorder, principally, depression; undischarged guilt tends to evoke thought disorder, particularly, obsessive and compulsive symptoms, and paranoia" (89). Punter claims that it is "impossible to make much sense out of Gothic fiction without continual recourse to the concept of paranoia" (*The Literature of Terror*, vol. 2, 183).
67. Léon Wurmser, *The Mask of Shame* (Northvale NJ: Jason Aronson, 1994; 2nd edn), 54.
68. Kerridge, "Meat is Murder," 10.
69. Lewis, *Shame and Guilt*, 200.
70. Wurmser, *The Mask of Shame*, 44.
71. Lewis, *Shame and Guilt*, 32.
72. Donald L. Nathanson, "Shaming Systems in Couples, Families, and Institutions," in *The Many Faces of Shame*, ed. Donald L. Nathanson, (New York: Guildford Press, 1987), 250.
73. Wurmser, *The Mask of Shame*, 93.
74. Wurmser, *The Mask of Shame*, 84.
75. Arthur G. Nikelly, "The Anatomy of Nostalgia: From Pathology to Normality," *International Journal of Applied Psychoanalytical Studies*, 1:2 (2004), 183.
76. Nikelly reminds us that the severance of the refugee from the homeland is seen by some as "a reenactment of the trauma of weaning from the warmth of the nurturing mother," and that the loss of the motherland "represented

symbolically the analogous loss of the mother's breast that sustains the craving for narcissistic gratification of nostalgic memories" ("The Anatomy of Nostalgia," 186).

77. Joe and Francie's shared affection for the chickenhouse as a place of dependable sanctuary where "Nothing can ever go wrong" (131) suggests its subliminal association with the security of the original safe house, the womb.
78. Wurmser, *The Mask of Shame*, 53.
79. Horton, "Absent from Home," 81.
80. Kristeva, *Powers of Horror*, 13.
81. Wurmser, *The Mask of Shame*, 81.
82. Wurmser, *The Mask of Shame*, xx, original emphasis.
83. See Peter Mulholland, "Moving Statues and Concrete Thinking," *Quaderns de l'Institut Català d'Antropologia: sèrie monogràfics*, 23 (2009), 162.
84. Cited in Elizabeth Butler Cullingford, "Virgins and Mothers: Sinead O'Connor, Neil Jordan and *The Butcher Boy*," *Yale Journal of Criticism*, 15:1 (2002), 193.
85. Carl Goldberg, *Understanding Shame* (Northvale, NJ: Jason Aronson, 1991), 8.
86. Nikelly, "The Anatomy of Nostalgia," 193. Nikelly explains: "While fantasy life over object loss, whether realistic or fictional, can have a compensatory purpose of enhancing self-esteem, it becomes pathological when used as an escape or evasion from responsibility or as a form of magical restitution in order to regain the love of the lost past and to restore the ego's self-regard" (188).
87. See Horton, "Absent from Home," 88–89.
88. Nikelly, "The Anatomy of Nostalgia," 186.
89. McCabe may be exploiting another oblique porcine reference here, as the missile crisis of October 1962 was precipitated by a disastrous invasion of Cuba in April 1961 by a CIA-trained brigade of Cuban exiles, which landed at the Bay of Pigs but was quickly detained by Fidel Castro's army.
90. Fergal Tobin, *The Best of Decades: Ireland in the 1960s* (Dublin: Gill and Macmillan, 1996; 2nd edn), 75.
91. L.C. Knights, *Some Shakespearean Themes* (Stanford: Stanford University Press, 1959), 98.
92. William Shakespeare, *King Lear*, in *The Arden Shakespeare: Complete Works*, eds Richard Proudfoot, Ann Thompson and David Scott Kastan (London: A&C Black, 2001), 652–653.

Chapter 4

Uncertain Terms, Unstable Sands: Colm Tóibín's *The Heather Blazing* (1992)

I

Since the early 1990s, Colm Tóibín has been at the forefront of attempts by Irish novelists to map the contours of a rapidly changing culture and society in prose fiction. His debut novel, *The South* (1990), set in Ireland and Catalonia, marked him out as a singular new voice, one already attuned to the predicaments of those who stand to one side of, or have little affinity with, traditional definitions and narratives of Irishness. *The Heather Blazing* delves more deeply into the contest between the forces of conservatism and change in contemporary Ireland by exploring the complex psychology of a senior Dublin magistrate who struggles to negotiate the widening gulf between his Catholic nationalist past and a present that is becoming increasingly secular and pluralist in complexion. Tóibín's next novel, *The Story of the Night* (1996), announced the theme of homosexuality in his work and, indirectly, in his life. In portraying Richard Garay's concealment of his hidden sexuality in the repressive political climate of 1980s Buenos Aires, Tóibín obliquely revealed his own gay identity. "Writing down and publishing *The Story of the Night* was a great personal liberation for me," he later recalled. "Putting it all in the first person felt almost like a confession."[1] He subsequently returned to "the drama of being gay in a fragile society"[2] in *The Blackwater Lightship* (1999), which deals with an AIDS-related illness and death in contemporary Ireland; in *The Master* (2005), which centers on key crises in the life of Henry James during his self-imposed exile in *fin de siècle* England; and in some of the short stories in his two collections to date,

---

Reading the Contemporary Irish Novel 1987–2007, First Edition. Liam Harte.
© 2014 Liam Harte. Published 2014 by John Wiley & Sons, Ltd.

Mothers and Sons (2006) and *The Empty Family* (2010). That Tóibín is much too varied in his themes and preoccupations to be pigeonholed as a gay writer, however, is evidenced by his sixth novel, *Brooklyn* (2009), which charts the fortunes of Irish emigrant Éilís Lacey as she seeks to adapt to 1950s New York, and by his novella, *The Testament of Mary* (2012), in which he rehumanizes that most iconic of religious figures, the mother of Christ.

While Tóibín's international reputation rests upon his novelistic output, it is important to remember that he has never confined himself to fiction. In fact, his novels are outweighed by his non-fiction corpus, which includes travelogues, essay collections, anthologies, and literary and historical studies. He first made his name as an independent-minded journalist in 1980s Ireland, most notably as editor of *Magill* magazine, in which role he championed a less deferential style of current affairs reporting. Journalism proved to be a valuable training ground for the fledgling novelist, providing him with the raw material for *The Heather Blazing*, the idea for which came to Tóibín when he was covering the Dublin courts in 1984.[3] Journalism also acted as a kind of intellectual catheter, helping to drain away the "poison" of his animus toward the forces of tradition and conservatism in contemporary Ireland.[4] Thus cleansed, the novels became "a return to self," a "reaching inwards."[5] But perhaps the most marked legacy of Tóibín's journalistic training is his distinctive style. Writing copy for a specific audience forced Tóibín to craft spare, precise sentences, devoid of figurative embellishment, thus teaching him that "in a plain statement you can bury emotion."[6] Stylistic colorlessness subsequently became one of his chief aims and hallmarks as a novelist; he is a master of expository, flat-voiced prose made up of sentences drained of moral judgment, whose slender means belie their "stark passion,"[7] to borrow a phrase Tóibín applied to the music of Frederick May. This austere prose is the vehicle for a wide arc of novelistic concerns, within which certain themes predominate: the complex and mysterious interplay of historical change and constancy; the question of how the past should be written about and remembered; the difficulties of reconciling individual freedoms with communal expectations; the combustible cultural effects of confusing history, memory, and mythology; and "the fierce addiction which love becomes within families."[8] Since his representation of each of these themes is deeply colored by his Irish experience, it is necessary to survey this background territory before turning our critical attention to *The Heather Blazing*.

Tóibín was born in 1955 in Enniscorthy, County Wexford, to a schoolteacher father and a mother who, though her formal education ended in her early teens, harbored a lifelong hunger for literature and learning. Enniscorthy is a town with a tangled history of settlement and rebellion that stretches back to Norman times. As the epicenter of the 1798 insurrection of the United Irishmen against

British rule, and one of the few towns outside Dublin that took part in the 1916 Easter rebellion, Enniscorthy occupies a particularly venerable place in the history of Irish nationalism. This past was, in Tóibín's words, "recent, alive, easy to get in touch with"[9] throughout his early years. He recalls: "The [1798] Rising was important for us: from our housing estate we could see Vinegar Hill where 'our side,' the rebels, had made their last stand."[10] Being "born on a battlefield," then, was deeply formative for him: "For me that Wexford landscape is resonant. It's where I'm from, where history has taken place that, in some way, had been fundamental for me."[11] Family life was also suffused with history. Tóibín's grandfather fought in the 1916 Rising, his uncle took the republican side in the Irish Civil War (1922–1923), and his father was a keen amateur historian who was instrumental in transforming Enniscorthy Castle – once "the bastion of English rule in the town"[12] – into Wexford County Museum in the early 1960s. But just as those inverted commas around "our side" signal Tóibín's skeptical distance from simplistic partisanship, his observation that his forebears were "complex men who had read a great deal of English literature, and [...] were not much given to Anglophobic outbursts, nor Anglophobia, however therapeutic,"[13] should deter us from reductive readings of bald facts. With Tóibín, appearances rarely reassure.

Catholicism was an equally pervasive presence in Tóibín's childhood. His travelogue, *The Sign of the Cross* (1994), begins with vivid vignettes of a boyhood steeped in the rituals and precepts of the faith: listening to adults' recount their pilgrimages to Lourdes, attending children's Mass at Easter in Enniscorthy cathedral, serving as an altar boy, and reciting the rosary each evening at home. However, the sudden death of Tóibín's father in 1967 meant that material self-sufficiency came to rival spiritual salvation in importance: "The need to find and keep a good job and the need to please God and save your soul at the same time were intrinsic parts of the same dream on which I was brought up, after my father's death, in that small town."[14] And although he still practised his faith, Tóibín gradually came to recognize the true extent of his unbelief:

· ·

I attended a seminar on vocations when I was sixteen and a theologian spoke about 'the paradox of faith', the idea that to believe you must first 'believe', that faith required a blind leap and then a more rational approach. In certain (and, indeed, uncertain) ways I came to realize that I had never believed. I had always known that the interest all around me in security, money, power and status was greater than my love of God or belief in his mercy. [...] I drifted away, I read Kafka and D. H. Lawrence, and by the time I reached university I had other things to think about.[15]

· ·

Tóibín's experience of studying history and English literature at University College Dublin (UCD) in the early 1970s precipitated an even more profound apostasy that would become central to his subsequent intellectual development. In a polemical and highly autobiographical 1993 review of Roy Foster's *Paddy and Mr Punch*, tellingly entitled "New Ways of Killing Your Father," Tóibín recalled his sudden awakening while at UCD into the light of a revisionist interpretation of Irish history that was rapidly gaining influence within and outwith the academy. This was in fact the second phase of Irish historical revisionism, an intellectual project that began in the 1930s under the aegis of the newly founded journal, *Irish Historical Studies*, which was committed to the publication of empirically detailed, "value-free" historical research. As Kevin Whelan points out, second-phase revisionism of the post-1960s period

. . . .

more explicitly attacked the received national narrative, questioned the independence project, and pronounced the failure of the postimperial state. The state-sponsored fiftieth anniversary of the Easter Rising in 1966 gave it impetus. Rather than identifying long-run historical explanations (notably colonialism) as the root cause of Irish difficulties, it sought instead to diagnose the difficulties within Irish society as self-generated, derived from the stifling narrowness of the combined effects of Catholicism and a Gaelic nationalism, allied to an entrenched Irish bourgeoisie's grasp on economic power, and symbolized by the Fianna Fáil Party, and notably by Charles J. Haughey, its leading figure from the 1960s to the 1980s. A modernization theme was endorsed, entirely detached from any constructive or transformative alternative, and the consensus developed that 'traditional' Ireland was itself alone the principal root of all Irish problems.[16]

. . . .

Tóibín himself remembers: "If there was a forbidden 'f' word or a forbidden 'c' word while we studied there, they were 'Fenian' and 'colonial': all the Irish history we studied was parliamentary and constitutional."[17] Context was all-important, of course. North of the border, the Troubles were in full spate at this time, and the murderous forces they unleashed posed a very real threat to the political status quo in the Republic, as evidenced by the carnage caused by the loyalist paramilitary bombings of Dublin and Monaghan in May 1974. Unsurprisingly, therefore, the issues of how the past should be interpreted and the political uses to which history should be put took on a pressing immediacy, and the teaching of history in the academy became a highly contentious matter because of its ideological implications for the political present:

Outside in the world there were car bombs and hunger strikes, done in the name of our nation, in the name of history. Inside we were cleansing history, concentrating on those aspects of our past which would make us good, worthy citizens who would keep the Irish 26-county state safe from the IRA and IRA fellow-travellers.[18]

In this same essay Tóibín recalled his euphoric response as a student to a critique of Henry Grattan's 1782 parliament, which debunked the view that it was an early form of Irish home rule. Tóibín's description is worth quoting at length, as it succinctly captures the defining elements of his historical consciousness: his implacable antipathy toward IRA militancy; his deep-seated desire to be free of the Irish past and its burdensome ideological backlog; his perception of history as a form of fiction; and his fascination for the "complications or ironies or half-truths"[19] of received versions of events:

I remember feeling a huge sense of liberation. I photocopied the piece and made everyone else read it. I was in my late teens and I already knew that what they had told me about God and sexuality wasn't true, but being an atheist or being gay in Ireland at that time seemed easier to deal with as transgressions than the idea that you could cease believing in the Great Events of Irish nationalist history. No Cromwell as cruel monster, say; the executions after 1916 as understandable in the circumstances; 1798 as a small outbreak of rural tribalism; partition as inevitable. Imagine if Irish history were pure fiction, how free and happy we could be! It seemed at that time a most subversive idea, a new way of killing your father, starting from scratch, creating a new self.[20]

Invigorating though these new possibilities were, however, they could not simply negate existing interpretations or inherited allegiances – his own included. Tóibín goes on to recall being invited to take part in a Wexford commemoration of the seventy-fifth anniversary of the Rising in 1991. Although he declined and went to Seville that Easter as planned, he found himself distracted by the vestigial pull of home and history, "wishing things were simpler, wishing that I was not in two minds about everything."[21] The dissenting nationalist found that he was still his father's son, yet also discovered that uncertainty is not necessarily an ignoble condition. In fact, Tóibín ends his review of Foster's book by prescribing double-mindedness as an enabling antidote to hidebound, zero-sum thinking:

....

I know that ambiguity is what is needed in Ireland now. No one wants territory, merely a formula of words ambiguous enough to make them feel at home. [...] Foster's position is clear: he wants Ireland to become a pluralist, post-nationalist, all-inclusive, non-sectarian place. So do I. But there are other (I hesitate to use the word 'atavistic') forces operating within me too that I must be conscious of.[22]

....

Tóibín's affirmation of the complicating power of nuance and ambiguity – in one interview he speaks of his interest in characters who exude "moral mistiness"[23] – and his corresponding refusal to impose closure where ambivalence prevails are governing principles of his work and thought. As several critics have noted, he typically finds a liberating potential in interpretive openness and the complex truths that emerge when prescriptive myths are sabotaged and convenient beliefs brushed against the grain.[24] Even the much-admired Foster is chided for his occasional blind spots and ideological bias in the aforementioned review article. Tóibín's resistance to fundamentalist paradigms and refusal to harmonize the present or the past into a fixed, abstract philosophy are especially marked in his attitude toward the shibboleths that surround notions of Irishness. "The only point in recognizing and trying to describe a [literary] tradition is then to fuck it up – to take it and throttle it," he declared in one interview, and went on to observe: "In Ireland, whatever you write, you have to be so alert as to what the stereotypes are, and exercise your intelligence enormously in combating them or at least giving into them in a new way."[25]

Such comments indicate Tóibín's restless desire to wriggle free of the straitjacket of inherited categories and fashion new modes of self-definition, for himself as much as for his protagonists. His characterization of his own cultural identity as protean and sheddable is a calculated riposte to exacting equations of Irishness with fixity and stability: "One of the things about being Irish is that you can lose your identity very easily – when you open your mouth you don't have an immediate cultural baggage and it gives you a chameleon face, it's lovely."[26] One corollary of his resistance to simplicity and singularity is an affinity for conflicting textures; another is a receptivity to difference, which appears to have begun as a fascination for the most intimate Irish Other, the Protestant double that defines, and undermines, the Catholic self. In a 2000 newspaper article Tóibín spoke of the allure that Protestant Dublin held for him when he moved to the capital in the early 1970s. As a Catholic boy from a Wexford housing estate, he became so intrigued by the déclassé remnants of "the race who had built Georgian, Victorian and Edwardian Dublin" that he experienced a fundamental reversal of perspective: "One of those Sundays when

I was 18 or 19 I realised that I would never be able to go back to my small town. I had found displacement. I had found home."[27]

One of the key benefits of this paradoxical state of dwelling in displacement is that is makes for a certain fertile detachment and an openness to life as process. Tóibín's vivid recreation of place is one of his most admired literary qualities. "All of us have a landscape of the soul, places whose contours and resonances are etched into us and haunt us," he reflects in his short memoir, *A Guest at the Feast* (2011), and for him this landscape is a certain section of the Wexford coastline, "remote, oddly lonely and desolate."[28] Yet his imagination also thrives on a kind of determined homelessness and dialectic of departure and return. Even as a boy, he relished "the sense of elsewhere"[29] that assailed him whenever he was allowed to wander the streets of Wexford town on his own. This dynamic is evident in his response to Richard Canning's questions about his relationship to his native landscape, which the novelist frames in highly specific, almost microscopic, terms:

> It's the inside of about three houses; the stretch of a cliff; two lanes, and another that connects them. Nothing else. It's a tiny stretch of childhood territory very clearly fixed in the memory. And any time you try and describe anything else, you tend to use that anyway.[30]

Almost immediately, however, Tóibín reminds his interlocutor that he gladly escaped from this locale and goes on to underline the point that "The feeling of unbelonging is as important as that of belonging: the idea of being there, of being immersed in the feeling surrounding these rooms and lanes also has its exact opposite: the sheer pleasure of being thousands of miles away from it, geographically and physically."[31] So while some critics regard Tóibín as an "in-between" writer "making a virtue of his own ambivalences towards notions of tradition, community and nationhood,"[32] I believe that his affinity for deracination is a function of imaginative necessity as much as intellectual disposition. Alterity, anomaly, strangeness, equivocation, transgression – these are important creative stimuli for Tóibín. Certainly, the need to displace or annihilate the ego and to test the known self against the unknown Other are fundamental to his literary imagination. His statement that "all fiction writing is, in some way, a way of playing with the self, of stretching the self, of imagining the self in various guises,"[33] suggests that his imagination is essentially fluid, maritime, and feeds off the defamiliarizing perspectives opened up by dislocation and alienation.[34] Much of his fiction, indeed, is constituted by the experience of estrangement or outsiderness. The figure of the watchful, detached observer is one of his favorite archetypes and provides all of his novels to date with their central organizing perspective. The fact that outsiderness is often linked to hidden sexual difference, as in the case of Richard Garay and Henry James, doubtless speaks to Tóibín's own experience of growing up gay in provincial Ireland, at a time when male homosexual acts were still unlawful in the Republic. More fundamentally, a sense of being "unhoused"[35] shapes the psychological processes of each of his chief protagonists, all of whom, to varying degrees, exude a "puzzling presence in the world."[36] In the case of Judge Eamon Redmond in *The Heather Blazing*, this quality is overlaid by an emotional remoteness and retentiveness that are the marks of a personality shaped by loss, repression and fear.

II

In the years since its publication, *The Heather Blazing* has secured an elevated place in the canon of contemporary Irish fiction. Substantial critical claims have been made for it by, among others, Neil Corcoran and Tom Herron, both of whom regard the novel as an important work of Irish literary revisionism. Corcoran's praise for Tóibín's "measured and temperate, but still-vigilant portrayal of a society some of whose most cherished ideals are now in a state of terminal collapse,"[37] is endorsed by Herron, who characterizes the novel as "a revisionist attempt to debunk the nationalist meta-narrative," which embodies "an understated but nonetheless damning critique of the republican nation-state and its effects upon discursivity, upon what may be said and what must be silenced."[38] Ray Ryan and Conor McCarthy, meanwhile, unravel the ideological implications of Tóibín's particular brand of liberal postnationalism by reading the novel alongside Tóibín's travelogue, *Bad Blood: A Walk Along the Irish Border* (1994), as a polemical narration of the "end of history" thesis in an Irish context.[39] Most recently, Kathleen Costello-Sullivan has cogently examined the figure of the lost mother in *The Heather Blazing*, arguing that the novel "offers a scathing judgment on the Irish national self-construction that sacrifices women – and generations of Irish – to a non-representative and incomplete vision of Irish society."[40] While each of these analyses illuminates aspects of the novel's central concerns, none takes proper account of the precise nature and complexity of Tóibín's revisionist critique, which, I want to argue, lies in his interrogation of the disjunctive, problematic relationship between republican ideology, constitutional discourse, and social reality in modern Ireland.

As I read it, *The Heather Blazing* is a critical yet compassionate exploration of the multiple tensions, ironies, and anxieties that stem from living in a state preoccupied with being rather than becoming, a state in which the values of an imagined, textualized nation are prioritized over those of a materially and morally changing society. Through his central character, a Dublin High Court judge, Tóibín dramatizes the personal and societal consequences of cleaving too rigidly to institutional and constitutional imperatives rather than responding reflexively to the evolving rights and demands of a diverse citizenry. Eamon Redmond's character and identity have been determined by a seemingly immutable set of interlinked theological, historical, and constitutional narratives. Born into a staunchly republican Catholic family in 1930s Wexford, Eamon grew up under the twin auspices of a sentimental nationalism and a bucolic anti-materialism, the staple orthodoxies of de Valera's Ireland, which period spanned the 1930s to the 1950s. His conservative conditioning was reinforced by his loyalty to the Fianna Fáil party and his party-endorsed legal training, both of which inculcated in him a solemn regard for the supreme textual expression of de Valeran nationalism, the 1937 Irish Constitution (*Bunreacht na hÉireann*). As a senior judge, however, he is troubled by cases that expose profound discrepancies between the authorized narratives of moral and constitutional meaning laid down by church and state and the growing liberalism of a society from which he feels increasingly alienated. Yet his obligation to adjudicate on such cases compels him to confront his own crisis of religious, political, and constitutional faith, as well as his deep-seated fear of change. Unable to admit his doubts and fears, he conceals them behind socially reactionary legal judgments and a formidably austere public persona. In the process, Eamon suppresses the unenunciated ambiguities and contradictions of the constitutional text – aporias, in Derrida's terms – thereby restricting its potential to be interpreted in ways that might enable the development of a more pluralist, inclusive Irish identity.[41]

One of the most compelling facts about Eamon Redmond is that his subjectivity is defined discursively, in and through the acts of reading and writing. Eamon is preeminently a man of the written word who, in his professional life as a judge, exhibits a scrupulous regard for textual authority. His textualist mindset has its origins in his childhood, the graphic character of which is evoked through a matrix of autographical images that suggests the complex ways in which the past underwrites and ensnares the present. For example, one of his earliest memories shows him mapping his surroundings on the school blackboard: "He drew maps of main roads and side roads, using different coloured chalk; he drew squiggles and matchstick figures."[42] This rudimentary cartography has an oblique analogue in the map of the 1798 rebellion in the new museum in Enniscorthy Castle, the dungeon of which contains another, remote adumbration of the boy's drawings in the shape of a sword-clad figure etched on the wall by an imprisoned rebel.[43] Other signatures inscribe a more personal indwelling of the past in the present. Eamon sees the vestigial presence of his father's "strange, indecipherable" handwriting in his own hand, which "had become exactly the same as his father's, a set of round squiggles, indecipherable to most others" (4). This autographic inheritance is linked to other iterative gestures. Michael Redmond, a teacher of Irish and history, spent part of his summer holidays marking examination scripts; his son spends part of his reading and annotating law reports. Indeed, it may not be too fanciful to see in Eamon's memory of rain-blurred ink on one of his father's scripts a symbolic prolepsis of the dissolution of his own religious and ideological certainties and the fading of his faith in the letter of the constitutional law.

The chapters that recreate Eamon's upbringing not only establish the centrality of Irish republican history to the formation of his identity but also the ways in which that history has been memorialized and mythologized into a fixed narrative of cultural meaning. Growing up with miles of Vinegar Hill, site of the pivotal battle of the 1798 uprising, Eamon's natal landscape was littered with republican totems, from the pike heads rusting in remote farmhouses to the monument to Father John Murphy in the town square. More significant still is the fact that his own family was and is a living embodiment of this revolutionary tradition. His grandfather and uncles were active Fenians who were interned for their part in the 1916 Rising, while his father fought in the War of Independence and subsequently took the anti-Treaty side in the Civil War. It is this illustrious republican lineage, more than any words or deeds of his own, that speaks for and through Eamon, inherently determining and proclaiming his identity. During the de Valera dispensation, Eamon's father dedicated himself to the preservation and transmittance of a strongly nationalist interpretation of Wexford's revolutionary past through his work as a history teacher, a Fianna Fáil activist, and a writer of historical articles for the local newspaper, each of which he carefully preserved in a scrapbook. This same custodial impulse underpinned his desire to convert Enniscorthy Castle, "the headquarters of the English down all the years" (18), into a county museum.[44] All of this commemorative activity represents a strategic attempt to memorialize the past by fixing its meaning to accord with a triumphalist contemporary nationalist agenda and, by implication, to elide those interpretations that do not fit with this agenda. The imposition of a nationalist interpretation on the events of 1798 was a crucial part of Eamon's father's mission, especially since the meaning of the rebellion was hotly contested by subsequent generations. As Kevin Whelan points out, the rebellion "never passed into history, because it never passed out of politics," thereby creating a "constantly shifting narrative of '98 after '98."[45] In the novel, Michael Redmond plays a key role in the effort to stabilize this shifting narrative and from an early age his son is enlisted in this battle for custody of the collective memory, a battle which is primarily pursued in and through the written word.

Destined from birth to uphold traditional republican values, Eamon – who was named after the republican revolutionary Éamon de Valera but whose surname is the same as that of John Redmond, leader of Irish constitutional nationalism during the early 1900s – has been taught to read history as a closed text comprising a stable narrative of reliable truths: "There was never anything to learn in history, Eamon forgot nothing that his father said" (106). The influence of this naive, uncomplicated view of history is audible in the young boy's precocious address to a 1951 Fianna Fáil election rally in Enniscorthy in the presence of de Valera and his deputy, Seán Lemass. Reading from a prepared script, Eamon invokes a shared historical knowledge, preparing the crowd for de Valera's own brief address. This speech effectively launches Eamon on the path toward a distinguished legal career, during which he continues to fulfill his textualist destiny by "working as a speech writer and campaign organizer in the 1959 presidential election and in the general elections of 1961" (190). With Fianna Fáil in power, he is busily employed representing the state in constitutional cases and is eventually rewarded with a High Court judgeship, in which office he enters fully into the determinative orbit of the written word of the revolution as embodied in the "sacred text" (90) of Irish nationhood, the 1937 Constitution. True to his upbringing and training, Eamon initially regards the Constitution as a closed text of fixed meanings that posits a definitive narrative of Irish citizenship and identity. Over time, however, he sees the "word" become flawed and its authority undermined by a succession of cases that expose latent inconsistencies and ambiguities in this framework document, which in turn mirror hidden tensions in the received narratives of nationalism, religion and belonging.

These cases, each of which reflects the shifting moral, social, and political landscape of contemporary Ireland, highlight a fundamental disjunction between the imagined version of Irishness posited in the Constitution and the changing identity of the citizens who make up the nation state. The imbrication of the fictional and the historical is particularly thematically significant at this point in the novel, since it is here that Tóibín engages most deeply with the social and legal history of modern Ireland. Eamon's judicial elevation in the mid-1960s coincides with a period of epoch-making cultural, economic, and attitudinal change in Irish society. Such change was an important contributory factor in the rise of judicial activism in the same period, which occurred under the auspices of a new generation of reforming judges. Up to that point, Irish judges had been generally slow to recognize and exploit the powers of constitutional interpretation conferred upon them by *Bunreacht na hÉireann*. As Basil Chubb explains, they were men "trained in the British system with its emphasis on the common law, the sovereignty of parliament and judicial precedent," and as such "tended to interpret the rights of the citizen conservatively, to give judgements that bestowed considerable powers and discretion on governments and to leave the extension of social and economic rights to the Oireachtas."[46] The early

115

1960s, however, saw the emergence of a more self-confident, innovative judiciary headed by Chief Justice Cearbhall Ó Dálaigh and Supreme Court judge Brian Walsh, who between them inaugurated what one legal historian describes as

a revolution in constitutional jurisprudence, most particularly in the area of fundamental rights. The most spectacular conquest of this revolution was the recognition – which an earlier generation of judges would have thought fantastic – that the Constitution implicitly protected an indefinite range of citizens' rights over and above those specifically enumerated in one or other article, and that the courts were entitled to identify such latent rights, whenever the occasion arose, by reference to their understanding of a standard such as 'the Christian and democratic nature of the state'.[47]

The judiciary's "discovery" of hitherto undisclosed citizens' rights in the 1937 charter had far-reaching social and political consequences. For example, as the number of innovative judgments grew, so too did the tensions between the judicial and the executive organs of government.[48] Yet as Chubb points out, this trend benefited citizens insofar as it helped to maintain the normative character of the Constitution, whereby it is "capable of being constantly adjusted, and perhaps occasionally recast, to reflect alterations in political practice and changes in community values."[49] Seen from another perspective, however, this development foregrounded a crucial fact about this, or indeed any, foundational text, namely, that it is inherently open and unstable. As Patrick Hanafin puts it: "the Constitution is not a petrified document. Writing a constitution or inscribing a collective identity is just the beginning of an unending dialectic between text and people."[50] It follows, therefore, that

the very notion of a founding document is riven with complexity. What de Valera [in 1937] was doing, in effect, was founding an Ireland of the imagination, an Ireland in which certain values were to prevail and others were to be excluded. However, the permanence of this project was to be stymied by the constitutional text's own inherent contradictions. The mingling of dominant and subordinate ideologies in the constitutional text was to lead to its transformation through the medium of textual exegesis.[51]

In *The Heather Blazing* Judge Eamon Redmond is forced to perform just such an act of textual exegesis when called upon to adjudicate on cases that expose discrepancies both *within* Irish constitutional discourse and *between* that discourse and the values of a changing society. His recognition of these discrepancies, and the unease that they engender, compel him to read the

Constitution as a deconstructionist critic would, as social process rather than immutable truth. Interpretive uncertainty thus emerges as the hallmark of his textual practice. Under his close scrutiny, *Bunreacht na hÉireann* undergoes a fundamental shift from coherence to complexity, as seemingly stable meanings and clear distinctions begin to collapse: "How hard it was to be sure! It was not simply the case, and the questions it raised about society and morality, it was the world in which these things happened which left him uneasy, a world in which opposite values lived so close to each other" (90). The closer Eamon comes to the postcolonial nation's textualized essence, therefore, the more dispersed that essence becomes, and the greater his sense of disorientation and distress. What he once thought of as an authoritative text he now sees as a tissue of multiple readings; what purports to be a fixed inscription of a collective identity is in reality a legal fiction; what appears to be a definitive narrative of citizenship is in fact always open to disruption in a reflexive reaction to social change; what proclaims to be a finished story is merely the beginning of an unending dialectic between text and people. Most unsettling of all is the realization that he, as a senior judge, has a crucial mediatory role to play in this dialectic, since it is his duty not simply to uphold the Constitution and its laws, but to *interpret* them for "a changing world" (89).

The legal case that crystallizes and personalizes many of these dilemmas and anxieties involves a pregnant schoolgirl who is challenging the decision of the Catholic school authorities to expel her. The case, which reminds Eamon of his strained relationship with his daughter Niamh, who is herself an unmarried mother, discomfits him because the principle at stake is a moral rather than a legal one: "the right of an ethos to prevail over the right of an individual" (90). In order to reach a judgment, therefore, he is forced to leave the known territory of the law and enter a treacherous moral terrain where he is no longer sure of his footing. Acting on his textualist instincts, he seeks to establish points of origin and order through writing, only to be plunged into deeper levels of uncertainty and doubt:

. . . .

He took a biro from a drawer and began to make squiggles on a pad of paper. What was there beyond the law? 'Law'; he wrote the word. There was natural justice. He wrote the two words down and put a question mark after them. And beyond that again there was the notion of right and wrong, the two principles which governed everything and came from God. 'Right' and 'wrong'; he wrote the two words down and then put brackets around them and the word 'God' in capitals beside them.

Somehow here in the middle of the night with the moths and midges drawn to the window, the idea of God seemed more clearly absurd to him than ever

117

before; the idea of a being whose mind put order on the universe, who watched over things, and whose presence gave the world a morality which was not based on self-interest, seemed beyond belief. He wondered how people put their faith in such a thing, and yet he understood that the courts and the law ultimately depended for their power on such an idea. He crossed out the word 'God'. He felt powerless and strange as he went back to read random passages of his judgment. (85–86)

This passage compelling evokes Eamon's fearful realization that there is no infallible system for measuring right and wrong, which casts him adrift from all his known moorings. The answers will not be *written*: each textual attempt to establish an absolute source of moral and metaphysical authority ends in an impasse that exposes insoluble doubts and hesitations. To cite Roland Barthes: "writing ceaselessly posits meaning ceaselessly to evaporate it, carrying out a systematic exemption of meaning."[52] No sooner have these aporetic fissures opened up, however, than Eamon seeks to conceal them and his own lack of "strong moral views" (90) through the very activity – writing – by which they were revealed. Confronting the definitional uncertainty that surrounds the term "family" in the Constitution is even more agonizing for this faithless judge, since it forces him to act as a moral arbiter, working from an incomplete text that calls on him to exercise his interpretive powers:

What was a family? The Constitution did not define a family, and at the time it was written in 1937 the term was perfectly understood: a man, his wife and their children. But the Constitution was written in the present tense, it was not his job to decide what certain terms – he wrote 'certain terms' in his note-pad, underlined it and wrote 'uncertain terms' below that – such as 'the family' had meant in the past. It was his job to define and redefine these terms now. Could not a girl and her child be a family? And if they were, did the girl have rights arising from her becoming a mother, thus creating a family, greater than the rights of any institution? (91)

Here we see Eamon poised between a readerly and a writerly approach to the Constitution, between being a consumer and a producer of the text. On the one hand, his deconstructive reading highlights the repressive strategies that exist within the structure of the document's narrative and conceptual forms by revealing how the ghostly, unwritten 1930s understanding of what constitutes a family has the potential to prevent the toleration of disparate types of family units in the present. On the other hand, however, Eamon is keenly conscious of his authority and duty to interpret the Constitution to provide a more inclusive definition of family that would take account of prevailing social realities. John Kelly's succinct gloss on the interpretation of constitutional grammar is pertinent here: "The courts see the Constitution as a contemporary fundamental law that speaks in the present tense. As a document it speaks from 1937, but as law it speaks in the present tense."[53] Eamon's eventual decision to endorse a restrictive family ideal by deciding in favor of the school authorities reveals that he is too fearful of change, too much a prisoner of an imagined past to disclose the pluralist potential of this founding document. The repressed subconscious of the text is kept hidden, therefore, and the opportunity to develop a more inclusive narrative of Irish citizenship is foreclosed. Having had silence imposed upon him as a child, Eamon Redmond now imposes silence upon the (female) children of the nation.

This is not the first or only time that Eamon's fear of change has caused him to suppress discrepancies between the textual and the actual versions of Ireland in order to preserve the social and political status quo. In the early 1970s he produced a number of confidential reports for the Irish government, advising it on how best to respond to the threat to state security posed by IRA violence. His recommendations were pragmatically partitionist, premised on the assumption that Northern sectarianism was an "internal" six-county problem unconnected to wider questions of state formation and legitimation. He warned the government "never to allow public opinion to become inflamed in the Republic by events within its own borders. The North, he argued, must be presented as a different society, a place apart" (178). Such advice effectively obfuscated the politically contentious reality of the border and sought to establish congruence between the Irish nation and the Irish state, thereby suppressing the claims of Northern nationalists to be part of that same nation. As such, his advice was technically unconstitutional in that it contravened the Republic's territorial claim to the whole island at that time, as expressed in Articles 2 and 3 of the Constitution, although neither article actually defined the "nation."[54] Yet the fact that Eamon's advice helped shape the government's policy of military containment of the Northern conflict shows that it merely confirmed the gap between irredentist rhetoric and partitionist practice in the Southern state. Then as now, however, Eamon recoils from confronting the implications of such disquieting aporias and conceals the precise nature of his advice from an inquiring historian. This concealment is compounded by his refusal to discuss his father's Civil War record with the same man, preferring instead to "consign it to the past, to silence, as his father had done with the names of the men who did the killings in Enniscorthy" (180).

This latter detail is a telling one, since it draws attention to a crucial fact about the nationalist version of Irish history that Eamon was taught to cherish as a child: what purported to be a seamless narrative of immutable truths turned out on closer inspection to be riven by a host of troubling lacunae and occlusions. This realization dawns on him during a visit to his elderly Aunt Margaret in Wexford:

There was a great deal he wanted to know, of which he possessed only snatches now, things which would disappear with her death. At times he felt that he had been there, close by, when his grandfather was evicted, and that he had known his father's Uncle Michael, the old Fenian, who was too sick to be interned after 1916. Or that he had been in the bedroom, the room above where they were now, when his grandfather came back to the house on Easter Monday 1916 and had sat watching him as he pulled up the floorboards under which he had hidden a number of rifles. Or that he had witnessed his grandfather being taken from the house at the end of the Easter Rising. These were things which lived with him, but he could only imagine them.

Some of these events were so close, they had been recounted and gone over so much. He realized that he would never know fully what went on, there were too many details left out. (61)

Thus, the more Eamon seeks the essence of this venerated past, the more he finds himself in recession from historical "truth." Gaps and elisions frustrate his search for definitive meaning and lead him to the unsettling, and again unspoken, conclusion that the text of history, like that of the Constitution, will yield to no authoritative reading. Rather, every reading generates a supplementary reading. The most troubling absence of all, however, is the one that fissures his own narrative of identity: the death of his mother when he was a child. In one of the most moving passages in the novel, Eamon admits to his wife Carmel that this death, above all other bereavements, shaped him into a repressed, insecure, undemonstrative man: "I learned never to need anything from anybody. [...] I don't believe that anyone has ever wanted me" (228). His aphasia is most conspicuous when he tries to communicate emotionally. Although he reads law reports "as avidly as though the pages were full of easy gossip," he cannot speak of love, loss, or loneliness: "It's really hard for me to talk" (58, 227). This primary absence is the emotional fault line that Eamon has spent his private and professional life passing over in silence, cloaking his centerless identity behind a "plausible," "eminently sensible" public persona (92). This is the haunting aporia that precedes and foreshadows all other aporias, the original rupture that insists there can be no single, definitive narrative of the self any more than there can be a unified reading of the received narratives of nation, history, or religion. Nor can there be social and political equality or inclusive citizenship, the absence of the mother in the domestic sphere being symbolically linked to the eclipse of a maternal femininity by a patriarchal ideology in the public realm.

Eamon's non-articulation of his faithlessness and the turmoil it engenders is absolute. His uncertainty and unbelief are hermetically sealed in, as is the cumulative grief occasioned by the deaths of his mother, father, and wife Carmel. Only in water, and in thoughts of water, does Eamon find a measure of release from his doubts and dilemmas and a salve for his grief. From the novel's opening sentences – which are repeated, wavelike, at the beginning of Part Three – water is a pervasive presence in *The Heather Blazing*, and there is a distinctive tidal rhythm to the narrative oscillation between scenes from Eamon's emotionally costive adulthood and his republican upbringing. Several scenes show the judge contemplating the River Liffey from his law offices, drawn by the prospect of its soothing allure. But his real Lethean element is the sea, specifically the coastal waters near the Wexford village of Cush, where he and Carmel have a holiday home. Eamon's link to this site is quasi-umbilical. Cush is where he was taken as a baby after his mother's death, a fact that seems to have caused a kind of emotional transference to occur within him, making the sea a mothering refuge, in contradistinction to houses, which are consistently figured as bare, unwelcoming emblems of motherless absence.

This marine locale – the same ground that is the anchor of Tóibín's imagination and the place where he himself has built a house – provides a resonant topographical analogue of the dualities of concealment and exposure, constancy and change that permeate Eamon Redmond's public and private worlds. Whereas Dublin is the place where Eamon is obliged to act as an official state arbiter of the moral and political complexities of a changing Ireland, Cush is a site of sanctuary where he can let "the landscape seep towards him" and "rid himself of everything that had happened" in the city (97). The more onerous the demands of judicial office, the greater his need to immerse himself in this landscape and in the sea itself, where he luxuriates in fleeting moments of oblivion. In this familiar space he is visited by epiphanies of immutability that allow him to believe "that nothing in him had changed since he first saw these buildings" (97). However, these intimations are counterpointed by his awareness of "how vulnerable the land here was to change, how the sand levels shifted each year" (206). The deceptive nature of this topographical drift is captured by the process of coastal erosion. Eamon is continually reminded that the site upon which the 1798 insurgents staged their rebellion, the very land they died defending, is inexorably crumbling into the advancing sea:

· ·

It had been so gradual, this erosion, a matter of time, lumps of clay, small boulders studded with stones becoming loose and falling away, the sea gnawing at the land.

> It was all so strange, year after year, the slow disappearance of the one contour to
> be replaced by another, it was hard to notice that anything had happened until
> something substantial, like Mike's house, fell down on to the strand. (32)

....

This image of a disappearing coastline, which the novelist himself knows intimately, is perfectly weighted to evoke the incremental processes of social change and the erasure of seemingly immutable orthodoxies and allegiances.[55] Yet the sea is also the element that binds successive generations of male Redmonds in a patrilineal chain. We first see this in Chapter 4 when, as a reluctant youngster, Eamon is initiated into the pleasures of swimming by his father. In adulthood, Eamon's recollection of this bonding experience is "more real and vivid and focused than anything that had happened since" (55), suggesting that each subsequent swim is in some way shadowed by the "texture" and "thrill" (55) of that first watery embrace. As we have already noted, such reiterations are deeply embedded in the novel's architecture, so much so that the recurring motifs and recursive movements of *The Heather Blazing* are as integral to its emotional and metaphoric power as the circular patternings are to that of *Amongst Women*, a novel Tóibín greatly admires. That the correspondences do not end there is shown by the way Tóibín follows McGahern's example in fashioning a denouement in which subtle suggestions of newness and change qualify the persistent emphasis on continuity, re-enactment, and recall.

For Eamon, the lure of the shoreline and the sea grows ever more insistent in the immediate aftermath of Carmel's death. Struggling to come to terms with the finality of her absence, he shuns the memory-saturated interiors of their beach house and instead divides his time between swimming, reading and going on marathon walks, as if wanting to be possessed by the landscape: "He walked: took step after step and allowed himself to think only about the ground he had already walked along" (210). If the bodily experience of walking suggests a turning outwards to the world and a shedding of cultural perceptions and beliefs, we are also shown this elderly servant of the state "going over old [legal] cases and the implications of recent legislation" (216), thus reminding us of the persistence of ingrained habits of mind. The judge's unreconstructed conservatism shows in other ways too, such as his needling reference to his infant grandson, Michael, as a "small recently-born feminist" (239). And yet it is Michael – bearer of his great-grandfather's name – who becomes the focus for Eamon's renewed attention to, and revaluing of, human relations as the ground of meaning, a reawakening that, significantly, is realized in and through water.

Having initially been wary of his grandson, Eamon slowly builds a wordless rapport with him through water-play, acting on a memory from his own children's childhood by bringing him a basin of tap water with which to amuse himself. This non-verbal bonding gesture is later repeated on Cush strand, where grandfather and grandson play with a basin of seawater while Niamh goes for a swim. The novel ends with Eamon taking Michael into the sea for the first time, gently raising and dousing him in a quasi-baptismal gesture that obliquely reprises Eamon's own marine "baptism" by his father. However, as critics have observed, Eamon's actions are altogether more tender and more equivocal than his father's were, and as such seem to be less to do with inheritance and imitation than with the reaffirmation of the bonds of family – single-parent as well as nuclear. While this ending does not absolve Judge Eamon Redmond of his responsibility for retarding the evolution of a more inclusive and equitable Irish body politic, it does suggest that he may be beginning to acknowledge that the pluralist, postnational future must not be bound by dictates and definitions forged from the exclusivist ideologies of the past. An accommodation must be made so that, in the novelist's own words, "opposites can join"[56] and cohabit, without necessarily destabilizing or neutralizing each other. *The Heather Blazing* ends not with a vision of wholeness or completeness but with a scene of ambiguity and open-endedness that concentrates our attention on the challenges and possibilities that lie ahead.

Notes

1. Richard Canning, *Hear Us Out: Conversations with Gay Writers* (New York: Colombia University Press, 2003), 182. There is a distinctly Wildean quality to Tóibín's use of the mask of fiction to reveal truths that cannot be uttered in the first person. In *Love in a Dark Time: Gay Lives from Wilde to Almodóvar* [2001] (London: Picador, 2002) he recalls his response to being asked in 1993 by an editor at the *London Review of Books* to write a pamphlet about his homosexuality: "I told him instantly I couldn't do that. It was a matter, I said, which I did not think that I could write about. [. . .] My sexuality [. . .] was something about which part of me remained uneasy, timid and melancholy" (2).

2. Tóibín, *Love in a Dark Time*, 2.

3. See Canning, *Hear Us Out*, 173. Pre-echoes of the novel's themes are discernible in a 1985 *Magill* article in which Tóibín examined the development of Irish constitutional jurisprudence since the 1960s. It is clear from the tone and tenor of this article that he greatly admired the reforming zeal of the post-1960 generation of Irish judges, especially Cearbhall Ó Dálaigh, who later served as President of Ireland from 1974 to 1976, and Brian Walsh, whom Tóibín described as "one of the most significant figures in the history of the Irish state." In Eamon Redmond, however, Tóibín created a conservative character who is in many ways the antithesis of Walsh. See Colm Tóibín, "Inside the Supreme Court," *Magill*, 8:7 (February 1985), 8–35.

4. See John McCourt, "Colm Tóibín," in *The UCD Aesthetic: Celebrating 150 Years of UCD Writers*, ed. Anthony Roche (Dublin: New Island Books, 2005), 229–238.

5. Canning, *Hear Us Out*, 174.

6. Fintan O'Toole, "An Interview with Colm Tóibín," in *Reading Colm Tóibín*, ed. Paul Delaney (Dublin: Liffey Press, 2009), 187.

7. Colm Tóibín, *A Guest at the Feast: A Memoir* (London: Penguin Shorts eBook, 2011), unpaginated.

8. O'Toole, "An Interview with Colm Tóibín," 200.

9. Colm Tóibín, *The Sign of the Cross: Travels in Catholic Europe* [1994] (London: Picador, 2001), 3.

10. Colm Tóibín, "New Ways of Killing Your Father," *London Review of Books*, November 18, 1993, 3.

11. Lynne Tillman, "Colm Tóibín," *Bomb*, 38 (Winter 1992), 22–23.

12. O'Toole, "An Interview with Colm Tóibín," 184.

13. Tóibín, "New Ways of Killing Your Father," 6.

14. Tóibín, *The Sign of the Cross*, 5.

15. Tóibín, *The Sign of the Cross*, 6.

16. Kevin Whelan, "The Revisionist Debate in Ireland," *boundary 2*, 31:1 (Spring 2004), 188–189.

17. Tóibín, "New Ways of Killing Your Father," 3.

18. Tóibín, "New Ways of Killing Your Father," 3.

19. Tóibín, "New Ways of Killing Your Father," 3.

20. Tóibín, "New Ways of Killing Your Father," 3.

21. Tóibín, "New Ways of Killing Your Father," 6.

22. Tóibín, "New Ways of Killing Your Father," 6.

23. Joseph Wiesenfarth, "An Interview with Colm Tóibín," *Contemporary Literature*, 50:1 (Spring 2009), 8.

24. See, for example, Paul Delaney's "Introduction" and R. F. Foster's "'A Strange and Insistent Protagonist': Tóibín and Irish History," both in Delaney, *Reading Colm Tóibín*, 1–20, 21–40.

25. Canning, *Hear Us Out*, 198.

26. Alex Clark, "Songs of Experience," *Guardian*, March 13, 2004, review section, 22.

27. Colm Tóibín, "Colm Tóibín's Dublin," *Daily Telegraph*, April 15, 2000, travel supplement, 1, 4.

28. Tóibín, *A Guest at the Feast*, unpaginated.

29. Tóibín, *A Guest at the Feast*, unpaginated.

30. Canning, *Hear Us Out*, 192.

31. Canning, *Hear Us Out*, 192.

32. Michael Böss, "'Belonging without Belonging': Colm Tóibín's Dialogue with the Past," *Estudios Irlandeses*, 0 (2005), 23.

33. O'Toole, "An Interview with Colm Tóibín," 197.

34. For a discussion of liminal seascapes in Tóibín's novels, see Liam Harte, "Colm Tóibín's Marine Imaginary," *Critique: Studies in Contemporary Fiction*, 51:4 (2010), 333–349.
35. Colm Tóibín, *The Master* (Toronto: McClelland and Stewart, 2004), 121.
36. Colm Tóibín, *The Master*, 49.
37. Neil Corcoran, *After Yeats and Joyce* (Oxford: Oxford University Press, 1997), 98.
38. Tom Herron, "ContamiNation: Patrick McCabe and Colm Tóibín's Pathographies of the Republic," in *Contemporary Irish Fiction: Themes, Tropes, Theories*, eds Liam Harte and Michael Parker (Basingstoke: Macmillan, 2000), 171, 183–184.
39. See Ray Ryan, *Ireland and Scotland: Literature and Culture, State and Nation, 1966–2000* (Oxford: Oxford University Press, 2002), 250–288, and Conor McCarthy, "Geographies of Liberalism: The Politics of Space in Colm Tóibín's *Bad Blood: A Walk along the Irish Border* and *The Heather Blazing*," in *Landscape and Empire 1770–2000*, ed. Glenn Hooper (Aldershot: Ashgate, 2006), 207–223.
40. Kathleen Costello-Sullivan, *Mother/Country: Politics of the Personal in the Fiction of Colm Tóibín* (Bern: Peter Lang, 2012), 66.
41. The term "aporia," literally meaning an impasse, is central to Derrida's theory of *différance* (meaning both "difference" and "deferral"). In *An Introduction to Literature, Criticism and Theory* (Harlow: Prentice Hall, 1999; 2nd edn) Andrew Bennett and Nicholas Royle define an aporia as "an impassable moment or point in narrative, a hole or opening that produces a hermeneutic abyss" (57).
42. Colm Tóibín, *The Heather Blazing* [1992] (London: Picador, 1993), 14. Subsequent page numbers are cited parenthetically in the text.
43. Tóibín recalls seeing just such a figure in the castle dungeon as a child. See Colm Tóibín, "Introduction: The Stones of Enniscorthy," in *Enniscorthy: History and Heritage*, Micheál Tóibín (Dublin: New Island Books, 1998), 11.
44. Here again, the fictional details are factually based. As already mentioned, Micheál Tóibín was the prime mover behind the purchase and transformation of the castle into a county museum.
45. Kevin Whelan, *The Tree of Liberty* (Cork: Cork University Press, 1996), 133, 174. Tóibín himself makes a similar point in his introduction to *Enniscorthy: History and Heritage*: "The Rising in Wexford, more than any other event in Irish history, is open to interpretation: it can be explained as one thing and also explained as exactly the opposite" (13). See also R. F. Foster, "Remembering 1798," in his *The Irish Story: Telling Tales and Making it Up in Ireland* (London: Allen Lane, 2001), 211–234.
46. Basil Chubb, *The Politics of the Irish Constitution* (Dublin: Institute of Public Administration, 1991), 64. The Oireachtas is the Gaelic term for the Irish national parliament, which consists of the President and two Houses, Dáil

Éireann (the House of Representatives) and Seanad Éireann (the Senate). The Houses of the Oireachtas are situated at Leinster House in Dublin.

47. John Kelly, "Fundamental Rights and the Constitution," in *De Valera's Constitution and Ours*, ed. Brian Farrell (Dublin: Gill and Macmillan, 1988), 167–168. Tóibín makes a similar point in "Inside the Supreme Court."

48. In "Inside the Supreme Court" Tóibín points out that the relationship between the Supreme Court and the Department of Justice deteriorated throughout the 1960s as the Court increasingly came to be seen as working against the interests of the Fianna Fáil establishment.

49. Chubb, *The Politics of the Irish Constitution*, 60.

50. Patrick Hanafin, "Legal Texts as Cultural Documents: Interpreting the Irish Constitution," in *Writing in the Irish Republic: Literature, Culture, Politics, 1949–1999*, ed. Ray Ryan (Basingstoke: Macmillan, 2000), 148.

51. Hanafin, "Legal Texts as Cultural Documents," 150.

52. Roland Barthes, *Image-Music-Text* (London: Fontana, 1977), 147. Quoted in *Untying the Text: A Post-Structuralist Reader*, ed. Robert Young (London: Routledge and Kegan Paul, 1981), 18.

53. Kelly, "Fundamental Rights and the Constitution," 195.

54. As J. J. Lee explains in *Ireland 1912–1985: Politics and Society* (Cambridge: Cambridge University Press, 1989): "The very structure of the constitution betrays the difficulties of the de Valera dialectic on the crucial question of identity. Articles 1–3 deal with 'The Nation'. Articles 4–11 deal with 'The State'. But de Valera makes no attempt to define 'the Nation'. The definition contained in Article 2 is not of the nation, only of the national territory. That so scholastic a thinker, so punctilious a draftsman, as de Valera, who would consult a dictionary to define 'republic', should avoid the fundamental issue of definition, in a constitution laden with definitions, suggests that even he could find no definition that could not be turned by the Protestant people into a definition of their own 'nation'" (205). Articles 2 and 3 were amended by referendum in 1998, following the signing of the Belfast Agreement. "The Nation" remains undefined in the new wording.

55. Tóibín's own reflections make it clear that his primary interest is in the reality of the crumbling coastline rather than the landscape's symbolic potential: "For some miles the cliffs are eroding. Each year some land falls into the sea. My godfather's house fell in, and so did Keatings' house. I suppose this is an interesting image of time, and a metaphor for what time does. But I am more interested in the exact thing itself – the actual detail of bits of this landscape which I have known for so long falling, dissolving, being washed away, not being there any more" (*A Guest at the Feast*, unpaginated).

56. Jacob Urup Nielsen, "An interview with Colm Tóibín," Nordic Irish Studies Network (1998). http://www.hum.au.dk/engelsk/nisn/reviews/toibininterview.html

Chapter 5

Unbearable Proximities: William Trevor's *Felicia's Journey* (1994)

I

The residual culture of déclassé Protestant Ireland to which the young Colm Tóibín was drawn in early 1970s Dublin, and through which he discovered his own sense of displacement, is one that William Trevor knew intimately from the inside, and which began in him "the process of being an outsider,"[1] as he himself put it. Born William Trevor Cox in Mitchelstown, County Cork in 1928, he has described himself as belonging to "that little sliver of Irish life which is poor and Protestant."[2] In his introduction to *Excursions in the Real World* (1993), a volume of occasional essays, he situates himself more precisely:

I was fortunate that my accident of birth actually placed me on the edge of things. I was born into a minority that all my life has seemed in danger of withering away. This was smalltime Protestant stock, far removed from the well-to-do Ascendancy of the recent past yet without much of a place in de Valera's new Catholic Ireland.[3]

Growing up, Trevor's sense of being on the cultural periphery was compounded by his family's peripatetic circumstances, during which he came to know many places while belonging fully to none. Trevor's father worked for Bank of Ireland, whose policy it was to relocate its employees on promotion, which meant that young William's 1930s childhood was spent moving from

Reading the Contemporary Irish Novel 1987–2007, First Edition. Liam Harte.
© 2014 Liam Harte. Published 2014 by John Wiley & Sons, Ltd.

posting to posting in a succession of small towns in counties Cork, Tipperary, and Wexford. His parents' unhappy marriage made for a lonely as well as a rootless upbringing. He later wrote of their joyless relationship that

> They were victims of their innocence when chance threw them together and passion beguiled them, leaving them to live with a mistake and to watch their field of battle expanding with each day that passed. They gave their love to their children and were loved in return, fiercely, unwaveringly. But not for a moment could that heal the wounds they carried to their graves.[4]

This passage bears many of the signatures of the humane vision that informs so much of Trevor's fiction: a steady empathy for the complex emotional contours of ordinary lives; an elliptical intimation of unassuaged yearnings; a muted admiration for the human capacity for adaptation and fortitude.

Unsurprisingly, this unsettled upbringing would later supply fuel for the fiction. Love and its deceptions and disillusionments are recurring themes in Trevor's novels and short stories, themes often played out in the context of crumbling middle-class marriages. Like his disenchanted mother, Trevor took to "creating drama out of the unpromising splinters of everyday life."[5] As he explained in a 1983 interview:

> I don't really have any heroes or heroines. I don't seem to go in for them. I think I am interested in people who are not necessarily the victims of other people, but simply the victims of circumstance, as they are in *Fools of Fortune*. I'm very interested in the sadness of fate, the things that just happen to people.[6]

Yet despite harboring a desire to write from early adolescence, it was many years before Trevor acted upon it. On completing his "fragmentary education"[7] in a Dublin boarding school, he entered Trinity College Dublin in 1946 to study medicine but transferred to a history degree after just one day in medical school. However, his principal interest during his student days was in sculpting, to which he had been introduced by his school art teacher, the distinguished sculptor Oisín Kelly. He carved his first piece of commissioned art in his rooms at Trinity and had his work exhibited under the name Trevor Cox while still a student.[8] Public recognition came in 1953, when he was joint-winner of the Irish section of the International Unknown Political Prisoner competition. Within months, however, the newly married artist decided to move to England, having failed to find work in the impoverished Republic.

Trevor and his wife Jane settled in Somerset, from where he worked as a church sculptor for several years until the birth of the couple's first child led him to take a job with a London advertising agency in 1960 in order to boost the family's income.

By now, the sculptor Trevor Cox had become William Trevor the novelist, *A Standard of Behaviour* having appeared in 1958. Although he would later dismiss this London-set novel as having been "written entirely for profit and of no literary merit,"[9] it nonetheless represents Trevor's first attempt to make sense, through fiction, of "a country that was totally strange" and "very fascinating" to him.[10] In a 2000 interview he reflected: "England was this extraordinary country that I had found myself in, a place I didn't want to be, but I was there. The great, mahogany establishment of it was so extraordinary and so different from Ireland, I wanted to know more and more about it."[11] This process of satisfying his outsider curiosity continued over his next three novels, *The Old Boys* (1964), *The Boarding-House* (1965), and *The Love Department* (1966), in which he explores, through a tragicomic lens, the inner lives of a picaresque collection of sub-Dickensian character types, from emotionally stunted septuagenarians to scheming philanderers. In later novels, such as *Elizabeth Alone* (1973), *Children of Dynmouth* (1976), and *Other People's Worlds* (1980), we see him digging ever deeper into the soil of English domestic, family, and social life, excavating fresh layers of emotional torment and moral bankruptcy, and in the process becoming "one of the greatest evokers of suburban England in the third quarter of the twentieth century."[12]

It was not until the late 1960s that Trevor began to turn his emigrant gaze on the country of his birth. *Mrs Eckdorf in O'Neill's Hotel* (1969) is his first "Irish" novel, though the eponymous protagonist is in fact a London-born photographer who has convinced herself that a rundown Dublin hotel harbors a secret tragedy that she is determined to unearth. Only with his second short story collection, *The Ballroom of Romance* (1972), did Trevor began to lay claim to a specific segment of Irish society, the material surfaces and moral interiors of which he has probed repeatedly ever since. The fictional space known as "Trevor's Ireland" has been summarized thus by Dolores MacKenna:

· ·

This is rural and small town Ireland, a bleak place where people endure life rather than live it; a place of loneliness, frustration and undramatic suffering. Timeless, except in its details, its moral climate remains constant whether its people live in the 1940s or the 1990s. Public events have little impact upon the inhabitants of the isolated farms, drab small towns, or, less often, dreary suburbs where individuals exist in states of unarticulated desperation.[13]

· ·

Intriguingly, this territory cannot be located with any certainty on a map of Ireland. Even though Trevor's Irish settings exude verisimilitude, he is a writer who, in the main, depicts a particular kind of Ireland rather than any particular Irish locale, as if the evocation of the *idea* of place appeals to him more than the recreation of a specific location. Whereas John McGahern's novels and short stories serially memorialize a very specific stretch of Leitrim–Roscommon countryside, Trevor tends to shy away from being quite so precise in his settings. Although actual place names and topographical landmarks anchor the novels and short stories in certain regions of Ireland – his native Munster and south Leinster are favorite locations – he usually stops short of using named towns and villages as his settings. Why this is so is hard to fathom, though it may be Trevor's subtle way of expressing the metaphorical homelessness that afflicts so many of his protagonists.[14] But whatever the reason, this approach imbues his fictive landscapes with a tantalizing, paradoxical quality: "Trevor's Ireland" is at once uncannily familiar and yet somehow "atopical," to use a J. Hillis Miller term, "a place that is everywhere and nowhere, a place you cannot get to from here."[15]

This is a feature of Trevor's work commented upon by Tóibín, who, with a sniff of condescension toward the displaced writer, contends: "Unlike writers such as John McGahern and Eugene McCabe, whose work takes place in an exact and contoured landscape, Trevor has no fiefdom in Ireland, no landscape which he knows in detail. He is more at home in boarding houses, shops, public houses, or in the minds of his characters."[16] Tóibín elaborated on this point in a 2002 interview, saying of Trevor: "Yes – no place that he's from, that he can describe in any detail: where the ditch was; which tree; where the shadows fell. It's deeply disabling not to have that."[17] Perhaps so. But Trevor's placelessness has not proved so disabling as to prevent him from being hailed as "one of the principal novelists in English at the end of the twentieth century,"[18] or judged "the most astute observer of the human condition currently writing in fiction."[19] In any case, it is altogether too reductive in the first instance to pigeonhole Trevor as a prospector of a single seam of Irish life. "Trevor's Ireland" can be readily disaggregated into several component parts, chief among which are "Trevor's Northern Ireland" – based largely on selected stories in the volumes *Angels at the Ritz* (1975), *Lovers in Their Time* (1978), *Beyond the Pale* (1981), and *The News from Ireland* (1986) – and "Trevor's Big House Ireland," which takes in the novels *Fools of Fortune* (1983), *The Silence in the Garden* (1988), and *The Story of Lucy Gault* (2002), all three of which center on the revolutionary period of 1916–1923. One could also make a case for a "Trevor's Dublin," given that he set *Mrs Eckdorf in O'Neill's Hotel* in the city and has since returned to it as the setting for several short stories, including "Two More Gallants," "The Third Party," "Faith," and "Bravado." The novel that is the subject of this chapter, *Felicia's Journey* (1994), forms the keystone of a further category,

"Trevor's Emigrant Ireland," which is mainly composed of fictions of the Irish in Britain.

The novelist himself, of course, has lived in England since the early 1950s and has compared the creative benefits of exile to "see[ing] Ireland more clearly through the wrong end of a telescope,"[20] although in *Felicia's Journey* it is his "binocular English-Irish vision"[21] that holds the reader's attention. The core theme of this novel is also that which holds his larger mosaic of fictional landscapes in place: history's coercive power or, more precisely, the complex and debilitating legacies of Britain's protracted history of colonialism in Ireland. As Mary Fitzgerald-Hoyt has noted, the recrudescence of political violence in Northern Ireland in the 1970s prompted Trevor to expend much sympathy and irony on dramatizing and appraising the effects of the colonial past on individual lives and intimate personal relations on both sides of the Irish Sea.[22] Often, particularly in his short stories, he draws on the resources of allegory to represent the psychic scars of this history of military occupation, political violence, and cultural deformation. Of his novels, *Felicia's Journey* is certainly his most richly nuanced allegorical drama of domination and resistance, in which the literal shades into the figurative throughout. It is, moreover, Trevor's "subtlest, most deeply ironic reading of Anglo–Irish relations to date."[23]

Set in the early 1990s, *Felicia's Journey* tells the story of a young Irish Catholic girl's travels through the English Midlands in search of Johnny Lysaght, the father of her unborn child. Lysaght, who comes from the same provincial town as Felicia, has led her to believe that he works in a lawnmower factory somewhere "north of Birmingham;"[24] in fact, he is a soldier in the British Army. Shortly after her arrival in England, Felicia comes within the ambit of a middle-aged catering manager, Joseph Hilditch, who insinuates himself into her life and exploits her desperate credulity, his genteel paternalism masking a sinister intent. Hilditch stalks Felicia relentlessly, steals her money to make her dependent upon him, and pretends throughout to be someone he is not: a retired military officer with a terminally ill wife. As this suspenseful cat-and-mouse chase escalates, it becomes clear that Hilditch is in fact a psychotic befriender and killer of vulnerable young women. The roots of his violent psychosis are shown to lie deep in his childhood relationship with his mother, who sexually preyed upon her son after she was abandoned by the last in a long line of casual lovers, a shadowy figure whom Hilditch knew as "Uncle" Wilf. Wilf himself was a powerful formative influence on the young Hilditch, who never knew the identity of his own father. Wilf's story is that, having fought in the First World War, he was sent to Ireland in 1920 to quell IRA militancy and came back with "army tales" (20) that would later sow the seeds of military ambition and colonial contempt for the neighboring island in his "nephew." Hilditch's dreams of a heroic regimental career were summarily dashed, however, when the Army rejected him. The festering disappointment of this rejection was subsequently compounded by his devastating discovery that Wilf's whole military persona was a sham, a smokescreen for his affair with Hilditch's promiscuous mother, who colluded in the fiction of Wilf's avuncular status. "Everything fell to bits then" (200), leaving Hilditch with a deeply traumatized psyche, which he hides behind a mask of affability, "simulating a calmness that does not reflect this inner tumult" (112). This placid veneer is tested to breaking point by his involvement with Felicia and the cultural baggage she brings with her from a country that excited strong feelings in Hilditch's duplicitous former mentor: "The Black and Tans should have sorted that island out, his Uncle Wilf said, only unfortunately they held back for humane reasons" (149).

Trevor's depiction of this tense, edgy duel between psychopathic eccentric and innocent waif is marked throughout by a masterly delineation of character, a superb control of narrative suspense, and a skilled management of point of view, all qualities that attracted the Canadian director Atom Egoyan to film the novel in 1999. The film adaptation, however, neutralizes key aspects of the novel's intricate fusion of the optics of psychoanalysis and postcolonialism to illuminate the tangled webs within which Hilditch and Felicia are trapped. It also misses the subtlety with which Trevor uses the natural and built environments to convey meaning, the way he makes space and place act as determinants of character, agency, and action. In this context, it is notable that novelist and film director clashed over the latter's intention to transpose the story to Canada when adapting it for the screen. Egoyan explained:

· ·

> I talked to William and there was a subtext to the story which he is very guarded
> about speaking about, but which he felt was very important to preserve. He felt
> the history of violence between Britain and Ireland is not something you could
> just transpose to Canada, and he was quite right.[25]

· ·

As Christine St. Peter notes, however, the fact that Egoyan was more interested in the novel's gender politics than its representation of Anglo-Irish power relations meant that he made substantial changes to the text in order to create space for "his own characteristic artistic concern: the deforming effects of media on the human psyche."[26]

In what follows, I wish to examine more closely the spatial or geographical imaginary of *Felicia's Journey*: that is, how Trevor's treatment of material and symbolic geographies affects the novel's merging of personal stories with public histories. If the novel's title suggests a plot animated by physical displacement, then the narrative itself extends this to cultural and psychic unsettlement, showing Hilditch to be much more troublingly "out of place" in contemporary Britain than migrant Felicia. The figure of the journey influences the novel's form and style in other ways too. Not only does the narration oscillate between Ireland and England (just as it shifts between the perspectives of Hilditch and Felicia), but the heroine's treacherous journey across the water is itself proleptic of her metaphysical "migration" from one "state" to another. Probing more deeply, we can see that the geographical spaces in the novel are symbolically freighted, marked by various historical trajectories and inscribed by social and political relationships, particularly those between Ireland and Britain. This means that the private and public spaces within which Felicia and Hilditch move and interact are charged with specific meanings and marked by residual discourses that have a crucial bearing upon Trevor's treatment of the persistence of the unresolved past in the consciousness of the living. In fact, as I will show, both Felicia and Hilditch are located and produced within social spaces that are so thoroughly shaped by colonial hierarchies and postcolonial pathologies that both protagonists inhabit powerfully *subjected* subjectivities.

It helps to remember here that Trevor's sensibility has always been closely attuned to the physical imprint of history in Ireland. In his *A Writer's Ireland: Landscape and Literature* (1984), for example, the profound and ineradicable traces of the colonial past are never far from view: "In Ireland you can escape neither politics nor history, for when you travel through the country today the long conflict its landscape has known does not as readily belong in the far-away past as Hastings or Stamford Bridge does for the English."[27] But this does not mean that he sees this colonial relationship in simple, dichotomous terms. Of far greater imaginative interest to Trevor are the reciprocities, interpenetrations, and cross-cultural movements between the two islands – hence the novel's echoing subplots of an English Black and Tan soldier fighting the IRA in 1920s Ireland and an Irish-born British Army soldier in 1990s England, who may yet be deployed against the IRA in Northern Ireland. Such a close engagement with the colonial and postcolonial spaces wherein Irish and British identities are contested and reconfigured means that character and locale are inextricably intertwined in *Felicia's Journey*, in ways that the following geographically inflected reading of the novel will seek to elucidate.

II

The opening chapter of *Felicia's Journey* establishes the central protagonist not so much as a conventional homesick emigrant but as one who is escaping the engulfment of home, its laws and its expectations, its limits and its boundaries. In a sense, Felicia's "homesickness" is no less severe than Francie Brady's, though she carries a different burden of gendered subjectivity. Here and elsewhere in the novel, Trevor highlights the perils of inhabiting a female body in a patriarchal postcolonial society that is profoundly inimical to women's self-regulation and self-assertion. The place that Felicia has stealthily exited exudes an air of claustrophobic, moralistic masculinity in her recollections of it during her lonely night-time crossing of the Irish Sea. Paternalistic arbiters of religious codes of sexual and moral behavior dominate her memories and dreams, from her stony-faced father to Father Kilgallen and Mr Scaddan the butcher, who is seen sharing his disapproval of a local courting-place with a young Christian Brother. Pregnant, jilted, and fearful, Felicia is a young woman in flight from judgmental, reprimanding voices and the stigma of unmarried motherhood in small-town Ireland. Only when the ship leaves the quayside does she feel "safe" (1).[28] From this point onward, we learn of Felicia's formative experiences through her fragmentary memories and the many flashback scenes that provide a window on her family background and social situation. The portrait that emerges is a decidedly dismal one that asks searching questions of the state of Irish society seventy-five years after the 1916 Easter Rising.

Far from "revers[ing] all the labels and stereotypes applied to the Irish in his twist on the traditional emigration narrative,"[29] Trevor actually reinforces pejorative perceptions of provincial Irish life through his negative rendition of it. For all that Felicia cherishes her memory of her first encounter with Johnny Lysaght, this is shown to be but a mirage in a landscape of narrowing horizons. In fact, Lysaght's opportunistic exploitation of her naivety merely compounds the existing constraints under which Felicia labors. Motherless and jobless, she lives as a virtual domestic slave to her father, brothers, and ninety-nine-year old great-grandmother – a fossilized, anachronistic *Sean Bhean Bhocht*, personification of the feminized nation – whose "aura" (25) binds the family to a solemn veneration of the nationalist faith for which her husband sacrificed himself in 1916.[30] Since the old woman has "outlived her own rational thought" (25), it has fallen to her grandson to honor this blood sacrifice on his own, and there is no mistaking his bewitchment by the transcendental romance of sacrificial nationalism. The image of Felicia's father poring over "his scrapbooks of those revolutionary times, three heavy volumes of wallpaper pattern books that Multilly of the hardware had let him have when their contents went out of date" (25–26), calls to mind what F. S. L. Lyons termed "the great enchantment" of Irish history, "which for too long has made myth so much more congenial than reality."[31] Moreover, the allusion to redundancy and emphasis on the private and solitary nature of such patriotic devotion hint at the unease surrounding the public remembrance of 1916 in 1990s Ireland.[32] Within the family, however, the torch of republican pride burns strongly, the flames fanned by Felicia's father's discovery that his daughter has been keeping company with "a member of the occupying forces" (58), which prompts a bitter sermon on the evils of British colonial rule in Ireland, past and present. The image of this patriarch advancing "on to the territory that mattered to him most" (58) subtly reinvokes the trope of the national landscape as feminine and implies a link between the political control of territory and the control of women's sexuality, now no longer disguised. To suggest, however, as Linden Peach does, that Felicia is "exiled by sectarianism"[33] is rather overemphatic, as the "pull" factor of finding Lysaght consistently counterbalances the social and familial "push" factors acting upon her.

Growing up, Felicia, who was herself named in honor of a 1916 insurgent, received a gentler instruction in republican history through those same sedulously preserved scrapbooks, which include a handwritten copy of the Easter Proclamation and the text of Prime Minister de Valera's 1943 radio broadcast on "The Ireland that we dreamed of." Trevor typographically divorces a key passage of this speech from the main narrative in order to underline the "hallowed" (26) nature of the symbolic landscape conjured up:

. . . .

The Ireland which we have dreamed of would be the home of a people who valued material wealth only as the basis of right living, of a people who were satisfied with frugal comfort and devoted their leisure to things of the spirit; a land whose countryside would be bright with cosy homesteads, whose fields and villages would be joyous with the sounds of industry, with the romping of sturdy children, the contests of athletic youths, the laughter of comely maidens; whose firesides would be forums for the wisdom of old age. It would, in a word, be the home of a people living the life that God desires men should live. (26-27)

. . . .

This broadcast, more than any other during de Valera's premiership, consolidated landscape's ideological role in the creation of a postcolonial Irish national identity. In it, the quintessence of nationhood is located in an idealized rural space, constructed as the source and locus of national cohesion, cultural authenticity, and moral and spiritual purity.[34] Immediately, however, Trevor exposes the stark disparity between this vision of uncompromisable bucolic harmony and the depressed reality that Felicia inhabits, a disparity symbolized as much by the tarnished brass nameplates that adorn the surgeries of dentist and doctor as by the heroine's unemployed status. Revealed, too, is the fact that her father would privately prefer her to gain part-time employment so that she could continue her domestic duties and tend to his bedridden grandmother. Such chauvinist thinking suggests that Felicia is destined to repeat the old woman's grim experience, without even the "aura" of patriotic widowhood as consolation, a vista that represents a painful commentary on women's progress toward socioeconomic emancipation in postrevolutionary Ireland.

Nor is this the only moment in the novel where women are shown to be the victims of strictly policed patriarchal Catholic values, particularly in the sphere of sexuality and reproduction. There is more truth than he realizes in Felicia's father's assertion that "A vision was born on the streets of Dublin seventy-five years ago during those Easter days. It was not fulfilled, the potential has not been realized: you have only to look around you" (58). The fate of a local woman, Miss Furey, whom Felicia seeks out as a potential confidant in her hour of need shows how far short Irish society has fallen from the Proclamation's socialist pledge "to pursue the happiness and prosperity of the whole nation and all of its parts, cherishing all the children of the nation equally."[35] Middle-aged and unmarried, Miss Furey is described as "a woman to whom no man had been known to pay attentions, yet about whom there had once been a rumour that she was pregnant. When abruptly her condition changed and she returned to normal it was said with certainty that no child existed in the farmhouse where she lived" (56). Despite being shunned by her, Felicia remains haunted by the rumors of incest and infanticide that surround this spinster, never more so than after her own abortion, when her guilt-ridden mind hallucinates an image of Miss Furey and her brother burying an infant's corpse in the corner of a field, under cover of darkness. This nightmarish scene recalls the real-life case of Kerrywoman Joanne Hayes, who on an April night in 1984 secretly gave birth in a field to a baby boy, conceived as a result of an extramarital affair, whose body she initially covered with hay.[36] The next stage of Felicia's delirium recalls another tragic episode of concealed pregnancy in what Fintan O'Toole called the "secret history of modern Ireland,"[37] that of Ann Lovett, a fifteen-year-old Longford schoolgirl who died in February 1984 while giving birth in front of a grotto to the Virgin Mary.[38] Felicia's feverish pleading for forgiveness in Chapter 17 from a blind and heedless Virgin – potent icon of traditional Irish womanhood and signifier of sexual and moral purity – powerfully captures the perdition that grips the soul of a Catholic girl who has internalized the shame and blame ascribed to Irish women who contravene religiously inspired social and sexual norms.

Viewed against this canvas of constrictive forces, Felicia might well be considered fortunate to be escaping a land of domineering fathers and custodial mothers, whose harsh censure she can vividly imagine were she to return. Yet this is not the full story by any means. For all its suffocating drudgery and despair, the small town that she has left is still home, the embodiment of a particular, sensual way of life rooted in a humanly meaningful landscape, enriched by a distinctive sense of tradition and creative of social community. Although no utopia, Felicia's natal place is depicted as a storied social space, one layered with human relationships and memories and embedded with a sense of family history and ancestral bonds. It is, moreover, positioned within a rurally-based Ireland, as yet lightly touched by the transformative forces of transnational, European, and global capital. While this is something of a curse economically, insofar as industrial underdevelopment exposes Ireland's continuing economic dependency on the former colonial power across the water, it is a blessing in terms of enhanced *gemeinschaft*. There is a distinctive village-like quality to Felicia's experience of her home town, a sense of organic communality and comforting neighborliness that suffuses her recurring memories of her brother's wedding day, for example. This kind of environment corresponds to what ethnologist Marc Augé calls "anthropological place,"[39] where human relations, history, and tradition are centrally constitutive of collective and individual identities. Such places stand at the opposite end of the spectrum to "non-places," the term Augé uses to designate "two complementary but distinct entities: spaces formed in relation to certain ends (transport, transit, commerce, leisure), and the relations that individuals have with these spaces."[40] He goes on to observe: "As anthropological places create the organically social, so non-places create solitary contractuality."[41] Such generic, asocial spaces are both everywhere and nowhere within the era of "supermodernity," a term Augé prefers to late modernity or postmodernity: "Non-places are the contemporary spaces where supermodernity can be found, in conflict with identity, relationship and history. They are the spaces of circulation, communication and consumption, where solitudes coexist without creating any social bond or even a social emotion."[42] For Augé, sites such as shopping malls, airport lounges, motels, motorways, industrial estates, and retail distribution centers are frequently experienced as non-places, their homogeneity and anonymity breeding feelings of isolation and detachment in those who pass through them.

Augé's theoretical observations have a compelling relevance for Trevor's treatment of place and landscape in the novel, since the material spaces of the natural and built environments that Felicia and Joseph Hilditch move through are presented as being central to their respective relationships to the world. Certainly, Felicia's journey from provincial Ireland to the English Midlands can be conceptualized as a movement from anthropological place to non-place. Having departed her morally stifling but intimately known Irish locale, where people and place coexist in mutual nurture, she enters a postindustrial landscape that seems emptied of organic, human community. Trevor's studious refusal to name the Midlands towns she visits is itself designed to underline the pervasive homogeneity of landscape, culture, and consumption, and so make the reader share in Felicia's sense of disorientation and alienation. The first thing she notices from her train window is a characterless terrain cluttered by cars, pylons, and aerials, and we later see through her eyes a compressed landscape subsumed by a burgeoning culture of industry and commerce: "Factories seem like fortresses, their towers protecting an ancient realm of iron and wealth. Terracotta everywhere has blackened to the insistent local sheen. The lie of the land is lost beneath a weight of purpose, its natural idiosyncrasy stifled, contours pressed away" (34). But it is in desolate commercial zones, where human interactions are as functionalist as the bland infrastructure, that Felicia most often finds herself searching for her caddish seducer, her hesitant inquiries typically receiving a breezy rebuff from employees busily engaged in "buying and selling, disposal and acquisition, discount for cash" (14). Blackbarrow industrial estate is the novel's archetypal non-place, "an endless repetition of nondescript commercial buildings, each with a forecourt for parking. Trade names blazon: Toyota, Ford, Toys 'Я' Us, National Tyre and Autocare, Kwik-Fit, Zanussi, Renault Trucks, Pipewise, Ready-bag, Sony, Comet" (14). It is upon such topographies that the condition of contemporary England is revealed. Toward the end of the novel, Trevor evokes a sense of the vast carelessness that characterizes this new England in which Felicia finds herself, depicting a society in which there are many lost and missing girls, not all of whom are missed by those close to them.

For Hilditch, conversely, such globalized commercial spaces are constitutive of the place he calls home. In his initial characterization of Hilditch, Trevor foregrounds key aspects of this psychopathic loner's relationship to a social environment that has been fundamentally reshaped by Britain's rapid postwar decline as an imperial and military power; by large-scale migration from the former colonies; by the rise of a multicultural society; by the collapse of consensus politics; and by accelerated globalization. None of these forces penetrate the walls of number three Duke of Wellington Road, however, an address that slyly warns us against seeing colonialism as a one-way street, so to speak.[43] Hilditch's suburban residence, a spacious detached manor house "built in 1867 to the designs of a tea merchant" (7), is an imperial time capsule which, since his mother's death, he has furnished with ivory, marble, and mahogany items, commodities redolent of the spoils of Britain's nineteenth-century colonial conquests.[44] The outdatedness of this fabricated, monocultural England – "portraits of other people's ancestors" (150) line his walls – is underlined by the cultural diversity of the townscape through which Hilditch drives on his daily commute to work. Since the 1950s, the town's social and spatial transformation has been driven by the growth of new industries, which have attracted large numbers of immigrant workers, some of whom are Hilditch's fellow employees. The eclipse of an older England by this multiethnic influx is graphically symbolized by the presence of a synagogue, a mosque, and churches of different denominations in the town, but no cathedral. Later, Hilditch summarizes these changes for Felicia during their first car journey together, explaining how "the motorways have changed the face of England, how new towns have come to these parts, how people from Pakistan and the West Indies have begun to settle, changing the look of things also, how prosperity has given way to poverty in certain areas" (65). Later still, after Felicia has escaped his clutches, Hilditch's detachment from this multicultural reality collapses when, symbolically unvehicled, he is compelled to roam "the neighbourhoods the Indians and Pakistanis have taken over" (179) in search of his quarry. Wandering at night through a postcolonial bazaar of ethnic shops and restaurants, this devotee of "the old ways" (97) becomes a stranger in a transformed England, a man out of place as well as out of time. Unable to recognize himself or "home" in this streetscape, Hilditch is as disorientated by the geography of the new as any immigrant from the former colonies.

Paradoxically, as civic society has grown in diversity, so the town's physical appearance has become more homogenous, assuming the character of "a placeless geography, a labyrinth of endless similarities."[45] The correlation between environmental, cultural, and political soullessness is deftly insinuated, the brutalist architecture symbolizing the brutalism of free-market economics and the social inequality, deprivation, and violence they have fostered. The novel's critique of the devastating social impact of the New Right policies of the 1980s is both subtle and caustic. The spiritual vacancy of Thatcher's Britain is artfully framed in the panoramic views of the town's breezeblock walkways and arcades, where actual humans have been replaced by hieroglyphs, the brown concrete showing "a sculptured group – man, woman and child in a stylized lumbering gait, *en route* from the post office to a multi-story car park" (8). At night, these dehumanized non-places are colonized by those without a place, the homeless, the ultimate outgroup in the Thatcherite dream of a property-owning democracy. Trevor's characterization of this disparate underclass as "maggots" (102) who, when night falls, crawl into makeshift shelters in building sites, alleyways, and courtyards, piquantly captures the neoliberal contempt in which they are held. Although personally shielded from this underworld, Hilditch is increasingly agitated by sensationalist tabloid accounts of gratuitous acts of criminality and depravity, symptoms of a pervasive moral and social barbarism. That he should recoil from this dystopia, blind to his own complicity in it, is of course intensely ironic, since this outwardly respectable suburbanite is himself a deadly prowler of unmonitored interstitial zones, forever on the lookout for troubled and homeless young women to befriend, control, and kill. Thus, the anonymous locales that so alienate Felicia are appropriated by Hilditch in his ghoulish Morris Minor, a "voyeur-voyager in his car"[46] if ever there was one:

. . . .

The snapshot memories begin again: weekend appearances in towns and places where no one knows he is Hilditch, a catering manager: hours spent in the car, watching from a vantage point near a disco that is due to end, or just parked anywhere on the off chance; up and down the motorways, alert on the approach roads in case there is another vehicle to keep close to; fatherly conversations with waitresses in bed-and-breakfast places, an invitation offered but not accepted. (51–52)

....

Once a "fatherly" invitation has been accepted (fatherhood being a role this psychologically castrated predator can only ever play at), it is Hilditch's habit to take his female prey to places of transient, superficial sociality where, to reprise Augé, "solitudes coexist without creating any social bond." Being seen – but, crucially, not known – by strangers in the company of young women in such places as motorway cafes and sales showrooms satisfies his deep psychic need to experience a frisson of the masculine potency that was stolen from him in childhood by his sexually abusive mother. The role of food and eating in such behavior is by no means incidental. Food imagery, which is ubiquitous in the novel, is not linked to Rabelaisian earthiness or the carnivalistic spirit. Unlike Bakhtin, who views the act of eating in joyful, hedonistic terms, Trevor extracts a much darker symbolism from Hilditch's pathological habits of consumption, connecting his relish for food with his appetite for misogynistic power and control.[47] His prodigious capacity for eating is not to be understood comically or even satirically, therefore, but as a function of traumatic personality disturbance.

From the moment of his introduction – "Although he does not know it, Mr Hilditch weighs nineteen and a half stone" (6) – right through to his hanging himself from a ham hook in Chapter 23, the primacy of Hilditch's corpulent body and its rapacious appetites is continually before us. In fact, the spectacle of his gluttonous overeating is so pervasive that his epicureanism forms the nexus of his characterization. The superabundant rolls of fat that loll about his paunch testify to much more than an "interest in meals and comestibles" (6). Prodigious consumption, psychological trauma, and moral depravity are deeply enmeshed in him. Morbidly obese, it is inferred that Hilditch overeats as a coping strategy to repress memories of incest, reflexively cramming food into his ever-ravenous maw in a hopeless attempt to sate the emotional malnourishment of childhood and the stigmatizing fear, shame, and helplessness that went with it. Food alone, however, cannot still the chaos within. The tumultuous swirl of shame and rage engendered by his sexual victimization is directed toward the women he befriends, whom he "consumes" in order to repair his terminally damaged sense of masculinity.[48] The same psychotic dynamic plays itself out each time the fatal tipping point is reached, his neurotic paranoia persuading him that his secret stigma, his dreaded sense of lack, has somehow been intuited by his companions:

. . . .

You could see Beth thinking it; you could see her searching her thoughts and finding it. And Elsie Covington, then the others: they broke in somehow. They trespassed on his privacy even though he took them places and lavished a bit on them in their time of need, the Irish girl too. (196)

. . . .

Dread provokes panic, which triggers in turn Hilditch's "executioner's compulsion" (212).[49]

Hilditch believes that his "friendship" with Felicia is "destined to be special" (51), however: "She is the ultimate in passing trade, more than just a new face for the A522 Burger King or the Forest East Services, or the Long Eaton Little Chef" (52). Her exceptionality lies in her ethnicity and in her pregnant state: Felicia is not just Other but peculiarly and disturbingly so. The presence of this postcolonial figure of transgression and excess on Hilditch's "home ground" (93) is so hauntingly unbearable and obsessively attractive to this thwarted imperialist that it propels him toward reckless acts of transgression and excess of his own. Roger Bromley's reflections on the way the symbolic presence of the unassimilable Other amplifies fears and anxieties in the reactionary nationalist mind are pertinent here:

. . . .

The outsider, the migrant, the visibly different are seen as being beyond/outside localisation and territorial ordering, threatening indistinction because he or she is not symbolically identified with, or by, the rigorously mediated power of distinguishing which is the 'national' ground. Strangers threaten because they lack the vestments of the local or national territory – colour, language, accent, religion, cuisine and so on. The more the 'localised' have invested in the 'sovereign' nation and drawn 'power' from it, the more densely mediated, or overcoded, their lives become and a kind of territorial fundamentalism is produced – very often an effect of powerlessness.[50]

. . . .

Hilditch's territorial fundamentalism is activated from the moment he first lays eyes on Felicia. A broiling cesspool of racism and misogyny is stirred by this foreigner from "the back of beyond" (180), whose quaintness and exoticism instantly excite a kind of ocular gluttony in him, reminding us of Derek Gregory's point that imperialism is "a discourse which privileges vision."[51] Hilditch's voracious gaze has already devoured the outward markers of this newcomer's alterity – her dress, demeanor, and carrier bags – before she has even opened her mouth: "'I don't know am I in the right place,' the girl says as he is about to pass her by, and Mr Hilditch smiles in his usual way. Irish, he says to himself"

(11). With that, the fuse of an incendiary stream of consciousness is ignited: "Funny the way your thoughts go round, Mr Hilditch reflects. Funny the way they begin with a girl's face lingering and then get back to Uncle Wilf and that recruiting sergeant. Number 19 she went into" (20). The knowledge that the father of Felicia's unborn child is himself an army man intensifies Hilditch's torment, Lysaght having succeeded on fronts where Hilditch failed. Psychotically aroused by this loop of invasion anxieties and fantasies of forceful masculinity, Hilditch feels "impelled" (125) to improvise an elaborate life story and then to take the unprecedented risk of inviting Felicia into the sanctum of his museum-like home, as a prelude to his ultimate "recolonisation" of her. The "potency of remembering" (42) – the only form of potency of which Hilditch is capable – reaches new levels of intensity as he imagines this "runaway from the Irish boglands" (127) alone in his house, her sexualized exoticism merging with his own sexual defilement at the hands of his mother,[52] who is now cast as his deceased wife in the apocryphal autobiography he has fashioned to entrap his guest:

Pregnant in his house, examining his mother's likeness draped in mourning on the dining-room mantelpiece, going from room to room upstairs, eventually at her strip wash. [...] Her clothes draped over the chair and the towel-rail in the bathroom: not since his mother was alive has there been anything like that in Number Three. (128)[53]

From this moment onward, Hilditch's voyeuristic, libidinal fascination for this pregnant postcolonial trespasser, whose culture he secretly scorns yet is also bewitched by, grows ever more psychically overwhelming. Felicia's proximity to the locus of his psychological gelding breeds excruciatingly masochistic feelings in Hilditch, the anxiety that she might intuit his secret shame flirting with the exhilarating prospect that she might also catalyze his fantasy of vigorous masculinity. That neither emotion can withstand this emasculated imperialist's frustrated need to cannibalize this excolonial subject is confirmed when Hilditch manipulates Felicia into having an abortion, the buildup to which gives him a quasi-orgasmic "tremor" (137) of virility. Hilditch has always proprietorially referred to his companions as "girlfriends" when out of earshot of them; but only Felicia affords him the opportunity to experience the exquisite thrill of having strangers regard him as a red-blooded, procreative male:

It is then that the excitement begins, creeping through him, like something in his blood. He is the father of an unborn child, no doubt in any of their minds. The girl they have all seen, who was here not ten minutes ago, whey-faced and anxious, is at this very moment being separated from their indiscretion. A relationship has occurred, no way you can gainsay it. [. . .]

Mr Hilditch closes his eyes and the indiscretion that occurred is there, an episode in his car. It's dark; they can't see one another; nothing could be nicer, the Irish girl is whispering to him; she wants to be with him for ever. (136–137)

The violent pathology that underpins such excitement inevitably reasserts itself, however, convincing Hilditch that Felicia has somehow divined his hidden trauma and therefore must be prevented from spreading such ruinous knowledge. Yet her specialness continues to oppress him, embodying as she does both the primal lure and the vertiginous fear of the Other. Felicia "blur[s] what he is trying to say to himself" (150) at the same time as she provokes in him an uncontainable confessional impulse, her "innocence" (189) drawing secrets out of him. Hilditch's anguished disclosure of his former "friendships" in Chapter 19 is symptomatic of the progressive loss of control Felicia engenders in him, which is compounded by her dramatic escape from his house and by the arrival at his door of another postcolonial immigrant, Miss Calligary, an itinerant Christian evangelist from Jamaica who previously offered Felicia shelter. With consummate skill, Trevor evokes the reversal of sexual–political power relations that occurs under the aegis of these mutinous postcolonial twins, whose ungovernability moiders Hilditch into delusional insanity and suicide. Desperate "to know what was said" (181) about him, he begins to search for Felicia as desperately as she once searched for Lysaght, while at the same time trying to evade the obsessive Miss Calligary, who wishes to "gather" him in for Jesus. The reversal of power brought about by Hilditch's vision of a free, unmonitored Felicia wandering "his" territory is exacerbated by the Jamaican woman's repeated visits to his house, which transform the invigilator into the invigilated. As his paranoid derangement deepens, so too does Hilditch's invasion complex. No longer caught in his dissecting gaze, Felicia now becomes imperially male in his febrile imagination, violating his allegorically feminine borders: "One morning, having fallen into an exhausted doze soon after dawn, he awakes with the eccentric notion that the Irish girl has invaded him, as territory is invaded" (179). This arresting image recalls Anne McClintock's claim that "the erotics of imperial conquest were also an erotics of engulfment," a discursive doubling that she sees as "the simultaneous dread of catastrophic boundary *loss* (implosion) associated with fears of impotence and infantilization and attended by an *excess* of boundary order and fantasies of unlimited power."[54]

In this crisis-ridden state, memory becomes a torment rather than a balm to Hilditch. Because he cannot visualize Felicia in his "Memory Lane" (42), "merciful oblivion" (193) eludes him. Instead, he is visited by a destructive torrent of scenes from an abused childhood. The juxtaposition of the little boy's trusting innocence and the mother's callous, sexually motivated duplicity forms part of Trevor's wider solicitation of the reader's compassion for this psychopathic protagonist in the closing chapters of the novel. Hilditch is first seen sobbing like "an animal suffering beyond endurance" (151), then pausing to contemplate his own flesh and blood – site of both his common humanity and his stigmatizing trauma – when he accidentally cuts his finger on a tin of pilchards. This cut is proleptic of his final fate, after which Felicia bestows the grace of merciful understanding on him, her retroactive gesture of clemency being heightened by Trevor's masterful use of free indirect narration: "Lost within a man who murdered, there was a soul like any other soul, purity itself it surely once had been" (212). That Hilditch is not a murderer but "a man who murdered" fuses suffering with compassion, revulsion with forgiveness, and thus makes him fully our fellow human being.

And what of Felicia herself? The final chapter reveals her to be a homeless derelict, a bag lady who drifts between towns and cities, gravitating to others of her kind wherever she finds herself. Presently in London, she is drawn towards the Thames, her thoughts and memories eddying like the currents as she makes her way riverward. Trevor extracts a final piece of oblique symbolism from Felicia's geographical location by having her recall an occasion when a fellow vagrant, Tapper, marveled at London's capacity to encompass both military valor and criminal depravity, the former represented by the statue of Sir Charles James Napier in Trafalgar Square, the latter by John Reginald Christie.[55] As St. Peter points out, Christie was another serial killer of women, who was eventually arrested near where Felicia now stands and hanged for his crimes in 1953.[56] Thus, the city becomes a geographical metaphor for the chasm between fantasy and reality that Hilditch inhabited. As for Felicia, her proximity to water, with its rich range of symbolic meanings, forms an important part of Trevor's valedictory characterization of her. Seeing her sitting beside the Thames, the river and mother of life, reminds us of the watery circumstances in which we first met her, aboard a ferry on the Irish Sea, racked by morning sickness. Although Felicia's baby has long since been aborted, the novel's subtle cyclical structure hints that her journey may have regenerative dimensions. And while her enduring homelessness is not romanticized, there is much authorial tenderness in the closing portrait of Felicia as a quasi-monastic nomad who is shown to have achieved a degree of Zenlike calm and equanimity.

Trevor's deployment of free indirect discourse in the closing scenes becomes markedly more concentrated, the voice and judgment of a compassionate narrator blending with Felicia's idiom and idiolect to imbue her thoughts with a contemplative tone. The value judgments that are communicated by the amplification of this narrative mode are decidedly kind to the heroine. Alienated from her mother culture yet by no means an assimilated immigrant, there are suggestions that Felicia has evolved a "contrapuntal"[57] mindset that, in its ability to tolerate contradictions, is reminiscent of what Gloria Anzaldúa calls a *mestiza* or border consciousness. In her seminal work, *Borderlands/La Frontera* (1987), Anzaldúa uses the frontier between Texas and Mexico as a metaphor to explore the fractures of her own identity as a multilingual, polyethnic, lesbian feminist of working-class origins. Rather than repress the contradictions of her plural subjectivity or be cowed by patriarchal systems of domination, however, Anzaldúa insists on the need "to shift out of habitual formations," to move from "convergent thinking" to "divergent thinking."[58] Her objective is to work towards an inclusive "synthesis" or "third element" that *la mestiza* embodies:

> The new *mestiza* copes by developing a tolerance for contradictions, a tolerance for ambiguity. [...] She learns to juggle cultures. She has a plural personality, she operates in a pluralistic mode – nothing is thrust out, the good the bad and the ugly, nothing rejected, nothing abandoned. Not only does she sustain contradictions, she turns the ambivalence into something else.[59]

As Yvonne Yarbro-Bejarano points out, in *Borderlands*, "this new consciousness is created through writing; Anzaldúa's project is one of discursive self-formation."[60] In *Felicia's Journey*, on the other hand, the heroine's altered state is the fruit of a modest, empathetic existentialism that consists of an openness to dwelling-in-contingency, a recognition of life's fragility, and a humility before "the chance that separates the living from the dead" (213):

> She knows she is not as she was; she is not the bridesmaid at the autumn wedding, not the girl who covered herself with a rug in the back of the car. The innocence that once was hers is now, with time, a foolishness, yet it is not disowned, and that same lost person is valued for leading her to where she is. Walking through another morning, fine after a wet night, she accepts without bewilderment the serenity that possesses her, and celebrates its fresh new presence. (207)

Felicia's compassion has been enhanced rather than diluted by her close encounter with "a man who murdered girls" (209). Her serenity has its source in her almost saintlike surrendering of the illusion of human control over arbitrary fate. There is also a certain beatific quality to the "happiness in her solitude at dawn" (213) and to her letting go of the compulsion to find purpose or pattern in her journey. Appreciative of the accident of being alive, her "mourning" (209) is to try to understand the humanity of the wicked, without which we are all diminished, and to contemplate the fate of the girls who died at Hilditch's hands: "Chosen for death because no one would know when they were no longer. What trouble made victims of them?" (209). The question coils back upon Felicia's own fate, and that of her nemesis who, as a victim of lies, cruelty, and deception himself, is also her obscure doppelgänger.

As George O'Brien succinctly observes, Felicia, at the point in her journey where we leave her, has found "a space and latitude beyond the binaries of Irishness and Englishness."[61] She may even be said to have gained a measure of exilic enlightenment of the kind described by Edward Said: "The exile knows that in a secular and contingent world, homes are always provisional. Borders and barriers, which enclose us within the safety of familiar territory, can also become prisons, and are often defended beyond reason or necessity."[62] There is certainly nothing fixed about the heroine's physical, psychic, or spiritual state at the novel's end. Although she remains in England, Felicia is metaphysically beyond "home" and "nation," beyond rigid notions of territoriality, especially as embodied in inherited nationalist and imperialist discourses. Trevor's final spatial gesture, therefore, is to show Felicia's identity as one that is formed and re-formed on the move. Her sovereign status, we might say, now lies in her goalless, open-ended journey. As a permanent transient, her sense of self is experienced in and through the act of movement itself, within which space she is content to let the mysteries of life and death be.

Notes

1. Mira Stout, "The Art of Fiction CVIII: William Trevor," *Paris Review*, 110 (1989), 131.
2. Tom Adair, "An Interview with William Trevor," *Linen Hall Review*, 11:3 (Winter 1994), 8.
3. William Trevor, *Excursions in the Real World* [1993] (London: Penguin, 1994), xiii.
4. Trevor, *Excursions in the Real World*, 24–25.
5. Trevor, *Excursions in the Real World*, 23–24.
6. Amanda Smith, "*PW* Interviews William Trevor," *Publishers Weekly*, April 23, 1983, 80. *Fools of Fortune* won the 1983 Whitbread Novel Award.
7. Trevor, *Excursions in the Real World*, 41.
8. Homan Potterton, "'Suggestions of Concavity': William Trevor as Sculptor," *Irish Arts Review Yearbook*, 18 (2002), 95.
9. Potterton, "Suggestions of Concavity," 101.

10. Stout, "The Art of Fiction CVIII," 131.

11. Mike Murphy, "William Trevor," in *Reading the Future: Irish Writers in Conversation with Mike Murphy*, ed. Clíodhna Ní Anluain (Dublin: Lilliput Press, 2000), 235.

12. Bernard O'Donoghue, "Houses of Troubles: The bleak morality of William Trevor," *Times Literary Supplement*, August 30, 2002, 3.

13. Dolores MacKenna, *William Trevor: The Writer and his Work* (Dublin: New Island Books, 1999), 139.

14. See Rónán McDonald, "Without heroes: alcohol, adultery and other forms of survival in the short fiction of William Trevor," *Times Literary Supplement*, June 18, 2010, 3.

15. J. Hillis Miller, *Topographies* (Stanford: Stanford University Press, 1995), 7.

16. Colm Tóibín (ed.), *The Penguin Book of Irish Fiction* (Harmondsworth: Viking, 1999), xxxi.

17. Richard Canning, *Hear Us Out: Conversations with Gay Writers* (New York: Colombia University Press, 2003), 191.

18. O'Donoghue, "Houses of Troubles," 3.

19. Tim Adams, "William Trevor, the keen-eyed chronicler," *Observer*, February 8, 2009, 35.

20. Murphy, "William Trevor," 224.

21. McDonald, "Without heroes," 4.

22. Mary Fitzgerald-Hoyt, *William Trevor: Re-imagining Ireland* (Dublin: Liffey Press, 2003), 55–56.

23. Fitzgerald-Hoyt, *William Trevor*, 161.

24. William Trevor, *Felicia's Journey* [1994] (London: Penguin, 1995), 29. Subsequent page numbers are cited parenthetically in the text.

25. Michael Dwyer, "Atomic Power," *Irish Times*, August 21, 1999, *Weekend* section, 5.

26. Christine St. Peter, "Consuming Pleasures: *Felicia's Journey* in Fiction and Film," *Colby Quarterly*, 38:3 (September 2002), 330.

27. William Trevor, *A Writer's Ireland: Landscape in Literature* (London: Thames and Hudson, 1984), 51.

28. In addition to subverting the archetype of the tearful Irish emigrant, Trevor punctures assumptions that Felicia is travelling to Britain for an abortion. Though pregnant and unmarried, she has no thoughts of terminating her pregnancy until it is suggested to her by Hilditch in Chapter 13. This aspect of her characterization deters us from reading Felicia's plight in relation to the highly controversial "X" case of 1992, in which a fourteen-year-old Irish girl, pregnant as a result of rape, was legally prevented from leaving the country for an abortion. In an online interview Trevor explicitly denied that this episode had any influence on the novel. See interview with William Trevor, Penguin Reading Group, http://us.penguingroup.com/static/rguides/us/felicias_journey.html.

29. Derek Hand, *A History of the Irish Novel* (Cambridge: Cambridge University Press, 2011), 272.

30. The *Sean Bhean Bhocht*, which translates as "Poor Old Woman," is one of a number of female personifications of Ireland in nationalist tradition. A character named "The Poor Old Woman" is the central protagonist in W. B. Yeats's most stirring nationalist drama, *Cathleen ni Houlihan* (1902), which is set in County Mayo in August 1798, on the eve of the landing of French troops sent to support the rebellion of republican militants against British rule in Ireland. The play ends with the Poor Old Woman's miraculous transmutation into a young queen through the shedding of patriotic male blood. The fact that no such rejuvenation awaits Felicia's great-grandmother may be read as a subtle comment on the barrenness of the mythology of republican nationalism in contemporary Ireland.

31. F. S. L. Lyons, "The Meaning of Independence," in *The Irish Parliamentary Tradition*, ed. Brian Farrell (Dublin: Gill and Macmillan, 1973), 223.

32. In *Revising the Rising*, eds Theo Dorgan and Máirín Ní Dhonnchadha (Derry: Field Day, 1991), Declan Kiberd characterized the Irish government's commemoration of the seventy-fifth anniversary of the Rising as "a brief, sheepish ceremony" (1), and Seamus Deane argued that the events of 1916 had become so thoroughly revised as to be "a matter of official embarrassment" (91).

33. Linden Peach, *The Contemporary Irish Novel: Critical Readings* (Basingstoke: Palgrave Macmillan, 2004), 194.

34. This myth of the rural was itself an extension of the preindependence cultural nationalist project, which, as Kevin Whelan explains, eulogized the West of Ireland as "an idyllic prelapsarian blending of culture and environment, creating a distinctive society and landscape, which had been saved from the pernicious effects of industrialisation, urbanisation and modernisation" ("The Bases of Regionalism," in *Culture in Ireland – Regions: Identity and Power*, ed. Proinsias Ó Drisceoil (Belfast: Institute of Irish Studies, 1993), 42).

35. "Proclamation of an Irish Republic," in *On the Easter Proclamation and Other Declarations*, Liam de Paor (Dublin: Four Courts Press, 1997), 10.

36. See Stephanie McBride, *Felicia's Journey* (Cork: Cork University Press, 2006), 25, 41–42. This event, which coincided with the discovery of another newborn baby's body with multiple stab wounds on a Kerry beach, resulted in a much-criticized police investigation, which led in turn to a protracted tribunal of inquiry in 1985, in which Hayes's sexual behavior was subjected to detailed public scrutiny. For further details, see Joanne Hayes and John Barrett, *My Story* (Dingle: Brandon Press, 1985) and Nell McCafferty, *A Woman to Blame: The Kerry Babies Case* (Dublin: Attic Press, 1985).

37. Fintan O'Toole, *A Mass for Jesse James* (Dublin: Raven Arts Press, 1990), 174.

38. See Nell McCafferty, "The Death of Ann Lovett," in her *The Best of Nell: A Selection of Writings over Fourteen Years* (Dublin: Attic Press, 1984), 48–54. In

the weeks after the death of this schoolgirl and her infant baby, hundreds of women came forward to speak (often anonymously) of their hidden extramarital pregnancies in the Irish media.

39. Marc Augé, *Non-Places: Introduction to an Anthropology of Supermodernity*, trans. John Howe (London: Verso, 1995), 51.

40. Augé, *Non-Places*, 94.

41. Augé, *Non-Places*, 94.

42. Marc Augé, "Paris and the Ethnography of the Contemporary World," in *Parisian Fields*, ed. Michael Sheringham (London: Reaktion Books, 1996), 178.

43. The first Duke of Wellington was Sir Arthur Wellesley (1769–1852), British military hero and prime minister from 1828 to 1830. The fact that he was Dublin-born and Irish-raised makes him illustrative of the sometimes overlooked fact that the Irish have historically been the agents as well as the subjects of British imperialism. Wellesley himself, however, scornfully repudiated his connection with Ireland. As D.J. Hickey and J.E. Doherty point out in *A Dictionary of Irish History* (Dublin: Gill and Macmillan, 1980): "With reference to his Irish birth, he was reputed to have remarked that being born in a stable did not make one a horse" (603).

44. In her discussion of the novel, Stephanie McBride makes the insightful point that "Hilditch's little collections, fragments of his own little empire, are a version in miniature of the imperial archive and, more significantly, are his attempts to construct a unified self and identity" (*Felicia's Journey*, 32).

45. Edward Relph, *Place and Placelessness* (London: Pion, 1976), 141.

46. Paul Virilio, *The Aesthetics of Disappearance*, trans. Philip Beitchman (New York: Semiotext(e), 1991), 67.

47. See St. Peter, "Consuming Pleasures," 332 and McBride, *Felicia's Journey*, 54–59.

48. St. Peter, "Consuming Pleasures," 332.

49. I can find no textual evidence to support Linden Peach's assertion that Hilditch rapes his victims before killing them (*The Contemporary Irish Novel*, 194). On the contrary, the whole tenor of Trevor's characterization of this murderer suggests that he is so psychically damaged as to be incapable of having sexual intercourse of any kind with women.

50. Roger Bromley, *Narratives for a New Belonging: Diasporic Cultural Fictions* (Edinburgh: Edinburgh University Press, 2000), 12.

51. Derek Gregory, *Geographical Imaginations* (Oxford: Blackwell, 1994), 171.

52. McBride draws persuasive parallels between Hilditch and Norman Bates in Alfred Hitchcock's *Psycho*, arguing that their shared fear of the possessive, devouring mother lies at the heart of their identity crises and their inability to form adult relationships with women. See her *Felicia's Journey*, 5–53.

53. Later, in Chapter 18, Hilditch's sublimated memories of incest are again disturbed by a glimpse of Felicia's "inadequate nightdress" (145), which brings to mind a night-time conversation with his mother before he left her to visit a

prostitute, which in turn triggers thoughts of the curtly dismissive recruiting sergeant who "ruled out the career that all through childhood had been taken for granted" (147).

54. Anne McClintock, *Imperial Leather: Race, Gender and Sexuality in the Colonial Contest* (New York: Routledge, 1995), 24, 26, original emphasis.

55. Like his contemporary, the aforementioned Duke of Wellington, Napier's (1782–1853) status as a British imperial hero conceals the decisive role of his Irish upbringing in shaping his outlook and actions. Though London-born, Napier's family moved to Ireland in 1785, and it was there that he began his military career. Young Charles helped his father defend their estate against republican rebels during the 1798 United Irish rebellion and he was part of the government forces that put down Robert Emmet's insurrection in Dublin in 1803. Coincidentally, Napier died from a cold caught when he was a pallbearer at Wellington's funeral in August 1853. See Ainslie T. Embree, "Napier, Sir Charles James (1782–1853)," in *Oxford Dictionary of National Biography*, eds H.C.G. Matthew and Brian Harrison (Oxford: Oxford University Press, 2004), online edition, ed. Lawrence Goldman. Jan. 2008. http://www.oxforddnb.com/view/article/19748.

56. St. Peter, "Consuming Pleasures," 337.

57. Edward W. Said, "Reflections on Exile," in his *Reflections on Exile and Other Essays* (Cambridge, Massachusetts: Harvard University Press, 2000), 186.

58. Gloria Anzaldúa, *Borderlands/La Frontera: The New Mestiza* (San Francisco: Aunt Lute Books, 1987), 79.

59. Anzaldúa, *Borderlands/La Frontera*, 9.

60. Yvonne Yarbro-Bejarano, "Gloria Anzaldúa's *Borderlands/La frontera:* Cultural Studies, 'Difference' and the Non-Unitary Subject," *Cultural Critique*, 28 (Autumn 1994), 13.

61. George O'Brien, "Contemporary prose in English: 1940–2000," in *The Cambridge History of Irish Literature, Volume 2: 1890–2000*, eds Margaret Kelleher and Philip O'Leary (Cambridge: Cambridge University Press, 2006), 432–433.

62. Said, "Reflections on Exile," 185.

Chapter 6

History's Hostages:
Edna O'Brien's
House of Splendid Isolation (1994)

I

If William Trevor has just claim to the mantle of most celebrated expatriate Irish male novelist still writing, then Edna O'Brien is certainly the country's most famous female equivalent. Like Trevor, O'Brien is a product of that foreign country now known by its short-hand appellation "de Valera's Ireland," though her roots are rural and Catholic rather than small-town and Protestant. The youngest of four children, she was born in 1930 in Tuamgraney in County Clare and raised in a house called Drewsboro in "semi-grandeur,"[1] a reference to that fact that by the time of her birth, her father had squandered much of the fortune he had inherited from entrepreneurial uncles who were priests in Boston. An unhappy home life contributed to this air of calamitous dissipation. As she reminisces in her memoir, *Country Girl* (2012): "We were all lonely in that house, lonely and sometimes at loggerheads."[2] Her father's drinking and gambling were the source of much domestic discord, which caused young Edna to cleave ever more intensely to her mother. In her memoir she recalls the ferocity of her feelings for her mother, which fluctuated between adoration and hatred, and which appear to have engendered a matricentric relationship with her own embryonic creativity as a girl:

. . . .

I would go out the fields to write. The words ran away with me. I would write imaginary stories, stories set in our bog and our kitchen garden, but it was not

---

Reading the Contemporary Irish Novel 1987–2007, First Edition. Liam Harte.
© 2014 Liam Harte. Published 2014 by John Wiley & Sons, Ltd.

enough, because I wanted to get inside them, in the same way as I was trying to get back into the maw of my mother. Everything about her intrigued me: her body, her being, her pink corset, her fads and the obsessions to which she was prone.[3]

. . . .

The twin governances of nationalism and Catholicism dominated O'Brien's childhood. "It was borne in on me at a very young age," she recalls, "that I came from fierce people and that the wounds of history were very raw and vivid."[4] Christ's weeping wounds, as depicted in the Stations of the Cross, were rawer still, and "The flames of Hell seemed as real as the turf burning in the fire. Sometimes, if a sod fell out, my mother would catch it with her bare hand to test her strength for the future and possible flames of eternity."[5] Homilies against all worldly temptations punctuated her convent education in Loughrea, County Galway where, with her fellow "little recruits for heaven,"[6] she learned the habits of self-restraint and self-mortification. Yet despite such suffocations and narrow conformism, O'Brien remembers being "very blessed as a child and [having] a great inner life,"[7] and she continues to cherish her childhood sensibility as the whetstone of her work. When invited to offer an inscription for a commemorative plaque in her home town, she wrote: "Tuamgraney / Home of my home and fount of my fictions / *Ta mé bhuíoch díot.*"[8] Antipathy tempered by affection, "a richness and an unquenchable grief"[9] – O'Brien's perspective on the forces that shaped her is marked by a contradictory concentration of impulses, just as Ireland itself embodies the tugs and tensions she encounters in what she refers to as the "monastic activity"[10] of writing.

In the mid-1940s O'Brien moved to Dublin to begin a four-year apprenticeship to a pharmacist, though her deepest desire was to meet writers and "be admitted into the world of letters."[11] It was in Dublin, appropriately, that she first encountered the work of James Joyce in a slim, one-volume selection of his prose. This she carried everywhere with her, "so that I could read it at will and copy out the sentences, luminous and labyrinthine as they were."[12] Reading Joyce was a crucially inspiring experience, one that encouraged the aspiring writer to look to her own experiences and emotions for the raw materials of fiction. The Christmas dinner scene in *A Portrait of the Artist as a Young Man* became an instant exemplum:

. . . .

Up to then, I had been writing rather fancifully, with a lot of adjectives. When I read that, I realized one thing: that I need go no further than my own interior, my own experience, for whatever I wanted to write. It was truly, without sounding like St. Paul, an utter revelation to me.[13]

. . . .

This seed took time to germinate, however. In the early 1950s O'Brien first eloped with and then married a man many years her senior, the novelist Ernest Gébler, with whom she had two sons (one of whom, Carlo, is now an established novelist in his own right). She dates the beginning of her "real apprenticeship as a writer"[14] to this time, though publication lay in the future. In November 1958 the family moved to London, where O'Brien initially found work as a manuscript reader for the Hutchinson publishing house. Although her marriage proved to be short-lived (the couple separated in 1963 and an acrimonious custody battle over the children ensued), London has remained her home ever since, apart from a period spent in remote Donegal in the 1990s. But like Joyce, O'Brien didn't so much escape *from* Ireland as *with* it: its fascinations and infuriations melted into her and formed the crust of her creativity. And while she has often acknowledged the losses and loneliness that dislocation brings, physical detachment from her home culture also sharpened her understanding of its debilitating effects. In her powerful memoir-cum-cultural history, *Mother Ireland* (1976), she reflected:

The real quarrel with Ireland began to burgeon in me then; I had thought of how it had warped me, and those around me, and their parents before them, all stooped by a variety of fears – fear of church, fear of gombeenism, fear of phantoms, fear of ridicule, fear of hunger, fear of annihilation, and fear of their own deeply ingrained aggression that can only strike a blow at each other, not having the innate authority to strike at those who are higher. Pity arose too, pity for a land so often denuded, pity for a people reluctant to admit that there is anything wrong. That is why we leave. Because we beg to differ. Because we dread the psychological choke. But leaving is only conditional.[15]

Emigration was also a powerful stimulus to O'Brien's creativity. Having received an advance of £50 from Iain Hamilton at Hutchinson, she set to work on her first novel, *The Country Girls* (1960), which she said "took three weeks, or maybe less, to write. [...] It was as if I was merely a medium for the words to flow. The emotional crux hinged on Ireland, the country I had left and wanted to leave, but now grieved for, with an inexplicable sorrow."[16] This chronicle of the social and romantic adventures of Caithleen Brady and Baba Brennan, two rebellious youngsters in flight from puritan provincialism, scandalized conservative Ireland. The novel's depiction of the girls' fitful sexual awakening reportedly caused one unwary Limerick reader to have a seizure and prompted O'Brien's former parish priest to carry out a public burning of copies in Tuamgraney.[17] The local postmistress advised that a "fitting punishment" would be for the novelist "to be kicked naked through the town."[18]

Such reactions, coupled with the book's banning by the Irish Censorship Board on grounds of obscenity, transformed this unknown literary debutant into an *enfant terrible* overnight. The author herself reflected: "I offended several fashions. I offended the Catholic church. I betrayed Irish womanhood. They even used that phrase – I was a 'smear on Irish womanhood.' I betrayed my own community by writing about their world. I showed two Irish girls full of yearnings and desires. Wicked!"[19]

The moral indignation that *The Country Girls* provoked set the tone for much of the literary career that was to follow. O'Brien's name became so indelibly associated with scandal and sensationalism that readers and reviewers came to her work with primed eyes. Her next four novels – the first two of which, *The Lonely Girl* (1962) and *Girls in their Married Bliss* (1964), trace the deepening disillusionment of Kate and Baba in swinging London – confirmed her status as "a standing annoyance to the small-town Irish literary male"[20] and were duly banned for their perceived sexual explicitness, although they bolstered O'Brien's readership and reputation abroad. The author's gender and glamorous image were undoubtedly contributing factors in these developments, as they were in later patronizing dismissals of her work as being beneath serious scholarly attention.[21] That a good-looking, convent-educated product of holy Ireland could be so bold as to besmirch the country's "colleen image"[22] by graphically portraying "unhappy married life – a young girl yearning and, indeed, eventually having sex with a much older married man,"[23] tested the limits of the nation's newfound liberalism. It was as if O'Brien was, in Anne Enright's words, "the first Irish woman ever to have sex",[24] and unsatisfying sex at that, to judge from the unfulfillment of the allegorically named Mary Hooligan in *Night* (1972).

Only later did it become apparent that what made O'Brien's fiction so incendiary to conservative minds was her willingness to depart so emphatically from the accepted cultural scripts and challenge a whole spectrum of moralities and ideologies that governed national discourse in Ireland. That, and her intently human explorations of the perplexities of social and sexual relationships. O'Brien herself encapsulated the jolt her fiction delivered to complacent conventions when she observed: "Heroines don't have to be good anymore, because women are writing fiction and are eager to express the more volatile part of themselves; equally they are less beholden to men."[25] That "less" is important: none of O'Brien's women are ever fully free of patriarchal constraints. On the contrary, her female protagonists are emotionally complex creations, whose lives are a protracted and often unsuccessful struggle to reconcile their disparate needs and desires with the ideals, expectations, and restrictive gender roles available to them in society. The barriers to independence and self-realization take many and varied forms, from prescriptive myths about women's subordination to seductive romantic fantasies that deliver hollow dividends. Thus, the same women who are resilient in their pursuit of self-determination are often fatally compromised by the manipulative power of patriarchal capitalism, leaving them vulnerable to exploitation by husbands and lovers, many of whom are themselves shown to be conflicted, dysfunctional, and without love.

The relationship between Baba Brennan and Frank Durack in *Girls in their Married Bliss* epitomizes this pattern of self-destructive female dependency on selfish and self-loathing men, which is a recurring feature of O'Brien's fiction. After eighteen months in London waiting for "the Mr Right that was supposed to come along," Baba settles for a man she thinks of as "Thick. But nice, too."[26] O'Brien's unflinching depiction of the casual humiliations this young woman must privately endure starkly exposes the asymmetric power relations that the much-trumpeted sexual freedoms of the 1960s merely papered over:

· ·

An Irishman: good at battles, sieges and massacres. Bad in bed. But I expected that. It made him a hell of a sight nicer than most of the sharks I'd been out with, who expected you to pay for the pictures, raped you in the back seat, came home, ate your baked beans, and then wanted some new, experimental kind of sex and no worries from you about might you have a baby, because they liked it natural, without gear.[27]

· ·

By the time Baba reappears in the "Epilogue" to *The Country Girls Trilogy* (1987), the carnivore world of urban life has made her a feminist of sorts. Whereas Kate's trusting nature proved to be her undoing, Baba has learned to live by the motto, "Put thy trust in no man."[28] Yet neither age nor cynicism has lessened her appetite for physical pleasure. "I'd commit adultery twice a day if I could,"[29] she confesses in the course of her Molly Bloom-like internal monologue, and lustfully recalls the sex she enjoyed with a stranger during a solo holiday paid for by her husband. Yet even though she recalls telling Kate that the heart is "only a pump,"[30] her own susceptibility to romantic sentiment shows in her decision to stop off on her way to the airport to say goodbye to her holiday fling: "Pure slop. I don't know why I do things like that."[31]

O'Brien's refusal to transform such "yearning heroines"[32] into card-carrying feminists meant that much of her 1970s fiction swam against the cultural and intellectual tide. As she acknowledges in her memoir, feminist critics frequently berated her for her "supine, woebegone inclinations."[33] But the point is that O'Brien knew her fallible women (and men) too well to unburden them of all contradictions and self-sabotaging tendencies. Rather than indulge in moralistic object lessons, her deeper purpose has always been to try to understand the twisted roots of hypocrisy as well as hurt, the ambiguities of human nature, the doubleness of who we are and what we do. She has aired her aversion to polemical fiction on more than one occasion, asserting: "Fiction is not about taking a stance. Fiction is about exploring in detail the full human range of people's lives."[34] Yet by the time she spoke these words in 2000, O'Brien had published what she herself described as an "openly and overtly political" trilogy of novels about "three themes important to Ireland and to me: politics, sex, and land."[35] The first of the set, *House of Splendid Isolation*, was widely seen as marking a significant new departure for O'Brien. For the first time in her long literary career she turned to the fractious political situation in Northern Ireland, at a point where the possibility of a historic settlement was beginning to emerge. The novel explores the Northern conflict through the emotional bond that develops between two outsider figures, Josie O'Meara, the widowed chatelaine of a Big House in Munster, which is recast as a contemporary version of the ruined gothic castle, and McGreevy, a notorious Northern-born republican, who commandeers her crumbling mansion as part of his plan to assassinate a visiting English judge. *Down by the River* (1996) reports from a different battlefront, that of the so-called "abortion wars" that flared up intermittently in the Republic during the 1980s and 1990s, and violent conflict is also central to the final novel in the trilogy, *Wild Decembers* (1999), which centers on a protracted land dispute between two farmers.

In interviews, O'Brien acknowledged the distance she had travelled between early and late trilogies, explaining: "Things get more complex, more searing. The early books were more personal, accessible. Now the subjects are about the country of Ireland and it entails more rummaging around."[36] In the case of *House of Splendid Isolation*, her research included interviews with republican inmates in Portlaoise prison, including Dominic "Mad Dog" McGlinchey, the notorious leader of the Irish National Liberation Army in the 1980s. She also spoke to a Clare policeman who was responsible for shooting dead a masked gunman, presumed to be an IRA member, who tried to rob a local bank.[37] Although her research methods drew inevitable criticism from some quarters – one critic dismissively dubbed her "the Barbara Cartland of long-distance Republicanism,"[38] and she claims the playwright Hugh Leonard publicly accused her in a Dublin restaurant of "sleeping with Provos"[39] – O'Brien insisted that her intention was not to produce an apologia for paramilitary violence but rather to probe the psychology and motivation of a committed militant:

. . . .

In the case of *House of Splendid Isolation*, I wanted to write about an IRA soldier, not from perceived opinion of him, but to explore his thinking, rationale, conflict, ruthlessness vs. idealism, etc. and for this I saw many prisoners who talked to me openly. The character of McGreevy is more rounded, complex, and probably truthful than any of my former male characters.[40]

. . . .

The novel does indeed confront us with uncomfortable questions about what motivates an IRA gunman, about how cultural enmities are socially encoded and transmitted, and about the extent to which contemporary Irish society, especially in the Republic, has matured beyond tribal, nationalist sentiments. In addition, the novel offers a salutary warning against precipitously consigning the Troubles to history's skip and presuming that historic handshakes between political adversaries will magically transform Northern Ireland into a harmonious, non-sectarian statelet. Yet there are also aspects of O'Brien's narrative style, characterization, and overall orchestration of the story that present formidable interpretive challenges and raise troubling questions that are as much to do with narrative ethics as aesthetics. Two particular strategies will concern us here: the novel's tragic perspectivism, which best expresses itself in the oracular, chorus-like narrative voice, and O'Brien's extended use of free indirect style to render her protagonists' unspoken thoughts and feelings. Working in tandem, these structuring devices are central to the novel's powerful impact and have a decisive bearing on the reader's interpretive and affective responses to its paramilitary protagonist. But while these stylistic techniques are meant to enlarge the reader's ability to see this insurgent from multiple perspectives, including his own subjective point of view, they seem to me to complicate and ultimately frustrate O'Brien's arduous and hazardous objective of exploring McGreevy's complex humanity. In what follows, I want to tease out some of the reasons why I think this is so, starting with the novel's short elegiac opening chapter.

II

House of Splendid Isolation begins with a brief incantatory prologue spoken by a nameless child, revealed subsequently to be Josie O'Meara's aborted baby, who returns to narrate the novel's equally synoptic epilogue. This structural use of a ghost-child immediately alerts us to the fact that we are entering the haunt of unquiet revenants, the realm of the contemporary gothic, where primal forces proliferate. This impression is confirmed by the view of history outlined in the prologue's opening sentences, which are set off from the rest of the text like an epigraph: "History is everywhere. It seeps into the soil, the sub-soil. Like rain, or hail, or snow, or blood. A house remembers. An outhouse remembers. A people ruminate. The tale differs with the teller."[41] This emotionally intense evocation of a people and society trapped within a continuous past, in thrall to a monolithic history that is as durable as a force of nature, establishes a mood of tragic fatalism that colors everything that follows, not only in this novel but in the trilogy as a whole. The ruminative gothic note struck in these lines reverberates through the rest of the prologue, which, through its allusions to the dead who "do not die" (3), the generations of young men blinded by patriotic devotion, and a prophesied apocalyptic showdown between sectarian armies, solemnly elaborates a sense of "history written according to a certain logic: a logic of the phantom, the revenant, a logic of haunting."[42] Here, then, is a conception of history as a pathological condition and a portrait of the nation as an ever-filling charnel house – the very antithesis of that found in the revisionist fiction of Colm Tóibín, for example. Although the spectral narrator might pray for an end to bloodshed, the prologue's vista of recursive violence in a vendetta-stricken land, coupled with the novel's circular form, suggest that history's grasp is ineluctable. This is a lesson not to be forgotten as we proceed.

This fatalistic, folkloric opening section bears the distinct impress of a brand of historical interpretation that professional historians of Ireland have striven to debunk for decades: an oversimplified, mythological view of the past, which is seen as being inherently generative of the tradition of physical-force nationalism that stretches back to the Fenians. Indeed, the prologue's pronounced accent on the negation of progressive change makes the ghost narrator sound as if he or she is channeling the mythic rhetoric of cyclical, sacrificial renewal that has sustained this tradition since its inception. This doom-laden note is further amplified by the inference that ethnicity is destiny in this benighted land. An entire population seems to be frozen in a state of intellectual disablement, permanently at the mercy of "something fateful that is to be" (201). The author's persistent use of the passive tense embeds this sense of fatedness into the novel's style. As Hermione Lee notes in her instructive review of the novel: "One particular mannerism, of turning verbs and adjectives into nouns – meant perhaps to sound vaguely Irish – makes everything feel passive and inert. [...] No one sets his or her jaw or feels feckless, everyone endures the condition of jaw-setness or fecklessness."[43] Josie herself feels the icy touch of this predeterminism when she recalls the circumstances of her husband's violent death: "History holding them ransom, when it should all be put to rest in the annals. [...] Yes, the dark threads of history looping back and forth and catching her and people like her in their grip, like snares" (53–54). Such syntax mocks the idea that the individual has any control over "history" or any say over their destiny. And it is not only the present that is controlled by the spectral legacy of the blood-bespattered past: the lines of demarcation between ancient history and present-day politics are also blurred. The narrator's rehearsal of dark instinctual passions and marmoreal enmities leaves no room for choice or agency. There is no sense that a liberating future might be fashioned from a selective use of the past, nor is there any hope that generationally nurtured hatreds might be amenable to rational resolution.[44] This, then, is the mood music that prepares us for the arrival on the scene of the latest son of this strife-torn soil to be taken "hostage" by history, McGreevy, a man with "war in his heart" (7).

O'Brien's paramilitary protagonist exudes an enigmatic, mythic aura from the moment of his introduction, when he is shown dramatically escaping police custody in Northern Ireland and stealthily heading across the border into the Republic. He is pointedly framed as both alive and dead during this scene, "scarcely breathing, curled up inside the hollow of a tree once struck by lightening; cradle and coffin, foetus and corpse" (7). McGreevy's betwixt-and-between characterization here is not only another hallmark of his gothic affiliation. It also identifies him as a living ghost and carrier of the unvanquishable spirit of Irish revolutionary republicanism, which is figuratively as well as literally "on the run" in the Republic. This protean quality is again on show in the scene where McGreevy is seen hiding in a farmyard barn. At first he is likened to Jesus, then to a creature made of rain, and finally to a cow.[45] Meanwhile, we have heard Rory Purcell, the policeman who is tasked with McGreevy's capture, think of him as a pimpernel, his daughter imagine him as a spaceman, and his young son compare him to the mythological Celtic hero Cúchulainn, around whom Patrick Pearse wove a mythology that combined revolutionary nationalism with Christian martyrdom.

These early intimations of McGreevy's elusive, polymorphous character are the prelude to O'Brien's portrayal of him as a culturally incendiary figure who excites starkly divergent emotions in the wider populace. Throughout the novel, we are presented with a kaleidoscopic array of perspectives on this ungraspably chameleonic fugitive and what he represents, such that he comes to resemble a kind of cultural hologram whose meaning and significance lie in the mind of the beholder. Although there are some, such as the young IRA sympathizer Creena Burke, who harbor Heathcliffean fantasies about McGreevy, the commonest public reaction to him is one of fear and revulsion. The press cast him as a dangerous criminal and he is variously denounced by local people as a "murderer" (16), a "maniac" (69), an "Out and out savage," and "a pervert to boot" (151). By contrast, several policemen waver between degrees of admiration and loathing, with some even seeing McGreevy as a reincarnation of a 1916 insurgent. Not so the professional classes. Josie's reflections on what her GP, Dr D'Arcy, would think of this Northern escapee encapsulates the antipathy of the

Southern middle classes as a whole toward militant republicans and what they stand for in the contemporary era:

....

For her visitor he would have no time. Like most people he called them thugs, sickos, and said if the country were to be united in the morning he and his kind would be criminals out of a job. [...]

'Psychopaths' he had called them. Well there was one in her kitchen, her spick and span kitchen which he had cleaned. Delft and jugs that he had washed were on the draining board and the windows had miniature rainbows in them where he had shone them (96).

....

Even though it stretches the reader's credulity, this vignette of a highly domesticated, even feminized, terrorist making himself at home in the house he has commandeered is clearly intended to counterbalance McGreevy's pervasive demonization by various others and foreground Josie's growing sympathy for him, an emotion which the novel controversially suggests is as culturally symptomatic as Dr D'Arcy's antipathy. The aforementioned passage, indeed, marks an important milestone in the humanization of this unreconstructed extremist, whose precise paramilitary affiliation is never actually disclosed. The more Josie interacts with McGreevy, the more inclined she becomes to empathize with the man behind the balaclava, and the greater her sense of emotional vacillation. After the initial shock and fear of being taken hostage, Josie tries to reason with McGreevy and posit, in a stereotypically gendered fashion, the life-giving qualities of the feminine maternal against his death-dealing masculinism.[46] At this stage, her view that McGreevy is fuelled by misconceived political beliefs outweighs her burgeoning admiration for his personal qualities. But a more profound process is also set in train by their forced cohabitation and by Josie's deepening sense of being under a death sentence.

Gradually, there wells up in this dowager a desire for "wholeness" (79) that has been dulled by years of subordination to her brutish late husband, James O'Meara, whose maltreatment of her is recapitulated at length in flashback chapters. The fact that this desire echoes McGreevy's dream of reuniting Ireland establishes a strange reciprocity between hostage and captor that plays itself out as a Mills & Boon–like romance, with distinct polemical and allegorical overtones. At times, this hostage situation resembles a seminar in which a suffering North seeks to educate an indifferent South. Thus, Josie's dawning awareness of the damage done to natural affinities by the partition of Ireland – "The saddest bit is that we're the same stock, the same faith, we speak the same tongue and yet we don't" (87) – is quickened by McGreevy's complaint about the Free State's abandonment of the Catholic minority within a new, militantly Protestant Northern statelet after 1922: "'The South forgot us,' he said. Forlorn. Aggrieved. A likeness to those children in fable banished, exiled in lakes for hundreds of years, cut off from the homeland" (99). Elsewhere in the text, O'Brien indulges her Yeatsian side, framing Josie as a latter-day Cathleen ni Houlihan in the scene in which she dreams of McGreevy piercing her ear and drawing blood, all the while reassuring her that it is "for the nicest possible reason" (99).[47] This motif of blood sacrifice later resurfaces when McGreevy tells Josie that he would like to have children "when the fight was over and the country one" (195). The description of her ostentatious inner response – "a great lunatic fork of longing rose up in her, to be young again, to have wains" (195) – recasts her as a version of the Celtic goddess of sovereignty, a *puella senilis* who will be restored to fertility only when young men willingly shed their blood for her.

And so this curious couple act out a halting minuet, she eliciting intimate confessions from him, he reawakening the dormant Fenian in her. Following some tense exchanges about the prevailing political situation in the North, Josie resurrects a fragment of a diary that belonged to her republican uncle, who was shot dead by the Black and Tans in 1921. She shows this to McGreevy, ostensibly to persuade him that she and he are "on the same side" (85), yet her internal monologue reveals that this is more than a ploy. The diary reanimates feelings of nationalist grievance and injustice that Josie felt as a young woman and that are "still there like spores, lurking" (85), despite the fact that she had once bitterly protested against her husband's decision to allow their land to be used for an IRA arms dump. Such apparently contradictory behavior would seem to imply that for Josie, emotions steer allegiances: the personal ultimately determines the political. Although still vacillating between terror and defiance, this lonely widow becomes ever more mesmerized by McGreevy's inner power and his unyielding commitment to his political principles, her empathy deepened by the knowledge that he is still mourning the murder of his wife and daughter by a loyalist killer gang. Josie's diary entries chart the mental turmoil caused by the tension between her distaste for this driven outlaw's murderous deeds and her slow bewitchment by his impenetrable poise, primal energy, and dark romanticism, which eventually wins out.[48] On cue, O'Brien ratchets up the hyperbolic language and emotive imagery. Despite repeated reminders of his ruthlessness and the knowledge that he has killed in cold blood, we see Josie falling for McGreevy like a lover, even gifting him a cherished fishing bait of her late husband's: "Everything happens then, his eyes grateful and shy, like magnets brushed with gold, and something soft and yielding in her bearing as if drenched in moonlight" (92–93). When he too is shown struggling to compose himself, McGreevy's transformation into a charismatic killer with a compassionate heart is almost complete.

161

Unlike the republican martyrs memorialized in Yeats's "Easter 1916," O'Brien makes clear that too long a sacrifice has *not* made a stone of this fanatic's heart. Hardened on the "anvil of circumstances" (75) he may be, but there is a softness beneath the steel that is calculated to prevent us from seeing him as an unalloyed monster. And as so often in O'Brien, love of the mother is adduced as the ultimate touchstone of humanity and goodness, though never more problematically than here.[49] This feature comes most fully into view when, just before the climactic police ambush, Josie, who long ago refused motherhood when she terminated her only pregnancy, convinces herself that she has seen "the secret source" (193) of McGreevy when he implies that his deepest love is reserved for the woman who bore him. Even though she goes on to reprove him again for his misguided political beliefs, Josie's awestruck response to this killer's hesitant allusion to his mother strikes a decidedly mawkish note that induces feelings of moral queasiness, at least in this reader.

In fashioning such provocative scenarios to humanize her central protagonist and solicit the reader's sympathy and understanding for him, O'Brien treads a very fine line between tragic realism, mythic fantasy, and special pleading; and her footing becomes more treacherous still as she adds layer upon layer to McGreevy's purist political outlook and motivation. This is largely because of the peculiar tone and effects of free indirect style, the mode of narration O'Brien uses to evoke McGreevy's point of view. As we have already seen in our discussion of the Barrytown trilogy in Chapter 1, free indirect style is a complex and subtle method of rendering a character's unvoiced thoughts from their own perspective and in their distinctive idiom, while remaining within a framework of third-person narration. It is a style that typically results in a fluid narrative voice – some theorists speak of a dual-voice effect – that moves in and out of characters' consciousness, allowing the reader freer access to their mental processes and what Bakhtin calls "inner speech."[50] Yet free indirect style can also create narrative ambiguity, not only because the dividing line between the narrator's perspective and that of a given character is blurred but also because this narrative mode allows for the infusion of subtle shades of sympathy or irony into the narrator's voice, which require careful decoding. The effects of this complex merging of voices and viewpoints can be seductive and unsettling in equal measure. Seductive, because free indirect style can significantly enhance the narrator's sympathetic identification with a character, which may in turn influence the reader's emotional involvement with, and moral attitude toward, that character; unsettling, because this style often destabilizes the reader's sense of narrative "truth" by making it difficult to distinguish the narrator's opinion and identify the source of statements and value judgments, especially when the latter are implicit rather than explicit. As H. Porter Abbott notes:

....

When the narrative voice is so free and fluid, it makes you wonder about the
status of the narrator and whether one can even speak of *a* narrator in the case
of free indirect style. Also, because it is so fluid, free indirect style can at times
present quite a challenge for interpreters who are trying hard to locate a unified
sensibility on which to base their interpretation.[51]

....

The challenge Abbott identifies here is palpably present in *House of Splendid
Isolation*, where any interpretation of narrative perspective and its influence on
characterization must wrestle with the tantalizingly elusive effects of O'Brien's
use of free indirect style. Consider, for example, this passage in which we are
afforded an insight into McGreevy's state of mind shortly after his escape from
police custody:

....

He scrapes the muck off with an end of a spade, drinks water from a pan that
he found under a barrel, brackenish and tasting of galvanise and then he lies
down. His hunger has gone. If they come and find him that's it. But they won't
break him. They know they won't. They know that. Jumpy lads, all lip, giving
statements, one statement and then another and another. Can't take the heat. He
can take anything, heat, cold, even the electric wires flaring his inner temples. The
certainty runs deep. It has to. It's all he has left. (13)

....

The passage begins in a straightforward third-person narrative voice, but then,
beginning with the sentence "But they won't break him," the narrator modu-
lates her voice to imitate McGreevy's silent contempt for his pursuers and his
corresponding faith in his supreme powers of resistance. This imitative narration, which obscures the origin of utterances and makes the attribution of
authority uncertain, becomes more complex in the final four sentences, as the
narrator mimics McGreevy's speaking style and effectively adopts his perspective to create the impression of unmediated access to his thought processes.
This results in what Dorrit Cohn calls "stylistic contagion," whereby "a reporting syntax is maintained, but where the idiom is strongly affected (or infected)
with the mental idiom of the mind it renders."[52] The effects of such intimate
ventriloquism are multivalent. By bringing narrator and protagonist into such
close empathetic alignment, it obscures attitudinal differences between them
and makes it difficult to determine where McGreevy's perspective begins and
the narrator's ends. At the same time, this narrative style forcefully draws us into
this gunman's mental universe and effectively implicates us in his emotional and
psychological predicament – all the more so because O'Brien has her narrator

163

speak in the same tense as her protagonist rather than switching to the past or conditional tense, as is the norm in free indirect style. Furthermore, at an intuitive level, the narrator's continual empathetic appropriation of McGreevy's voice, vocabulary, and idiom carries with it a certain affirmatory force that, to my ear at least, has the effect of amplifying the sense of certainty and superiority that informs his perspective.

In such passages, and there are many in the novel, it does sound as if the narrator is doing more than merely tuning into the thoughts of this hardened paramilitary so that we might better understand him. One senses that she is tacitly taking his side and subtly inviting the reader to empathize with him at a human, if not a political, level. The fact that such scenes pass without qualifying comment from the narrator reinforces the impression that she is more inclined to endorse than critique McGreevy's insurgent politics, even though she never openly solicits our pity or approval for them. Vituperative condemnation of McGreevy's terrorism is expressed by others but never by the narrator, who scrupulously avoids overt moral evaluation of his deadly deeds. Moreover, in marked contrast to other modern Irish novels that probe paramilitary mindsets – Benedict Kiely's *Proxopera* (1977), for example, or Bernard MacLaverty's *Cal* – *House of Splendid Isolation* puts no ironic distance between narrator and central protagonist, hence the verdict of one critic that what we have here is the "most sympathetic treatment of an IRA character in women's fiction."[53]

Politically partisan writing is nothing new in Irish literature, of course, nor is it sufficient grounds on which to denigrate or dismiss a work, unless we wish to reinstate the regime of state censorship that O'Brien herself fell foul of as a debut novelist. What concern me more are the ramifications of the author's decision to eschew moral or ironic scrutiny of McGreevy's political outlook and activism in the course of her sustained humanization of him. What we are left with, it seems to me, is a portrait of a modern-day republican that is so denuded of nuance and complexity that it smacks of implausibility, anachronism, and one-dimensionalism.

Let us take, as an example, the scene in the "Captivity" chapter where McGreevy writes a note to Josie in which he reminds her of the social and political inequities that first led him to take the path of violence:

· ·

Not to grow up in hate, not to have been Papist leper scum, not to have been interned at fourteen and fifteen and sixteen, not to have been in the Crum and Long Kesh and waiting to go on the blocks, now that would have been out of this world. To be an ordinary bloke with a wife and kids – I just can't imagine it. (113)

· ·

Now, these lines present a compelling snapshot of the systematic discrimination and harassment that many working-class Northern Catholics had to endure during the darkest days of unionist rule and the early years of the Troubles.[54] What jars is their overreliance upon a reactive cause-and-effect model of paramilitary activism from which the role of human choice and agency is excluded. As O'Brien presents it, the coercive, determinative power of socio-historical circumstance is as irresistible as the brooding sense of fatalism and helplessness that perpetually stalks the land, a point underlined in the subsequent scene in which McGreevy fleetingly considers his predicament prior to his eventual arrest:

> If he quit and ran now, what would he do, what was there – nothing else, nothing else. His life was graphed by others and his deeds punished or rewarded by others, but that was not why he did it, it was his oath to himself, made long ago, drunk at the breast. (164)

These are the ventriloquized thoughts of a man who is subject to, rather than the subject of, his history, a man who is not an actor in his own right but driven by mythic forces beyond his understanding and control. His destiny having been scripted in advance by nameless others, McGreevy's only task is to act his part. By representing him – and history – in such stock, starkly monolithic terms, nuance and complexity leach away to leave little more than a passive automaton caught in the undertow of irresistible agencies.

What is also conspicuously absent from this depiction of a committed republican is any sense of McGreevy having wrestled with the morality of his actions, let alone their political efficacy – an ironic omission in a text that purports to offer a rounded, multidimensional portrait of the contemporary IRA mind. Without this ingredient, McGreevy is reduced to a time-warped extremist of the crude "Brits Out" variety, one whose platitudinous talk belongs to an earlier era. With every uncompromising political utterance he seems more parrotlike and more out of sync with the times. For example, when challenged by Josie to state his organisation's purpose he replies, in knee-jerk fashion, "'To get the British out of Ireland,'" the achievement of which will, in some unspecified way, bring about "'Justice for all. Peace. Personal identity. Racial identity'" (77). Tellingly, he does not address the small matter of if and how the million-strong Protestant unionist majority in the North might feature in this fantasy utopia, let alone the sizeable Catholic minority, which polls indicate wish to remain part of the United Kingdom. Instead, the shifting social and political realities of Northern Ireland and the complexities of its contested sovereignty are simplified into a zero-sum struggle from which all gray areas have been silently airbrushed.

The novel's failure to address such blind spots and archaic delusions is compounded when McGreevy's aggressive irredentism is allowed to go unchallenged by both Josie and the narrator, the latter maintaining a studious silence whenever the gunman expounds his dogmatic, messianic views. At key junctures such as this, O'Brien falls well short of illuminating the intricacies of the IRA's political and tactical thinking in the late 1980s and 1990s, at which time inherited pieties were rapidly being jettisoned by the Northern republican leadership en route to Sinn Féin's signing up to the 1998 Belfast Agreement and subsequently taking office in a devolved power-sharing government, thus acknowledging that the problems of the province can only be resolved through political dialogue. As Candice Rodd points out in her review of the novel, the Ireland of *House of Splendid Isolation* "is not a country where, McGreevy notwithstanding, you could ever imagine Gerry Adams, deadly-eyed and deadly serious in camera-conscious tailoring, ever seeming relevant."[55]

Nor do the novel's implausibilities end there. Having romanticized McGreevy to the point where he is "decorousness itself" (99), Josie's mood and outlook change dramatically following a visit from a neighbor who recites this paramilitary's murderous history. In a discordant plot lurch designed to reinstate the push–pull dynamic of attraction and revulsion within Josie, the widow is shown turning on her captor, calling him and his "lot" "maggots" (110) and deriding his homilies about truth and justice. Not only does she now sense "Something wiped out in his nature" (113), Josie also actively wishes to blot out "his presence and what he stood for" (115).[56] Although McGreevy is visibly unsettled by Josie's outburst, it is in fact she who falls apart after she discovers that he has absconded. Improbably, rather than make good her escape, Josie proceeds to search frantically for her captor in the mist and fog of "a timeless, placeless, featureless world" (115). McGreevy's mysterious magnetism appears to have bred in her a peculiarly Irish version of Stockholm syndrome, such that by the time the police come to search her house we hear that "Nothing would make her betray him now" (153). Revealingly, the precise reasons for such implacable loyalty are beyond her understanding; Josie simply cannot explain to herself or others why she is acting this way: "How many would understand why she had hidden McGreevy, how many would do it themselves and like her not know why" (151). The mesmeric force of "history," it seems, has compromised rational thought and action yet again, and not only within the addled consciousness of a smitten old widow, as the closing section of the novel shows.

Arguably, the most hard-to-credit aspect of O'Brien's portrayal of attitudes toward militant republicanism in 1990s Ireland is her depiction of a police force in which members' statutory duty to uphold the civil law is compromised by the siren call of martyred voices from the mythicized past and a residual, sentimental sympathy for present-day paramilitaries, who are seen as the heirs to a glorious revolutionary tradition. However plausible Rory Purcell's expression of admiration for McGreevy's audacious escape from custody – "Even in his outrage he gave the fella credit and said 'That's my boy, McGreevy, that's my baby'" (11) – the response of his colleagues to the shooting dead of one of the fugitive's paramilitary accomplices in a police ambush stretches credulity. While they await the arrival of a priest and ambulance, two nervous gardaí inexplicably succumb to dark, atavistic feelings. Ned suddenly breaks into a ballad about the death of Michael Collins, which prompts Tommy to intone over the body of the dead gunman:

. . . .

'Half of you hopes you got him and the other half hopes you didn't,' and then he puts the jacket back and the slow sad guttural drops in the aftermath of rain fall onto it, like softly tempered, funeral gongs.
    'I know . . . I'd be the same . . . We're all Irish under the skin,' Ned says, quiet. (177)

. . . .

Such piously deluded talk suggests that beneath the veneer of civilized outrage there exists a deep-rooted tribalist dynamic in Irish culture that is unsusceptible to argument and which determines the thoughts and actions of all Irish people, who are presumed to sympathize with the ideology of militant republicanism. Variations on this totalizing theme come thick and fast in the closing pages of the novel, as O'Brien's melodramatic narration rises to its highest pitch. We witness the private torment of one Sergeant Cleary, the only garda present who has shot and killed a subversive, and who managed "to black it out" (197) until the strains of a rebel ballad suddenly unmanned him. "The songs get to one" (198), we are solemnly informed by a narrative voice of indeterminate provenance. Another garda, Cormac, tells his partner Matt that "'if you'd been in 1916 you'd be on their side'" (187), which provokes the latter to put the case for the prosecution: "'That's different . . . that's a totally different ball game . . . These guys are without conscience, without ideals and with only one proclamation, money and guns and murder, guns and money'" (187). However, when weighed against the "Bits of history, bits of folklore" (197) that pepper the conversations of his colleagues, this unequivocal denunciation of IRA violence sounds like a marginal, if not downright aberrant, viewpoint among the rank and file of the Republic's police force.

In all of this, one struggles to reconcile O'Brien's maudlin, misty-eyed police-men with the professionally trained men and women who patrol the streets of the modern nation. Rodd astutely notes the absence of specialist counterterrorist officers from the scene of McGreevy's capture, "not for any very plausible reason, but because the sentimental landscape of the novel could not take the strain of too much modernity."[57] Instead, we are treated to even greater levels of sentimental narration as O'Brien's mythologizing impulse pushes the novel's climactic events toward the interface of the historical and the visionary. This makes for a heady brew, so much so that events seem to be played out in the borrowed (twi)light of the Celtic revival. The mythic and fated nature of what we are about to witness is signalled when a police van hits and injures a young doe, which is subsequently put down by a garda. But this is no ordinary deer: its blood is imagined as "life-giving" (200), an adjective that again recalls the spiritually charged rhetoric of Pearse, who explicitly linked Christ's sacrificial death to the need for a sacred blood sacrifice on behalf of Ireland. These quasi-religious resonances are heightened by the sight of McGreevy being anointed by the meltwater dripping from the trees and by the mysterious bird that swoops down to sip the blood on Josie's mortally wounded body, an image that returns us to the heroic figure of Cúchulainn, whose death, according to legend, was confirmed when a raven alighted upon him.[58] The reference to Josie's corpse having "a stilled twitch around the mouth, suggesting an unfinished utterance" (208), resuscitates her as a nationalist emblem by obliquely associating this slain widow with the motif of incompletion within the epistemology of the Provisional republican movement, for which the ultimate achievement of a united Ireland is still pending. Although this sacral mood is briefly pierced by the suggestion that Josie died for "feck all" (208), McGreevy is shielded from such cynicism, as he is from the jubilant mockery of his captors, by "the blind impervious aura of a martyr" (211) that surrounds him. Enclosed within "a thin nimbus of rain" (209), he exudes "the cold unswerving conviction of a Messiah" (211), a description that aligns his fate with the nationalist myth of sacrificial renewal, thus implying that the "salvation" of "the land that he was pledged to since birth" (207) may yet be the offspring of his terrorism.

The ghostly voice of the epilogue reiterates the plea of the prologue, empha-sizing that death can never be a midwife to life. Rather, the perpetrator must be made to feel the victim's pain: "When we take life we cry out in one voice but when we lose it we cry out in another. Two chords that must meet" (215). The evidence suggests that the likelihood of reconciliation is remote, however. The very fact that this message is uttered by an aborted child underlines its self-cancelling nature. The prospect of an end to the cyclical patterns of vio-lence is therefore deferred as, in place of closure, the undead narrator offers us a prescription for future change: "To go right into the heart of the hate and the wrong and to sup from it and be supped. It does not say that in the books. That is the future knowledge. The knowledge that is to be" (216).

Whatever hope may be gleaned from the narrator's departure from the received script of history, it is more than offset by the herculean nature of the task outlined in these final sentences of the novel. Furthermore, this bold prescription recalls optimistic but self-deluding predictions of an end to violent conflict in Ireland from the recent and distant past, two of which are sewn into the narrative in the form of epigraphs. The first is taken from a letter of 1606 by Sir John Davies, an influential colonial administrator in early seventeenth-century Ireland and author of *A Discovery of the True Causes Why Ireland was Never Entirely Subdued until the Beginning of His Majesty's Reign* (1612). Davies's sanguine assertion that "his Majesty's blessed genius will banish all those generations of vipers" from Ireland is echoed by the second epigraph, which comes from a speech by the British premier, David Lloyd George, in November 1920, in which he expressed satisfaction at the counterinsurgency activities in Ireland of the notorious Black and Tans, at a time when the War of Independence was about to enter its bloodiest phase. "Unless I am mistaken," Lloyd George told his audience, "by the steps we have taken we have murder by the throat." Both declarations are indicative of British politicians' perennial presumption to know the "solution" to the Irish "problem," and both were shown by subsequent events to be hopelessly misguided. There is little in *House of Splendid Isolation* to suggest that the recommendations of a native voice from beyond the grave will fare any better. In the land of the unappeasable past, social healing remains a chimera.

Notes

1. Edna O'Brien, *Country Girl* (London: Faber and Faber, 2012), 61.
2. O'Brien, *Country Girl*, 324.
3. O'Brien, *Country Girl*, 61. Later in her memoir, O'Brien revisits her mother's premarital life in New York, where she worked as a cutter in the tailor room of a department store, and reveals that she still keeps her mother's rusted scissors in a drawer, "a prized possession, as if between us there is still something to be cut" (253).
4. O'Brien, *Country Girl*, 29.
5. O'Brien, *Country Girl*, 53.
6. O'Brien, *Country Girl*, 62.
7. Edna O'Brien, *Mother Ireland* [1976] (London: Penguin, 1978), 143.
8. Eileen Battersby, "Mother Ireland," *Irish Times Magazine*, September 16, 2006, 18. "Ta mé bhuíoch díot" translates as "I am grateful to you."
9. O'Brien, *Mother Ireland*, 88.
10. Nicholas Wroe, "Country matters," *Guardian*, October 2, 1999, review section, 6.
11. O'Brien, *Country Girl*, 82.

12. O'Brien, *Country Girl*, 96.

13. Interview with Edna O'Brien, *Salon Magazine*, December 2, 1995.

14. O'Brien, *Country Girl*, 117.

15. O'Brien, *Mother Ireland*, 87.

16. John Mullan, "Guardian book club," *Guardian*, April 19, 2008, review section, 7.

17. Rachel Cooke, "The first lady of Irish fiction," *Observer*, February 6, 2011, 13.

18. O'Brien, *Country Girl*, 141.

19. Julia Carlson (ed.), *Banned in Ireland: Censorship and the Irish Writer* (London: Routledge, 1990), 76. This did not mean that her work went unread in Ireland. At a public meeting in Limerick in 1966, O'Brien asked how many in the audience had read her banned books. A forest of hands went up, amid much laughter. See Sean McMahon, "A Sex by Themselves: An Interim Report on the Novels of Edna O'Brien," *Éire-Ireland*, 2:1 (1967), 80.

20. Anne Enright, "Fabulous and infuriating," *Guardian*, October 13, 2012, review section, 6.

21. See Rebecca Pelan, "Reflections on a Connemara Dietrich," in *Edna O'Brien: New Critical Perspectives*, eds Kathryn Laing, Sinéad Mooney, and Maureen O'Connor (Dublin: Carysfort Press, 2006), 12–37. In *Country Girl* O'Brien recalls how, after her marriage failed, her husband's jealousy of her talent led to a nakedly misogynistic article by the novelist John Broderick, who, "in a journal called *Hibernia*, quoting my husband's exact words, [. . .] said that my 'talent resided in my knickers'" (168).

22. Carlson, *Banned in Ireland*, 73.

23. Carlson, *Banned in Ireland*, 71.

24. Anne Enright, "Murderous loves," *Guardian*, October 14, 2006, review section, 16.

25. Edna O'Brien, "Why Irish Heroines Don't Have to be Good Anymore," *New York Times Book Review*, May 11, 1986, 13.

26. Edna O'Brien, *Girls in their Married Bliss* [1964] in *The Country Girls Trilogy* [1987] (London: Penguin, 1988), 383.

27. O'Brien, *Girls in their Married Bliss*, 384.

28. O'Brien, *The Country Girls Trilogy*, 531.

29. O'Brien, *The Country Girls Trilogy*, 525.

30. O'Brien, *The Country Girls Trilogy*, 530.

31. O'Brien, *The Country Girls Trilogy*, 523.

32. O'Brien, *Country Girl*, 252.

33. O'Brien, *Country Girl*, 204.

34. Mike Murphy, "Edna O'Brien," in *Reading the Future: Irish Writers in Conversation with Mike Murphy*, ed. Clíodhna Ní Anluain (Dublin: Lilliput Press, 2000), 212.

35. Helen Thompson, "Edna O'Brien," in *Irish Women Writers Speak Out*, eds Catriona Moloney and Helen Thompson (Syracuse: Syracuse University Press, 2003), 200.

36. Wroe, "Country matters," 6.

37. O'Brien, *Country Girl*, 244. O'Brien reveals that her conversation with this policeman inspired the opening lines of *House of Splendid Isolation*, and one of the remarks she attributes to him in her memoir ("we're all Irish under the skin") is spoken by a garda named Ned in the novel.

38. Edward Pearce, "Words with no wisdom," *Guardian*, July 12, 1994, review section, 18. Cited in Amanda Greenwood, *Edna O'Brien* (Tavistock: Northcote House, 2003), 2 and by O'Brien herself in *Country Girl*, 249.

39. O'Brien, *Country Girl*, 236.

40. Quoted in Sophia Hillan King, "On the Side of Life: Edna O'Brien's Trilogy of Contemporary Ireland," *New Hibernia Review*, 4:2 (2000), 55.

41. Edna O'Brien, *House of Splendid Isolation* [1994] (London: Phoenix, 1995), 3. Subsequent page numbers are cited parenthetically in the text.

42. David Punter and Glennis Byron, *The Gothic* (Oxford: Blackwell, 2004), 55.

43. Hermione Lee, "The Terror and the Pity," *The New Republic*, June 13, 1994, 53.

44. The novel's evocation of a culture steeped in cyclical, atavistic violence recalls earlier renditions of this theme, such as that found in section XVI of Louis MacNeice's *Autumn Journal* (1939) – "And each one in his will / Binds his heirs to continuance of hatred" – and in Seamus Heaney's "bog poems" of the 1970s, which were controversially criticized for giving the reprehensible impression that the suffering of victims of IRA violence in Northern Ireland is somehow normal and understandable when viewed through a mythic lens.

45. When McGreevy subsequently helps a cow to calf, he cannot help but hear in her cries "the moans of the cows and cattle of ancient times, for which land and fiefdoms were fought over" (14), an allegorical allusion that calls to mind O'Brien's statement at the beginning of *Mother Ireland* that "Ireland has always been a woman, a womb, a cave, a cow, a Rosaleen, a sow, a bride, a harlot, and, of course, the gaunt Hag of Beare" (11).

46. In this, Josie is following the example of the wife of a farmer who discovers McGreevy hiding in their barn, and who asks her pro-IRA husband and McGreevy "to think for an instant on the killing instinct of man as opposed to the child-bearing instinct of womankind" (17). The irony, of course, is that Josie lives with the secret knowledge that she too has taken an incipient life, that of her unborn baby.

47. There are clear overtones here of Pearse's impassioned sentiments in his 1913 article, "The Coming Revolution," which include his famous assertion that "bloodshed is a cleansing and a sanctifying thing, and the nation which regards it as the final horror has lost its manhood." For the full text of this article, see

The Field Day Anthology of Irish Writing, vol. 2, ed. Seamus Deane (Derry: Field Day, 1991), 556–558.

48. There is a faint echo here of Rose Brady's attraction to the outlaw qualities in ex-IRA man Michael Moran. See McGahern, *Amongst Women*, 24–25.

49. O'Brien's romance with mothering and mother-love bears distinct Freudian overtones. Freud himself hypothesized in *An Outline of Psychoanalysis* (London: Hogarth Press, 1938) that "The relationship to the mother is unique, without parallel, laid down unalterably for a whole life-time, as the first and strongest love-object, and as the prototype of all later love relations" (56).

50. Mikhail Bakhtin, *The Dialogic Imagination: Four Essays*, trans. Caryl Emerson and Michael Holquist, ed. Michael Holquist (Austin: University of Texas Press, 1981), 319.

51. H. Porter Abbott, *The Cambridge Introduction to Narrative* (Cambridge: Cambridge University Press, 2002), 71, original emphasis. As a widely studied mode of narration, free indirect style has long been a subject of contention and debate among narratologists, and theorists still argue about its function and effect.

52. Dorrit Cohn, *Transparent Minds: Narrative Modes for Presenting Consciousness in Fiction* (Princeton: Princeton University Press, 1978), 33.

53. Christine St. Peter, *Changing Ireland: Strategies in Contemporary Women's Fiction* (Basingstoke: Palgrave, 2000), 185.

54. Remarks O'Brien made in her interview with Mike Murphy in *Reading the Future* suggest that McGreevy's back story is closely modeled on that of Dominic McGlinchey: "He told me a great deal about his life, growing up in Bellaghy, Catholic families such as his victimized in all sorts of ways. He was fourteen when he was first interned without having committed any crime, and that instilled in him the resolve to join the IRA" (215).

55. Candice Rodd, "Mouldering mansions," *Times Literary Supplement*, April 22, 1994, 22.

56. Interestingly, Josie's complaint that McGreevy is devoid of feelings directly echoes the accusation leveled at Skeffington, the IRA mastermind in *Cal*, and touches the same raw nerve. However, McGreevy's knee-jerk retort – "I have plenty of feelings" (112) – lacks the ironic subtlety of Skeffington's response, in which he recites Pearse's poem, "A Mother," and so unwittingly confirms the truth of the allegation.

57. Rodd, "Mouldering mansions," 22.

58. The most famous sculptural representation of the Celtic hero, Oliver Sheppard's *The Death of Cuchulainn*, features a striking raven perched on the dying figure's shoulder. In 1935 this statue was unveiled as an official memorial to the 1916 Rising in Dublin's General Post Office, the headquarters and focal point of the rebellion.

Chapter 7

Shadows in the Air: Seamus Deane's *Reading in the Dark* (1996)

I

House of Splendid Isolation shares its central motif – that of a people, culture, and society held hostage by history and memory – with *Reading in the Dark*, Seamus Deane's only novel to date, which won the 1996 *Guardian* Fiction Prize and was short-listed for that year's Booker Prize. Both works depict the past as a haunting, maddening presence in the lives of those whom it ensnares, but whereas O'Brien's novel is imbued with a view of history as a heritable monolith of established facts and teleological drives, Deane's constitutes a sustained meditation on the very nature of history, one that dramatizes the problematic relationship between facts, representation, and truth in a community that has endured "repeated violations."[1] The community in question is that of working-class nationalist Derry – or Londonderry, to give the city its official name – in the decades after the Second World War, an era of unionist hegemony in Northern Ireland during which the sectarian tensions that erupted in civil violence in the late 1960s were incubated. The novel is arranged into two parts, within which there are six chapters, each of which consists of several shorter sections, all titled and dated, which cover the period from February 1945 to June 1961, with a final subchapter, "After," dated July 1971. But this chronological linearity is at odds with the retroactive movement of the plot, which keeps shifting the reader back in time through its focus on the unnamed narrator's obsessive quest to solve the mysteries that lie at the core of his family's republican past, and which continue to be the source of much anguish and grief in the present, particularly

Reading the Contemporary Irish Novel 1987–2007, First Edition. Liam Harte.
© 2014 Liam Harte. Published 2014 by John Wiley & Sons, Ltd.

for his mother. The protagonist's all-consuming desire to uncover the unspeakable secrets of this violent history turns him into a kind of family detective and propels him on a painful journey out of ignorance and confusion, though it ultimately leaves him with more guilt and sadness than closure or release.

As critics have noted, this continual return to events that have not been processed into familial or communal memory is one of many clues to the novel's status as a contemporary trauma narrative, which also has a distinct postcolonial gothic coloration about it, since trauma in the novel is shown to have its ultimate source in structural and symbolic colonial oppression and its lingering effects.[2] In fact, at the risk of sounding overly parochial, it is fair to say that *Reading in the Dark* is as prime a slice of Derry gothic as *House of Splendid Isolation* is Clare gothic and *The Butcher Boy* Monaghan gothic. Deane himself invoked one of the defining tropes of the Irish gothic tradition when he explained that the plot of his novel is bound up with

. . . .

the notion that the past will keep revisiting you in a demonic form if you don't find a way of dealing with it – which is not a way of dismissing it, but a way of internalising it. But if you don't internalise it within yourself, then it will externalise itself around you in some way.[3]

. . . .

To readers familiar with Deane's voluminous literary criticism, the novel's preoccupation with the legacies of historical trauma and emphasis on the difficulty of establishing any stable notion of truth or subjectivity in such circumstances will come as no great surprise, since there are strong deconstructive energies running through an *oeuvre* that extends from *Celtic Revivals: Essays in Modern Irish Literature* (1985), to his general editorship of the landmark *Field Day Anthology of Irish Writing* (1991), to *Foreign Affections: Essays on Edmund Burke* (2005). Born in 1940 in the economically deprived Bogside district of Derry, Deane studied English and history at Queen's University Belfast, after which he completed his doctorate in English at the University of Cambridge in 1966. After a short period working as an academic in the United States, he returned to Ireland in the late 1960s and joined the English department at University College Dublin, where he served as Professor of Modern English and American Literature from 1980 until 1993, in which year he was appointed Keough Professor of Irish Studies at the University of Notre Dame, a post he held until 2004. In addition to producing three accomplished volumes of poetry – *Gradual Wars* (1972), *Rumours* (1977), and *History Lessons* (1983) – Deane has been an influential contributor since the 1970s to the abrasive intellectual debates surrounding the writing of Irish history, which took place against the backdrop of the calcified political conflict in the North. His trenchant criticism of Irish historical revisionism, whose practitioners he attacked for their "pretentions to objectivity"[4] and propensity to define nationalism "in terms of an irrationality for which it [revisionism] is the saving alternative,"[5] has coexisted with a critically self-reflexive revisionism of his own, whereby the problematic relationship between tradition and modernity in Ireland has been subjected to sustained and provocative critique. Conor McCarthy's synopsis of Deane's historicist understanding of this relationship clarifies the deconstructionist interpretive model that underpins much of his literary revisionism:

Deane has a sense that Irish literary and political history is characterized by 'the experience of rupture, discontinuity, break and breakdown'. He recognizes that 'tradition' emerges to impose a continuity on this shattered narrative and that 'tradition' is as much answerable to the political and social needs of the moment of its production as to its content-matter. But he also and at the same time recognizes that all critical or scholarly work amounts to a re-interpretation or a re-narration of the evidence of cultural history, and that to try to step outside this circle is to try to escape from a Borgesian labyrinth.[6]

Joe Cleary endorses McCarthy's analysis and, in the fullest appraisal yet of Deane's complex critical value system, emphasizes the contrary currents that permeate his work, arguing that interpretation is for Deane "in the end its own reward even when all it yields is a renewed sense of how difficult it is to awaken from the nightmare of Irish history particularly or from that of modern history more generally."[7]

Much of Deane's reinterpretation of Irish literary and cultural history has been produced under the auspices of the Field Day Theatre Company, an artistic initiative founded in Derry in 1980 by dramatist Brian Friel and actor Stephen Rea.[8] As befitted its geographical location, there was a frontier feeling about Field Day from its inception, and what began as a theatre project intent on bringing new plays dealing with issues of history, language, and identity to audiences throughout Ireland quickly expanded into a more ambitious cultural and political enterprise.[9] Populist in ethos and anti-establishment in outlook, the Field Day collective was committed to opening up a new intellectual space or "fifth province of the mind" – a metaphysical supplement to the four territorial provinces – in which the prevailing political crisis might be reappraised. Although Field Day issued no formal manifesto, one of its foundational ideas is contained in a remark made by Hugh O'Donnell, the hedge-schoolmaster in Friel's *Translations* (1980), the company's hugely successful inaugurating play:

"it is not the literal past, the 'facts' of history that shape us, but images of the past embodied in language. [...] [W]e must never cease renewing those images; because once we do, we fossilize."[10] Field Day's politics were nationalist in complexion, premised on the desirability of a culturally if not a politically united Ireland, though with a keen appreciation of the obstacles, contradictions, and ambiguities inherent in so lofty an aspiration. Friel expressed the hope in a 1982 interview that the group's activities "should lead to a cultural state, not a political state. And I think out of that cultural state, a possibility of a political state follows."[11] These sentiments were echoed by Deane himself in a 1988 television documentary: "Our desire would be to create through Field Day, and through certain kinds of writing and theatre, a vision of [...] the cultural, social, political unification that is possible in Ireland between all the different groupings and sects."[12]

The most impactful result of this commitment to a new critical praxis was a succession of plays with such distinctly political subtexts that the company's output to some extent "bore all the traces of attempting to bear the burden of representing an entire nation, much as the Abbey [Theatre] had done before it."[13] However, Deane made clear in a program note to Friel's 1981 adaptation of Chekhov's *Three Sisters* (1901) that the cultural resurgence Field Day set out to sponsor was not a veiled version of unreconstructed nationalism, let alone a covert means of justifying the IRA's armed struggle. Nevertheless, these were precisely the accusations leveled at the project by critics such as Conor Cruise O'Brien, Colm Tóibín, and Edna Longley, who regarded Field Day as an enterprise fatally freighted with doctrinaire nationalist assumptions and prejudices, and as such dismissed it as "old whines in new bottles."[14] Deane's own argument was that more inclusive paradigms were needed, including comparative ones, to replace the outmoded nationalist rhetoric and mythology of previous decades, notably those promoted by Yeats and his fellow literary revivalists of the early 1900s. Field Day, Deane explained, is "like the Abbey in its origin in that it has within it the idea of a culture which has not yet come to be in political terms. It is unlike the Abbey in that it can no longer subscribe to any simple nationalism for the basis of its existence."[15]

The corollary of Deane's rejection of nationalist essentialism was a heightened awareness of colonization's continued effects in Ireland and a critical belief in the potential of postcolonial theory to provide a productive alternative to the intractably oppositional terms within which Irish culture and history were traditionally viewed. His conviction that postcolonial frameworks could help redeem the Northern conflict from "the realm of the irrational, the purblind, the atavistic"[16] and deepen political understandings of it was shared with Friel, who insisted that "the decolonisation process of the imagination is very important if a new Irish personality is to emerge."[17] On foot of such beliefs, Field Day broadened its activities by launching an influential pamphlet series in 1983 that eventually ran to fifteen essays in total, two of which, *Civilians and Barbarians* (1983) and *Heroic Styles: The Tradition of an Idea* (1984), were written by Deane. In these, he sought to reconfigure received political narratives of Irishness by critiquing the complex myths, stereotypes and representational paradigms that flourished on both sides of the colonizer/colonized binary, especially those that shaped notions of contrasting Irish and British national characters, which he saw as still having a "dangerous applicability [. . .] to the situation in the North."[18] Deane's poststructuralist emphasis on the socially constructed nature of such blighting stereotypes went hand in hand with a postcolonial reading of the North's embattled factions, and with a bold call for a wholesale reevaluation of existing value systems: "Everything, including our politics and our literature, has to be rewritten – i.e. re-read. That will enable new writing, new politics, unblemished by Irishness, but securely Irish."[19]

Deane further elaborated his postcolonial approach in his introduction to *Nationalism, Colonialism and Literature* (1990), in which the final series of Field Day pamphlets (by Terry Eagleton, Fredric Jameson, and Edward Said, respectively) were republished in a single volume. Arguing from the premise that the conflict in the North "is, above all, a colonial crisis," which involves all of Ireland and the United Kingdom, he called for a "fresh analysis, stimulated by the pressure of the existing political crisis," of "the interaction between the political and cultural zones and of the interaction between the British and the Irish that has done so much to produce the present complex and stymied situation in which we find ourselves."[20] Predictably, vituperative objections to this reading of the Northern situation were not slow to emerge, though Deane remained unapologetic a decade and half later:

. . . .

[W]e never said that 'one size fits all'; we knew more about colonial theory than that; but we also knew that Northern Ireland was one of the many varieties of colonialism and one of the foulest because it was so deeply entrenched within the United Kingdom system itself that it could pretend to be part of a liberal democracy rather than the one-party sectarian statelet that it truly was. We were the first group to say it was necessary to look at Northern Ireland as a colonial society, certainly a unique one, and therefore different from other colonies of the Ukanian State. If people thought we were being anti-unionist, that's fine; we were anti-unionist. Unionism is one of the versions of colonialism. We believed we needed to show this and help to destroy it.[21]

. . . .

The mutually illuminating relationship between Deane's critical and creative endeavors is underlined by the fact that several of the key themes that he elucidates in his introduction to *Nationalism, Colonialism and Literature* also inform *Reading in the Dark* at a fundamental level, particularly his emphasis on colonialism as "a process of radical dispossession," which produces in the colonized a crisis of self-representation and "search for a legitimating mode of nomination and origin."[22] Reviewers were quick to spot the weave of the author's theoretical insights in the novel's narrative fabric, as they were to note the bright threads of autobiography there.[23] Yet while Deane himself openly acknowledged the novel's allegiance to autobiography – "I felt how the child in the fiction feels,"[24] he told one interviewer – he was also keen to proclaim its distance from bare biographical details, reminding readers that "family histories like this, if not exactly common, are at least widespread in our part of the world. I knew three families in Derry with that sort of history."[25] Not for the first time in this study, then, we are confronted with a work that self-consciously kneads liberal amounts of history and autobiography into the dough of fiction to produce a richly evocative *Bildungsroman* in which a Catholic protagonist's youth and early manhood are freighted with allegorical and symbolic import, in a manner that inevitably calls to mind the *locus classicus* of the genre, Joyce's *A Portrait of the Artist as a Young Man*, an author and work about which Deane has written eloquently and extensively.[26] Like *Portrait*, *Reading in the Dark* is at once a specific and a representative text, a meditation on a young man's painful struggle to free himself from his parental and cultural origins and authorize his own story in his own place. In fact, as Robert Garratt points out, "so pervasive and suggestive is the Joycean presence in Deane's imagination, that it is tempting to claim *Reading in the Dark* as a post-colonial rewriting of *A Portrait of the Artist as a Young Man*."[27]

This is one of the bases of my own analysis, though it is important to attend to the contrasts as well as the continuities in the patterns of complicity and resistance the novels trace, many of which stem from the cultural and locational specificities to which both authors are so precisely tuned. While Joyce's Stephen and Deane's unnamed protagonist are both straining after self-definition in cities that bear the impress of violent colonial subjection, there are marked differences in their respective socioeconomic and political circumstances. Deane's narrator's laconic reflection that "The Protestants had more than we had" (33) encapsulates the undisputable fact of Catholic disadvantage in a society where structural inequities and sectarian discrimination, particularly in the areas of housing and jobs, were widespread. The alienation of the Derry nationalist community is a constant bass note throughout *Reading in the Dark* and the agents of state power are shown to exude an air of brooding menace whenever they encroach on nationalist territory. Such sectarian animosity had much deeper roots, of course, stretching back to the epoch-defining siege of Williamite Londonderry by the Catholic forces of King James II in 1689, and beyond that to the primal scene of Catholic dispossession, the Protestant plantation of Ulster that began in 1609. Acutely aware of this history, Deane once stated that Derry's peculiar symbolic importance lay in its being "a place small enough to be understood and big enough to be typical of others, as the North's, maybe the whole island's exemplary town."[28]

By the 1950s, Catholic Derry's distrust and antagonism towards the "Orange state" was particularly intense, the city's nationalist majority having found itself in a permanent minority in local government as a result of unionist gerrymandering of electoral boundaries. Within this same close-knit community, memories of the political division of the island in the early 1920s remained raw, the arbitrary line on the map being a perpetual reminder of the damage done to the integrity of the region by an undemocratic partition settlement that severed Derry city from its natural Donegal hinterland. Grief and grievance, then, have long been intimate bedfellows in this benighted "city of bonfires" (33), and Deane makes this hemmed-in community's restive psychohistorical condition emblematic of the whole city in the "Fire" episode of the novel, deftly invoking the Joycean trope of history as nightmare in the process: "The town lay entranced, embraced by the great sleeping light of the river and the green beyond of the border. It woke now and then, like someone startled and shouting from a dream, in clamour at its abandonment" (36).

"Place, then," in the words of Stephen Regan, "is not a neutral entity or simply a convenient setting for the narrative of *Reading in the Dark*. It is where the long, protracted struggle for meaning and definition goes on."[29] Place also exerts a powerfully shaping and censoring pressure on the individual. Postwar Derry, with its peculiar mix of oral and literate cultures, was in the grip of forces that were every bit as fossilizing as those that gripped Joyce's Dublin, and the novel vividly illustrates how this sense of entrapment was exacerbated by the city's smallness and stiflingly enclosed social life. The task of disentangling self and soul from the nets that impede their flight is all the more arduous as a result, but it is not only politics and religion that threaten to compromise the intellect and freedom of Deane's autobiographical alter ego. Like *Portrait*, *Reading in the Dark* is a novel that tackles the links between turbulent postcolonial situations and the plight of the traumatized. But whereas historical trauma lurks in the recesses of Joyce's novel, in Deane's it bears down upon the narrator with such insistent, irresistible force that it arrests his progress towards self-definition at every turn. This is because trauma and the foreclosure of mourning that is its concomitant are constitutive elements of this Catholic boy's familial and cultural life, and the novel's governing themes. They constitute the youth's toxic patrimony, the legacies of a troubled family history that has been relegated to secrecy by his parents, just as the wider nationalist community has repressed the unresolved legacies of colonial trauma, this being a society where the personal is inseparable from the political and where "every political question becomes a sectarian question."[30] The narrator's experiences of the effects of traumatic loss and denial are therefore not merely personal; they are symptomatic of larger national struggles that are still ongoing. Moreover, by conceptualizing history and trauma as inherently relational, *Reading in the Dark* resonates with what Cathy Caruth identifies as a key insight of Freud: "that history, like trauma, is never simply one's own, that history is precisely the way we are implicated in each other's traumas."[31]

The novel makes clear that if this inheritance is not to become the corrosive foundation of the narrator's identity, he must plumb the interior labyrinths of a not-fully-knowable past, excavate its secrets, and facilitate their psychic and narrative integration into his own story. Only then can he begin the necessary work of secondary or vicarious mourning and develop a way of living with the memory of the dead rather than with their ghostly traces. But as the following analysis will show, Deane, like Joyce, is committed to expressing the impossibility of authoring one's own subjectivity, of knowing and naming oneself in circumstances where the consequences of colonial subjugation and discrimination are still felt, and where the larger political crisis is not only unresolved but intensifying. In the process, he draws attention to the intergenerational and intersubjective nature of traumatic experience and emphasizes its social dimension, thus recalling the central concerns of *The Butcher Boy*, although stylistically speaking, Deane eschews McCabe's comic anarchy for a meditative realism. As an inscription of postcolonial trauma, *Reading in the Dark* implicitly challenges theorizations of traumatic incidents as singular, extraordinary, and chronologically bounded, and instead dramatizes the extent to which transgenerational haunting can determine the destiny of an entire family line and stymie a subject's potential to be himself in relation to others and to his own history.

II

There are few more emotionally intense opening sequences in contemporary Irish fiction than those of *Reading in the Dark*. A seemingly inconsequential everyday scenario – a young boy climbing a staircase while his mother looks on from the landing – suddenly takes on a charged strangeness when the woman tells her son not to move because she senses "something there between us. A shadow" (5). This ghostly interposition throws the boy-narrator's pitch-perfect attunement to his surroundings into disarray and alerts him to the intrusive presence of unresolved grief in his mother's life. Although the boy doesn't yet know it, this specter on the stairs is symptomatic of a deep-seated psychic obstruction in his mother, an impediment to speech produced by years of repressed mourning. Roger Luckhurst's gloss on ghosts and their narrative import helps to elucidate the nature of this impediment:

> Ghosts are the signals of atrocities, marking sites of untold violence, a traumatic past whose traces remain to attest to the lack of testimony. A haunting does not initiate a story; it is the sign of a *blockage* of story, a hurt that has not been honoured by a memorializing narrative.[32]

Soon, we shall come to realise the symbolic significance of the mother seeing this shadow in the space that separates her from her son, as the latter's all-consuming desire to discover the source of her hurt and unblock its expression causes a widening rift between them. We shall also come to understand why the narrator expresses a wish to partake of his mother's haunting and the reasons behind her discouraging response.

This pivotal opening encounter in liminal space (a favourite haunt of the gothic) also signals the end of what we might call the narrator's phenomenological innocence, his unquestioning faith in the reliability of his affective relationship to the visible world. If absence can be a symptom of palpable presence, what then is the status of the actual objects of sensuous experience and perception, and what is his proper relationship to them? In the wake of such disturbing thoughts, experience ceases to be the only basis of knowledge for the narrator and taken-for-granted reality assumes a strange and elusive new aspect. Appearances no longer reassure; the realization dawns that the evidence of one's senses is not always to be trusted, any more than the world of fixtures and fittings is to be taken at face value. The "clear, plain silence" (5) on the stairwell has been replaced by a mother's oppressive silence and a son's relationship with her and with his surroundings has been irrevocably transformed.

Thus begins the narrator's protracted inquiry into the origin of his mother's chronic psychic suffering, a search that draws him ever deeper into the labyrinthine maze of his family's hushed-up history of republican activism in a society where the past remains steadfastly alive in the present and shapes individuals' self-recognition and relational lives in deeply damaging ways. At the heart of this suppressed past is the mystery surrounding the disappearance of Eddie, the boy's father's older brother, following a shoot-out between the IRA and the Derry police in April 1922, a time when Northern Ireland was in its troubled infancy and "the 'meaning' of the city in geopolitical terms was being contested."[33] The correlation of the private with the political here brings into focus the constitutive role of traumatic, unredeemable loss in this nationalist community and its centrally determinative role in the narrator's deepening crisis of subjectivity as he vainly struggles to produce a truthful account of Eddie's fate. Like the stairwell shadow, which hovers between being and unbeing, the enigma of his uncle's disappearance gestures towards a "radical privation" or "missing agency,"[34] which Deane identified as a defining feature of the self's relationship to society in Ireland. This sense of missing agency is a deeply engrained feature of the sites of memory and history in the novel and is shown to be an intractable bar to self-articulation, since the more the catastrophic past is disavowed, the more it remains troublingly alive, petrifying time in an endless present. Whenever the narrative lens opens out beyond the tight confines of the narrator's family home, we see a landscape of ruins and scars that resounds with the aftershocks of myriad ruptures and betrayals:

. . . .

So there it was, our territory, with the old fort of Grianan on one hill overlooking Lough Foyle, the feud farmhouse on another hill, gazing on Lough Swilly, the thick neck of the Inishowen peninsula between, Derry gauzed in smoke at the end of Lough Foyle, the border writhing behind it. (59)

. . . .

The lingering, unbearable past that the ghosts of the missing represent exerts such a powerfully disintegrative hold over the cultural unconscious of this region that it resists absorption into cognitive memory. It persists instead in disguised or displaced form, as supernatural legends and tales of demonic possession, which register truths that are incommensurate with any simple statement of facts. The proliferation and reiteration of such tales reveal how deep-seated repressed psychological suffering is in this border territory and how pervasive are the ghosts that refuse final interment. Such collective dissociative behavior blurs the dividing lines between past and present, imagination and reality, and means that the sense of crisis expressed in the city's two names is reproduced at every level, from the temporal and the political to the discursive and the psychic. In short, there is nothing, no state, entity, or identity in this trauma-filled space that is not marked by partition, absence, and incompletion.

Like Joyce's Stephen, then, Deane's nameless narrator is subject to forces he cannot fully grasp but which are powerfully coercive in his subject-formation. Not only must he determine the truth of his family's history in circumstances of chronic historical trauma, he must also try to define himself in a present that is dominated by a constant political struggle to fix the meaning of the past in order to lay claim to the future. At home and on the streets, the boy is inducted into a culture of aggrieved republicanism that seeks to mold him into a defiantly oppositional form of Irish subjectivity. At school, conversely, he is subjected to lessons and lectures designed to interpellate him and his fellow

Catholic classmates into loyal and compliant (second-class) British citizens. The "Political Education" section dramatizes this contest *in parvo*. The date is November 1956 and a British Army chaplain has been dispatched by the Ministry of Education to the narrator's secondary school to deliver a talk on the need for collective action to defeat the communist foe. This strategically timed speech, which coincided with the start of "Operation Harvest," the IRA's six-year guerrilla campaign against military and police targets in Northern Ireland, is a master class in political revisionism in which divided Derry is represented as a homogeneous community of freedom-loving citizens committed to maintaining the "democratic system in which we all have the good fortune to live" (196). The history teacher endorses the chaplain's emphasis on "global vision" and "the irrelevance of our own internal differences in the face of the demands of world history" (199–200), leaving it to one of the narrator's classmates to decode the political subtexts of both men's position: "'Propaganda,' said Irwin. 'That's all that is. First, it's the Germans. Then it's the Russians. Always, it's the IRA. British propaganda. What have the Germans or the Russians to do with us? It's the British who are the problem for us'" (200).

If this episode demonstrates that no narrative is ideologically innocent in a divided society, then "Accident" proves that no event is immune from politicization. In one of the novel's shortest and most artful subchapters, the narrator recalls witnessing the accidental death of a local boy and the traumatizing shock that followed: "For months, I kept seeing the lorry reversing, and Rory Hannaway's arm going out as he was wound under" (11). Each involuntary mental replaying of this event churns up feelings of guilt and betrayal in the narrator, who privately felt more sympathy for the policeman called to the scene of the accident than for Rory's mother or the hapless lorry driver. His sense of treachery is eventually allayed when, months later, a friend described "in detail how young Hannaway had been run over by a police car which had not even stopped" (12). Although the narrator stays silent, this object lesson in propagandist falsification forces him to confront troubling questions about the knowability of historical truth and the correspondence between an event and its representation, questions that have a direct bearing on his incessant probing of his family's secret past.

The more this barely comprehending narrator tries to separate truth from falsity in this overdetermined social space, the more he looks to his family for leads, since in order to represent himself completely he must first represent his parents and reconstruct their pasts. But whereas the narrator's maternal uncles repeatedly mull over the circumstances of Eddie's vanishing, his father Frank is conspicuously evasive: "I wanted him to make the story his own and cut in on their talk. But he always took a back seat in the conversation, especially on that topic" (10). This early expression of frustration is a telling clue to the burgeoning impact of inherited historical trauma in the life of this child, a pointer to the fact that *Reading in the Dark* is as much about the legacies of unspeakable violent histories as it is the primary suffering of the parental generation. Frank is somewhat more forthcoming about other early tragedies, telling his son how Eddie's disappearance occurred a short time after he and his siblings were orphaned, which led to the children being divided up between relatives in Derry and Donegal. The two girls, Ena and Bernadette, were sent to live with their mother's sister (the narrator's grandaunt) in a farmhouse near Buncrana, where they were maltreated. This discovery, coupled with a later dispute over property inheritance that also involved Eddie's memory, led Frank to sever ties with his relations and shun the "feud farmhouse" (46) thereafter. But even after hearing this disclosure, the narrator is left with a "half-sense" of discrepant knowledge, of there being "a deeper sorrow in the family than I could yet know" (51).

Gradually, it emerges that Frank's anguished silence derives from his belief that his brother was a police informer who was interrogated and shot by the IRA in 1922. But Frank does not have the full story. What he doesn't know is that his brother was executed in error on the orders of the man who later became his father-in-law. Neither does he know that the actual informer was Tony McIlhenny, with whom the narrator's mother was in love before she married Frank but who jilted her to marry Katie, her younger sister. McIlhenny's betrayals did not end there. In 1926 he fled Derry following a tipoff from the narrator's mother that his cover was about to be blown, leaving behind his wife and their unborn child. He also left the boy's mother in his wake, not only heartbroken but also guilt-ridden, a guilt she carried into her marriage to Frank in 1933, after which she remained "haunted forever" (229). All through marriage and motherhood she silently bore "the sharpness of a grief that could so pierce the heart" (51), since "everything that was precious to her was so bound up with betrayal" (224). Yet her understanding of events was also partial. Not until much later did her dying father tell her of his role in her brother-in-law's death, a revelation that effectively retraumatized the boy's mother and pitched her into a chronic state of inner desolation and stasis from which she never recovered. Acute grief, mute shame, and searing guilt, then, are central to the interlocking traumatic silences that enclose husband and wife in the novel, and to the sorrowful secrets that paradoxically divide and unite them. Their sealed-off pain is all the more intense because neither parent, for different reasons, has been able to mourn openly let alone publicly. Their losses can only ever be experienced as absences – Eddie's body was never found; McIlhenny's precise whereabouts remain unknown – and, in the words of trauma theorist Gabriele Schwab, "Where there is no grave, one cannot mourn properly; one remains forever tied to a loss that never becomes real."[35]

These interlinked issues of inexpressible secrets and unending mourning are central to a proper understanding of the traumatic amnesia of the parental generation in *Reading in the Dark* and its mute intrapsychic transmission to the next. The complex psychic burdens of parents and son are illuminated by the work of psychoanalysts who have studied the effects of repressed secrets and failed mourning in the context of catastrophic loss or injury, and applied their insights to the interpretation of trauma in literature. The most obvious theoretical framework for a discussion of unfinished or diverted grief is Sigmund Freud's concept of melancholia, which emphasizes the pathological nature of mourning that, because of an enduring, ambivalent attachment on the part of the bereaved to a lost love object, resists the kinds of closures and restitutions that "healthy" grieving implies. However, it strikes me that equally fruitful insights can be derived from the work of post-Freudian psychoanalysts Nicolas Abraham and Maria Torok, who drew on their years of clinical experience and philosophical reflections to develop a theory of psychic concealment as part of their larger thesis that unworked-through trauma is transmitted between individuals and generations, with damaging psychic and somatic consequences.

Rejecting Freud's notion of "dynamic" repression in favor of a theory of "preservative" repression, Abraham and Torok argued that torment which is "untellable and therefore inaccessible to the gradual, assimilative work of mourning" causes a shift in the psyche that leads to "the establishment of a sealed-off psychic place, a crypt in the ego,"[36] in which the lost love object is kept like a living corpse. They linked the formation of such mental tombs, which typically leave the bearer in a fugue or death-in-life state, to specific kinds of traumatic silences: "Crypts are constructed only when the shameful secret is the love object's doing and when that object also functions for the subject as an ego ideal. It is therefore the *object's* secret that needs to be kept, *his* shame covered up."[37] The interpersonal consequences of the silencing of such shameful histories show themselves psychically in the form of the phantomatic return of the past, a concept Abraham and Torok derived from folklore and which led them to hypothesize that "only certain categories of the dead return to torment the living: those who were denied the rite of burial or died an unnatural, abnormal death, were criminals or outcasts, or suffered injustice in their lifetime"[38] – categories into which Eddie and McIlhenny fit with uncanny precision. Only when trauma has been psychically assimilated do phantoms and the economy of haunting they sustain begin to fade, since "laying the dead to rest and cultivating our ancestors implies uncovering their shameful secrets, understanding their nameless and undisclosed suffering."[39] Otherwise, the dead will continue "to lead a devastating psychic half-life in us,"[40] a haunting that can extend across the generations.

As I have already intimated, these psychoanalytical theories provide a useful pathway into understanding the complex manifestations of the traumatic foreclosure of mourning in *Reading in the Dark*. Certainly, the form of psychic haunting that afflicts the protagonist's parents, which is suffused with a palpable sense of interiority, bears many of the hallmarks of inexpressible or cryptic mourning. Frank's behavior leaves his son with the feeling of living "in an empty space with a long cry from him ramifying through it. At other times, it appeared to be as cunning and articulate as a labyrinth, closely designed, with someone sobbing at the heart of it" (43). Similarly, the narrator's mother's inertia suggests that the living ghosts of the violent past are deeply encrypted within her, leaving her in the grip of "the most resistant of pathologies: the blocked expression of a memory trace which cannot tell the submerged history of its own (traumatic) origins."[41] Her inability to mourn sometimes gives her the appearance of a living corpse, as references to her having a "dead mouth" (119) and moving "as though there were pounds of pressure bearing down on her" (139) imply. Furthermore, she "buries" her secret in language and speech in ways that are analogous to the psychological dynamic proposed by Abraham, who hypothesized that the entombed ghosts of the past are often paradoxically concealed and revealed through disturbances in speech. The changes the narrator detects in his mother's speech patterns after the deathbed revelations of her father are consistent with this form of psychic functioning:

. . . .

This was her new conversation. Connected remarks separated by days, weeks, months, but always in her new voice. I knew she was getting stranger; she was telling herself a story that only appeared now and again in her speech. [. . .] She had been in love with someone else, not quite my father. That's what she was telling, and not telling, him. And she was telling me. Most of all, she was telling herself. (145–146)

. . . .

But it is what psychoanalytical theory has to say about the wider transgenerational effects of the silencing of traumatic memories that is most strikingly illustrated by the psychic topographies in the novel. One of the basic premises of Abraham and Torok's work is that "the unsettling disruptions in the psychic life of one person can adversely and unconsciously affect someone else."[42] More specifically, Abraham argued that "It is the children's or descendants' lot to objectify these buried tombs through diverse species of ghosts. What comes back to haunt are the tombs of others. The phantoms of folklore merely objectify a metaphor active in the unconscious: the burial of an unspeakable fact *within the love-object*."[43] As Esther Rashkin observes, this theory of intrapsychic haunting subtly differs from that of the return of the repressed, in that "What returns to haunt is the 'unsaid' and 'unsayable' of *an other*. The silence, gap, or secret in the speech of someone else 'speaks,' in the manner of a ventriloquist, through the words and acts (readable as words) of the subject."[44] In essence, then, the ghost is the effect of another's crypt in the unconscious of the haunted individual. To cite Rashkin again: "The child haunted by a phantom becomes a living tomb or repository in which an unspeakable drama, experienced as traumatic by someone else, lies buried yet alive, exerting its disruptive influence in a potentially infinite number of ways on the existence of the child or on the child grown to adulthood."[45]

The relevance of this theory to the transmission of trauma in *Reading in the Dark* is evident right from the opening shadow play on the stairs, the internal psychic dynamics of which come into clearer focus when viewed through this theoretical lens. It is the entombed secrets of McIlhenny and the boy's grandfather that intrude in spectral form upon the everyday activities of his mother, and it is this unspoken knowledge, combined with her own encrypted secrets, that infiltrates and haunts the narrator in turn, from the moment he sees "a darkness" (6) leaving the stairs window. Further evidence of what Abraham terms the "phantom effect"[46] emerges as the child becomes increasingly entangled in the effects of his parents' repressed mourning, which leads his perturbed mother to regard him as "possessed" (42) and him to reach a point where he cannot properly distinguish between what he has been told, what he remembers, and what he imagines. At this moment, the narrator's relationship to his parents' pasts recalls Marianne Hirsch's influential concept of "post-memory," whereby an individual is so "dominated by narratives that preceded one's birth or one's consciousness" that they become "shaped, however indirectly, by traumatic events that still defy narrative reconstruction and exceed comprehension."[47] After his dying grandfather has freed his own buried ghosts, the narrator believes that his secret "could not but re-embed itself in my mother and go on living. We were pierced together by the same shaft" (127) – an image that vividly identifies the son as a carrier of family phantoms. Later, faced with his mother's unremitting grief, he fingers strands of her hair and he feels a "tightness [...] travelling inside, looking for a resting place, a nest to live in and flourish, finding it in the cat's cradle of my stomach and accumulating there" (143). This denied pain eventually becomes "swollen" (194) inside him, demanding release in speech, in testimony, by which point it is clear that what is a "memory crisis" for the parents has become an "identity crisis" for their son, who must break through the barrier of silenced histories and confront the ghosts of an unworked-through past in order to discover what the word "I" means.

Of course, the process of making silenced parental trauma audible and concrete in the son's own life is not quite as simple as this reading might suggest.

For one thing, the youth's struggle for self-definition is shadowed by a subtle paradox, whereby his compulsion to testify to events that defy representation coexists with a contrary impulse to avoid this difficult knowledge. This paradox first surfaces in the section entitled "The Feud," when he responds ambivalently to his father's need to talk – "keep your secrets, I said to him inside my closed mouth, keep your secrets, and I won't mind. But, at the same time, I wanted to know everything" (46) – and it later reemerges when the son eventually hears his father's "confession" in a country church. Such contradictory responses are in fact entirely consistent with the legacies of traumatic experience, one of which is a feeling of "being caught between the compulsion to complete the process of knowing and the inability or fear of doing so."[48] The predicament of children who inherit parental phantoms is even more acute, since "the parent transmits to the child not only the unspeakable content of the secret, but also the unstated obligation to keep the secret invisible and unreachable and to prevent anyone from discovering it, including the child."[49] Meanwhile, the boy's Aunt Katie encapsulates the dynamic of cryptic mourning and transmission that the narrative as a whole enacts when she describes some families as "devil-haunted":

Maybe it's something terrible in the family history, some terrible deed that was done in the past, and it just spreads down the generations like a shout down that tunnel, the secret passage, in the walls of Grianan, that echoes and echoes and never really stops. It's held in those walls forever. (66)

This image of an echo frozen in the crypt-chamber of the ancient hillfort that overlooks the city is powerfully suggestive of a national topography of encrypted shameful secrets, as is the fact that Katie's analogy transposes the echo from the private realm of the family to a public space that is saturated with historical and mythic associations. Abraham and Torok's notion of cryptic mourning is thus extended from the individual to the community and beyond. A similar movement can be traced in the story of a man who was traumatized by the death of his infant daughter, which the narrator retells his mother, who first heard it from her sister. The original source of the story was McIlhenny, who anticipated his own fate when he remarked that

the worst punishment of all was the one Sean from Malin had created for his child – not being able to let it die properly, getting it caught between this world and the next. The air of Donegal, of all Ireland, was full of such people, he had claimed, because of our bad history. (210)

Abraham and Torok's theorization of transgenerational trauma has recently been augmented by Gabriele Schwab, whose *Haunting Legacies: Violent Histories and Transgenerational Trauma* (2010) examines the effects on children of parents' disavowal of post-traumatic mourning. One of the points she makes about such children is that they "become avid readers of silences and memory traces hidden in a face that is frozen in grief, a forced smile that does not feel quite right, an apparently unmotivated flare-up of rage, or chronic depression."[50] Deane's narrator evolves into just such a reader after his stairwell experience, and the more attuned he becomes to the disintegrative effect of repressed emotion in his parents' lives, the more he notices disturbances in their expressive functions, such as his father "knowing something about Eddie, not saying it, not talking but sometimes nearly talking, signalling" (43). Schwab also follows Abraham and Torok in arguing that children of traumatized parents are often haunted by disturbances of identity and experience problems with self-knowledge. The key insight here comes in the form of an explanatory note by Abraham and Torok on the phenomenon of the psychic phantom:

Should a child have parents 'with secrets,' parents whose speech is not exactly complementary to their unstated repressions, the child will receive from them a gap in the unconscious, an unknown, unrecognized knowledge – a *nescience* – subjected to a form of 'repression' before the fact. The buried speech of the parent will be (a) dead (gap) without a burial place in the child. This unknown phantom returns from the unconscious to haunt its host and may lead to phobias, madness, and obsessions. In effect it can persist through several generations and determine the fate of an entire family line.[51]

This hypothesis has such compelling applicability to the dynamics of traumatic possession in *Reading in the Dark* that the novel could almost be said to be a literary instantiation of it. The haunting nature of the phantom of repressed history is evident throughout the novel, as is its capacity to breed obsessions and even a kind of madness, as demonstrated in the "Roses" episode when, in a fit of manic fury, the narrator destroys his father's rose beds, barely stopping for breath until his "nausea and dread" subside to leave him in a "trance" (105). At the root of such frenzied behavior is the nescience or lacuna in knowledge that is the narrator's inheritance, the crisis of self-knowing that obsessively drives him to unpick the lock on his parents' encrypted secrets and end the silence. By attempting "to make the story his own," the youth is effectively seeking to make unbearable historical losses real by vicariously mourning them, not out of a mere curiosity-satisfying impulse but in order to complete the gapped circle of his subjectivity. Deane's remarks about his protagonist's predicament underline this need to gain some form of narrative control and affective mastery over experience that is at once unspeakable and undeniable:

....

My view of the novel [. . .] is that it's about a young child who never earns a name. He never achieves sufficient identity (to use that terrible word!) to deserve the name or the sense of self he's looking for in relation to his parents. [. . .] One way of coming into self-possession, of overcoming any kind of oppression, colonial or otherwise, is to take charge of interpretation yourself, not to allow yourself to be interpreted by others. This novel is a kind of parable of that attempt (and a painfully abortive attempt) on the part of a young kid.[52]

....

Interpretation and disclosure, then, are an inextricable part of the journey towards self-definition and self-possession that the narrator is embarked upon. Burdened with the legacy of his parents' traumatic foreclosure of mourning, he is both obligated and compelled to become a historian of his own family in order to authenticate himself and settle his origin of being. Only knowledge, understanding, and articulation will enable him to do the necessary work of mourning and live without ghosts, thereby avoiding the catastrophic fate of his parents and so many others in his community who, because of denied memories of violence, exist in a state of living death, "never alive, never dead, just shadows in the air" (211). The protagonist's situation corresponds in many ways to that of the subaltern within colonial discourse theory, in that his desire for interpretative agency signifies his struggle for subjectivity, for an effective name and voice, since without understanding and enunciation there can be no agency or self-realization for the colonized indigene. Frantz Fanon wrote that a culture under colonial domination "quickly becomes a culture condemned to secrecy"[53] and Deane's own comments on the clandestine mores of his narrator's community are in a similar vein: "If you have something suppressed, if you have great pressure bearing down upon a community there is going to be all sorts of ways of dealing with that pressure of which secrecy is one. And secrecy's other face is always betrayal."[54] So whereas secrecy, silence, and treachery are forms of mutilation produced by political pressure and oppression from within and outwith this tight-knit nationalist community, utterance is figured as an essential prerequisite for self-definition. At an important level, therefore, Deane's preoccupation in the novel can be said to be with that most characteristic of Field Day concerns, the process of translation, which he conceptualized as "the adaptations, readjustments, and reorientations that are required of individuals and groups who have undergone a traumatic cultural and political crisis so fundamental that they must forge for themselves a new speech, a new history or life story that would give it some rational or coherent form."[55]

What the novel demonstrates, however, is that for the child of a family whose traumatic history remains silenced and reenactive, and who grows up in a society conditioned by the enduring ramifications of colonization, the process of forging a new speech is an urgent yet necessarily incomplete endeavor. Because there is no working-through of trauma and its resonant after-effects – no open acknowledgement of guilt, shame, or responsibility on the part of the narrator's mother, no "enlightenment" of the father by the son – the cycle of encryptment, silencing, and suffering goes "on and on and on" (203), fuelled by the complications of love, fidelity, and betrayal. No sooner has the narrator begun to penetrate the walls of his inherited tombs and disinter their secrets than he begins to bury this knowledge in his own mental crypt so as to protect his parents' feelings, yet the more he does so, the more tightly his resentful mother seals in her own unmourned secrets. The agonizing and increasingly wordless "pact" (228) that forms between mother and son reaches its apotheosis in October 1968, when she suffers a stroke and loses the power of speech:

....

I would look at her, sealed in her silence, and now she would smile slightly at me and very gently, almost imperceptibly, shake her head. I was to seal it all in too. Now we could love each other, at last, I imagined. Now we could have the luck for each other. (230)

....

The habit of repressing painful experience is thus continued into the next generation: just as the mother encrypted McIlhenny's shameful secret out of love, so does the son cover up his mother's shame by interring it in an inaccessible mental grave. The convergence of this reenactive behavior with the recrudescence of the Troubles in the late 1960s signals a crisis that extends beyond this one family and underscores the wider destructive costs of the collective or communal silencing of violent histories.

Cyclical entrapment, then, is the dominant trope of the closing sections of the novel and it carries with it the implication that, until losses are mourned and history named, the "crisis of truth"[56] that Shoshana Felman claims is a fundamental part of the legacy of traumatic experience will persistently thwart the desire for secure self-identity. And so despite the narrator's concentrated efforts to exercise agency over the past through the narrative assemblage of Eddie's story, definitive knowledge and (self-)definition continue to elude him. The more he tries to possess "the one story that cancelled all the others" (206), the more he finds that there can be no single authoritative narrative of what really happened, only endlessly recomposable fragments, versions, interpretations. The narrator's crippling lack of intellectual mastery and agency are powerfully borne in on him when, as punishment for absconding from the annual school retreat, he is forced to study Ignatius of Loyola's *Spiritual Exercises* under the guidance of the dean of studies (a scene that is resonantly intertextual with the famous encounter between Stephen and his dean of studies in the fifth chapter of *Portrait*). There he discovers the Ignatian method of discernment, a mode of integrated thought and disciplined decision-making that exudes a sense of resolute assurance and which is the antithesis of the narrator's own sense of chronic deficiency and etiolation:

> The *Exercises* were clean and tonic. A man grew out of them, one whom I had never seen nor known, in all perfection, making choices in accord with that perfection. He was a star, sure and yet troubled, but always reducing his trouble gradually by accumulating certainty, by making decision after decision, knowing the more, the more trouble it took him to know. But when I imagined him so, then I would see myself again in a dither of light and dark, see my father again, see Eddie, re-recognise my mother, see them blur and fade, know that I too was blurred, was astray for not knowing how to choose. (168)

This lack stays with the narrator to the end, as do the behavioral and affective disruptions caused by the phantomatic transmission of unspeakable trauma. Appropriately, the deferral of narrative closure is enacted in multiple ways, from the question mark in the subchapter title "All Of It?" to the way the narrator becomes inexorably taken over by an aura of incompletion. His sense of dither eventually convinces him that he has morphed into his mother's phantom – "Now the haunting meant something new to me – now I had become the shadow" (217) – at which point he comes to share in the fate of the traumatized, who "become themselves the symptom of a history that they cannot possess."[57] The novel ends with the death of the narrator's "innocent" father, which coincides with the imposition of a curfew by the British Army. As troops move in to dismantle the improvised street barricades, the narrator watches a gypsy boy riding bareback through the debris. The appearance of this figure of shadowy ambiguity, who trails associations of aboriginal outsiderness and freedom from material and political concerns, suggests that the narrator's quest for a unified subjectivity will go on in the face of escalating sectarian violence. Unmarked mental graves retain their living specters, phantomatic family secrets their affective power.

Notes

1. Seamus Deane, *Reading in the Dark* [1996] (London: Vintage, 1997), 49. Subsequent page numbers are cited parenthetically in the text.

2. The episodic nature of the novel can be taken as another sign that we are reading a trauma text, insofar as each subchapter resembles a decontextualized memory fragment of a kind common in trauma narratives.

3. Seamus Deane and Maurice Fitzpatrick, "An Interview with Seamus Deane," *Journal of Irish Studies*, 22 (2007), 90.

4. Seamus Deane, "Wherever Green is Read," in *Revising the Rising*, eds Theo Dorgan and Máirín Ní Dhonnchadha (Derry: Field Day, 1991), 100.

5. Seamus Deane, *Strange Country: Modernity and Nationhood in Irish Writing Since 1790* (Oxford: Clarendon, 1997), 193.

6. Conor McCarthy, "Seamus Deane: Between Burke and Adorno," *The Yearbook of English Studies*, 35 (2005), 235.

7. Joe Cleary, "Dark Fields of the Republic: Seamus Deane's Sundered Provinces," *boundary 2*, 37:2 (2010), 8, 11.

8. Deane joined the Field Day board of directors in 1981, along with musicologist David Hammond and poets Seamus Heaney and Tom Paulin. The board membership remained exclusively Northern Irish until 1988, when Kilkenny-born playwright Thomas Kilroy was invited to join.

9. On average, the company staged one new Irish play or adaptation per year during the 1980s, with sixteen productions in total being toured between 1980 and 1998, mostly in non-theatrical and makeshift venues. Since the early 1990s, Field Day has been more visible as a publishing enterprise, sponsoring the Field Day Critical Conditions book series in association with Cork University Press and publishing an annual journal, the *Field Day Review*, in association with the Keough Institute for Irish Studies at the University of Notre Dame. Deane has coedited the *Review* with Breandán Mac Suibhne since its inception in 2005.

10. Brian Friel, *Selected Plays* (London: Faber and Faber, 1984), 445.

11. Cited in John Gray, "Field Day Five Years On," *Linen Hall Review*, 2:2 (Summer 1985), 5.

12. Cited in Stephen Regan, "Ireland's Field Day," *History Workshop Journal*, 33 (Spring 1992), 26.

13. Christopher Morash, "Irish theatre," in *The Cambridge Companion to Irish Culture*, eds Joe Cleary and Claire Connolly (Cambridge: Cambridge University Press, 2002), 336.

14. Cited in Gray, "Field Day Five Years On," 6. For a flavor of the heated polemic that Field Day provoked, see the reviews of *The Field Day Anthology of Irish Writing* by Anthony Bradley, Enda Longley, and Colm Tóibín in *Canadian Journal of Irish Studies*, 18:2 (December 1992), 117–124.

15. Seamus Deane, "What is Field Day?," program note for the Field Day production of Brian Friel's adaptation of *Three Sisters* (1981).

16. Seamus Deane, "Introduction: The Longing for Modernity," *Threshold*, 32 (Winter 1982), 1. Cited in Morash, "Irish theatre," 334.

17. Brian Friel, quoted in Ulick O'Connor, "Friel Takes Derry by Storm," *Sunday Tribune*, September 6, 1981, 2.

18. Seamus Deane, "Heroic Styles: The Tradition of an Idea," in *Ireland's Field Day*, ed. Field Day Theatre Company (London: Hutchinson, 1985), 57.

19. Deane, "Heroic Styles," 58. The eventual fruit of this project of collective self-redefinition, the three-volume *Field Day Anthology*, is not only the most ambitious work of modern Irish literary scholarship but also the most controversial. Feminist critics attacked it for its serious underrepresentation of female authors, whereas revisionist-minded critics resented its conscription of Northern Irish Protestant writing into an expanded Irish canon, which they read as evidence of Deane's republican irredentism. For assessments of the *Anthology* and the disputes it provoked, see Helen Thompson (ed.), *The Current Debate about the Irish Literary Canon: Essays Reassessing "The Field Day Anthology of Irish Writing"* (Lewiston, NY: Edwin Mellen Press, 2006) and Cleary, "Dark Fields of the Republic," 33–49. Two substantial additional volumes were added to the *Anthology* in 2002, both of which were exclusively devoted to Irish women's writings and traditions.

20. Seamus Deane, "Introduction," in *Nationalism, Colonialism and Literature*, ed. Seamus Deane (Minneapolis: University of Minnesota Press, 1990), 10.

21. Yu-chen Lin, "Field Day Revisited (I): An Interview with Seamus Deane," *Concentric: Literary and Cultural Studies*, 33:1 (March 2007), 206.

22. Yu-chen Lin, "Field Day Revisited (I)," 10, 12. Deane has said on more than one occasion that he does not think of his critical and creative endeavors in oppositional terms, and indeed the novel's long gestation coincided with the publication of several of his major critical works. The earliest extract from what would become *Reading in the Dark* was published in *Granta* magazine in spring 1986, and subsequent extracts appeared there in 1988, 1991, and 1994.

23. See, for example, Edna Longley, "Autobiography as History," *Fortnight* (November 1996), 34; Eamonn Hughes, "Belfastards and Derriers," *Irish Review*, 20 (Winter–Spring 1997), 151–157.

24. Seamus Deane, "*Reading in the Dark*: An Interview with Seamus Deane," *English & Media Magazine*, 36 (Summer 1997), 18.

25. Nick Fraser, "A kind of life sentence," *Guardian*, October 28, 1996, 9. Family sensitivities delayed the book's appearance. Deane explained: "I couldn't publish it when other people were alive, not only my parents. I could have written it, but I couldn't have *published* it before their death" (Deane, "*Reading in the Dark*," 18, original emphasis).

26. In addition to his many articles and essays on Joyce, Deane edited and annotated *A Portrait of the Artist as a Young Man* for the Penguin Twentieth-Century Classics series on the works of Joyce, of which he was the general editor.

27. Robert F. Garratt, *Trauma and History in the Irish Novel: The Return of the Dead* (Basingstoke: Palgrave Macmillan, 2011), 101. Garratt's illuminating account

of the place of trauma in *Reading in the Dark*, which pays close attention to the ideas of the uncanny and the return of the repressed in the novel, differs from my own reading, as will become clear when we come to discuss the concept of the phantom in relation to the narrator's mental topography.

28. Seamus Deane, "Derry: City Besieged within the Siege," *Fortnight* (October 1983), 18.

29. Stephen Regan, review of *Reading in the Dark*, *Irish Studies Review*, no. 19 (Summer 1997), 38.

30. Lin, "Field Day Revisited (I)," 208.

31. Cathy Caruth, *Unclaimed Experience: Trauma, Narrative, and History* (Baltimore: Johns Hopkins University Press, 1996), 24.

32. Roger Luckhurst, *The Trauma Question* (London: Routledge, 2008), 93, original emphasis.

33. Gerry Smyth, *Space and the Irish Cultural Imagination* (Basingstoke: Palgrave Macmillan, 2001), 140. Northern Ireland, which came into being in May 1921, had a violent gestation and, in the words of Sergeant Burke, "a cruel birth" (205), as intercommunal violence flared up repeatedly between 1920 and 1922. The first six months of 1922 witnessed particularly intense fighting between loyalists and nationalists, which resulted in the deaths of over 200 people in Belfast alone.

34. Seamus Deane, "Autobiography and Memoirs, 1890–1980," in *The Field Day Anthology of Irish Writing*, vol. 3, ed. Seamus Deane (Derry: Field Day, 1991), 383.

35. Gabriele Schwab, *Haunting Legacies: Violent Histories and Transgenerational Trauma* (New York: Columbia University Press, 2010), 3.

36. Nicolas Abraham and Maria Torok, *The Shell and the Kernel: Renewals of Psychoanalysis*, vol. 1, trans. Nicholas T. Rand (Chicago: University of Chicago Press, 1994), 141.

37. Abraham and Torok, *The Shell and the Kernel*, 131, original emphasis.

38. Abraham and Torok, *The Shell and the Kernel*, 167.

39. Abraham and Torok, *The Shell and the Kernel*, 167.

40. Abraham and Torok, *The Shell and the Kernel*, 167.

41. Abraham and Torok, *The Shell and the Kernel*, 7.

42. Abraham and Torok, *The Shell and the Kernel*, 166.

43. Abraham and Torok, *The Shell and the Kernel*, 172, original emphasis.

44. Esther Rashkin, *Family Secrets and the Psychoanalysis of Narrative* (Princeton: Princeton University Press, 1992), 28, original emphasis.

45. Esther Rashkin, *Unspeakable Secrets and the Psychoanalysis of Culture* (Albany: State University of New York Press, 2008), 94.

46. Rashkin, *Unspeakable Secrets and the Psychoanalysis of Culture*, 176.

47. Marianne Hirsch, "The Generation of Postmemory," *Poetics Today*, 29:1 (Spring 2008), 107.

48. Dori Laub and Nanette C. Auerhahn, "Knowing and not knowing massive psychic trauma: forms of traumatic memory," *International Journal of Psycho-Analysis*, 74:2 (1993), 288.
49. Rashkin, *Unspeakable Secrets and the Psychoanalysis of Culture*, 106.
50. Schwab, *Haunting Legacies*, 14.
51. Abraham and Torok, *The Shell and the Kernel*, 140, original emphasis.
52. Carol Rumens, "Reading Deane," *Fortnight* (July/August 1997), 29–30.
53. Frantz Fanon, *The Wretched of the Earth* [1961], trans. Constance Farrington (London: Penguin, 1990), 191.
54. Deane, "*Reading in the Dark*," 19.
55. Deane, "Introduction," in *Nationalism, Colonialism and Literature*, 14. Thinking about the novel in these terms returns us to *Translations*, Field Day's classic drama of cultural dispossession, abandonment, and adaptation under the impetus of colonial government in 1830s Ireland. Both play and novel focus on protagonists in complex social circumstances who find themselves having to mediate between cultures at key transitional moments, when their own communal and cultural systems are on the cusp of irreversible transformation. Through the intermediary figures of Deane's unnamed narrator and Friel's principal character, Owen O'Donnell, these writers ask searching questions about the extent to which the translator or interpreter is intrinsically a traitor, and about the deeper ideological problems associated with translation and interpretation in a politically contested place.
56. Shoshana Felman and Dori Laub, *Testimony: Crises of Witnessing in Literature, Psychoanalysis, and History* (London: Routledge, 1992), 5–6.
57. Cathy Caruth (ed.), *Trauma: Explorations in Memory* (Baltimore: Johns Hopkins University Press, 1995), 5.

Chapter 8

The Politics of Pity: Sebastian Barry's *A Long Long Way* (2005)

I

Sebastian Barry's literary career differs from those of the other eight novelists featured in this book in several respects, one of the most notable of which is his persistent refusal to limit himself to a single genre. While none of the writers discussed here is faithful only to prose fiction, Barry is more promiscuous than most in his sustained flitting between genres. Born in Dublin in 1955, he studied English and Latin at Trinity College Dublin and spent the late 1970s and early 1980s living and teaching for periods in France, Switzerland, England, Greece, and Italy. In 1984 he held an honorary fellowship in writing at the University of Iowa. By the time Barry returned to settle in Ireland in the mid-1980s, he was already the author of a coming-of-age novel, *Macker's Garden* (1982); a pair of novellas, *Time Out of Mind* (1983) and *Strappado Square* (1983); two volumes of poetry, *The Water-Colourist* (1983) and *The Rhetorical Town* (1985); and a children's novel, *Elsewhere: The Adventures of Belemus* (1985). In 1986 he turned to drama, which gave him "an almost literal sense of coming home,"[1] in that he was now entering territory successfully inhabited by his actress mother Joan O'Hara, who would later appear in several of his plays.[2] *The Pentagonal Dream*, an experimental piece for a single performer, was followed by *Boss Grady's Boys*, which was first produced by the Abbey Theatre in August 1988 and won the inaugural BBC/Stewart Parker Award. The play's enthusiastic reception set Barry on a more determinedly theatrical course in the 1990s, during which decade he produced five plays – *Prayers of Sherkin* (1990), *White Woman Street*

Reading the Contemporary Irish Novel 1987–2007, First Edition. Liam Harte.
© 2014 Liam Harte. Published 2014 by John Wiley & Sons, Ltd.

(1992), *The Only True History of Lizzie Finn* (1995), the multiaward-winning *The Steward of Christendom* (1995), and *Our Lady of Sligo* (1998) – that were at once intimately personal and, in the words of Fintan O'Toole, "emphatically public plays, up to their necks in the matter of Ireland."[3] Yet fiction was not abandoned. This quintet of plays was bookended by the novels *An Engine of Owl-Light* (1987) and *The Whereabouts of Eneas McNulty* (1998), the latter of which marks the beginning of Barry's mature style. Since then, he has alternated between drama and fiction with near metronomic regularity, interspersing plays such as *Hinterland* (2002), *Whistling Psyche* (2004), and *The Pride of Parnell Street* (2007) with the novels *Annie Dunne* (2002), *The Secret Scripture* (2008), *On Canaan's Side* (2011), and *A Long Long Way*, which is widely regarded as one of the finest historical novels of the contemporary era.

It is tempting to link Barry's oscillation between genres to his aversion to other forms of fixity and confinement, particularly his uneasy connection to Ireland and Irishness as prescribed political and cultural concepts. Although I have referred to him settling in Ireland in the mid-1980s, the term is perhaps too definitive-sounding, since his disposition is closer to that of an internal exile. He has spoken of "struggling to be at home in my own place"[4] after returning to Ireland in his early thirties and of being "at odds with the official nature of the present country."[5] Indeed, Barry's suggestive remarks on the inspiration behind what he refers to as his "ghost plays" – "I am interested not so much in the storm as the queer fresh breeze that hits suddenly through the grasses in the ambiguous time before it"[6] – alert us to his imaginative fascination for the disregarded, the idiosyncratic, the uncanny. Little wonder, then, that his fiction and drama should be populated by characters who exceed traditional categorization. As O'Toole has pointed out, Barry specialises in "history's leftovers, men and women defeated and discarded by their times. [. . .] They are misfits, anomalies, outlanders."[7] His particular affinity is for historically obscured individuals who, because of their personal choices, public duties, or political allegiances, have been excluded from the Irish nationalist master-narrative. The biblical epigraph to *The Whereabouts of Eneas McNulty* – "And whosoever was not found written in the book of life was cast into the lake of fire"[8] – speaks to the restorative and corrective impulses that undergird his entire *oeuvre*.

Virtually all of the prodigal protagonists through whom Barry explores these themes of historical erasure and ambiguous belonging have their origins in his own family history, which he has recursively mined for transgressive forebears whose experiences he reimagines as both singular and representative, "exception[s] to a general rule of Irishness, but at the same time not as rare as one might think."[9] The most critically acclaimed of his "family of plays about a family"[10] is *The Steward of Christendom*, loosely based on the life of his great-grandfather, a Catholic who rose to the rank of chief superintendent in the

Protestant-dominated Dublin Metropolitan Police (DMP) during the 1910s. Although the political opprobrium attached to this ancestor made Barry fearful of the consequences of wrenching him from "the dead grip of history and disgrace,"[11] the elegiac drama he fashions transforms him into an unabashedly tragic figure, a noble survivor from "a vanished world,"[12] the ghosts of which are his only companions in the nursing home where he languishes in his dotage. As a Catholic loyalist, Thomas Dunne found himself on the "wrong" side of history in the nationalist state that emerged from the rubble of revolution and civil war in 1922. Ten years on, he bitterly laments the violent eclipse of the colonial structures that sustained his proud record of service to crown and country. Yet despite being branded a traitor for his complicity in colonialist domination, Dunne refuses to renounce his loyalty to Queen Victoria, whom he eulogizes as "the very flower and perfecter of Christendom."[13] Through its unrepentant protagonist, the play challenges Irish audiences in particular to respect the imperial values Dunne embodies and to afford him the same "mercy"[14] and forgiveness his father showed Thomas as a child, when he returned home after sheltering an errant sheepdog that he feared would be put down.

Despite their broadly factual basis, Barry is keen to deter audiences from expecting historical exactitude from his "familiar" plays and novels. He tends to downplay his scholarly credentials and disavow polemical intent, presenting himself as a benign redeemer of suppressed histories. Commenting on the central figure in *The Secret Scripture*, he explained:

....

I'm afraid of the damage that is caused by not speaking of people like Roseanne, the unmentioned first wife, like so many families' old uncle Jacks who died in the First World War fighting for England. I'm concerned these silences leave a gap in yourself which then leaves a gap in your children and can ultimately lead to a hole in the country's sense of itself. Ireland's history is so much more rich, exciting, varied and complicated than we had realised. What I'm trying to do is gather in as much as I can. It's not to accuse, it is just to state that it is so.[15]

....

In spite of such conciliatory remarks, Barry's ongoing imaginative rehabilitation of the tradition of Irish Catholic unionism cannot be divorced from fractious debates about historiography and the politics of remembrance in contemporary Ireland. His determined efforts to queer the pitch of traditional nationalist history has led to him being firmly identified with the revisionist strand of Irish historical and cultural discourse. Elizabeth Cullingford, for example, forcefully argues that "Barry borrows the rhetoric of silencing from radical critics and appropriates it for conservative ends: his desire to give voice to the historically occluded native collaborator is a literary extension of the project of historical revisionism."[16] The dedication of *A Long Long Way* to

the leading revisionist historian, Roy Foster, appears to copper-fasten this association, yet the dedicatee is himself quick to defend the novelist against crude
accusations of "Raj revisionism," even though he acknowledges that there are
"several points where Barry's work chimes with recent preoccupations in Irish
historiography: the many ways in which Irish Catholics, often middle-class
nationalists, made their careers through imperialist channels."[17]

Foster's defense forms part of a sympathetic reading of what is, to date,
Barry's most historically informed use of the specificity of individual experience
to counter the prejudicial force of abstract categories and fixed stereotypes.
Through the story of Private Willie Dunne in *A Long Long Way*, Barry seeks
to honor the contribution to the Allied cause of southern Catholic Irishmen
during the First World War, many of whom enlisted in the British Army in the
belief that their actions would yield the dividend of Irish self-government when
the war ended. The spur to memorialization lies in the fact that these soldiers'
sacrifice has until recently been officially unacknowledged by the Irish state,
loyalty to the former imperial power being traditionally regarded as an affront
to the authorized narrative of nationalist resistance to British rule. Such strategic
forgetting stands in stark contrast to the recurrent ceremonial remembrance in
Northern Ireland of the sons of Protestant Ulster, whose sacrifice at the Somme
in 1916 as part of the 36th (Ulster) Division has long been woven into a tapestry
of deep-dyed loyalty to British monarchical Protestantism that stretches back
to the Battle of the Boyne in 1690 – and this despite the fact that in 1914 many
of those same Ulstermen were threatening armed rebellion against the British
authorities in Ireland, using German-sourced rifles. It was not until the late
1980s and 1990s that the contribution of nationalist Ireland to the British war
effort began to be investigated by historians, and Barry formally acknowledges
his debt to a number of pioneering studies at the novel's close.[18]

As a memorial gesture, then, *A Long Long Way* complements other public
expressions of the Irish Republic's newfound respect for its "unknown soldiers,"
including the Irish National War Memorial at Islandbridge in Dublin, officially
opened in 1995, and the Irish "Peace Tower" at Messines in Belgium, jointly
dedicated by Irish President Mary McAleese and Queen Elizabeth II in 1998.[19]
The novel's special contemporary relevance is also attested by its enthusiastic
critical reception – it was shortlisted for the 2005 Man Booker Prize and the 2007
International Impac Dublin Literary Award, and was chosen for the "Dublin:
One City, One Book" event in 2007[20] – and by the repressed personal histories
it has released, sometimes in the presence of the author himself: "I was down
in Kilkenny and this woman in her 70s stood up and said in a trembling voice
how her grandfather was the chaplain in the Royal Dublin Fusiliers. It was
probably the first room she had ever been in where she could stand up and
say that."[21]

In righting this lopsided Irish culture of remembrance and retrieving experiences that have previously been excluded from official historiographies, Barry seeks not only to advance his project of enlarging the terms upon which Irishness is constituted but also to elevate the Great War to a tragic status it has never attained within postcolonial Irish culture. In this chapter I wish to examine the textual strategies he employs to achieve these ends. Unlike a number of notable recent Irish historical novels, such as Roddy Doyle's *A Star Called Henry* (1999) and Joseph O'Connor's *Star of the Sea* (2002), *A Long Long Way* eschews the postmodern techniques of self-reflexivity, irony, subversion, and pastiche in its critical re-visioning of the Irish past. Despite its proximity to revisionist historiographic culture and its creation of protagonists who complicate simplistic antinomies of heroism and villainy, the novel cannot be straightforwardly categorized as historiographic metafiction, defined by Linda Hutcheon as "fictionalized history with a parodic twist."[22] Even though it is marked by a fundamental concern with the questions of "*whose* history survives" and "*whose* truth gets told"[23] in historical narratives, *A Long Long Way* lacks "theoretical self-awareness of history and fiction as human constructs,"[24] being in many respects closer to the nineteenth-century model of historical fiction in its realistic interleaving of the fictional and the factually historic. That is to say, Barry does not self-reflexively interrogate the myth-making tendencies of Irish historiography nor does he foreground the unknowability of the past other than through its textualized remains. What is at issue is not how we come to know and represent the past *per se* but rather the substance of the received narrative of Irish history and the blind spots and elisions it contains. We might therefore characterize *A Long Long Way* as well-researched, politically engaged, unironic historiographic fiction that actively solicits the reader's sympathy for its anomalous and decidedly innocent protagonists, to whom the author wishes to extend full humanity. The rhetorical means by which Barry garners and sustains such sympathy will be a key part of our explorations, because this is a novelist who wants as few barriers as possible to his readers' identifying with his pitiful protagonists and succumbing to narrative illusion. In the process, however, Barry's political agenda of not merely recuperating but exalting the sacrifice of the ordinary Irish volunteer in the First World War causes him to take a number of rhetorical risks that, I will argue, result in the simplification of the novel's subjects and a diminishment of its empathic and experiential power.

II

"He was born in the dying days:"[25] the novel's opening sentence proleptically encapsulates Dubliner Willie Dunne's fleeting existence, the very brevity of the statement enacting the shortness of his life's span. Here is a child of a transitional generation, born in 1896 in a city poised on the threshold of monumental change, who is destined to be crushed by history's "ferocious" (4) jaws. This is a protagonist whose story is effectively over before it begins, consciousness of which is forever with us as we read. Although Willie's naming (after William of Orange) and surroundings (Great Britain Street) identify him with the imperial forces that sought to bind Ireland to a unitary British state since the 1690s, the blood that "gathered on the nurses' white laps like the aprons of butchers" (3) and the storm that sluiced it down to the sea portend the tumultuous events that will soon violently sever those bonds. This leaking blood also presages that which will be shed at the western front by Private Dunne and "all those boys of Europe born in those times" (4), who succumbed to the cataclysmic events of 1914–1918.

These sentiments form part of a sudden amplification of tone and elevation of narrative perspective in which time is telescoped and a stately voice of lofty omniscience elegizes all the forgotten fallen of the Great War. It is from this Olympian vantage point that Barry posits his humane, compassionate aesthetic. He explicitly invokes the familiar motifs of the "lost generation" and the futility of war, thus aligning his novel with the canonical works of Britain's soldier–poets, notably Wilfred Owen, whose late war lyrics comprehensively repudiate the persistent idealization of battle and glorification of death found in much popular poetry of the 1914–1918 period.[26] By borrowing the plangent idiom of Owen's trench lyrics, Barry leaves us in no doubt but that *A Long Long Way* is to be read as a belated anthem for Ireland's forgotten doomed youth, channeled through the experiences of one raw recruit. Thus, in the space of a mere twenty sentences, the narrator whisks us from an evocation of Willie's inauspicious, meaningless birth to a view of his inauspicious, meaningless death, compressing his fate with that of countless hapless others. Before we are allowed even a glimpse of his heart and mind, the lens of historical inevitability strips this common soldier of all individuality and particularity, casting him as an anonymous atom of history predestined to be "milled by the mill-stones of a coming war" (4).

With this opening, Barry performs a calculated trade-off, forfeiting dramatic tension in order to purchase the reader's sympathy and pity for his benighted protagonist, whose heavily accentuated paltriness – Willie is "provisional and bare" (3), "a scrap of a song" (4), "a featherless pigeon" (5) – seals the deal. Again, Owen comes to mind, particularly his excoriation of the meaningless horror and searing inhumanities of mechanized warfare, pithily expressed in the preface to his *Poems* (1920): "The subject of it is War, and the Pity of War."[27] Yet Barry also primes us for the next turn of his narration, where this requiem for the senselessly sacrificed is counterpointed by the image of Willie's mother being stilled by her son's singing voice and made to marvel at "the power of mere words, the mere things you rolled around in your mouth, the power of them strung together on the penny string of a song, how they seemed to call up a hundred vanished scenes, gone faces, lost instances of human love" (5). This scene is deftly metonymic for the historical novelist's own relationship to history: "human stories told for nothing" (4) may yet be redeemed from history's "mighty scrapheap" (4) and the "secret Scripture"[28] of the faceless dead memorialized in prose fiction. With this, we are ready to witness Private Willie Dunne's symbolic resurrection from the no-man's-lands of both Flanders fields and twentieth-century Irish history.

The condensed narration of Willie's childhood and adolescence continues over the rest of Chapter 1, glancingly taking in the death of his mother in childbirth; his family's move to Dublin Castle, the epicenter of British rule in pre-independence Ireland; the involvement of his father, James Dunne, a DMP chief superintendent, in the baton-charging of striking workers during the 1913 Dublin lockout; Willie's burgeoning secret passion for Gretta Lawlor, whose father was among those injured by the police; and his decision to enlist in the Royal Dublin Fusiliers, a regiment of the 16th (Irish) Division, in August 1914, thereby becoming one of the estimated 58,000 Irish servicemen who were mobilized at the start of hostilities.[29] Such abbreviated treatment of Willie's first eighteen years gives the chapter – which, like the novel as a whole, is replete with proleptic detail – the feel of an overture to the defining action to come. In keeping with this anticipatory mood, Gretta's father, to whom Willie ferries unwanted gifts from his own guilt-ridden father, broaches some of the novel's governing themes when he berates Willie for not having an opinion on the police's rough treatment of the protesting workers: the necessity of knowing one's own mind; the conflict between personal feeling and public duty; the difficulty of reconciling individual conscience with the dictates of state and civil society.[30] Furthermore, in questioning whether James Dunne "knew his own mind" (10) when he led the fateful baton charge, Mr Lawlor disabuses Willie of his ignorance of his father's culpability for the deaths of the four men who were killed in the fracas.

Following this episode, a troubled awareness of his father's guilt lodges in Willie's mind "like a rat and made a nest for itself there" (11). This knowledge constitutes the first mote in his naive political outlook. Hitherto, he appears to have acquiesced in the general consensus that "the police had acted bravely and had won the day" (7); now he stands "marooned" (11) by the force of an unsettling counter version, the whole episode being proleptic of his final, stateless fate on Flanders fields. Thus discomfited, Willie reflexively answers Lord Kitchener's call for Irish recruits and is plunged into a much more disorienting "deep, dark maze of intentions" (15): the complex motives, tangled emotions, and divided allegiances that surrounded Irish military participation in the First World War, an event that both intensified and transformed the country's already acute political tensions. Given the centrality of the tumultuous politics of the 1912–1918 period to the novel, it is necessary to summarize the historical contexts of *A Long Long Way* at this point, before proceeding to examine the textual strategies and ideological implications of Barry's representation of his central characters and their dilemmas.

The impassioned conflict over Irish Home Rule dominated British politics in the immediate prewar period. When the Parliament Act of 1911 removed the House of Lords' absolute veto over legislation, the way was cleared for the third Home Rule Bill, which was introduced in the House of Commons by the Liberals in April 1912, to be passed into law within two years. Outraged Ulster unionists responded by marshaling all of their resources to prevent Irish self-government from becoming a reality, publicly threatening to defy, by any means necessary, the authority of any parliament forced upon them. The implicit threat of militancy represented by the signing of a Solemn League and Covenant by just under 240,000 Ulstermen in September 1912 was made explicit four months later with the formation of the Ulster Volunteer Force, a citizen militia committed to the preservation of the Union. Irish nationalists responded to this extremist move by setting up the Irish Volunteers in Dublin in November 1913 to defend the Home Rule cause. Each paramilitary organization professed loyalty to the crown, while at the same time threatening armed revolt if their political demands were not met. Such threats were not merely rhetorical. By the summer of 1914 both militias were in possession of significant quantities of arms and ammunition smuggled in from Germany. Tensions were heightened by the passage of the Home Rule Bill by the Commons in May 1914, which allowed for six of Ulster's nine counties to opt out of a self-governing Irish parliament for a six-year period only. When the Lords responded by amending the Bill to enable all nine counties to exclude themselves forever, the political situation became seriously deadlocked. With no resolution in sight, civil war in Ireland seemed to many to be inevitable until, on August 3, 1914, Germany's invasion of Belgium defused the "Ulster crisis" by sweeping Britain and Ireland into the twentieth century's first global war, bringing about a radical realignment of Anglo-Irish politics in the process.

The immediate effect of the outbreak of war was to prompt the political leaders of both Irish citizen militias publicly to pledge their respective followers to the Allied cause. Unionist leader Sir Edward Carson did so because he saw an opportunity to demonstrate Ulster's unyielding loyalty to the Union; Irish Party leader John Redmond, because he strategized that common sacrifice for the British war effort would ensure the implementation of the Home Rule Bill, which was signed into law as the Government of Ireland Act in September 1914 but had its operation suspended for the duration of the war. Redmond also believed that collective action by Irishmen of diametrically opposed political persuasions would lay the foundations for a postwar reconciliation of the country's warring traditions. He wrote:

· ·

I pray that whenever a battalion of the Irish Brigade goes into action there may be a battalion of the Ulster Division alongside them. I need not point out the moral to you. This is the way to end the unhappiness and discords and confusion of Ireland. Let Irishmen come together in the trenches and spill their blood together and I say there is no power on earth when they come home can induce them to turn enemies one upon the other.[31]

· ·

And so, in an impromptu speech at Woodenbridge, County Wicklow on September 20, 1914, Redmond unconditionally pledged the Irish Volunteers to the British war effort, announcing that they would go "wherever the firing line extends, in defence of right, of freedom and of religion in this war."[32] This declaration had seismic political ramifications in that it led directly to a split in the Volunteer movement, pitting the pro-war Redmondite majority against a minority of militant republican separatists who were guided by the ancient Fenian dictum that "England's difficulty is Ireland's opportunity." Nor was the irony lost on this minority that Britain, the nation now purporting to be the protector of "gallant little Belgium," was still Ireland's oppressor. So while recruits to Redmond's mainly nationalist "Irish Brigade," formally constituted as the 16th (Irish) Division, marched off to Belgium and France to fight alongside the other two Irish divisions of Kitchener's new army – the 10th (Irish) and the 36th (Ulster) – the breakaway separatists remained at home, secretly planning for an insurrection that would eventually materialize in April 1916.

At the front, Willie Dunne – who, as a Catholic loyalist, simultaneously stands apart from these fierce internecine tensions and straddles mutually exclusive categories of Irishness – encounters volunteers from many different parts of Ireland who harbor varying degrees of fealty to crown and shamrock. The spectrum stretches from the patrician Captain George Pasley, scion of landed Wicklow Protestants with a proud history of imperial loyalty, to Sergeant-Major Christy Moran, who curses both the army in which he serves and the 1916 rebels, to Private Jesse Kirwan, a Redmondite nationalist whose entire *raison d'être* for enlisting is so undermined by the Easter Rising and the execution of its leaders that he shrinks, literally and figuratively, from the very fabric of his uniform, before being court-martialed and shot for "cowardice." It is a key part of Barry's revisionist agenda to give voice to such varied ideological positions and to show how many of them were radically destabilized by the overlapping force fields of the First World War and the Rising. Thus, the contradictions and complexities of allegiance that conventional nationalist versions of this period of Irish history have tended to elide are densely woven into the narrative, to underline the point that history is subtle and ambiguous and not "all threads going one way only" (22), to adapt a phrase applied to Christy Moran. Moran himself, indeed, highlights the hybrid realities that monochromatic exteriors conceal when he declares that the British Army should be renamed the "Irish-British" Army (55), in view of the ubiquity of khaki-clad Irishmen at the front.

While this assertion rests on sound historical evidence, there is a somewhat tendentious flavor to some of the novel's other challenges to the biases and elisions of nationalist historiography.[33] For example, Barry's insistent reminder that it was not only the sons of senior metropolitan policemen who volunteered for war service in 1914 results in a disproportionate number of Willie's comrades – Joe McNulty, Joe Kielty, Pete O'Hara – being of Connaught origin, the province that "invariably had the lowest provincial rate of enlistment"[34] during the war. Clearly, it suits Barry's aesthetic and political purposes to foreground such regional diversity, not least because it enables him to endow Willie with a belief in the pervasiveness of "his father's fervent worship of the King" as "the lynchpin that held down the dangerous tent of the world," thus convincing him "that all Ireland was, and all that she had, should be brought to bear against this entirely foul and disgusting enemy" (22–23). This evocation of universal Irish sacrifice for a common cause undoubtedly heightens the pathos of hundreds of "Catholic, Protestant and Jewish Irishmen" (54) succumbing to chlorine gas at St Julien alongside English, French, and African troops, their bodies pestled together in death. Such mass chemical slaughter seems to erase the very markers of national, ethnic, and ideological difference, giving the soldiers who survive this carnage the composite appearance of imperial Everymen: "They stripped to the waist and got black as desert Arabs. The white skins were disappearing. Mayo, Wicklow, it didn't matter. They might be Algerians now, some other bit of the blessed Empire" (54).

The St Julien gas attack, which claims the life of Captain Pasley and several of Willie's closest pals, marks a crucial stage in the young Dubliner's declension from proud volunteer to disillusioned combatant. The invigorating "euphoria" (23) he felt on completing his basic training in Fermoy is as distant a memory as the quasi-epiphanic sense of fearlessness he experienced during his first, night-time excursion into no-man's-land. Sorrow had now "gone rancid in him, he thought; it had boiled down to something he didn't understand. The pith of sorrow was in the upshot a little seed of death" (59). The more Willie atrophies inwardly, the more *unheimlich* the verdant Flanders landscape appears. When, in the aftermath of the gas attack, a "strange teem of rain" (53) falls on the ragged survivors with a degenerative rattle, it seems that even nature's restorative potency has been debased. Although he still tries to calibrate the horrors of "this new world of terminality and astonishing dismay" (52) against seemingly temperate Irish realities, his propensity to domesticate the Belgian landscape can no longer be sustained in the charnel house of the front. To the contrary, when Irish realities become blood-darkened after Easter 1916, Flanders becomes an uncanny facsimile of home. When Willie stops to bury the German soldier he killed, he realizes that "Dublin and Ypres were all the one" (124), a phrase that echoes the title of a post-Rising souvenir picture postcard, "Ypres on the Liffey," published by Bairds of Belfast.[35]

The full extent of this mirroring reveals itself only gradually. It is not just a matter of events imitating each other in these two sites of war, though the execution by firing squad of Jesse Kirwan, who is too weak to stand unsupported, bears obvious similarities to that of the wounded insurgent James Connolly, who had to be propped up in a chair before being executed by firing squad in Kilmainham Gaol in May 1916. More fundamentally, Dublin and Ypres exist as polar points of an echo chamber in which reciprocal truths and treacheries ramify disconcertingly. Thus, Willie feels like a "traitor" (73) in his father's presence because he cannot banish the knowledge of Chief Superintendent Dunne's betrayal of the Dublin populace's trust in him during the 1913 riots. Yet he himself is subsequently accused by his father of having a "treacherous gob" (247) when he dares to express tentative, ambivalent sympathy for the 1916 rebels, whose own act of national "treachery" haunts "loyal" Irishmen at the front: "The executed men were cursed, and praised, and doubted, and despised, and held to account, and blackened, and wondered at, and mourned, all in a confusion complicated infinitely by the site of war" (144). Ultimately, it is Willie's belated appreciation of the truth of words spoken by the doomed Kirwan, who is the living embodiment of this complicated confusion, which constitutes the most tragic echo of all: "Now we won't have a country at all. Now everything you and me and the others were trying to do is useless" (156).

Willie's descent into grim disaffection further underlines the novel's affinity with experiential First World War literature produced by frontline witness–participants, one of the most pronounced traits of which is that it is "a literature of brutally disappointed expectations,"[36] which exposes the cruel myths of heroic warfare and patriotic sacrifice. In this respect, it is interesting to note Barry's admission that the book that served as his "talisman"[37] during the composition of *A Long Long Way* was *All Quiet on the Western Front* (1929), since the structural and thematic impress of Erich Maria Remarque's anti-war classic on Barry's text is quite marked. The young protagonists of both novels follow a similar trajectory: basic training on enlistment followed by swift immersion in the horrors of the trenches; intervals of rest and recuperation, including visits to brothels; going on home leave and returning to the front as changed men; killing an enemy soldier in hand-to-hand combat; being wounded and sent on convalescent leave; and being killed in action in October 1918, on the eve of the Armistice. The deeper affinities between the novels center on the core theme of war as a wholly destructive and degrading experience, the harrowing effects of which are heightened by the youthfulness of the protagonists. Eighteen-year-old Willie Dunne's "sense of youth not vanishing but being submerged in a killing sea from which no one might emerge, bathed in the acid blood of bomb or bullet" (130), resonates with Paul Bäumer's bleak reflections on what war did to his German school friends: "We were eighteen years old, and we had just begun to love the world and to love being in it; but we had to shoot at it. The first shell to land went straight for our hearts."[38] Both Dunne and Bäumer are also devastated by their shared awareness of the senselessness and insignificance of their sacrifice and the indelibility of their feelings of existential lostness, such that the former's climactic realization that "he had no country now" (286) echoes the latter's sense of his generation as "superfluous even to ourselves."[39] Yet both novelists also strive to deny death complete dominion. The courageous comradeship of the doomed acts as a temporary "reserve against the onslaught of oblivion"[40] for both of these common soldiers, and that "nameless active force that we call life"[41] continues to assert itself right up to the moment when the snipers' bullets find their respective marks. Willie dies with an antiphonal hymn on his lips, Bäumer, wearing a tranquil expression, both soldiers having ceased to believe that those in the opposing trenches are enemies, only suffering fellow human beings.

It is, however, the novels' contrasting treatment of the emotion that is most synonymous with the literature of the First World War – pity for a whole generation of young men, condemned to routinized slaughter by ignorant and negligent elites – that brings the problematic aesthetic and polemical aspects of *A Long Long Way* into sharp focus. Whereas Remarque's rendering of the brutal reality of battle relies on lapidary sentences that plainly convey subjective individual experience with a minimum of emotion, Barry's emotionally charged prose not only evokes the felt reality of war but also relentlessly solicits our pity for the Irish volunteers on the basis of their enduring innocence and harmlessness. As it does so, the novel indulges in a kind of rhetorical excess, sentimentalizing and sanctifying these benighted young men to such a degree that the suasive force of the work is significantly blunted. Readers who are familiar with Barry's *oeuvre* will not be at all surprised by this feature of his characterization, which has drawn plaudits from critics such as Christina Hunt Mahony, who explains:

....

Barry endows ordinary people with a degree of sustained innocence and a purity of soul and spirit which seems to defy any negative experience life might have dealt them. [. . .] Barry's often ornately poetic language is used to cultivate a lush aural environment in which such intensity and purity can thrive, forcing audience or reader to suspend disbelief, even while it remains steadfastly at odds with the realism of Barry's historical and geographical settings.[42]

. . . .

But whereas Mahony clearly admires Barry's poetics of innocence and the liberal humanist ideology it posits, I find that the pronounced accentuation of the protagonists' naivety distorts the imaginative integrity of *A Long Long Way* because it sacrifices much moral, psychological, and political complexity in order to press home the *parti pris* point that the protagonists are to be seen as irreproachable paragons of goodness. In this, I find myself in sympathy with key aspects of Cullingford's critique of *The Whereabouts of Eneas McNulty* and *The Steward of Christendom*, the affective power of which is significantly diminished, she argues, by the author's subordination of his protagonists to a schematic political allegory which insinuates that "the history of Ireland in the twentieth century has been bedeviled by the patriotic idea of 'freedom': decolonization spells disaster."[43] While I regard *A Long Long Way* as a less ideologically programmatic text than either of these earlier works, I nevertheless believe that Barry's polemically driven exaltation of the Irish volunteer relies on a set of rhetorical strategies that, by placing undue emphasis on the cultivation of sympathy, leads to simplifying acts of representational selectivity.

Of particular relevance here is the way Barry deploys a decidedly sentimental and exonerative narrative idiom to elicit the reader's uncritical pity for his durably innocent central protagonist. Mark Jefferson's remarks about the nature and implications of sentimentality are highly pertinent in this context, insofar as they help us to understand better the special character of narratives that employ this particular emotion. Jefferson argues that what chiefly distinguishes sentimental works is

. . . .

their emphasis upon such things as the sweetness, dearness, littleness, blameless-ness, and vulnerability of the emotions' object. The qualities that sentimentality imposes on its objects are the qualities of innocence. But this almost inevitably involves a gross simplification of the nature of the object. And it is a simpli-fication of an overtly moral significance. The simplistic appraisal necessary to sentimentality is also a direct impairment to the moral vision taken of its objects. [. . .] The unlikely creature and moral caricature that is someone unambiguously worthy of sympathetic response has its natural counterpart in a moral caricature of something unambiguously worthy of hatred.[44]

. . . .

Now, we have already noted the pervasive emphasis in the opening chapter on Willie's diminutive size, his "'damnable' height" (6) being a mark of his failure to live up to his father's expectations of him.[45] As the narrative develops, the cluster of mental and emotional experiences associated with puniness is systematically exploited to deepen the pathos and sentimentality of his plight in the midst of "a human nowhere" (231). The most obvious of these associations is the childlike neediness and vulnerability that "little Willie" exhibits throughout. For example, after he escapes the lethal cloud of chlorine gas in Chapter 4, we are told that he "wanted his sergeant and his captain and his mates the way a baby wants its home, no matter how provisional" (49). This metaphor is effectively literalized during his first furlough, when the motherless recruit is deloused, washed, and swaddled by his father, as if "they were still in Dalkey and he was a little lad" (74). On his return to the front, the horrors of trench warfare infantilize him further. One of the novel's most harrowing scenes shows Willie childishly gripping the coattails of Christy Moran as they cross a field of high corn on their approach to village of Guillemont, which is clogged with the pulverized corpses of Allied and German troops. Willie's rejection by his father and by Gretta during his final furlough diminish him to ghostly status, so that he is "just wisps and scraps of a person" (252) on rejoining his regiment for what proves to be the last time. This imagistic seam reaches an appropriate apotheosis in the final chapter when, on the threshold of death, the starkness of Willie's utterly forlorn predicament is exposed: "He had no country, he was an orphan, he was alone" (289).

Although he is the beneficiary of most authorial sentiment in the novel, Willie is not the only volunteer to be represented in this way. Joe Kielty, to whom the epithet "gentle" is applied as consistently as the adjective "poor" is to the fusiliers in general, is compared to a sleeping baby, the wounded Captain Sheridan to a six-month-old infant, and Pete O'Hara to "a child thrown among blood and broken souls" (169). In fact, Barry persistently infantilizes the volunteers as a means of accentuating their piteous simplicity and divesting them of the messy complexities of adult agency. This motif is established early in the narrative when five of Willie's regiment go for a swim in a river near their billet. They immediately revert to boyish behavior, setting paper boats on the water and playing football in their long johns before taking a skinny-dip. Afterwards, they dispose themselves in a chillingly vulnerable fashion on the riverbank: "They were naked as babies. A little breeze played about in the willows. The five penises lay like worms in their nests of pubic hair" (40). The sense of innocuous sexuality conjured up by this pastoral interlude is reinforced by the sanitized quality of many of the volunteers' sexual thoughts and deeds – Pete O'Hara's complicity in the horrific rape of a Belgian woman notwithstanding. For example, the foul-mouthed Christy Moran's fantasy of a romantic rendezvous in Kingstown is improbably non-sexual, stopping at "how clean and good and sweet-smelling" (30) his girl would be, and Willie himself harbors remarkably chaste thoughts about Gretta, despite being "plagued" by "endless" erections (7). Furthermore, for all that the war marks his transition to "bloody manhood" (21), there remains much of the passive, pure-hearted naïf about Willie. It is telling that even though he loses his virginity to an Amiens prostitute, it is she who is pointedly shown to be taking the initiative throughout, obliging the submissive youth to surrender helplessly to her "graceful heat" (63). This episode is one of several in which Willie is absolved of mature agency and intentionality, be it sexual or ideological. Like Eneas McNulty, his unimpeachable goodness precedes him. Indeed, a key point of contrast between the two protagonists merely serves to underline their similarity. Whereas "Simple, innocent, foolish Eneas is unable to kill even when he gives it a shot,"[46] Willie slays a German soldier in hand-to-hand trench combat. Yet even as he does so, the narrative exonerates him by having him react almost involuntarily, as if acting unbeknown to himself:

. . . .

For some reason, without himself actually registering it, he had got the funny tomahawk into his left hand and when he raised the hand the spike at the top of the short stick horribly drove into the underchin of the German. The man now clawed there himself and to Willie's surprise tore off the saving mask, which looked a very much more admirable design than Willie's. Now Willie again almost on instinct struck at the man's face with the hatchet and it opened the cheek from the side of the mouth to the eye above. (114)

. . . .

Such persistent use of an exculpatory idiom means that Willie and his fellow volunteers exist as angels of history in the midst of diabolical grand carnage, a sentimental characterization that jars somewhat beside the unflinching fidelity with which the rest of the novel conveys the physical and psychological miseries of modern industrial warfare. The volunteers' almost holy humility strikingly manifests itself in Chapter 8, by which point Willie is back in Flanders, his mind still reeling from the disorientating events of Easter week in Dublin, during which he comforted a dying rebel. Although the young rebel's death had "shifted his very heart about" (102), its indelibility symbolized by the stubborn bloodstain on Willie's uniform, his scorn for the rebels' "violent ignorance" (110) reasserts itself as the Hulluch gas attack looms. In an epiphanic moment just before the "familiar ogre" (111) descends, the "unsullied truth" (111) of his comrades' sacrifice forcefully strikes Willie, such that he sees his companions frozen in a *tableau vivant*, their pose supplicatory, their ghosthood immanent (to purloin a phrase of Seamus Heaney's). The pathos of the scene is overpowering, not least because the crouching troops are explicitly denied heroic status, being "only poor Tommies of Irishmen, Joe Soaps of back streets and small lives" (110). Yet despite being stripped of all emotional and spiritual comforts, a strange kind of grace inheres in these pitiable pawns of history, a quasi-metaphysical quality that, like the soothing power of the *Ave Maria*, "could not be rendered meaningless even by slaughter, the core inviolable, the flame unquenchable" (134). For all that they see and do, none of these volunteers become overtly brutalized or emotionally inured by war. Unlike Bäumer and his fellow recruits, these soldiers do not grow "tough, suspicious, hard-hearted, vengeful and rough."[47] Willie himself never seems to harden fully, emotionally or morally, despite his telling Gretta that "you do end up here as hard as a nut" (64). Like the horses that "looked even in death faithful and soft" (231), a pith of refined feeling and fidelity to humane values remains intact in him. To the rhetorical questions that punctuate the narrative – "What of such hearts and souls? Could the soul hold good, could the heart?" (169), "Could they not all be holy" (289) – the novel posits poignantly affirmative answers.

Aesthetically, Barry's pervasive beatification of Willie's innocence, and that of most of his companions, undoubtedly succeeds in engaging the reader's pity and sympathy for "these wretched fools of men come out to fight a war without a country to their name" (134). One has only to scan the encomia that festoon the paperback edition of the novel to appreciate this. Ideologically, however, Barry's poetics of innocence seems to me to veer toward a rather heavy-handed polemic, insistently promoting the message that these once-vilified volunteers should now be seen only as tragic victims of historical circumstance, thus leaving the novel open to the charge that it refutes one partial version of history with an equally partisan rebuttal. The protagonists' staggering naivety and innocuousness are so heavily ring-fenced by the exonerative narration and sentimental characterization that psychological verisimilitude and historical plausibility are sometimes stretched to breaking point. This is perhaps most evident when we examine the men's motives for enlisting in the first place. Barry's volunteers are, in the main, "loyal, unthinking and accepting sort of men" (26), few of whom appear to be motivated by deep ideological conviction. On the contrary, some of their reasons for joining up are markedly contingent, even whimsical. Christy Moran reveals he enlisted because his wife burned her hand while drunk, Joe Kielty says he did so because he was presented with a white feather in Ballina, and Joe McNulty appears to have followed suit simply to keep his cousin company.[48] Even the nationalist Jesse Kirwan is made to disavow full-blooded political commitment when, after telling Willie that he volunteered in order "to save Europe so that we might have the Home Rule in Ireland in the upshot," he proceeds to blame his father for lumbering him with "this rigmarole, this torment of talk of freedom" (157).

Willie's own motives for joining the Fusiliers are decidedly overdetermined. A number of impulses are shown to be acting upon him, primarily his being too short to join the DMP but also his wish to please his father and protect his sisters and his beloved Gretta, since "there were women like her being killed by the Germans in Belgium, and how could he let that happen?" (13).[49] However, the sense of patriotic duty that underpins the last named of these reasons is strikingly nebulous and barely intuited by him: "something in him had leaped forth towards this other unknown something. He could put it no clearer than that in his mind" (23). Like many of his fellow volunteers, Willie is understandably oblivious of the peculiar horrors and wrenching changes the war will wring. But if, as Christina Hunt Mahony argues, his naive idealism at the point of enlistment is "not out of place historically nor in literary historical terms" (90), Willie's utter consternation on being deployed to quell the 1916 Rising while on leave is harder to credit. Throughout his brief assignment, he remains completely baffled by events in Dublin, to the extent that he mistakes a fatally wounded rebel for a German. Even allowing for the fact that Willie has been away from his home city for two years, it stretches credulity to imagine that someone of his background, who has chosen to don khaki and fight in the empire's service, would be so drastically ignorant of Ireland's murderous political animosities as to require an impromptu history lesson from Jesse Kirwan. After all, we know that Willie read a "long account" (14) of Redmond's Woodenbridge speech in the *Irish Times*. Surely, then, he would have had at least an inkling of the bitter factionalism that subsequently racked the Volunteer movement and known of the existence of a dissenting minority of Dublin-based advanced nationalists intent on fermenting rebellion?

Contextualized thus, Private Willie Dunne's innocence seems more reprehensible than pitiable. So careful is Barry to protect his protagonist's political and moral inviolability that he freezes him a state of arrested development that tests the limits of the reader's suspension of disbelief. Although the authorial tenderness lavished on Willie and his fellow volunteers clearly appeals to many readers' sensibilities, there is to my mind an overly directive and ultimately self-defeating quality to the novelist's insistent attempts to persuade us to feel with him on this politically charged subject. By portraying this "featherless pigeon" as someone who is, in Jefferson's terms, "unambiguously worthy of sympathetic response," the novel's sentimental exaltation of its disenfranchised subjects distorts and detracts from what is otherwise a richly textured and deeply moving account of young Irishmen crushed by a conflict of Dantean ferocity.

Notes

1. Nicholas Wroe, "A Life in Writing: Sebastian Barry," *Guardian*, October 11, 2008, review section, 13.
2. Barry's decision to write for the stage could even be construed as a return to the prenatal home. In "Following the Steward," his prefatory essay to *The Steward of Christendom* (London: Methuen, 1997), Barry revealed: "My only experience actually on stage was in my mother's womb at the Abbey while she was doing a pantomime" (xiii–xiv).
3. Fintan O'Toole, "Introduction: A True History of Lies," in *Plays: 1*, Sebastian Barry (London: Methuen, 1997), x.
4. Barry, "Following the Steward," viii.
5. Maria Kurdi, "'Really All Danger': An Interview with Sebastian Barry," *New Hibernia Review*, 8:1 (2004), 49.
6. Barry, *Plays: 1*, xv.
7. O'Toole, "Introduction," vii.
8. Sebastian Barry, *The Whereabouts of Eneas McNulty* (London: Picador, 1998), unpaginated page.
9. Kurdi, "'Really All Danger,'" 42.
10. Kurdi, "'Really All Danger,'" 42.
11. Barry, "Following the Steward," ix.
12. Barry, *Plays: 1*, 246.
13. Barry, *Plays: 1*, 250.
14. Barry, *Plays: 1*, 301.
15. Wroe, "A Life in Writing," 13.
16. Elizabeth Cullingford, "Colonial Policing: *The Steward of Christendom* and *The Whereabouts of Eneas McNulty*," *Éire-Ireland*, 39:3&4 (2004), 12.
17. Roy Foster, "'Something of us will remain': Sebastian Barry and Irish History," in *Out of History: Essays on the Writings of Sebastian Barry*, ed. Christina Hunt Mahony (Dublin: Carysfort Press, 2006), 191.
18. Barry also had at least one contemporary source to hand, as he revealed in an online interview: "my wife's grandfather was in the Royal Army Medical Corps right through the war and came home safely. I had his Soldier's Small-Book, still pristine, on my table while I worked." See interview with Sebastian Barry, Penguin Reading Group, http://us.penguingroup.com/static/rguides/us/long_long_way.html.
19. The history of the Irish National War Memorial is itself indicative of the cultural neglect of those whom it commemorates. The memorial was completed in 1939 and dedicated "To the memory of the 49,400 Irishmen who gave their lives in the Great War, 1914–18." However, its formal opening was delayed by the outbreak of the Second World War and the site subsequently fell into disrepair until the Office of Public Works initiated a restoration program in the

1980s. Even then, no government representatives attended the blessing of the renovated park by church leaders in 1988 and it was not until April 1995 that the memorial received an official state opening. Sixteen years later, the memorial was one of the sites visited by Queen Elizabeth II during her historic four-day visit to Ireland in May 2011. See Yvonne Whelan, *Reinventing Modern Dublin: Streetscape, Iconography and the Politics of Identity* (Dublin: UCD Press, 2003), 185–191.

20. Launched in 2006, this annual event is designed to encourage as many people as possible to read the same book during a nominated month.

21. Wroe, "A Life in Writing," 13.

22. Linda Hutcheon, *The Politics of Postmodernism* (London: Routledge, 2002), 50.

23. Linda Hutcheon, *A Poetics of Postmodernism: History, Theory, Fiction* (London: Routledge, 1988), 120, 123, original emphasis.

24. Hutcheon, *A Poetics of Postmodernism*, 5.

25. Sebastian Barry, *A Long Long Way* [2005] (London: Faber and Faber, 2006), 3. Subsequent page numbers are cited parenthetically in the text.

26. See Paul Norgate, "Wilfred Owen and the Soldier Poets," *Review of English Studies*, 40:160 (1989), 516–530.

27. Owen Wilfred, *The Collected Poems of Wilfred Owen*, ed. Cecil Day Lewis (London: Chatto and Windus, 1963), 31.

28. This phrase, which is also the title of Barry's 2008 novel, comes from a sonnet written by Tom Kettle, poet, professor of economics at University College Dublin, Irish nationalist MP, and British soldier, who was killed at the Somme in September 1916. Five days before his death he wrote a sonnet for his daughter Betty that ends: "Know that we fools, now with the foolish dead, / Died not for flag, nor King, nor Emperor, / But for a dream, born in a herdsman's shed, / And for the secret Scripture of the poor." Quoted in Terence Denman, *Ireland's Unknown Soldiers: The 16th (Irish) Division in the Great War, 1914–1918* (Dublin: Irish Academic Press, 1992), 176–177.

29. David Fitzpatrick, "The logic of collective sacrifice: Ireland and the British Army, 1914–1918," *Historical Journal*, 38:4 (1995), 1017.

30. James Dunne's "treats" are also rooted in an awareness of the class difference between the Dunnes and the Lawlors. This transmits itself to Willie, who feels he must keep his love for Gretta hidden from his sisters because she is "a slum dweller" (11).

31. Quoted in Denman, *Ireland's Unknown Soldiers*, 28–29.

32. Denman, *Ireland's Unknown Soldiers*, 26.

33. Ireland was a valued repository of British military manpower throughout the nineteenth century. In 1830 Irish-born soldiers comprised 42% of the British Army, and although the post-Famine decades witnessed a sharp decline in enlistment in numerical terms, Irish service in the British Army remained constant in proportional terms up until the First World War. See Kevin Kenny,

"The Irish in the Empire," in *Ireland and the British Empire*, ed. Kevin Kenny (Oxford: Oxford University Press, 2004), 104–106.

34. Fitzpatrick, "The logic of collective sacrifice," 1020.

35. Keith Jeffrey reproduces "Ypres on the Liffey" in his *Ireland and the Great War* (Cambridge: Cambridge University Press, 2000), 52. This may well have been the postcard Gretta sends Willie in Chapter 11, which is described as "showing poor Sackville Street in ruins" (140). Willie sends her one of Ypres in return.

36. Damon Marcel DeCoste, "The Literary Response to the Second World War," in *A Companion to the British and Irish Novel 1945–2000*, ed. Brian W. Shaffer (London: Blackwell, 2005), 4. Despite his chapter's title, DeCoste is referring here to the First World War.

37. Interview with Sebastian Barry, Penguin Reading Group.

38. Erich Maria Remarque, *All Quiet on the Western Front* [1929], trans. Brian Murdoch (London: Vintage, 1996), 63.

39. Remarque, *All Quiet on the Western Front*, 206.

40. Remarque, *All Quiet on the Western Front*, 193.

41. Remarque, *All Quiet on the Western Front*, 192.

42. Christina Hunt Mahony, "Children of the Light amid the 'risky dancers': Barry's Naïfs and the Poetry of Humanism," in Mahony, *Out of History*, 83.

43. Cullingford, "Colonial Policing," 35–36.

44. Mark Jefferson, "What is Wrong With Sentimentality?," *Mind*, 92:368 (1983), 526–527.

45. The proleptic significance of the marks on the wallpaper made by James Dunne's police pencil when ritually measuring his young son's height become clear in Chapter 6 when Willie notices these "ancient marks" while on leave from the front, and recalls the time "when his father used to put him up against the wall like a fella to be shot at dawn" (75).

46. Cullingford, "Colonial Policing," 28.

47. Remarque, *All Quiet on the Western Front*, 19.

48. The song "The Boys from the County Mayo" may be an intertext here, the chorus of which contains the lines: "So boys, stick together in all kinds of weather, / Don't show the white feather wherever you go."

49. Interestingly, one of the commonest motives of those who joined the Dublin Fusiliers in 1914, economic necessity (to which Father Buckley refers in Chapter 16), is not among Willie's reasons, presumably because of his relatively comfortable situation as a senior policeman's son.

Chapter 9

Mourning Remains Unresolved: Anne Enright's *The Gathering* (2007)

I

Anne Enright was born into a middle-class Dublin family in 1962 and graduated with a degree in English and philosophy from Trinity College Dublin in 1985, after which she completed an MA in creative writing at the University of East Anglia. On her return to Dublin in the late 1980s, she secured a job as a television producer in RTÉ, the national broadcaster, where she remained for six years. For most of this time Enright worked on *Nighthawks*, a late-night show set in a fictional diner that combined stand-up comedy, political satire, and live interviews. This "vanguard experiment in postmodernist programming"[1] is perhaps best remembered for a 1992 episode in which a former government minister revealed that Charles J. Haughey had authorized the phone-tapping of two political journalists when he was Irish prime minister in the early 1980s. The revelation led to Haughey's resignation as leader of the Fianna Fáil party in January 1992 and also sealed the fate of *Nighthawks*, which was axed later that same year. The program's demise provided Enright with the spur she needed to become a full-time writer in 1993, though she has also linked her decision to a nervous breakdown she experienced three years earlier, which made it clear to her that she "needed to write."[2] Having already made an auspicious debut with *The Portable Virgin* (1991), a short-story collection hailed by the *Irish Times* as "a real departure in women's fiction in this country,"[3] Enright focused her energies on what was to become her first novel, *The Wig My Father Wore* (1995), a satirical anti-*Bildungsroman* set in the cynical, exploitative world

Reading the Contemporary Irish Novel 1987–2007, First Edition. Liam Harte.
© 2014 Liam Harte. Published 2014 by John Wiley & Sons, Ltd.

of TV program production. This was followed by *What Are You Like?* (2000), which traces the convergent paths of twins separated at birth in the 1960s, and *The Pleasure of Eliza Lynch* (2002), a historical novel set in nineteenth-century Paris and Paraguay, as well as a volume of short stories, *Taking Pictures* (2008), and a book of essays about motherhood, *Making Babies* (2004). It was not until *The Gathering* won the Man Booker Prize in 2007, however, that Enright's work attracted the attention of the wider reading public. Such is the marketing power of the Man Booker brand that the novel, which was considered to have little chance of winning by bookmakers, was propelled to the top of the bestseller lists in the wake of the award, having sold a modest 3553 copies in Britain prior to that.[4] Since then, Enright has published a fifth novel, *The Forgotten Waltz* (2011), and edited *The Granta Book of the Irish Short Story* (2010).

From the start, Enright's fiction announced itself as both postmodernist and feminist, though both terms require nuanced application in her case. As regards the first, Enright's facility for formal inventiveness in her early works makes for a fiction of outlandish conceits, startling juxtapositions, idiosyncratic perspectives, and hallucinatory thought patterns.[5] Although this aspect of her work has become more muted as she has matured as a writer, it hasn't disappeared entirely. She reflected in a 2008 interview: "One of the pathways I have been negotiating as a writer has been my relationship with the real. So all these words like surreal, like *hyperréalisme* in French, I like hyperrealism, as a description of what I do."[6] There is, moreover, a persistent metafictional dynamic in operation, which means that Enright's ostensible narrative subject is shadowed by a deeper concern with the challenge of representing the subject, both linguistically and formally. Yet there is no postmodern disavowal of the realities of power and oppression or of the social and economic circumstances that determine choice, agency, and opportunity: "My impulse is towards lives as people live them. My impulse is towards the real. That's where I'm trying to get."[7]

Enright's feminism is equally complex and interrogative. On the one hand, her work is properly skeptical of gender antinomies and too self-reflexive to offer any simplistic critique of women's devaluation within misogynistic power relations; on the other, it is closely attuned to the profound damage done to women's physical and psychological well-being by the production and regulation of female subjectivity by the patriarchal symbolic order. Thus, most of the stories in *The Portable Virgin* are narrated by female protagonists who speak from various points on a spectrum that stretches from subjugation to empowerment. Some struggle to establish an authentic emotional connection with men and some strive to resist being engulfed by them, while others willfully disavow societal codes of female behavior. Several protagonists delight in mocking a culture that measures female value by a woman's physical shape and appearance, among them Clare in "The Brat," who wears her ugliness "like a badge,"[8] and the girl in "Fruit Bait," who rebels against respectability and refinement by transforming her body into a palette of tattoos. While many of these women are troubled, atomized, or socially unmoored, all know the value of feminine agency and refuse to capitulate to the pernicious imperatives of a sexualized social world. Like Angela Carter, one of her tutors at the University of East Anglia, Enright uses the tools of surrealism and fantasy to comment on the socialization of gender roles and relations and to question conventional assumptions about women's subordination and sexual passivity. "Fatgirl Terrestrial" is a *tour de force* of stereotype subversion in this regard, a wry postmodern fable about the triumph of feisty corpulence over the destructive power of social prejudice.

These early stories also reveal Enright's disposition toward a magical realist idiom, whereby everyday scenarios are playfully reimagined, without fluctuation of tone, in ways that mimic the fantastic logic of folk tales. "(She Owns) Every Thing," the opening story in *The Portable Virgin*, presents an impressionistic portrait of an emotionally unstable shop assistant whose subjectivity is dispersed among the handbags she sells, each of which is a token of unfulfilable desire and ineradicable loathing. In the title story, another handbag – this one stolen – acts as the catalyst for the volume's most symbolically suggestive scene, which challenges the long-standing, ideologically coercive trope of the virginal maternal in Irish culture. Sitting on Dollymount Strand, a betrayed wife finds in the stolen bag a plastic statuette of the Virgin Mary that bears the legend, "A present from Lourdes,"[9] and is filled with holy water. She drinks the contents and then launches this kitsch souvenir on the waves in the direction of where she imagines her unfaithful husband to be. This deftly orchestrated denouement neatly encodes the protagonist's ambivalent relation to inherently contradictory and psychologically damaging conceptions of Irish femininity, which idealize and objectify women as stoic, self-sacrificing, desexualized icons. This scene can also be read as a feminist reworking of one of the most iconic moments in Irish fiction, Stephen Daedalus' artistic epiphany in *A Portrait of the Artist as a Young Man*, which takes place in the same liminal Dublin space. But whereas the wading girl that Stephen sees is a kind of secularized version of the Virgin Mary, pregnant with ecstatic meaning for him, the plastic Madonna discarded by Enright's disillusioned housewife speaks only to its finder's gnawing feelings of inauthenticity and disposability.

As the religious undertones of this story imply, Enright's feminist fictions are inflected by a residual Catholicism that cannot easily be expunged. Her generation was, she said, "radical and had a sense of ownership and newness,"[10] yet she also acknowledges that although the Catholic Church no longer enrages her, "for anyone reared in that tradition, the problem of God does not go away."[11] Religious and metaphysical issues do not manifest themselves in any straightforward way in Enright's fiction. The winged angel who appears in *The Wig My Father Wore*, for example, is a much more magical realist in nature than biblical. In this novel Enright moves decisively beyond conventional realism to produce a full-blown metafictional work in which the influence of Carter's brand of gothic postmodernism is even more marked, although, as Patricia Coughlan notes, the novel's "rehearsal of female self-empowerment [. . .] scarcely replicates the prescriptions of naïve second-wave feminism, and in formal innovation and thematic irony it ranges well beyond the usual realist and Oedipal-confessional territory of Irish fiction at large".[12] Based around a romance between a neurotic television producer named Grace/Gráinne and Stephen, a reincarnated suicide, the novel's stream-of-consciousness style makes considerable demands on the reader and sometimes tapers off into whimsical, self-indulgent prose. Yet the staccato, fragmentary form is very well suited to conveying Grace's alienation from Irish popular culture, which is seen as being as depthless and artificial as the eponymous wig, and to capturing her absurdist take on weighty political issues, exemplified by the scene in which the shower of a TV newsreader literally becomes his mouthpiece when she uses it:

. . . .

'A crisis in the European Exchange Rate Mechanism,' says the showerhead. 'Minister for Agriculture moves on animal drug abuse,' as I soap between the perfection of my toes and back to the soft handful of my heel.

'Bishop says no to AIDS test.' There is no hair on my shin anymore. I soap the white swell of my thigh. It is not a modern body, wherever I got it from. And now it has no pubic hair.

'Ceasefire in Belfast,' says the water. I have no pubic hair.[13]

. . . .

In addition to testifying to Enright's capacity for unconstrained, ludic imaginings, this satiric passage also suggests the ways in which the female body serves as a site where biological, social, political, religious, and economic realities collide. The very title of Enright's debut collection draws attention to an anatomical detail, and the stories themselves show bodies in various states of distortion, whether bloated by appetite or "whittled into thinness."[14] As already indicated, the premise of *The Wig My Father Wore* pivots on a flesh/spirit dyad and Grace's body in particular "keeps thrusting itself forward in all its manifestations, grotesque, painful, or pleasurable."[15] The motif of feminine embodiment is equally pronounced in *What Are You Like?*, which features chapters entitled "Hands," "Blood," "Wrist," "Tissue," "Veins," "Lung," and "Skin." Throughout this novel, there is a sense in which protagonist Maria's pervasive sense of dislocation and fragmentation is corporeally displayed. The oddity of inhabiting a body is continually borne in upon her. "She had the right mouth, but the wrong voice might come out of it," we are told, and hear her describe an extra vein on her arm as a "mistake."[16] Even her sex is a mystery to be decoded, an "unreadable knot of anatomy between her thighs."[17] Bodily gratification, torment, and despoliation are also governing motifs in *The Pleasure of Eliza Lynch*, the forensic, anti-erotic first sentence of which sets the tone: "Francisco Solano López put his penis inside Eliza Lynch on a lovely spring day in Paris, in 1854."[18] "The sheer fleshliness of the body is always in evidence," observes Coughlan of this novel, and she goes on to argue that Enright is ultimately "reminding us of the fundamentally paradoxical relation between the incontrovertible fact of embodiment and the capacity for rational consciousness."[19]

This emphasis on embodied subjectivity assumes a much more sustained weight of thematic and symbolic significance in *The Gathering*, the most searing fictional representation to date of the devastating effects of the trauma of child sexual abuse in Ireland on identity, agency, and relationships, and of the corresponding, profoundly difficult need to counteract silence and forgetting through disclosure. According to Maria Luddy and James M. Smith, "the story of contemporary Irish society, a story that many claim signals unprecedented social and economic transformation, is a narrative with the child as its central trope."[20] Supportive evidence for this assertion exists in many forms, from the plethora of recent films, plays, art works, and autobiographies that anatomize Irish childhoods from plural perspectives to the litany of child abuse scandals – and their systematic concealment – involving religious- and state-run institutions, which have attracted a torrent of media attention since the mid-1990s.[21] The continuing proliferation of first-hand accounts of child physical, sexual, and psychological abuse, within individual Irish families as well as within the state's network of industrial and reformatory schools, bears vivid and disturbing testimony to this cultural confluence. The popular reception of such memoirs affirms the moral and emotional power of their truth-claims, yet the cultural representation of institutional, clerical, and familial child abuse has not been the sole preserve of real-life victims and survivors. Ireland's novelists and short-story writers have also given "eyes to the horrified narrator. Eyes to see and to weep."[22] Indeed, some of the most memorable and affective portrayals of child sexual abuse in contemporary Ireland have been in fictional form, from Dorothy Nelson's groundbreaking *In Night's City* (1982) through Jennifer Johnston's *The Invisible Worm* (1991) and Edna O'Brien's *Down by the River* (1996) to Patrick McCabe's *The Butcher Boy* and his even more phantasmagoric *Winterwood* (2006).

What distinguishes *The Gathering* from these works is the subtlety and complexity of its depiction of the trauma of child abuse as a collective as much as a personal experience; its nuanced attempt to build a critical and ethical consciousness in the reader by narrating what was formerly unspeakable; and its scrupulous refusal to redeem history by suggesting that the far-reaching effects of traumatic memory can be completely erased or transcended. Enright's elucidation of the interconnections between personal and national trauma is central to the moral force and finesse of the novel. By locating the human body as an operative site of trauma, she illuminates the myriad ways in which the psychological and somatic dissonance created by traumatic events reverberates outwards from the individual to the social group, from the body of the victim/survivor to that of the nation. "Trauma writers," observes Laurie Vickroy, "make the suffering body the small, focused universe of the tormented and a vehicle for rendering unimaginable experience tangible to readers,"[23] and Enright's approach certainly fits this template. In fact, so deftly does the condition of the individual body map onto that of the social collective that *The Gathering* can be read as an exemplum of Peter Stallybrass and Allon White's claim that

the body cannot be thought separately from the social formation, symbolic topography and the constitution of the subject. The body is neither a purely natural given nor is it merely a textual metaphor, it is a privileged operator for the transcoding of these other areas. Thinking the body is thinking social topography and vice versa.[24]

The social topography under scrutiny in *The Gathering* is one heavily obscured by cultural amnesia, concealment, and denial. Through her tormented and amnesiac central protagonist, Veronica Hegarty, Enright addresses the prodigious array of psychic, somatic, moral, and cultural ramifications of hidden child sexual abuse in modern Ireland, the fact of which is shown to be symptomatic of a pervasive devaluation and victimization of vulnerable individuals by church, state, and society. Veronica is a bereaved woman in search of a discourse through which to make sense of her difficult relationship to a traumatic past, the debilitating effects of which have deformed her personality, self-image, and her relational life. Hers is the story of a self formed under the burden of a trauma that has remained cognitively unprocessed until her brother Liam's suicide causes her to evaluate the origins and extent of her shattered subjectivity. It is this concealed narrative that Veronica, whose name is potent with religious symbolism,[25] is seeking to reconstruct and communicate as part of an arduous process of recovery, which is overlaid by searing grief and anger. She is also seeking to piece together and give voice to her dead brother's story: Veronica's post-traumatic *testimonio* contains within it Liam's ghosted memoir, the medium of his reincarnation, though this is no Christian resurrection. Rather, the narrator attempts to make her brother come alive as the dead man he was in life, his core being having been annihilated – mortified, in all senses of the word – by the trauma of sexual abuse, stripped "of voice, of life, of knowledge, of awareness, of truth, of the capacity to feel, of the capacity to speak."[26] Veronica's narrative can therefore be said to correspond to the "double telling" that Cathy Caruth identifies as a defining feature of trauma narratives, "the oscillation between a *crisis of death* and the correlative *crisis of life*: between the story of the unbearable nature of an event and the story of the unbearable nature of its survival."[27]

Read thus, *The Gathering* constitutes a powerful critique not only of patriarchal power in Irish society but also of the deeper ideologies upon which that society was founded and which continue to sustain it. In the following analysis I wish to examine how, in giving voice to traumatized victims and survivors, the novel indicts familial, communal, and state complicity in the perpetuation of abusive practices and the betrayal of vulnerable individuals. I will pay particular attention to Enright's formal and stylistic attempts to replicate the damaged psyche of the trauma survivor and the impediments that bedevil her protagonist's belated post-traumatic recuperation, central to which is Veronica's need to find, or impart, meaning to her suffering and that of her deceased brother. Ultimately, I suggest, the novel's moral urgency and grim tragic power derive from its careful delineation of the ramifying impact of traumatic wounds and violations, and the necessarily partial and protracted nature of the recovery process.

II

The Gathering is narrated from the Dublin of 1998 by Veronica Hegarty, who is thirty-nine at the time of telling. Outwardly, she has all the trappings of Celtic Tiger affluence, including a Saab and a large "Tudor-red-brick-with-Queen-Anne-overtones" house in an upmarket Dublin suburb, where she lives with her "high-maintenance" husband and their "two beautiful daughters in two beautiful bedrooms."[28] Inwardly, however, Veronica is in a state of emotional freefall as a result of the death by suicide in Brighton of her favorite brother, the wayward Liam. A mere eleven months younger than he, she sometimes thought of him as a kind of twin with whom she "overlapped" (11) in the womb, a thought that makes his death seem like a second – and final – untimely severance of bodies once entwined. His loss has brought about a radical disintegration of the certainties that had formerly sustained Veronica and exposed deep fissures beneath her life's affluent façade. But it is not just Liam's suicide that has undone her. Much of Veronica's pain and anguish come from the feeling that she failed her brother, both in childhood and in adulthood, leaving her with a burden of unappeasable guilt, unexpressed rage, and paralyzing depression. Since his death she has developed chronic insomnia and started to drink heavily. She has also become emotionally estranged from her children and her marriage seems to be edging inexorably toward dissolution. When, after another round of "the unhappiness game" (179), Veronica takes stock of the self-hatred, emotional numbness, and chronic self-fragmentation that bereavement has starkly laid bare, her life comes into focus as a defensive performance, a simulation of convention and control. She realizes, in short, that she has been surviving rather than experiencing life, hiding behind a protective persona, cut off from feeling in order to feel less pain:

....

> I was living my life in inverted commas. I could pick up my keys and go 'home' where I could 'have sex' with my 'husband' just like lots of other people did. This is what I had been doing for years. And I didn't seem to mind the inverted commas, or even notice that I was living in them, until my brother died. (181)

....

Destabilized thus by "a grief that is biological" (11), Veronica spends most of her sleepless nights in a state of melancholic entrapment, endlessly revisiting the events of her dysfunctional family's distant and recent past for clues to "the Hegarty conundrum, the reason we were all so fucked up" (85). In particular, she is desperate to fathom the origins of the causes that led to Liam's final act of self-destruction. Veronica's tortured broodings repeatedly circle the events of the summer of 1968, the time when she, Liam, and their sister Kitty were "farmed out" (86) to her grandmother, Ada Merriman, in Broadstone in Dublin's north inner city. It was here, she suspects, that Liam was sexually abused by the mysterious Lambert Nugent, a friend (and possibly lover) of Ada, widow of the recently deceased Charlie Spillane. Veronica soon realizes, however, that her search for causal factors requires her to probe more deeply into family history, to a time beyond the reach of personal memory: "The seeds of my brother's death were sown many years ago. The person who planted them is long dead – at least that's what I think. So if I want to tell Liam's story, then I have to start long before he was born" (13).

To unravel the knot of her family's disconnected dynamic, therefore, Veronica must establish a dialogue between memory, consciousness, history, and narrative. None of these terms is a given for her, however, nor is her access to them compatible with single, unified utterance. This immediately becomes clear in the short opening chapter, in which she tries to explain her urgent need to turn to writing, to story, in the midst of her bereavement. Her opening statement resonates with compacted layers of meaning:

> I would like to write down what happened in my grandmother's house the summer I was eight or nine, but I am not sure if it really did happen. I need to bear witness to an uncertain event. I feel it roaring inside me – this thing that may not have taken place. I don't even know what name to put on it. I think you might call it a crime of the flesh, but the flesh is long fallen away and I am not sure what hurt may linger in the bones. (1)

This confessional beginning exemplifies many of the central insights of trauma theory: the radical disruption of memory and its reliability; the imperfectly known past; the body as the site of an unnameable wounding; and the belated, overarching urge to testify to a dubious, haunting event that was not fully understood or integrated at the time it occurred – if occur it did – and which may or may not be susceptible to meaningful retrospective narrative formulation. Framed thus, Veronica's testimony presents itself as a form of traumatic memory, or as an expression of her desire to master such memory by translating it into narrative and linking it with feeling. Her words bring to mind Pierre Janet's distinction between "normal" or narrative memory, which is adaptive, improvisational, and oriented toward a listener, and traumatic memory, which he viewed as a "peculiar morbid disturbance"[29] that, because it is fixed in the patient's consciousness, has not been properly integrated into existing mental frameworks and remains beyond language, dissociated from consciousness. Working from the premise that memory is essentially *"the action of telling a story,"* Janet theorized that an event

> has not been satisfactorily liquidated, has not been fully assimilated, until we have achieved [...] an inward reaction through the words we address to ourselves, through the organisation of the recital of the event to others and ourselves, and through the putting of this recital in its place as one of the chapters in our personal history.[30]

In her study of trauma and testimony in women's autobiography, Suzette Henke gives this recital of events another name, "scriptotherapy – the process of writing out and writing through traumatic experience in the mode of therapeutic re-enactment."[31] Veronica's express need to recover autobiographical wholeness by narrating her story can be read precisely in these terms, notwithstanding the fact that she is speaking primarily as a witness rather than a victim of traumatic injury, though she may be both – the narrator's inability to know is itself classically symptomatic of traumatic injury. The distinction is in any case largely irrelevant, since witnessing abuse has been clinically correlated with experiencing it personally in real life, as the psychotherapist Judith Lewis Herman explains:

....

Witnesses as well as victims are subject to the dialectic of trauma. It is difficult for an observer to remain clearheaded and calm, to see more than a few fragments of the picture at one time, to retain all the pieces, and to fit them together. It is even more difficult to find a language that conveys fully and persuasively what one has seen.[32]

....

This struggle to give cohesive narrative shape to something that eludes speech and may in fact be non-existent is textually foregrounded throughout the novel, making Veronica's trauma story a highly self-reflexive one. By continually exposing the reader to the confusions and conflicts of traumatic memory, Enright seeks not merely to *present* trauma's effects but also to *encode* them in the novel's form and narration. In other words, the novelist re-creates the sense of disorientation inherent to trauma that thwarts knowledge and comprehension, so that as readers we partake of the protagonist's grueling struggle to make sense. The richly suggestive metaphor this witness–victim chooses to describe her project – "I lay them out in nice sentences, all my clean, white bones" (2) – presents her in the guise of forensic archaeologist, painstakingly attempting to reassemble the skeletal remains of the past, performing a figurative re-memberment of history, memory, and subjectivity. But because the bones of history will not stop "sliding around" (13) for her, Veronica is unable to situate herself properly in relation to the past. This is because the traumatized mind has no direct access to traumatic memory: there is no single, totalizing narrative waiting to be told, no "one story that would explain us all" (84). Indeed, as Marita Sturken explains, the term "traumatic memory" is itself oxymoronic: "the traumatic event is not initially remembered or represented but is held at bay by dissociation and reenacted without remembering. It is narrative integration that produces the *memory* of the traumatic event. It is when they become full-blown narratives that these memories tell stories of blame and guilt."[33] Veronica's attempts to knit together the bones of disrupted memory are shadowed, therefore, by an awareness of the inherent instability and fictionality of her enterprise. The provisional idiom that governs the narration ("maybe," "perhaps," "probably," "I assume," "is this possible?") has a pictorial analogue in the flame-singed family snapshot that adorns the cover of the original hardback edition of the novel, the partially obscured faces underscoring the problematic relationship between traumatic events and the individual's recollection and narration of them. Veronica's story is reliant on unreliable acts of remembrance, imagination, and speculation, with only shadows and traces to work with: rent books, photographs, and a "thick little fold of letters" (217) written by Lamb to Ada. The narrator's response to the latter epitomizes her recourse to novelistic methods to translate traumatic (non)memory into "normal" memory, at the same time as it questions the ethics of narrative and its therapeutic powers: "There are gaps and lapses, into which I read anger or desire. I would do that, that is what I do, but they are, at the very least, intriguingly mute" (233).

As a narrative structured on traumatic experience, then, Veronica Hegarty's scriptotherapeutic gesture is inherently suspect and may well be as wishful and fallible as "fancy" (21). Indeed, she pointedly underlines the arbitrariness of her project by choosing as her point of narrative entry the meeting of Ada, Lamb, and Charlie in the foyer of a Dublin hotel in 1925. The process of putting fictional flesh on conjectural bone is immediately literalised: Nugent "must be reassembled; click clack; his muscles hooked to bone and wrapped with fat, the whole skinned over and dressed in a suit of navy or brown" (14). The emotional content of the past is equally pliable, as Veronica's reflections on the instant passion she supposes must have burgeoned between Lamb and Ada attest. Paradoxically, the narrator begins to develop more faith in her imagined versions of events – "my little blasphemies" (66) – than in any so-called factual account, to the extent that she becomes seduced by the "romance" (27) of narrative possibility. This is crystallized in Chapter 21 when, driven by her relentless need to know if Lamb truly loved Ada, Veronica weaves a highly charged sexual encounter around a momentary "flaw in the air" between them (136). But the intoxication of being able to "twist them as far as you like, here on the page" (139) takes her no closer to emotional truth, and the essential unknowability of the irrecuperable past reasserts itself:

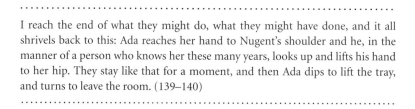

I reach the end of what they might do, what they might have done, and it all shrivels back to this: Ada reaches her hand to Nugent's shoulder and he, in the manner of a person who knows her these many years, looks up and lifts his hand to her hip. They stay like that for a moment, and then Ada dips to lift the tray, and turns to leave the room. (139–140)

When, in the following chapter, the irrefutable facts of Liam's death compel Veronica to put "an end to romance and just say what happened in Ada's house, the year that I was eight and Liam was barely nine" (142), the deeper psychological and somatic effects of her traumatic memories, and the radical challenges they pose to narrative integration and authoritative telling, powerfully manifest themselves. The scene in which she "recalls" her sudden, passive witnessing of Liam being abused by Nugent reveals both the indelibility and the ambiguity of her "memories" of pain and devastation, the simultaneity of knowledge and denial. The degree to which this experience has permanently marked Veronica's inner being without ever having been cognitively or emotionally processed into "normal" memory is registered by her anguished struggle to assert the veracity of this disturbing episode:

. . . .

And even though I know it is *true* that this happened, I do not know if I have a true picture in my mind's eye [. . .]. I think it may be a false memory, because there is a terrible tangle of things that I have to fight through to get to it, in my head. And also because it is unbearable. (144)

. . . .

Although writing about actual survivor trauma of a self-evidently much greater order, Dori Laub's reflections on the relation of personal witness to truth in the minds of Holocaust survivors cast helpful light on Veronica's defensive dissociation from painful memories here, and enable us to read it not as a case of "false memory" syndrome but as a product of the continuing power of traumatic memory to confound the meaning of reality and truth. Laub asserts that the horror of traumatic experience is "maintained in the testimony only as an elusive memory that feels as if it no longer resembles any reality. The horror is, indeed, compelling not only in its reality, but even more so, in its flagrant distortion and subversion of reality."[34] If we apply this insight to *The Gathering*, we can see that Veronica's incredulity underscores the extent to which she "failed to be an authentic witness to herself,"[35] a reading buttressed by her later inability not only to state categorically what she saw happen to Liam but to ascertain if she herself was sexually abused. The mental image she has of her younger self holding Nugent's penis comes, she says, "from a place in my head where words and actions are mangled. It comes from the very beginning of things, and I can not tell if it is true. Or I can not tell if it is real" (221–222). Thus, what constitutes the truth is so radically in doubt that the narrator can only bear witness to her *inability* to access fully her traumatic memory or achieve complete interpretive mastery over her past. Her evocation of her profound uncertainty recalls Caruth's claim that "For history to be a history of trauma means that it is referential precisely to the extent that it is not fully perceived as it occurs; or to put it somewhat differently, that a history can be grasped only in the very inaccessibility of its occurrence."[36]

Veronica's unreliable narration of her uncertain memory of her immediate response to the sight of Liam being abused is even more revealing of the disjunction between affect and understanding that attended this moment of traumatic witnessing, and its continuing psychic and somatic effects in the present. The image she presents in Chapter 22 of her eight-year-old self running "to the toilet upstairs, with an urge to pee and look at the pee coming out; to poke or scratch or rub when I was finished, and smell my fingers afterwards" (146), graphically evokes the way in which her trauma was processed somatically rather than cerebrally, so that the memory of it lodged more in the body than in the mind. This is further underlined by the narrator's seemingly involuntary physical response to her act of recall in the present: "I pause as I write this, and place my own hand over my face, and lick the thick skin of my palm with a girl's tongue. I inhale. The odd comforts of the flesh. Of being me" (146). Such highly enactive behavior accords with Susan Brison's explanation of the ways in which traumatic experience is viscerally embedded, remembered in and through the body, in ways that are not fully understood by the victim:

. . . .

A primary distinguishing factor of traumatic memories is that they are more tied to the body than are narrative memories. Indeed, traumatic memory can be viewed as a kind of somatic memory [. . .]. Traumatic memory blurs the Cartesian mind-body distinction that continues to inform our cultural narrative about the nature of the self. [. . .] The intermingling of mind and body is apparent in traumatic memories that remain in the body, in each of the senses, in the heart that races and skin that crawls whenever something resurrects the only slightly buried terror.[37]

. . . .

The conclusion of Chapter 22 further bears out Brison's observations by bringing into sharp focus how, without entering narrative memory, such somatic memory conditions thought and behavior long after the abuse has ceased. Not for the first time, Veronica alludes to her chronic propensity to self-harm, but the terms she uses on this occasion explicitly identify it as a pernicious symptom of her somatic storage of trauma since childhood: "You know everything at eight, but it is hidden from you, sealed up, in a way you have to cut yourself open to find" (147). Over thirty years later, Liam's suicide has become the metaphorical knife that has caused more and more of the body's sealed-up "memory-knowledge"[38] to seep from "the wound of family" (243), thereby exposing the underlying agony and all-pervasive psychosomatic repercussions of such abnormal processing of trauma. Now that the "imagined body" (223) of the violated child has become a felt presence through the "brute body" (223) of the drowned adult, Veronica's alienation from embodied human-ity in all its forms appears absolute. The more of her story we hear, therefore, the more evident it becomes that all life, all love, has been tainted by the effects of her traumatic witnessing, and that her painful connection to this trauma is displayed and replayed through the body. The shock of her brother's death has intensified this debilitating corporeal dynamic, simultaneously heightening her aversion toward human bodies and deepening her misanthropic disdain for all manner of "bodily events" (138).[39] A profound alienation from sexual desire, copulation, and procreation has taken root in her since Liam's suicide, fuelling her excremental vision of the fertile world. Veronica Hegarty belongs to one of the largest families ever seen in Irish fiction, not that this is a source of any pride to her. On the contrary, so overwhelming is this traumatized daughter's memory–knowledge of children's corruption by adults that she is revolted by her parents' sexual incontinence, their having "bred as naturally as they might shit" (25). The "sex that produced the twelve children and seven miscarriages inside my mother's body" (227) exists as a permanent affront to her, such that she is unable to forgive her mother for such obscene fecundity: "The stupidity of so much humping. Open and blind. Consequences, Mammy. *Consequences*" (8). Later, on Brighton seafront, Veronica almost vomits on seeing "The liv-ing, with all their smells and holes [...], while thinking of my own brother's flesh and how it will look in two months', then three months' time" (76), and moments afterwards she is consumed by a visceral revulsion not merely for her own maternal flesh but for the procreative potential of all humanity:

. . . .

I look at my hands on the railings, and they are old, and my child-battered body, that I was proud of, in a way, for the new people that came out of it, just feeding the grave, *just feeding the grave!* I want to shout it at these strangers, as they pass. (79)

. . . .

It is significant that Veronica's body nausea also extends to her husband, whose sexuality she no longer trusts, so blinded is she by the male body's latent capacity to inflict sexual suffering. The insidious intermingling of the psychological and the somatic effects of trauma are again visible here: the more Veronica inspects her uncertain memories of Liam's abuse, the more she real-izes that Nugent's selfish pleasure was "the most terrible thing in the room" (144), and the deeper her fear of sexual intimacy in the present. Hence her phallocentric patterns of thought and behavior, as evidenced by her contempt for what she sees as Tom's insatiable carnal appetites and her conviction that he desires her "annihilation" (145) when they have sex. Even though she subsequently acknowledges the irrationality of such views, and concedes that "this side-by-side business is all we've got" (220), it is clear from the scene in which she abruptly fellates her husband that her perspective on the most socially sanctioned form of sex – that which takes place between a married couple – is disturbed by its latent affinities with the most culturally forbidden kind, that between an adult and a child. The enactive aspects of Veronica's behavior during this scene constitute it as episode of transference, further exemplifying the ongoing affective power of traumatic experience to determine an individual's present-day memory and relational life. Herman provides an apt gloss on such reenactment without remembrance when she points out that there is "something uncanny about reenactments. Even when they are consciously chosen, they have a feeling of involuntariness" (41).

In all of this, we can see just how tainted by trauma Veronica Hegarty's relationship with the human body has become, right down to the most intimate form of human interaction, touch. To a woman who thinks of herself as being "beyond sex" (97), the words uttered by the risen Christ to Mary Magdalene after the Resurrection – "*Noli me tangere*," "Do not touch me" – have an awful, ironic appropriateness, not least because Nugent's nickname, Nolly May, is a corruption of this phrase. At its dark extremities, Veronica's haptic anxiety and aversion to human fleshiness mutate into a desire to transcend her own body entirely and become as ghostly as her brother, whose exile from Ireland can itself be read as a prolepsis of his final fate.[40] Clearly, this trauma survivor struggles with deep-seated feelings of dehumanization and worthlessness, frequently feeling herself to be reduced to animal status, "like meat that has been recently butchered" (219). Liam, too, appears in this light in one of Veronica's pivotal epiphanic moments:

· ·

What is written for the future is written in the body, the rest is only spoor. I don't know when Liam's fate was written in his bones. And although Nugent was the first man to put his name there, for some reason, I don't think he was the last. Not because I saw anything else going on, but because this is the way these things work. Of course, no one knew how these things *worked* at the time. We looked at the likes of Liam and had a whole other story for it, a different set of words.

Pup, gurrier, monkey, thug, hopeless, useless, mad, messer. (163)

· ·

Here, Veronica zones in on one of the cruxes of child sexual abuse, the way in which victims are simultaneously robbed of their subjectivity and condemned to a life of indelible social stigmatization. The erasure of the trauma victim's original identity by another person comprises a key part of this shattering of the self. This process of diminishment is then compounded by the judgments of the wider society, which further devalue the victim by turning them into a scapegoat or demonized Other, making them into "someone else's speech, the medium of another's agency," as Brison explains:

> The trauma survivor experiences a figurative dismemberment – a shattering of assumptions, a severing of past, present, and future, a disruption of memory. Piecing together a self requires a working through, or remastering of, the traumatic memory that involves going from being the medium of someone else's (the torturer's) speech to being the subject of one's own.[41]

Enright herself said of Liam that "He is the lost one, the scapegoat. In a very original sense, he is the sacrificial boy."[42]

Liam's inability to reclaim his own subjectivity by articulating his pain, then, makes Veronica's attempt to undo the silencing effects of trauma all the more urgent. Although she couches her recuperative drive in terms of personal indebtedness – "I owe it to Liam to make things clear – what happened and what did not happen in Broadstone" (223) – there is more at stake here than the fidelity to the dead that is a familiar feature of trauma survival. Paradoxically, Veronica's recognition of the impossibility of fully retrieving her dissociated memories crystallizes deeper truths about the relationship of private trauma to Irish national history. Gradually, the network of connections between the personal repression of traumatic memories and the cultural denial of the reality of child sexual abuse in modern Ireland is borne in upon Enright's tortured protagonist, enabling her to map the psychopathological signs and symptoms of traumatized individuals onto the society that produced them. That is to say, she begins to understand that individual memory is always at the same time collective memory and that repression is a social as well as a personal response to traumatic injury.

And so, as she gains a fresh perspective on the social matrix within which Liam's violation occurred, Veronica is struck by how fundamentally inhospitable patriarchal Irish society was to children's welfare and well-being. She recalls how, during her university days in the 1980s, "Children were being chucked out all over Dublin. All our parents were mad, in those days. There was something about just the smell of us growing up that drove them completely insane" (96). Going further back to her own 1960s upbringing, she remembers that her father "used to hit his children all the time," although such violence was, she wrily notes, "never personal" (226). But it is the knowledge that she, Liam, and Kitty were "farmed out" (86) to her grandmother that most starkly epitomizes the fact that "children in those days were of little account. We three Hegartys were manifestly *of little account*" (235–236). Small wonder, then, that a sexual predator such as Lamb Nugent should look upon other people's children, especially the children of the poor (Ada was, after all, financially indebted to Nugent, her landlord[43]) as instruments of pleasure or revenge, safe in the knowledge that no child's allegation could trump an adult's denial. The victimizer, no less than the victim, insists on the condition of silence, and the lack of a discursive space in which traumatic experience can be publicly articulated and communally acknowledged further reifies its unspeakability. Herman's clinical conclusions are again applicable to this fictional context: "When the victim is already devalued (a woman, a child), she may find that the most traumatic events of her life take place outside the realm of socially validated reality. Her experience becomes unspeakable."[44]

It was not until the endemic nature of sexual violence against Irish children surfaced into public consciousness during the 1990s, therefore, as a result of sustained media coverage of child abuse scandals and their associated official inquiries, that Veronica was able to see abuse and trauma as indices of the systemic betrayal of children on a national and historical scale. Her failure to realize that the unthinkable was happening in her midst is a crucial and immediate source of the unabsolvable guilt that haunts her. As is well documented, actual trauma survivors frequently take upon themselves the shame and guilt of their abusers, thereby compounding their "malignant sense of inner badness."[45] So it is with Veronica, in whose mind the deformations and disorders caused by this corrosive process of internalization are not confined to the consciousness of the individual victim. An entire social order stands indicted: "This is the anatomy and mechanism of a family – a whole fucking country – drowning in shame" (168). Significantly, she traces her own "betrayal" of her brother to the occasion when she mocked his teenage claim that he was beaten during a night in police custody, a mockery she now regards as lethally misplaced, being symptomatic of a whole culture of secrecy and denial, the diffusive effects of which now seem to her to be profoundly insidious:

· ·

If I believed in such a thing as confession I would go there and say that, not only did I laugh at my brother, but I let my brother laugh at himself, all his life. This laughing phase lasted through his cheerful drinking, and through his raucous drinking, and only petered out in the final stinking stage of his drinking. But he never gave it up completely – the idea that it was all a *complete joke*. (167)

· ·

The shock of Veronica's belated realization of the sheer scale and pervasiveness of covert sexual child abuse transforms Nugent into a malign "slick of horror" (215), a contaminating presence not unlike the "malignant fate"[46] that Freud found at work in traumatic neurosis. Reconstructed thus, Nugent becomes an archetype of commonplace evil, while at the same time ceasing to be the sole source of moral corruption:

....

I know he could be the explanation for all our lives, and I know something more frightening still – that we did not have to be damaged by him in order to be damaged. It was the air he breathed that did for us. It was the way we were obliged to breathe his second-hand air. (224)

....

This epiphany further enables Veronica to read the moral geography of hidden victimization in modern Ireland and the hegemonic forms of social control that underpinned it, such that we see her beginning to recognize the prejudices, practices, and institutions that facilitated the perpetration and repression of violence against vulnerable individuals at various state-sanctioned levels. Liam, she now understands, was far from alone in having his identity effaced, his dignity disregarded. His fate is linked to that of her "mad" Uncle Brendan, who was long ago committed to St Ita's psychiatric hospital in Portrane in north County Dublin. When, on visiting the hospital, Veronica comes upon a recently erected memorial to the nameless residents buried there since 1922, she is visited by a sudden awareness of the systemic erasure of generations of pain and suffering. The place seems to be "boiling with corpses" (160), none of which are "properly dead" (158), any more than Liam or Brendan are, precisely because their brutal truths have never been heard or their victimization acknowledged. From this point onward, Veronica finds it increasingly difficult to separate the individual's dissociation from the agony of unspeakable trauma from the pervasive denial of memory and responsibility by state and society. A crisis of personal subjectivity thus becomes a crisis of civic and national identity: Veronica's mourning of the bodily remains of her traumatized brother mediates a much larger grief and anger for the unacknowledged trauma endured by generations of unknown Irish bodies made abject by postcolonial nationalism and discarded anonymously in literal and metaphorical unmarked graves.

The profound, unresolved legacies of this crisis are graphically symbolized by the wretched ghosts that confront Veronica on the landing of her family home in Chapter 30. Up to this point, the enduring destructive effects of traumatic memory and survivor guilt have been represented by Liam's troubled ghost, which is Veronica's persistent interlocutor, mocking, haranguing, and accusing her by turn. Now, on the eve of his funeral, and with his body laid out in the corpse room downstairs, his ghost is displaced by a procession of other revenants, each an agitated manifestation of repressed histories into which Veronica regresses with every descending step on the stairs. The last and most disturbing of these symptomatic apparitions is Brendan as a small boy, his "knee socks and short pants" ominously reflecting Veronica's suspicion that the origins of his "madness" may lie in the abuse he suffered a generation before Liam. Brendan's head is

· ·

full to bursting with all the things he has to tell Ada, that she will not hear him say. Brendan's bones are mixed with other people's bones; so there is a turmoil of souls muttering and whining under his clothes, they would come out in a roar, were he to unbutton his fly; if he opened his mouth they would slop out over his teeth. Brendan has no rest from them, the souls of the forgotten who must always be crawling and bulging and whining in there; he reaches to scratch under his collar and handfuls come loose. (216)

· ·

Slavoj Žižek's insights into the archetype of the living dead enable us to understand the deeper symbolic significance of the restless, composite specter that assails Veronica in this seminal scene. The return of the dead, Žižek argues, is "a sign of a disturbance in the symbolic rite, in the process of symbolization; the dead return as collectors of some unpaid symbolic debt."[47] As such, they represent "the reverse of the proper funeral rite. While the latter implies a kind of reconciliation, an acceptance of loss, the return of the dead signifies that they cannot find their proper place in the text of tradition."[48] The improper dead will continue to haunt the cultural unconscious and stalk the living, therefore, until their repressed trauma is integrated into historical memory. For this to happen, the living must speak the truth; Liam's ghost has already insinuated as much by means of the "uncanny" look he gives his sister in Chapter 24: "The truth. The dead want nothing else. It is the only thing they require" (156). As we have already seen, however, the nature and value of truth are radically in doubt in the minds of the traumatized, and we are shown this again when Veronica tries and fails to inform her mother that "A dead man put his hand in a deader man's flies thirty years ago" (207). The very impulse to utter the truth is so nullified at source by the paralyzing question, "*What use is the truth to us now?*" (208), that she can only tell her mother indirectly. This tense encounter is charged with symbolic overtones, being shadowed by the Mother Ireland motif – one of the oldest and most recycled allegorical tropes in Irish nationalist culture – of which we are obliquely reminded by Veronica's earlier revelation that "*Don't tell Mammy*" was "the mantra of our childhoods" (9). Clearly, the coercive power of the social and psychological forces that render the traumatic memories of both daughter and nation untellable will not yield easily to disclosure.

There is also the latent symbolism attached to the body of the dead son to consider here. During Liam's wake, the Irish term *cam reilige* is invoked, meaning "the twist of the grave" (205), an expression that has a suggestive resonance in a novel about the wrenching effects of traumatic witnessing in the aftermath of death. In view of the gagging effects of traumatic stasis, it may not be too fanciful to detect here an echo of another Gaelic phrase, *marbhfháisc*, which refers to the strip of cloth placed around the face of a corpse to keep the mouth closed in Irish funerary tradition. If the dead are to be ungagged and the living healed, the witness is obliged to testify, an act that, as Shoshana Felman explains, takes on a distinct public and political urgency in the case of trauma victims: "To testify is thus not merely to narrate but to commit oneself, and to commit the narrative, to others: to *take responsibility* – in speech – for history or for the truth of an occurrence, for something which, by definition, goes beyond the personal, in having general (nonpersonal) validity and consequences."[49]

The denouement shows Veronica grappling with this necessary act of critical memory, on behalf of herself, her family and, implicitly, her nation. Initially, she takes flight to England, only to find that the imperative to testify is as insistent as it is fraught with difficulty. The logic of her traumatized condition dictates that the deeper complexities of her predicament remain beyond her full comprehension, yet now more than ever her desire for collective understanding and healing cries out for empathetic reception and response. It is an appeal that calls us, as (Irish) readers, to conscience, situating us within a web of social, ethical, and moral implications and forcing us to consider both our collective culpability for the repression that attends traumatic experience and the myriad ways in which we are still wounded by the concealment of this intimate and immediate history. Veronica's struggle – and ours – is, in Milan Kundera's oft-quoted terms, "the struggle of memory against forgetting."[50] More specifically, we might couch this call to conscience in terms of Dominick LaCapra's notion of "empathetic unsettlement," which involves "a kind of virtual experience through which one puts oneself in the other's position while recognising the difference of that position and hence not taking the other's place."[51] To articulate the truth to empathetic listeners is to answer back to those social and political systems of power that render the victims of violation voiceless. Personal, familial, and cultural amnesia must therefore be systematically undone by making the traumatized body's memories communicable in the present. Veronica derives added impetus to create open, unsettling, collective knowledge from Liam's three-year-old son, Rowan, whom she meets for the first time at his funeral. The mere sight of the boy enraptures and transfixes her, embodying as he does the anointed future, a new child for the new millennium – innocent, inviolable, and wholly without stain or stigma.

At the end of the novel, then, Veronica Hegarty appears poised on the threshold of speech, primed to bear historical witness to the trauma of "the mad and the inconvenient dead" (216), who are still struggling to find a meaningful voice in contemporary Irish society. Yet her valedictory resolution underlines the necessarily incomplete nature of her testimonial act. Traumatic memory may have been translated into narrative memory on the page but disclosure remains deferred at the level of speech:

. . . .

I know what I have to do – even though it is too late for the truth, I will tell the truth. I will get hold of Ernest and tell him what happened to Liam in Broadstone, and I will ask him to break this very old news to the rest of the family (but don't tell Mammy!) because I can not do it myself, I do not have the arguments for it. (259)

. . . .

By querying the power of articulation and communication to heal the unspeakable wounds of history, this equivocal, problematic pledge leaves open the extent to which Veronica's narrative has been therapeutic or cathartic. Equally, the closing image of a woman "falling" (261) into her life as her flight arrives at Dublin Airport simultaneously gestures toward and shies away from closure. If the implied symbolism of Veronica "touching down" suggests that she may soon allow herself to be caressed again – an interpretation supported by her fresh thoughts of a having a third child with Tom – her still-agitated consciousness shows that her struggles with being and telling are far from over. She may be reaching the point where she can be "less afraid" (261) and more future oriented, but there is no suggestion that her recovery will follow any simple, linear arc of progression.

With this ending, Enright remains true to the mournful, determinative logic of traumatic injury, balancing the potential for recovery against the reality of trauma's chronic destructive power. To do otherwise would be to revalidate the very forces of repression, dissociation, and entropy that have entrapped her protagonist for so long. Ultimately, *The Gathering* suggests that for this particular trauma survivor, testimonial acts are not inherently or facilely transformative, nor can they necessarily be taken to presage the complete reconstitution of personal subjectivity, let alone the social order of things. Recovery is never absolute; the past lingers beyond the reach of full understanding; mourning remains unresolved.

Notes

1. Helena Sheehan, "Television," in *The Blackwell Companion to Modern Irish Culture*, ed. W. J. McCormack (Oxford: Blackwell, 1999), 560.
2. Sarah Lyall, "Congratulations on the book award, and welcome to the scrutiny," *New York Times*, November 8, 2007. See also Kate Holmquist, "A very dark horse," *Irish Times*, October 20, 2007, *Weekend* section.
3. Mary Morrissy, "Surprising changes of light," *Irish Times*, March 2, 1991, 37.
4. Stuart Jeffries, "I wanted to explore desire and hatred," *Guardian*, October 18, 2007, 13.
5. Asked about her views on narrative in a 2011 interview, Enright replied: "Conventional novels are all about cause and effect: the idea that if you put one event followed by another event in a novel, then there is a link between the two. I have retained a kind of modernist impulse; I don't think that our lives are necessarily explicable in that simple way." See Miranda Popkey, "Anne Enright on *The Forgotten Waltz*," *The Paris Review Daily*, October 25, 2011. http://www.theparisreview.org/blog/2011/10/25/anne-enright-on-the-forgotten-waltz/
6. Hedwig Schwall, "Muscular Metaphors in Anne Enright: An Interview," *The European English Messenger*, 17:1 (2008), 21.
7. Schwall, "Muscular Metaphors in Anne Enright," 22.
8. Anne Enright, *The Portable Virgin* [1991] (London: Minerva, 1992), 159.
9. Enright, *The Portable Virgin*, 87.
10. Lyall, "Congratulations on the book award, and welcome to the scrutiny."
11. Catriona Moloney, "Anne Enright," in *Irish Women Writers Speak Out: Voices from the Field*, eds Catriona Moloney and Helen Thompson (Syracuse: Syracuse University Press, 2003), 59.
12. Patricia Coughlan, "Irish Literature and Feminism in Postmodernity," *Hungarian Journal of English and American Studies*, 10:1–2 (2004), 182–183.
13. Anne Enright, *The Wig My Father Wore* (London: Jonathan Cape, 1995), 137.
14. Enright, *The Portable Virgin*, 82.
15. Coughlan, "Irish Literature and Feminism in Postmodernity," 184.
16. Anne Enright, *What Are You Like?* (London: Jonathan Cape, 2000), 37, 188.
17. Enright, *What Are You Like?*, 22.
18. Anne Enright, *The Pleasure of Eliza Lynch* (London: Jonathan Cape, 2002), 1.
19. Patricia Coughlan, "'Without a Blink of Her Lovely Eye': *The Pleasure of Eliza Lynch* and Visionary Scepticism," *Irish University Review*, 35:2 (Autumn/Winter 2005), 355–356.

20. Maria Luddy and James M. Smith, "Editors' Introduction," *Éire-Ireland*, 44:1–2 (2009), 6.

21. The most damning evidence to date of the Irish state facilitating the cover-up of clerical sexual abuse is contained in the Report by the Commission of Investigation into the Catholic Archdiocese of Dublin, also known as the Murphy Report, published in November 2009 (http://www.justice.ie/en/JELR/Pages/PB09000504). The Report exposed the Irish Catholic hierarchy's sustained suppression of scandal and protection of pedophile priests at the expense of innocent children from 1975 to 2004. It also laid bare the failure of state agencies to fulfill their responsibilities by investigating complaints and prosecuting the perpetrators. The following year, the leader of the Catholic Church in Ireland, Cardinal Seán Brady, was directly implicated in a cover-up of clerical sexual abuse when it emerged that, as a young canon lawyer in 1975, he had participated in an internal church investigation that failed to inform the civil authorities of the activities of Father Brendan Smyth, a rapacious pedophile who went on to rape and sodomize dozens of children before being convicted on seventy-four charges of child sexual assault in 1993, for which he received a twelve-year prison sentence. Brady rejected widespread calls for his resignation in the wake of this revelation in 2010. For an overview of child abuse scandals of the 1990s, see Brian Lalor (ed.), *The End of Innocence: Child Sexual Abuse in Ireland* (Dublin: Oak Tree Press, 2001).

22. Paul Ricoeur, *Time and Narrative*, vol. 3, trans. Kathleen Blamey and David Pellauer (Chicago: University of Chicago Press, 1984), 188.

23. Laurie Vickroy, *Trauma and Survival in Contemporary Fiction* (Charlottesville: University of Virginia Press, 2002), 33.

24. Peter Stallybrass and Allon White, *The Politics and Poetics of Transgression* (New York: Cornell University Press, 1986), 192.

25. In the Christian tradition, Veronica is said to have been the pious woman who wiped Christ's face on the road to Calvary. His features were miraculously impressed on the cloth she used, which came to be known as the *vera icon*, meaning "true image." Veronica Hegarty explicitly invokes this legend in Chapter 19 of the novel when she says: "I am residually interested, in the bleeding face of Christ, and the woman who may have existed, but who was certainly not called Veronica, who wiped the blood away and with it some of the hurt" (130). Enright may be alluding here to the fact that the name Veronica is derived not from *vera icon*, as is widely supposed, but from the Latin form of Berenice, which is the name of the woman afflicted by a permanent menstruation who is cured by Jesus in the apocryphal account of Christ's trial contained in the fourth-century *Acts of Pilate*. See Ewa Kuryluk, *Veronica and her Cloth* (Oxford: Blackwell, 1991), 5.

26. Shoshana Felman and Dori Laub, *Testimony: Crises of Witnessing in Literature, Psychoanalysis, and History* (London: Routledge, 1992), 231.

27. Cathy Caruth, *Unclaimed Experience: Trauma, Narrative, and History* (Baltimore: Johns Hopkins University Press, 1996), 7.

28. Anne Enright, *The Gathering* (London: Jonathan Cape, 2007), 36, 70. Subsequent page numbers are cited parenthetically in the text.

29. Pierre Janet, *Psychological Healing: A Historical and Clinical Study*, trans. Eden and Cedar Paul (London: George Allen and Unwin, 1925), 669.

30. Janet, *Psychological Healing*, 661–662, original emphasis.

31. Suzette Henke, *Shattered Subjects: Trauma and Testimony in Women's Life-Writing* (Basingstoke: Macmillan, 1998), xii.

32. Judith Lewis Herman, *Trauma and Recovery* (London Pandora, 2001), 2.

33. Marita Sturken, "Narratives of Recovery: Repressed Memory as Cultural Memory," in *Acts of Memory: Cultural Recall in the Present*, eds Mieke Bal, Jonathan Crewe, and Leo Spitzer (Hanover: University Press of New England, 1999), 235.

34. Felman and Laub, *Testimony*, 76.

35. Felman and Laub, *Testimony*, 80.

36. Caruth, *Unclaimed Experience*, 18.

37. Susan J. Brison, "Trauma Narratives and the Remaking of the Self," in Bal *et al.*, *Acts of Memory*, 42.

38. Roberta Culbertson, "Embodied Memory, Transcendence, and Telling: Recounting Trauma, Re-establishing the Self," *New Literary History*, 26:1 (1995), 170.

39. The novel's core paradox is symbolically significant in this regard. The fact that the most palpably absent body in the novel – the "lost" body of Liam, whose repatriation stretches across the whole narrative – is also the most insistently present one in Veronica's narrative further testifies to the haunting nature of trauma.

40. There is a long tradition in Irish culture of equating emigration with metaphorical death. For a discussion of representations of emigration as self-effacement in Irish writing, see Liam Harte, "'You want to be a British Paddy?': The Anxiety of Identity in Post-war Irish Migrant Writing," in *The Lost Decade: Ireland in the 1950s*, eds Dermot Keogh, Finbarr O'Shea, and Carmel Quinlan (Cork: Mercier Press, 2004), 233–251.

41. Brison, "Trauma Narratives and the Remaking of the Self," 48.

42. Schwall, "Muscular Metaphors in Anne Enright," 19.

43. The letters written by Nugent to Ada expose the cash nexus that lay at the root of their relationship for almost four decades and which evidently reinforced his sense of sexual ownership of her and, by extension, her grandchildren.

44. Herman, *Trauma and Recovery*, 8.

45. Herman, *Trauma and Recovery*, 105.

46. Sigmund Freud, "Beyond the Pleasure Principle," in his *On Metapsychology: The Theory of Psychoanalysis* [1920], trans. James Strachey, ed. Angela Richards (London: Penguin, 1984), 292.

47. Slavoj Žižek, *Looking Awry: An Introduction to Jacques Lacan through Popular Culture* (London: MIT Press, 1991), 23.

48. Žižek, *Looking Awry*, 23.

49. Felman and Laub, *Testimony*, 204.

50. Milan Kundera, *The Book of Laughter and Forgetting*, trans. Michael Henry Heim (London: Faber and Faber, 1982), 1.

51. Dominick LaCapra, *Writing History, Writing Trauma* (Baltimore: Johns Hopkins University Press, 2001), 78.

Bibliography

Abbott, H. Porter. *The Cambridge Introduction to Narrative* (Cambridge: Cambridge University Press, 2002).

Abraham, Nicolas and Maria Torok, *The Shell and the Kernel: Renewals of Psychoanalysis*, vol. 1, trans. Nicholas T. Rand (Chicago: University of Chicago Press, 1994).

Adair, Tom. "An Interview with William Trevor," *Linen Hall Review*, 11:3 (Winter 1994), 4–8.

Adams, Tim. "William Trevor, the keen-eyed chronicler," *Observer*, February 8, 2009, 35.

Anzaldúa, Gloria. *Borderlands/La Frontera: The New Mestiza* (San Francisco: Aunt Lute Books, 1987).

Augé, Marc. *Non-Places: Introduction to an Anthropology of Supermodernity*, trans. John Howe (London: Verso, 1995).

Augé, Marc. "Paris and the Ethnography of the Contemporary World," in *Parisian Fields*, ed. Michael Sheringham (London: Reaktion Books, 1996), 175–179.

Bakhtin, Mikhail. *The Dialogic Imagination: Four Essays*, trans. Caryl Emerson and Michael Holquist, ed. Michael Holquist (Austin: University of Texas Press, 1981).

Banville, John. "In violent times," *New York Review of Books*, December 6, 1990, 22–23.

Banville, John. "Survivors of Joyce," in *James Joyce: The Artist and the Labyrinth*, ed. Augustine Martin (London: Ryan Publishing, 1990), 73–81.

Barry, Sebastian. "Following the Steward," in his *The Steward of Christendom* (London: Methuen, 1997), vii–xxi.

Barry, Sebastian. *Plays: 1* (London: Methuen, 1997).

Barry, Sebastian. *The Whereabouts of Eneas McNulty* (London: Picador, 1998).

Barry, Sebastian. *A Long Long Way* [2005] (London: Faber and Faber, 2006).

Barthes, Roland. *Image-Music-Text* (London: Fontana, 1977).

Barton, Ruth. "Feisty Colleens and Faithful Sons: Gender in Irish Cinema," *Cinéaste*, 24:2–3 (1999), 40–45.

Battersby, Eileen. "Mother Ireland," *Irish Times Magazine*, September 16, 2006, 18.

Reading the Contemporary Irish Novel 1987–2007, First Edition. Liam Harte.
© 2014 Liam Harte. Published 2014 by John Wiley & Sons, Ltd.

Beckett, Samuel. "Homage to Jack B. Yeats," in his *Disjecta: Miscellaneous Writings and a Dramatic Fragment*, ed. Ruby Cohn (London: Calder, 1983), 149.

Bennett, Andrew and Nicholas Royle. *An Introduction to Literature, Criticism and Theory* (Harlow: Prentice Hall, 1999; 2nd edn).

Bhabha, Homi K. *The Location of Culture* (London: Routledge, 1994).

Booker, M. Keith. "Late Capitalism Comes to Dublin: 'American' Popular Culture in the Novels of Roddy Doyle," *Ariel: A Review of International English Literature*, 28:3 (July 1997), 27–45.

Böss, Michael. "'Belonging without Belonging': Colm Tóibín's Dialogue with the Past," *Estudios Irlandeses*, 0 (2005), 22–29.

Bourke, Joanna. *An Intimate History of Killing* (London: Granta, 1999).

Brace, Marianne. "Comic cuts from the butcher boys," *Independent*, January 20, 2001, review section, 9.

Brison, Susan J. "Trauma Narratives and the Remaking of the Self," in *Acts of Memory*, eds Mieke Bal, Jonathan Crewe, and Leo Spitzer (Hanover: University Press of New England, 1999), 39–54.

Bromley, Roger. *Narratives for a New Belonging: Diasporic Cultural Fictions* (Edinburgh: Edinburgh University Press, 2000).

Brown, Terence. *Ireland: A Social and Cultural History 1922–2002* (London: Harper Perennial, 2004).

Bruhm, Steven. "The contemporary Gothic: why we need it," in *The Cambridge Companion to Gothic Fiction*, ed. Jerrold E. Hogle (Cambridge: Cambridge University Press, 2002), 259–276.

Canning, Richard. *Hear Us Out: Conversations with Gay Writers* (New York: Colombia University Press, 2003).

Carlson, Julia (ed.). *Banned in Ireland: Censorship and the Irish Writer* (London: Routledge, 1990).

Caruth, Cathy (ed.). *Trauma: Explorations in Memory* (Baltimore: Johns Hopkins University Press, 1995).

Caruth, Cathy. *Unclaimed Experience: Trauma, Narrative, and History* (Baltimore: Johns Hopkins University Press, 1996).

Chubb, Basil. *The Politics of the Irish Constitution* (Dublin: Institute of Public Administration, 1991).

Clare, Anthony. *On Men: Masculinity in Crisis* (London: Chatto and Windus, 2000).

Clark, Alex. "Songs of Experience," *Guardian*, March 13, 2004, review section, 22.

Cleary, Joe. *Outrageous Fortune: Capital and Culture in Modern Ireland* (Dublin: Field Day Publications, 2006).

Cleary, Joe. "Dark Fields of the Republic: Seamus Deane's Sundered Provinces," *boundary 2*, 37:2 (2010), 1–68.

Clifton, Harry. "A Visitor from the Future," in *The Faber Book of Best New Irish Short Stories 2006–7*, ed. David Marcus (London: Faber and Faber, 2007), 161–175.

Cobley, Paul. *Narrative* (London: Routledge, 2001).

Cohn, Dorrit. *Transparent Minds: Narrative Modes for Presenting Consciousness in Fiction* (Princeton: Princeton University Press, 1978).

Collinge, Linda and Emmanuel Vernadakis, "John McGahern—b.1934," *Journal of the Short Story in English*, 41 (Autumn 2003), online edition. http://jsse.revues.org/index314.html

Connor, Steven. *The English Novel in History: 1950–1995* (London: Routledge, 1996).

Coogan, Tim Pat. *Disillusioned Decades: Ireland 1966–1987* (Dublin: Gill and Macmillan, 1987).

Cooke, Rachel. "The first lady of Irish fiction," *Observer*, February 6, 2011, 13.

Corcoran, Neil. *After Yeats and Joyce* (Oxford: Oxford University Press, 1997).

Corkery, Daniel. *Synge and Anglo-Irish Literature* [1931] (Cork: Mercier Press, 1966).

Costello, Stephen J. (ed.). *The Irish Soul: In Dialogue* (Dublin: Liffey Press, 2001).

Costello-Sullivan, Kathleen. *Mother/Country: Politics of the Personal in the Fiction of Colm Tóibín* (Bern: Peter Lang, 2012).

Coughlan, Patricia. "Irish Literature and Feminism in Postmodernity," *Hungarian Journal of English and American Studies*, 10:1–2 (2004), 175–202.

Coughlan, Patricia. "'Without a Blink of Her Lovely Eye': *The Pleasure of Eliza Lynch* and Visionary Scepticism," *Irish University Review*, 35:2 (Autumn/Winter 2005), 349–373.

Coulter, Colin. "The end of Irish history: an introduction to the book," in *The End of Irish History?: Critical Reflections on the Celtic Tiger*, eds Colin Coulter and Steve Coleman (Manchester: Manchester University Press, 2003), 1–33.

Craig, Cairns. "Resisting Arrest: James Kelman," in *The Scottish Novel Since the Seventies*, eds Gavin Wallace and Randall Stevenson (Edinburgh: Edinburgh University Press, 1993), 99–114.

Cremin, Kathy. "The Dispersed and Dismissed: The World of Irish Women's Best-sellers," *Critical Survey*, 15:1 (2003), 60–76.

Cronin, Michael. *The Barrytown Trilogy* (Cork: Cork University Press, 2006).

Crotty, Patrick. "'All Toppers': Children in the Fiction of John McGahern," *Irish University Review*, 35:1 (Spring/Summer 2005), 42–57.

Culbertson, Roberta. "Embodied Memory, Transcendence, and Telling: Recounting Trauma, Re-establishing the Self," *New Literary History*, 26:1 (1995), 169–195.

Cullingford, Elizabeth Butler. *Ireland's Others: Ethnicity and Gender in Irish Literature and Popular Culture* (Cork: Cork University Press, 2001).

Cullingford, Elizabeth Butler. "Virgins and Mothers: Sinead O'Connor, Neil Jordan and *The Butcher Boy*," *Yale Journal of Criticism*, 15:1 (2002), 185–210.

Cullingford, Elizabeth. "Colonial Policing: *The Steward of Christendom* and *The Whereabouts of Eneas McNulty*," *Éire-Ireland*, 39:3&4 (2004), 11–37.

Cunningham, Justine. Review of *The Van, Sunday Business Post*, August 11, 1991.

Curtis, L. P. *Apes and Angels: The Irishman in Victorian Caricature* (Washington DC: Smithsonian Institution Press, 1997; 2nd edn).

D'Erasmo, Stacey. "About Colm Tóibín: A Profile by Stacey D'Erasmo," *Ploughshares*, 37:1 (Spring 2011), 165–168.

de Nie, Michael. *The Eternal Paddy: Irish Identity and the British Press, 1798–1882* (Madison: University of Wisconsin Press, 2004).

de Paor, Liam. *On the Easter Proclamation and Other Declarations* (Dublin: Four Courts Press, 1997).

Deane, Seamus. "What is Field Day?," programme note for the Field Day production of Brian Friel's adaptation of *Three Sisters* (1981).

Deane, Seamus. "Introduction: The Longing for Modernity," *Threshold*, 32 (Winter 1982), 1–7.

Deane, Seamus. "Derry: City Besieged within the Siege," *Fortnight* (October 1983), 18–19.

Deane, Seamus. "Heroic Styles: The Tradition of an Idea," in *Ireland's Field Day*, ed. Field Day Theatre Company (London: Hutchinson, 1985), 43–58.

Deane, Seamus. "Introduction," in *Nationalism, Colonialism and Literature*, ed. Seamus Deane (Minneapolis: University of Minnesota Press, 1990), 3–19.

Deane, Seamus. "Autobiography and Memoirs, 1890–1980," in *The Field Day Anthology of Irish Writing*, vol. 3, ed. Seamus Deane (Derry: Field Day, 1991), 380–383.

Deane, Seamus. "Wherever Green is Read," in *Revising the Rising*, eds Theo Dorgan and Máirín Ní Dhonnchadha (Derry: Field Day, 1991), 91–105.

Deane, Seamus. *Reading in the Dark* [1996] (London: Vintage, 1997).

Deane, Seamus. "*Reading in the Dark*: An Interview with Seamus Deane," *English & Media Magazine*, 36 (Summer 1997), 17–20.

Deane, Seamus. *Strange Country: Modernity and Nationhood in Irish Writing Since 1790* (Oxford: Clarendon, 1997).

Deane, Seamus and Maurice Fitzpatrick, "An Interview with Seamus Deane," *Journal of Irish Studies*, 22 (2007), 84–92.

DeCoste, Damon Marcel. "The Literary Response to the Second World War," in *A Companion to the British and Irish Novel 1945–2000*, ed. Brian W. Shaffer (London: Blackwell, 2005), 3–20.

Delaney, Paul. "Introduction," in *Reading Colm Tóibín*, ed. Paul Delaney (Dublin: Liffey Press, 2009), 1–20.

Denman, Terence. *Ireland's Unknown Soldiers: The 16th (Irish) Division in the Great War, 1914–1918* (Dublin: Irish Academic Press, 1992).

DiBattista, Maria. "Joyce's ghost: the bogey of realism in John McGahern's *Amongst Women*," in *Transcultural Joyce*, ed. Karen R. Lawrence (Cambridge: Cambridge University Press, 1998), 21–36.

Donnelly, Brian. "Roddy Doyle: From Barrytown to the GPO," *Irish University Review*, 30:1 (Spring/Summer 2000), 17–31.

Donoghue, Denis. "Together," in his *We Irish: Essays on Irish Literature and Society* (Berkeley: University of California Press, 1986), 148–152.

Dorgan, Theo and Máirín Ní Dhonnchadha (eds). *Revising the Rising* (Derry: Field Day, 1991).

Doyle, Roddy. *Brownbread* and *War* [1989] (London: Secker and Warburg, 1992).

Doyle, Roddy. *The Barrytown Trilogy* [1992] (London: Minerva, 1993).

Drewett, James. "An Interview with Roddy Doyle," *Irish Studies Review*, 11:3 (December 2003), 337–349.

Dwyer, Michael. "Atomic Power," *Irish Times*, August 21, 1999, *Weekend* section, 5.

Eagleton, Terry. *Heathcliff and the Great Hunger: Studies in Irish Culture* (London: Verso, 1995).

Editorial, "The savage reality of our darkest days," *Irish Times*, May 21, 2009, 19.

Eldred, Laura G. "Francie Pig vs. the Fat Green Blob from Outer Space: Horror Films and *The Butcher Boy*," *New Hibernia Review*, 10:3 (2006), 53–67.

Embree, Ainslie T. "Napier, Sir Charles James (1782–1853)," in *Oxford Dictionary of National Biography*, eds H.C.G. Matthew and Brian Harrison (Oxford: Oxford University Press, 2004), online edition, ed. Lawrence Goldman. Jan. 2008. http://www.oxforddnb.com/view/article/19748.

Engels, Friedrich. *The Condition of the Working Class in England* [1845] (London: Penguin, 1987).

Enright, Anne. *The Portable Virgin* [1991] (London: Minerva, 1992).

Enright, Anne. *The Wig My Father Wore* (London: Jonathan Cape, 1995).

Enright, Anne. *What Are You Like?* (London: Jonathan Cape, 2000).

Enright, Anne. *The Pleasure of Eliza Lynch* (London: Jonathan Cape, 2002).

Enright, Anne. "Murderous loves," *Guardian*, October 14, 2006, review section, 16.

Enright, Anne. *The Gathering* (London: Jonathan Cape, 2007).

Enright, Anne. "Fabulous and infuriating," *Guardian*, October 13, 2012, review section, 6.

Erikson, Kai. "Notes on Trauma and Community," in *Trauma: Explorations in Memory*, ed. Cathy Caruth (Baltimore: Johns Hopkins University Press, 1995), 183–199.

Fanon, Frantz. *The Wretched of the Earth* [1961], trans. Constance Farrington (London: Penguin, 1990).

Felman, Shoshana and Dori Laub, *Testimony: Crises of Witnessing in Literature, Psychoanalysis, and History* (London: Routledge, 1992).

Fitzgerald, Penelope. "Fried Nappy," *London Review of Books*, September 12, 1991, 16.

Fitzgerald-Hoyt, Mary. *William Trevor: Re-imagining Ireland* (Dublin: Liffey Press, 2003).

Fitzpatrick, David. "The logic of collective sacrifice: Ireland and the British Army, 1914–1918," *Historical Journal*, 38:4 (1995), 1017–1030.

FitzSimon, Christopher. "St Macartan, Minnie the Minx and Mondo Movies: Elliptical Peregrinations through the Subconscious of a Monaghan Writer Traumatised by Cows and the Brilliance of James Joyce," *Irish University Review*, 28:1 (Spring/Summer 1998), 175–189.

Fludernik, Monika. *The Fictions of Language and the Languages of Fiction* (London: Routledge, 1993).

Fogarty, Anne. "Uncanny Families: Contemporary Irish Women's Fiction," *Irish University Review*, 30:1 (Spring/Summer 2000), 59–81.

Foran, Charles. 'The Troubles of Roddy Doyle', *Saturday Night*, 111:3 (April 1996), 59–64.

Foster, R.F. "Remembering 1798," in his *The Irish Story: Telling Tales and Making it Up in Ireland* (London: Allen Lane, 2001), 211–234.

Foster, Roy. "Something to Hate: Intimate Enmities in Irish History," *Irish Review*, 30 (Spring–Summer 2003), 1–12.

Foster, Roy. "'Something of Us Will Remain': Sebastian Barry and Irish History," in *Out of History: Essays on the Writings of Sebastian Barry*, ed. Christina Hunt Mahony (Dublin: Carysfort Press, 2006), 183–197.

Foster, R. F. "'A Strange and Insistent Protagonist': Tóibín and Irish History," in *Reading Colm Tóibín*, ed. Paul Delaney (Dublin: Liffey Press, 2009), 21–40.

Fraser, Nick. "A kind of life sentence," *Guardian*, October 28, 1996, 9.

Freud, Sigmund. "Beyond the Pleasure Principle," in his *On Metapsychology: The Theory of Psychoanalysis* [1920], trans. James Strachey, ed. Angela Richards (London: Penguin, 1984), 269–338.

Freud, Sigmund. *An Outline of Psychoanalysis* (London: Hogarth Press, 1938).

Freud, Sigmund. *On Creativity and the Unconscious*, trans. Alix Strachey (New York: Harper & Row, 1958).

Friel, Brian. *Selected Plays* (London: Faber and Faber, 1984).

Garratt, Robert F. "John McGahern's *Amongst Women*: Representation, Memory and Trauma," *Irish University Review*, 35:1 (Spring/Summer 2005), 121–135.

Garratt, Robert F. *Trauma and History in the Irish Novel: The Return of the Dead* (Basingstoke: Palgrave Macmillan, 2011).

Genette, Gérard. *Paratexts: Thresholds of Interpretation*, trans. Jane E. Lewin (Cambridge: Cambridge University Press, 1997).

Gibbons, Luke, "Coming Out of Hibernation: The Myth of Modernity in Irish Culture," in *Across the Frontiers: Ireland in the 1990s*, ed. Richard Kearney (Dublin: Wolfhound Press, 1988), 205–218.

Gibbons, Luke. "The Global Cure?: History, Therapy and the Celtic Tiger," in *Reinventing Ireland: Culture, Society and the Global Economy*, eds Peadar Kirby, Luke Gibbons, and Michael Cronin (London: Pluto Press, 2002), 89–106.

Goldberg, Carl. *Understanding Shame* (Northvale, NJ: Jason Aronson, 1991).

González, Rosa. "'An Interview with John McGahern," in *Ireland in Writing: Interviews with Writers and Academics*, eds Jacqueline Hurtley, Rosa González, Inés Praga, and Esther Aliaga (Amsterdam: Rodopi, 1998), 39–50.

Gough, Julian. "The State of Irish Literature 2010." http://www.juliangough.com/journal/2010/2/10/the-state-of-irish-literature-2010.html

Gramsci, Antonio. *Selections from the Prison Notebooks*, eds and trans. Quintin Hoare and Geoffrey Nowell-Smith (London: Lawrence and Wishart, 1971).

Gray, John. "Field Day Five Years On," *Linen Hall Review*, 2:2 (Summer 1985), 4–10.

Greenslade, Liam. "White Skin, White Masks: Psychological Distress among the Irish in Britain," in *The Irish World Wide: History, Heritage Identity*, vol. 2., ed. Patrick O'Sullivan (London: Leicester University Press, 1992), 201–225.

Greenwood, Amanda. *Edna O'Brien* (Tavistock: Northcote House, 2003).

Gregory, Derek. *Geographical Imaginations* (Oxford: Blackwell, 1994).

Grossman, David. *On Killing: The Psychological Cost of Learning to Kill in War and Society* (New York: Back Bay Books, 1995).

Hanafin, Patrick. "Legal Texts as Cultural Documents: Interpreting the Irish Constitution," in *Writing in the Irish Republic: Literature, Culture, Politics, 1949–1999*, ed. Ray Ryan (Basingstoke: Macmillan, 2000), 147–164.

Hand, Derek. *A History of the Irish Novel* (Cambridge: Cambridge University Press, 2011).

Harte, Liam. "'You Want to be a British Paddy?': The Anxiety of Identity in Post-war Irish Migrant Writing," in *The Lost Decade: Ireland in the 1950s*, eds Dermot Keogh, Finbarr O'Shea, and Carmel Quinlan (Cork: Mercier Press, 2004), 233–251.

Harte, Liam. "Colm Tóibín's Marine Imaginary," *Critique: Studies in Contemporary Fiction*, 51:4 (2010), 333–349.

Haverty, Anne. *The Free and Easy* (London: Chatto & Windus, 2006).

Hayes, Joanne and John Barrett, *My Story* (Dingle: Brandon Press, 1985).

Hegarty, Shane. "Reading the Public," *Irish Times*, October 18, 2003, *Weekend* section, 11.

Henke, Suzette. *Shattered Subjects: Trauma and Testimony in Women's Life-Writing* (Basingstoke: Macmillan, 1998).

Herman, Judith Lewis. *Trauma and Recovery* (London Pandora, 2001).

Herron, Tom. "ContamiNation: Patrick McCabe and Colm Tóibín's Pathographies of the Republic," in *Contemporary Irish Fiction: Themes, Tropes, Theories*, eds Liam Harte and Michael Parker (Basingstoke: Macmillan, 2000), 168–191.

Hewson, Paul. "Bono: The White Nigger," in *Across the Frontiers: Ireland in the 1990s*, ed. Richard Kearney (Dublin: Wolfhound Press, 1988), 188–191.

Hickey, D. J. and J. E. Doherty. *A Dictionary of Irish History* (Dublin: Gill and Macmillan, 1980).

Hirsch, Marianne. "The Generation of Postmemory," *Poetics Today*, 29:1 (Spring 2008), 103–128.

Hogle, Jerrold E. "Introduction: the Gothic in western culture," in *The Cambridge Companion to Gothic Fiction*, ed. Jerrold E. Hogle, (Cambridge: Cambridge University Press, 2002) 1–20.

Holland, Siobhán. "Re-citing the Rosary: Women, Catholicism and Agency in Brian Moore's *Cold Heaven* and John McGahern's *Amongst Women*," in *Contemporary Irish Fiction: Themes, Tropes, Theories*, eds Liam Harte and Michael Parker (Basingstoke: Macmillan, 2000), 56–78.

Holmquist, Kate. "A very dark horse," *Irish Times*, October 20, 2007, *Weekend* section.

Horton, Patricia. "'Absent from Home': Family, Community and National Identity in Patrick McCabe's *The Butcher Boy*," *Irish Journal of Feminist Studies*, 3:1 (December 1998), 75–93.

Hughes, Eamonn. "Belfastards and Derriers," *Irish Review*, 20 (Winter–Spring 1997), 151–157.

Hurley, Kelly. "British Gothic fiction, 1885–1930," in *The Cambridge Companion to Gothic Fiction*, ed. Jerrold E. Hogle (Cambridge: Cambridge University Press, 2002), 189–207.

Hutcheon, Linda. *A Poetics of Postmodernism: History, Theory, Fiction* (London: Routledge, 1988).

Hutcheon, Linda. *The Politics of Postmodernism* (London: Routledge, 2002).

Interview with Edna O'Brien. *Salon Magazine*, December 2, 1995. http://www2.salon.com

Interview with Sebastian Barry. Penguin Reading Group. http://us.penguingroup. com/static/rguides/us/long_long_way.html

Interview with William Trevor. Penguin Reading Group. http://us.penguingroup. com/static/rguides/us/felicias_journey.html

Jackson, Joe. "Tales from the Darkside," *Hot Press*, November 14, 1991, 18–20.

Janet, Pierre. *Psychological Healing: A Historical and Clinical Study*, trans. Eden and Cedar Paul (London: George Allen and Unwin, 1925).

Jefferson, Mark. "What is Wrong With Sentimentality?," *Mind*, 92:368 (1983), 519–529.

Jeffrey, Keith. *Ireland and the Great War* (Cambridge: Cambridge University Press, 2000).

Jeffries, Stuart. "I wanted to explore desire and hatred," *Guardian*, October 18, 2007, 13.

Jordan, Neil. "Imagining Otherwise," in *Across the Frontiers: Ireland in the 1990s*, ed. Richard Kearney (Dublin: Wolfhound Press, 1988), 196–199.

Joyce, James. *Finnegans Wake* (New York, Viking Press, 1959).

Joyce, James. *The Letters of James Joyce*, vol. 2, ed. Richard Ellmann (New York: Viking Press, 1966).

Kelly, Aaron. *The Thriller in Northern Ireland since 1969: Utterly Resigned Terror* (Aldershot: Ashgate, 2005).

Kelly, John. "Fundamental Rights and the Constitution," in *De Valera's Constitution and Ours*, ed. Brian Farrell (Dublin: Gill and Macmillan, 1988), 163–173.

Kenny, Kevin. "The Irish in the Empire," in *Ireland and the British Empire*, ed. Kevin Kenny (Oxford: Oxford University Press, 2004), 90–122.

Kerridge, Richard. "Meat is Murder: Patrick McCabe talks to Richard Kerridge," *Irish Studies Review*, 3 (Spring 1993), 10–12.

Kerrigan, Gene. "Catching the Rhythm," *Magill* (April 1987), 43.

Kiberd, Declan. *Inventing Ireland: The Literature of the Modern Nation* (London: Jonathan Cape, 1995).

Kiberd, Declan. *The Irish Writer and the World* (Cambridge: Cambridge University Press, 2005).

Killen, John (ed.). *Dear Mr McLaverty: The Literary Correspondence of John McGahern and Michael McLaverty, 1959–1980* (Belfast: Linen Hall Library, 2006).

Kilroy, Thomas. "The steady pulse of the world," *Irish Times*, May 12, 1990, *Weekend* section, 9.

Kincaid, Andrew. *Postcolonial Dublin: Imperial Legacies and the Built Environment* (Minneapolis: University of Minnesota Press, 2006).

Kincaid, Andrew. "'Down These Mean Streets': The City and Critique in Contemporary Irish Noir," *Éire-Ireland*, 45:1&2 (Spring/Summer 2010), 39–55.

King, Sophia Hillan. "On the Side of Life: Edna O'Brien's Trilogy of Contemporary Ireland," *New Hibernia Review*, 4:2 (2000), 49–66.

Kirby, Peadar. "Contested Pedigrees of the Celtic Tiger," in *Reinventing Ireland: Culture, Society and the Global Economy*, eds Peadar Kirby, Luke Gibbons and Michael Cronin (London: Pluto Press, 2002), 21–37.

Knights, L. C. *Some Shakespearean Themes* (Stanford: Stanford University Press, 1959).

Kristeva, Julia, *Powers of Horror: An Essay on Abjection*, trans. Leon S. Roudiez (New York: Columbia University Press, 1982).

Kuhling, Carmen. "'Liquid Modernity' and Irish Identity: Irishness in Guinness, Jameson and Ballygowan Advertisements," *Advertising and Society Review*, 9:3 (2008), online edition. http://muse.jhu.edu/journals/advertising_and_society_review/v009/9.3.kuhling.html

Kundera, Milan. *The Book of Laughter and Forgetting*, trans. Michael Henry Heim (London: Faber and Faber, 1982).

Kurdi, Maria. "'Really All Danger': An Interview with Sebastian Barry," *New Hibernia Review*, 8:1 (2004), 41–53.

Kuryluk, Ewa. *Veronica and her Cloth* (Oxford: Blackwell, 1991).

LaCapra, Dominick. *Writing History, Writing Trauma* (Baltimore: Johns Hopkins University Press, 2001).

Lalor, Brian (ed.). *The End of Innocence: Child Sexual Abuse in Ireland* (Dublin: Oak Tree Press, 2001).

Langer, Lawrence. *Holocaust Testimonies: The Ruins of Memory* (New Haven: Yale University Press, 1991).

Laub, Dori and Nanette C. Auerhahn, "Knowing and Not Knowing Massive Psychic Trauma: Forms of Traumatic Memory," *International Journal of Psycho-Analysis*, 74:2 (1993), 287–302.

Lawrence, D. H. *England, My England and Other Stories* [1922], ed. Bruce Steele (Cambridge: Cambridge University Press, 1990).

Lee, Hermione. "The Terror and the Pity," *The New Republic*, June 13, 1994, 53.

Lee, J.J. *Ireland 1912–1985: Politics and Society* (Cambridge: Cambridge University Press, 1989).

Lentin, Ronit and Robbie McVeigh (eds). *Racism and Anti-racism in Ireland* (Belfast: Beyond the Pale, 2002).

Lewis, Helen Block. *Shame and Guilt in Neurosis* (New York: International Universities Press, 1971).

Lewis, Michael. *Shame: The Exposed Self* (New York: Free Press, Simon and Schuster, 1995).

Lin, Yu-chen. "Field Day Revisited (I): An Interview with Seamus Deane," *Concentric: Literary and Cultural Studies*, 33:1 (March 2007), 201–221.

Lloyd, David. *Anomalous States: Irish Writing and the Post-Colonial Moment* (Dublin: Lilliput Press, 1993).

Lloyd, David. *Irish Times: Temporalities of Modernity* (Dublin: Field Day, 2008).

Longley, Edna. "Autobiography as History," *Fortnight* (November 1996), 34.

Luckhurst, Roger. *The Trauma Question* (London: Routledge, 2008).

Luddy, Maria and James M. Smith, "Editors' Introduction," *Éire-Ireland*, 44:1&2 (2009), 5–8.

Lyall, Sarah. "Congratulations on the book award, and welcome to the scrutiny," *New York Times*, November 8, 2007.

Lynn, Christopher J. "Black Pig's Dyke," *The Encyclopedia of Ireland* ed. Brian Lalor (Dublin: Gill and Macmillan, 2003), 96.

Lyons, F. S. L. "The Meaning of Independence," in *The Irish Parliamentary Tradition*, ed. Brian Farrell (Dublin: Gill and Macmillan, 1973), 223–234.

MacKenna, Dolores. *William Trevor: The Writer and his Work* (Dublin: New Island Books, 1999).

Mackle, Joanna. "The publishing of *Amongst Women*," *The John McGahern Yearbook* 1, ed. John Kenny (Galway: NUI Galway, 2008), 88–91.

Maguire, Matt. "Dialect(ic) Nationalism?: The Fiction of James Kelman and Roddy Doyle," *Scottish Studies Review*, 7:1 (2006), 80–94.

Mahony, Christina Hunt. "Children of the Light Amid the 'Risky Dancers': Barry's Naïfs and the Poetry of Humanism," in *Out of History*, ed. Christina Hunt Mahony, 83–98.

Mantel, Hilary. "Booker winner Hilary Mantel on dealing with history in fiction," *Guardian*, October 17, 2009.

McArdle, Niam. "An Interview with Roddy Doyle," *New Orleans Review*, 21:3–4 (1995), 112–117.

McAuliffe, John. "Fiction's poetry," in *The John McGahern Yearbook* 4, ed. John Kenny (Galway: NUI Galway, 2011), 108–113.

McBride, Stephanie. *Felicia's Journey* (Cork: Cork University Press, 2006).

McCabe, Patrick. *The Butcher Boy* [1992] (London: Picador, 1993).

McCabe, Patrick. "The Republic of the Soul," *Irish Times*, December 29, 1999, 10.

McCabe, Patrick. "Ships and shadows and invisible men," *Guardian*, September 4, 2004, review section, 27.

McCabe, Pat and Maurice Fitzpatrick. "An Interview with Pat McCabe," *Journal of Irish Studies*, 23 (2008), 53–59.

McCafferty, Nell. "The Death of Ann Lovett," in her *The Best of Nell: A Selection of Writings over Fourteen Years* (Dublin: Attic Press, 1984), 48–54.

McCafferty, Nell. *A Woman to Blame: The Kerry Babies Case* (Dublin: Attic Press, 1985).

McCarthy, Conor. "Seamus Deane: Between Burke and Adorno," *The Yearbook of English Studies*, 35 (2005), 232–248.

McCarthy, Conor. "Geographies of Liberalism: The Politics of Space in Colm Tóibín's *Bad Blood: A Walk along the Irish Border* and *The Heather Blazing*," in *Landscape and Empire 1770–2000*, ed. Glenn Hooper (Aldershot: Ashgate, 2006), 207–223.

McCarthy, Dermot. *Roddy Doyle: Raining on the Parade* (Dublin: Liffey Press, 2003).

McClintock, Anne. *Imperial Leather: Race, Gender and Sexuality in the Colonial Contest* (New York: Routledge, 1995).

McCluskey, Dara (dir.). *Patrick McCabe: Blood Relations*, "Arts Lives," RTÉ One, June 3, 2008.

McCourt, John. "Colm Tóibín," in *The UCD Aesthetic: Celebrating 150 Years of UCD Writers*, ed. Anthony Roche (Dublin: New Island Books, 2005), 229–238.

McCoy, Daniel. "Ireland's Spectacular, If Delayed, Convergence," *Radharc: A Journal of Irish and Irish-American Studies*, 5–7 (2004–2006), 181–195.

McDonald, Rónán. "Without heroes: alcohol, adultery and other forms of survival in the short fiction of William Trevor," *Times Literary Supplement*, June 18, 2010, 3.

McGahern, John. *The Barracks* [1963] (London: Faber and Faber, 1983).

McGahern, John. *The Pornographer* [1979] (London: Faber and Faber, 1990).

McGahern, John. *Amongst Women* [1990] (London: Faber and Faber, 1991).

McGahern, John. "The Life, the Work and the Hurt," *Irish Times*, March 17, 1990, *Weekend* section, 9.

McGahern, John. "From a Glorious Dream to Wink and Nod," *Irish Times*, April 3, 1991, 9.

McGahern, John. "The Solitary Reader," *Canadian Journal of Irish Studies*, 17:1 (July 1991), 19–23.

McGahern, John. *That They May Face the Rising Sun* (London: Faber and Faber, 2002).

McGahern, John. *Memoir* (London: Faber and Faber, 2005).

McGahern, John. "What Is My Language?," *Irish University Review*, 35:1 (Spring/Summer 2005), 1–12.

McGlynn, Mary. "Why Jimmy Wears a Suit: White, Black, and Working Class in *The Commitments*," *Studies in the Novel*, 36:2 (Summer 2004), 232–250.

McGlynn, Mary M. *Narratives of Class in New Irish and Scottish Literature: From Joyce to Kelman, Doyle, Galloway, and McNamee* (Basingstoke: Palgrave Macmillan, 2008).

McLoone, Martin. *Irish Film: The Emergence of a Contemporary Cinema* (London: British Film Institute, 2000).

McMahon, Sean. "A Sex by Themselves: An Interim Report on the Novels of Edna O'Brien," *Éire-Ireland*, 2:1 (1967), 79–87.

Miller, J. Hillis. *Topographies* (Stanford: Stanford University Press, 1995).

Moloney, Catriona. "Anne Enright," in *Irish Women Writers Speak Out: Voices from the Field*, eds Catriona Moloney and Helen Thompson (Syracuse: Syracuse University Press, 2003), 51–64.

Morash, Christopher. "Irish theatre," in *The Cambridge Companion to Irish Culture*, eds Joe Cleary and Claire Connolly (Cambridge: Cambridge University Press, 2002), 322–338.

Morrissy, Mary. "Surprising changes of light," *Irish Times*, March 2, 1991, 37.

Mulholland, Peter. "Moving Statues and Concrete Thinking," *Quaderns de l'Institut Català d'Antropologia: sèrie monogràfics*, 23 (2009), 159–179.

Mullan, John. "Guardian book club," *Guardian*, April 19, 2008, review section, p. 7.

Murphy, Mike. "Edna O'Brien," in *Reading the Future: Irish Writers in Conversation with Mike Murphy*, ed. Clíodhna Ní Anluain (Dublin: Lilliput Press, 2000), 207–220.

Murphy, Mike. "John McGahern," in *Reading the Future: Irish Writers in Conversation with Mike Murphy*, ed. Clíodhna Ní Anluain (Dublin: Lilliput Press, 2000), 136–155.

Murphy, Mike. "William Trevor," in *Reading the Future: Irish Writers in Conversation with Mike Murphy*, ed. Clíodhna Ní Anluain (Dublin: Lilliput Press, 2000), 223–239.

Murray, Paul. "Partition and the Irish Boundary Commission: A Northern Nationalist Perspective," *Clogher Record*, 18:2 (2004), 181–217.

Nathanson, Donald L. "Shaming Systems in Couples, Families, and Institutions," in *The Many Faces of Shame*, ed. Donald L. Nathanson (New York: Guildford Press, 1987), 246–270.

Nielsen, Jacob Urup. "An interview with Colm Tóibín," *Nordic Irish Studies Network* (1998). *http://www.hum.au.dk/engelsk/nisn/reviews/toibininterview.html*

Nikelly, Arthur G. "The Anatomy of Nostalgia: From Pathology to Normality," *International Journal of Applied Psychoanalytical Studies*, 1:2 (2004), 182–199.

Norgate, Paul. "Wilfred Owen and the Soldier Poets," *Review of English Studies*, 40:160 (1989), 516–530.

O'Brien, Edna. *Mother Ireland* [1976] (London: Penguin, 1978).

O'Brien, Edna. "Why Irish Heroines Don't Have to Be Good Anymore," *New York Times Book Review*, May 11, 1986, 13.

O'Brien, Edna. *The Country Girls Trilogy* (London: Penguin, 1987).

O'Brien, Edna. *House of Splendid Isolation* [1994] (London: Phoenix, 1995).

O'Brien, Edna. *Country Girl* (London: Faber and Faber, 2012).

O'Brien, George. "Aspects of the Novelist," *Irish Review*, 10 (Spring 1991), 113–118.

O'Brien, George. "Worlds of Their Own: Autonomy and Anxiety in Contemporary Irish Fiction," *Colby Quarterly*, 35:3 (September 1999), 133–153.

O'Brien, George. "Contemporary prose in English: 1940–2000," in *The Cambridge History if Irish Literature, Volume 2: 1890–2000*, eds Margaret Kelleher and Philip O'Leary (Cambridge: Cambridge University Press, 2006), 421–477.

O'Connor, Joseph. Obituary for John McGahern, *Independent*, April 1, 2006, 44.

O'Connor, Ulick. "Friel Takes Derry by Storm," *Sunday Tribune*, September 6, 1981, 2.

O'Donoghue, Bernard. "Houses of Troubles: The bleak morality of William Trevor," *Times Literary Supplement*, August 30, 2002, 3.

O'Faolain, Sean. "The Dilemma of Irish Letters," *The Month*, 2:6 (1949), 366–379.

O'Hearn, Denis. "The Celtic Tiger: The role of the multinationals," in *Under the Belly of the Tiger: Class, Race, Identity and Culture in the Global Ireland*, eds Ethel Crowley and Jim Mac Laughlin (Dublin: Irish Reporter Publications, 1997), 21–34.

O'Mahony, John. "King of Bog Gothic," *Guardian*, August 20, 2003.

O'Toole, Fintan. "Brave New World," *Sunday Tribune*, April 12, 1987, 21.

O'Toole, Fintan. *A Mass for Jesse James: A Journey Through 1980s Ireland* (Dublin Raven Arts Press, 1990).

O'Toole, Fintan. "The family as independent republic," *Irish Times*, October 13, 1990, *Weekend* section, 2.

O'Toole, Fintan. "Introduction: On the Frontier," in *A Dublin Quartet*, Dermot Bolger (London: Penguin, 1992), 1–6.

O'Toole, Fintan. "Introduction: A True History of Lies," in *Plays: 1*, Sebastian Barry (London: Methuen, 1997), vii–xiv.

O'Toole, Fintan. "Writing the boom," *Irish Times*, January 25, 2001, 12.

O'Toole, Fintan. "Irish Culture in a Globalised World," in *Kaleidoscopic View of Ireland*, eds Munira H. Mutran and Laura P. Z. Izarra (São Paulo: Humanitas/FFLCH/USP, 2003), 75–93.

O'Toole, Fintan. "An Interview with Colm Tóibín," in *Reading Colm Tóibín*, ed. Paul Delaney (Dublin: Liffey Press, 2009), 183–208.

O'Toole, Fintan. "A very Irish box of tricks," *Irish Times*, December 31, 2011, *Weekend* section, 1.

Onkey, Lauren. "Celtic Soul Rebels," *Éire-Ireland*, 28:3 (Fall 1993), 147–158.

Owen, Wilfred. *The Collected Poems of Wilfred Owen*, ed. Cecil Day Lewis (London: Chatto and Windus, 1963).

Padley, Steve. *Key Concepts in Contemporary Literature* (Basingstoke: Palgrave Macmillan, 2006).

Paschel, Ulrike. *No Mean City?: The Image of Dublin in the Novels of Dermot Bolger, Roddy Doyle and Val Mulkerns* (Frankfurt am Main: Peter Lang, 1998).

Paulin, Tom. *The Strange Museum* (London: Faber and Faber, 1980).

Peach, Linden. *The Contemporary Irish Novel: Critical Readings* (Basingstoke: Palgrave Macmillan, 2004).

Pearce, Edward. "Words with no wisdom," *Guardian*, July 12, 1994, review section, 18.

Pearse, Patrick. "The Coming Revolution" [1913], reproduced in *The Field Day Anthology of Irish Writing*, vol. 2, ed. Seamus Deane (Derry: Field Day, 1991), 556–558.

Pelan, Rebecca. "Reflections on a Connemara Dietrich," in *Edna O'Brien: New Critical Perspectives*, eds Kathryn Laing, Sinéad Mooney, and Maureen O'Connor (Dublin: Carysfort Press, 2006), 12–37.

Pine, Richard. "Brian Friel and Contemporary Irish Drama," *Colby Quarterly*, 27:4 (December 1991), 190–201.

Popkey, Miranda. "Anne Enright on *The Forgotten Waltz*," *The Paris Review Daily*, October 25, 2011. http://www.theparisreview.org/blog/2011/10/25/anne-enright-on-the-forgotten-waltz/

Potterton, Homan. "'Suggestions of Concavity': William Trevor as Sculptor," *Irish Arts Review Yearbook*, 18 (2002), 93–103.

Potts, Donna. "From Tír na nÓg to Tír na Muck: Patrick McCabe's *The Butcher Boy*," *New Hibernia Review*, 3:3 (1999), 83–95.

Prone, Terry. "Bricks on the Road to Hell," in *Responding to the Ryan Report*, ed. Tony Flannery (Dublin: Columba Press, 2009), 84–94.

Punter, David. *The Literature of Terror: A History of Gothic Fictions from 1765 to the present day*, vol. 2 (London: Longman, 1996).

Punter, David and Glennis Byron, *The Gothic* (Oxford: Blackwell, 2004).

Quinn, Antoinette. "A Prayer for My Daughters: Patriarchy in *Amongst Women*," *Canadian Journal of Irish Studies*, 17:1 (July 1991), 79–90.

Quinn, Emma, John Stanley, Corona Joyce, and Philip J. O'Connell, *Handbook of Immigration and Asylum in Ireland 2007* (Dublin: Economic and Social Research Institute, 2008).

Randolph, Jody Allen (ed.). *Close to the Next Moment: Interviews from a Changing Ireland* (Manchester: Carcanet, 2010).

Rashkin, Esther. *Family Secrets and the Psychoanalysis of Narrative* (Princeton: Princeton University Press, 1992).

Rashkin, Esther. *Unspeakable Secrets and the Psychoanalysis of Culture* (Albany: State University of New York Press, 2008).

Regan, Stephen. "Ireland's Field Day," *History Workshop Journal*, 33 (Spring 1992), 25–37.

Regan, Stephen. Review of *Reading in the Dark*, *Irish Studies Review*, 19 (Summer 1997), 35–40.

Relph, Edward. *Place and Placelessness* (London: Pion, 1976).

Remarque, Erich Maria. *All Quiet on the Western Front* [1929], trans. Brian Murdoch (London: Vintage, 1996).

Report by the Commission of Investigation into the Catholic Archdiocese of Dublin (2009). http://www.justice.ie/en/JELR/Pages/PB09000504.

Richards, Shaun. "Northside Realism and the Twilight's Last Gleaming," *Irish Studies Review*, 2 (Winter 1992), 18–22.

Ricoeur, Paul. *Time and Narrative*, vol. 3, trans. Kathleen Blamey and David Pellauer (Chicago: University of Chicago Press, 1984).

Roche, Anthony. *Contemporary Irish Drama* (Dublin: Gill and Macmillan, 1994).

Rodd, Candice. "Mouldering mansions," *Times Literary Supplement*, April 22, 1994, 22.

Roth, Philip. "A Conversation with Edna O'Brien: 'The Body Contains the Life Story,'" *New York Times Book Review*, November 18, 1984, 38–40.

Rumens, Carol. "Reading Deane," *Fortnight* (July/August 1997), 29–30.

Ryan, Liam. "Irish Emigration to Britain since World War II," in *Migrations: The Irish at Home and Abroad*, ed. Richard Kearney (Dublin: Wolfhound Press, 1990), 45–67.

Ryan, Ray. *Ireland and Scotland: Literature and Culture, State and Nation, 1966–2000* (Oxford: Oxford University Press, 2002).

Said, Edward W. "Reflections on Exile," in his *Reflections on Exile and Other Essays* (Cambridge, Massachusetts: Harvard University Press, 2000), 173–186.

Sampson, Denis. "A Conversation with John McGahern," *Canadian Journal of Irish Studies*, 17:1 (July 1991), 13–18.

Sampson, Denis. *Outstaring Nature's Eye: The Fiction of John McGahern* (Dublin: Lilliput Press, 1993).

Sbrockey, Karen. "Something of a Hero: An Interview with Roddy Doyle," *Literary Review*, 42:4 (Summer 1999), 537–552.

Scarlata, Jessica. "Carnivals and Goldfish: History and Crisis in *The Butcher Boy*," in *Literature and Film: A Guide to the Theory and Practice of Film Adaptation*, eds Robert Stam and Alessandra Raengo (Oxford: Blackwell, 2005), 233–251

Scheff, Thomas and Suzanne Retzinger, *Emotions and Violence: Shame and Rage in Destructive Conflicts* (Lexington, MA: Lexington Books, 1991).

Schwab, Gabriele. *Haunting Legacies: Violent Histories and Transgenerational Trauma* (New York: Columbia University Press, 2010).

Schwall, Hedwig. "Muscular Metaphors in Anne Enright: An Interview," *The European English Messenger*, 17:1 (2008), 16–22.

Shakespeare, William. *King Lear*, in *The Arden Shakespeare: Complete Works*, eds Richard Proudfoot, Ann Thompson, and David Scott Kastan (London: A&C Black, 2001).

Sheehan, Helena. "Television," in *The Blackwell Companion to Modern Irish Culture*, ed. W. J. McCormack (Oxford: Blackwell, 1999), 559–561.

Shovlin, Frank. "The ghost of W. B. Yeats", in *The John McGahern Yearbook* 2, ed. John Kenny (Galway: NUI Galway, 2009), 42–51.

Smith, Amanda. "*PW* Interviews William Trevor," *Publishers Weekly*, April 23, 1983, 80.

Smyth, Gerry. "Appendix: An Interview with Roddy Doyle, September 16, 1996," in his *The Novel and the Nation* (London: Pluto, 1997), 98–112.

Smyth, Gerry. *Space and the Irish Cultural Imagination* (Basingstoke: Palgrave Macmillan, 2001).

Smyth, Gerry. *Music in Irish Cultural History* (Dublin: Irish Academic Press, 2009).

St. Peter, Christine. *Changing Ireland: Strategies in Contemporary Women's Fiction* (Basingstoke: Palgrave, 2000).

St. Peter, Christine. "Consuming Pleasures: *Felicia's Journey* in Fiction and Film," *Colby Quarterly*, 38:3 (September 2002), 329–339.

Stallybrass, Peter and Allon White, *The Politics and Poetics of Transgression* (New York: Cornell University Press, 1986).

Stout, Mira. "The Art of Fiction CVIII: William Trevor," *Paris Review*, 110 (1989), 119–151.

Sturken, Marita. "Narratives of Recovery: Repressed Memory as Cultural Memory," in *Acts of Memory*, eds Mieke Bal, Jonathan Crewe and Leo Spitzer (Hanover: University Press of New England, 1999), 231–248.

Sweeney, Ellen E. "Mrs Nugent's Little Piggy Went to Town: Abjected Identities and the Traumatic Return in Neil Jordan's *The Butcher Boy*," *Cultural Dynamics*, 15:3 (2003), 267–286.

Taylor, Timothy D. "Living in a Postcolonial World: Class and Soul in *The Commitments*," *Irish Studies Review*, 6:3 (1998), 291–302.

Thompson, Helen. "Edna O'Brien," in *Irish Women Writers Speak Out: Voices from the Field*, eds Catriona Moloney and Helen Thompson (Syracuse: Syracuse University Press, 2003), 197–205.

Thompson, Helen (ed.). *The Current Debate about the Irish Literary Canon: Essays Reassessing "The Field Day Anthology of Irish Writing"* (Lewiston, NY: Edwin Mellen Press, 2006).

Tillman, Lynne. "Colm Tóibín," *Bomb*, 38 (Winter 1992), 22–23.

Tobin, Fergal. *The Best of Decades: Ireland in the 1960s* (Dublin: Gill and Macmillan, 1996; 2nd edn).

Tóibín, Colm. "Inside the Supreme Court," *Magill*, 8:7 (February 1985), 8–35.

Tóibín, Colm. *The Heather Blazing* [1992] (London: Picador, 1993).

Tóibín, Colm. Review of *The Field Day Anthology of Irish Writing*, *Canadian Journal of Irish Studies*, 18:2 (December 1992), 121–124.

Tóibín, Colm. "New ways of killing your father," *London Review of Books*, November 18, 1993, 3–6.

Tóibín, Colm. *The Sign of the Cross: Travels in Catholic Europe* [1994] (London: Picador, 2001).

Tóibín, Colm. "Dublin's Epiphany," *The New Yorker Magazine*, April 13, 1995, 45–53.

Tóibín, Colm. "Introduction: The Stones of Enniscorthy," in *Enniscorthy: History and Heritage*, Micheál Tóibín (Dublin: New Island Books, 1998), 7–16.

Tóibín, Colm (ed.). *The Penguin Book of Irish Fiction* (Harmondsworth: Viking, 1999).

Tóibín, Colm. "Colm Tóibín's Dublin," *Daily Telegraph*, April 15, 2000, travel supplement, 1, 4.

Tóibín, Colm. *Love in a Dark Time: Gay Lives from Wilde to Almodóvar* [2001] (London: Picador, 2002).

Tóibín, Colm. *The Master* (Toronto: McClelland and Stewart, 2004).

Tóibín, Colm. *A Guest at the Feast: A Memoir* (London: Penguin Shorts eBook, 2011).

Trevor, William. *A Writer's Ireland: Landscape in Literature* (London: Thames and Hudson, 1984).

Trevor, William. *Excursions in the Real World* [1993] (London: Penguin, 1994).

Trevor, William. *Felicia's Journey* [1994] (London: Penguin, 1995).

Vice, Sue. *Introducing Bakhtin* (Manchester: Manchester University Press, 1997).

Vickroy, Laurie. *Trauma and Survival in Contemporary Fiction* (Charlottesville: University of Virginia Press, 2002).

Virilio, Paul. *The Aesthetics of Disappearance*, trans. Philip Beitchman (New York: Semiotext(e), 1991).

Walter, Bronwen. "From 'Flood' to 'Trickle': Irish Migration to Britain 1987–2006," *Irish Geography*, 41:2 (2008), 181–194.

Waters, John. "The smell of Appalachia," *Irish Times*, November 23, 1993. Reproduced in his *Every Day Like Sunday?* (Dublin: Poolbeg Press, 1995), 72–77.

Wheeler, Pat and Jenny Newman, "Roddy Doyle," in *Contemporary Irish and British Fiction: An Introduction Through Interviews*, eds Sharon Monteith, Jenny Newman, and Pat Wheeler (London: Arnold, 2004), 54–70.

Whelan, Kevin. "The Bases of Regionalism," in *Culture in Ireland – Regions: Identity and Power*, ed. Proinsias Ó Drisceoil (Belfast: Institute of Irish Studies, 1993), 5–62.

Whelan, Kevin. *The Tree of Liberty* (Cork: Cork University Press, 1996).

Whelan, Kevin. "The Revisionist Debate in Ireland," *boundary 2*, 31:1 (Spring 2004), 179–205.

Whelan, Yvonne. *Reinventing Modern Dublin: Streetscape, Iconography and the Politics of Identity* (Dublin: UCD Press, 2003).

White, Caramine. *Reading Roddy Doyle* (Syracuse: Syracuse University Press, 2001).

Whyte, James. "Appendix: An Interview with John McGahern," in his *History, Myth, and Ritual in the Fiction of John McGahern: Strategies of Transcendence* (Lewiston, NY: Edwin Mellen Press, 2002), 227–235.

Wiesenfarth, Joseph. "An Interview with Colm Tóibín," *Contemporary Literature*, 50:1 (Spring 2009), 1–27.

Wroe, Nicholas. "Country matters," *Guardian*, October 2, 1999, review section, 6.

Wroe, Nicholas. "A Life in Writing: Sebastian Barry," *Guardian*, October 11, 2008, review section, 12–13.

Wurmser, Léon. *The Mask of Shame* (Northvale NJ: Jason Aronson, 1994; 2nd edn).

Yarbro-Bejarano, Yvonne. "Gloria Anzaldúa's *Borderlands/La frontera*: Cultural Studies, 'Difference' and the Non-Unitary Subject," *Cultural Critique*, 28 (Autumn 1994), 5–28.

Young, Robert (ed.). *Untying the Text: A Post-Structuralist Reader* (London: Routledge and Kegan Paul, 1981).

Žižek, Slavoj. *Looking Awry: An Introduction to Jacques Lacan through Popular Culture* (London: MIT Press, 1991).

Index

Reading the Contemporary Irish Novel 1987–2007, First Edition. Liam Harte.
© 2014 Liam Harte. Published 2014 by John Wiley & Sons, Ltd.